WOMEN NOVELISTS, 1891–1920

GARLAND REFERENCE LIBRARY
OF THE HUMANITIES
(VOL. 491)

WOMEN NOVELISTS, 1891–1920
An Index to Biographical and Autobiographical Sources

Doris Robinson

GARLAND PUBLISHING, INC. • NEW YORK & LONDON
1984

Library of Congress Cataloging in Publication Data

Robinson, Doris.
Women novelists, 1891–1920.

(Garland reference library of the humanities ;
vol. 491)
Bibliography: p.
1. Women novelists—19th century—Biography—
Indexes.   2. Women novelists—20th century—Biography—
Indexes.   I. Title.   II. Series: Garland reference
library of the humanities ; v. 491.
Z7963.A8R62   1984   [PN471]   016.823′912′09 [B] 83-49334
ISBN 0-8240-8977-4 (alk. paper)

Printed on acid-free, 250-year-life paper
Manufactured in the United States of America

To
Susan, Vicki and Al
for their understanding and support
and to
Janet and William Grimes
for their friendship,
their encouragement,
and the use of their computer

CONTENTS

PREFACE

The purpose of this index is to identify English-language biographical and autobiographical works as well as obituary notices for women novelists who wrote at the turn of the century or whose novels were first translated into English during this period. This work was designed as a companion to *Novels in English by Women, 1891–1920*[1] and *Toward a Feminist Tradition.*[2]

In researching information about women writers one must look under various forms of each writer's name. There is no consistent rule one can follow, particularly with nineteenth-century women authors. Women may be listed under their maiden name, pen name, one or more married names, or, especially with obituary notices, under their husband's first and last name with just the individualizing designation "Mrs." to distinguish the subject from her husband. One woman can be listed under various names over the course of her career. Neither the Library of Congress nor the British Museum has been consistent in its cataloging treatment of womens' names. Moreover, the same woman may be listed differently in the two national catalogs.

The data base of 5,267 authors identified in *Novels in English by Women, 1891–1920* was used in compiling this work. There, the authors' names were entered under the fullest form available, including the latest married name with extensive cross references to pen names and pseudonyms. I have used the names as listed in *Novels in English* with the exception of hyphenated or compound names where I have listed the author under the first part of the name. Some biographical information has been found for 1,565 of

[1]Grimes, Janet, and Diva Daims. *Novels in English by Women, 1891–1920; A Preliminary Checklist.* New York: Garland, 1981.

[2]Daims, Diva, and Janet Grimes. *Toward a Feminist Tradition.* New York: Garland, 1982.

these authors. The information varies from entries of a few brief lines to complete books.

Additional married names discovered in the course of my research, generally through obituary notices, are indicated under the name as found in the above work. Pen names and pseudonyms, in addition to appearing as cross references, are also listed under the main entry. A search was made for birth and death dates and the country in which the author produced the majority of her works. Where this information could be found, it has been noted after the author's name. Sources have been listed in the following order: autobiography, collective biography, individual biography, obituary notice, and bibliography.

Following the main index are two supplemental indexes. Because it has been difficult to identify black women writing during this period, I have also listed them separately. An index by country has been provided.

Autobiographical works include published letters and diaries. Reminiscences and travel books have been included only if they contained information about the authors themselves. Biographical sources comprise 290 collective works as well as individual biographies. Books containing three or more biographies are referred to by code. Collective works, biographical dictionaries, encyclopedias, and other reference books selected for inclusion have been published since 1890. Works contemporary to the authors' time period as well as works published through 1983 have been indexed.

The two major sources for obituary notices were the *New York Times* and the London *Times.* A systematic search of *Nineteenth Century Readers' Guide to Periodical Literature, Readers' Guide to Periodical Literature, International Index to Periodicals, and Biography Index* was made and all obituaries thus identified were added.

The listing of individual bibliographies was not part of the original design for the book. I have cited those books I have found useful but no attempt has been made to be complete in this respect or to specifically seek this information. Manuscript collections, dissertations, and journal articles other than obituaries were excluded. A thorough search of the journal literature will require a separate index.

All entries have been verified using the OCLC data base and the National Union Catalog to obtain Library of Congress cataloging where available. The LC card number has been included in the citations as an aid to interlibrary loan. Where LC cataloging is not available, the OCLC number has been given or NUC indicated as the source.

All works which were not clearly identified as biographical by standard reference sources were examined before inclusion. Numerous obituary notices were also read to verify the entries. Many books have been reprinted. Editions listed were chosen on the basis of what was available for verification and examination. For reprints only the date of the original edition has been given.

ACKNOWLEDGMENTS

I would like to thank Janet Grimes, my colleague, at the Albany Campus Library of Russell Sage College for her encouragement and support throughout this project. Her enthusiasm for this subject first fired my own interest. I am grateful to Janet and Bill Grimes for all their aid and for their willingness to adapt their schedules to accommodate my use of their computer, without which this work would not have been possible.

A summer faculty grant from Russell Sage College allowed me to spend time at the Library of Congress in 1981. I am grateful to Jack and Barbara Ginsburg for their kindness and hospitality while I was in Washington. Access to an OCLC terminal at the college enabled me to verify all entries using the OCLC data base. I am indebted to the College for its support.

Throughout the project I have relied heavily on the Interlibrary Loan services of the Albany Campus Library. Deborah Priest has my special thanks for cheerfully and efficiently processing the numerous requests and for her support in many other ways. I appreciate the help given by the Capital District Library Council and by its couriers in identifying and delivering the local resources. I particularly wish to thank the Interlibrary Loan staffs at Union College, Schenectady, the State University of New York at Albany, and the Troy Campus Library of Russell Sage College for their fine services.

LIST OF ABBREVIATIONS

ILLUS. LONDON NEWS   *Illustrated London News*
m.   married name
NUC   *National Union Catalog*
pub.   published
SAT. REVIEW OF LIT   *Saturday Review of Literature*

KEY TO COLLECTIVE WORKS

ADC   Adcock, Arthur S. The Glory That Was Grub
Street; Impressions of Contemporary
Authors. 1928. Reprint. Freeport, N.Y.:
Books for Libraries, [1969]. LC72-99678.

ADE   Adelman, Joseph F. Famous Women, an
Outline of Feminine Achievement Through
the Ages with Life Stories of Five
Hundred Noted Women. New York: E.M.
Lonow, [c1926]. LC26-9917.

ALY   American Literary Yearbook. 1919. Reprint.
Detroit: Gale, 1968. LC68-21521.

AMH   American Humorists, 1800-1950, edited by
Stanley Trachtenberg. Vol. 11, Dictionary
of Literary Biography. 2 vols. Detroit:
Gale, 1982. LC81-20238.

AML   American Literature to 1900. New York: St.
Martin's, c1980. LC79-5251.

AMN   American Novelists, 1910-1945, edited
by James J. Martine. Vol. 9, Dictionary
Literary Biography. 3 vols. Detroit:
Gale, 1981. LC81-6834.

AMR   American Realists and Naturalists,
edited by Donald Pizer and Earl N.
Harbert. Vol. 12, Dictionary of Literary
Biography. Detroit: Gale, 1982. LC82-9258.

AMWRP   American Writers in Paris, 1920-1939,
edited by Karen L. Rood. Vol. 4,
Dictionary of Literary Biography.
Detroit: Gale, 1980. LC79-26101R.

APP   Appleton's Cyclopaedia of American
Biography. 7 vols. 1888. Reprint.
Detroit: Gale, 1968. LC67-14061.

APP-S   _____. Supplement, by John F. Kirk.
2 vols. 1891. Reprint. Detroit: Gale,
1965.

ASH   Ashley, Michael. Who's Who in Horror and
       Fantasy Fiction. New York: Taplinger,
       1978, c1977. LC77-4608.

AUC   Auchincloss, Louis. Pioneers and Care-
       takers; a Study of 9 American Women
       Novelists. Minneapolis: Univ. of
       Minnesota Press, [1965]. LC65-17016.

AUDB   Australian Dictionary of Biography. 8 vols.
       Melbourne: Melbourne Univ. Press, [1966-.]
       LC66-13723R.

AW   American Writers; a Collection of Literary
       Biographies. New York: Scribner, 1974-.
       LC73-1759.

AWO   American Women: the Standard Biographical
       Dictionary of Notable Women. 1939.
       Reprint. [Teaneck], N.J.: Zephyrus ,
       [1974]. LC73-20050.

AWW   American Women Writers: a Critical
       Reference Guide from Colonial Times to
       the Present. 4 vols. New York: Ungar,
       1979-1982. LC78-20945R.

BAN   Banta, Richard E., comp. Indiana Authors
       and Their Books, 1816-1916; Biographical
       Sketches of Authors Who Published During
       the First Century of Indiana Statehood....
       Crawfordsville, Indiana: Wabash College,
       1949. LC49-5434.

BAR   Barker, Nettie G. Kansas Women in
       Literature. Kansas City, Kansas:
       S.I. Meseraull, [c1915]. LC15-5173.

BARN   Barns, Florence E. Texas Writers of Today.
       Dallas, Texas: Tardy, [c1935]. LC35-11028.

BAS   Baskervill, William M. Southern Writers:
       Biographical and Critical Studies. 2 vols.
       1897-1903. Reprint. New York: Gordian,
       1970. LC70-93242.

BD   Bibliophile Dictionary.... 1904. Reprint.
       Detroit: Gale, 1966. LC66-15269.

BEATG   Beaton, Cecil and Kenneth Tynan. Persona
       Grata. [New York]: Putnam, [1954].
       LC54-8464.

BEI   Beilby, Raymond and Cecil Hadgraft. Ada
       Cambridge, Tasma, and Rosa Praed.
       Melbourne: Oxford Univ. Press, 1979.
       LC79-318364.

BEL   Bell, Mackenzie. Representative Novelists
       of the Nineteenth Century, Being Passages
       from Their Works with Brief Biographies....
       3 vols. New York: Dial, 1927. LC27-27948.

BENN   Bennett, Arnold. Books and Persons. New
       York: George H. Doran, [c1917]. LC17-21768.

BERE   Benet, William R., ed. The Reader's
       Encyclopedia. 2d ed. New York: Crowell,
       [1965]. LC65-12510.

BEY   Beyer, Harald. A History of Norwegian
       Literature. [New York]: New York Univ.
       Press for the American-Scandinavian
       Foundation, 1956. LC56-6801.

BICA   The Biographical Cyclopaedia of American
       Women.... New York: Halvord, 1924.
       LC24-7615.

BIN   Binheim, Max, ed. Women of the West; a
       Series of Biographical Sketches of Living
       Eminent Women in the Eleven Western
       States.... Los Angeles, Calif.:
       Publishers Press, [c1928]. LC28-21005.

BLA   Black, Helen C. Notable Women Authors of
       the Day. 1893. Reprint. Freeport,
       N.Y.: Books for Libraries, [1972].
       LC74-38758.

BLAP   _____. Pen, Pencil, Baton and Mask;
       Biographical Sketches. London:
       Spottiswoode, 1896. LC66-88066.

KEY

BOASE   Boase, Frederic. Modern English Biography:
Containing Many Thousand Concise Memoirs
of Persons Who Have Died Between the Years
1851-1900.... 6 vols. New York: Barnes &
Noble, [1965]. LC65-8551.

BOLS   Bolton, Sarah K. Successful Women.
1888. Reprint. Plainview, N.Y.: Books
for Libraries, [1974]. LC74-936.

BOOCA   The Book of Catholic Authors (Fourth Series)
Informal Self-Portraits of Famous Modern
Catholic Writers. Freeport, N.Y.: Books
for Libraries, [1971, c1948]. LC70-179740.

BOY   Boylan, Henry. A Dictionary of Irish
Biography. New York: Barnes & Noble,
1978. LC79-102572.

BOYS   Boynton, Percy H. Some Contemporary
Americans. 1924. Reprint. New York:
Biblo and Tannen, 1966. LC66-23516.

BREI   Breit, Harvey. The Writer Observed.
Cleveland: World, [1956]. LC56-5311.

BREN   Brenni, Vito J. West Virginia Authors: a
Bibliography. 2d ed. Morgantown: West
Virginia Library Association, 1968.
LC73-650336.

BRI   Brown, Stephen J. Ireland in Fiction; a
Guide to Irish Novels, Tales, Romances
and Folk-lore. Shannon, Ireland: Irish
Univ. Press, 1969, c1919.

BRIT   Brittain, Very M. The Women at Oxford; a
Fragment of History. New York: Macmillan,
[1960]. LC60-1109.

BRO   Browning, David C., ed. Everyman's
Dictionary of Literary Biography: English
and American. Rev. ed. New York:
Dutton, 1962. LCA58-2815.

KEY

BROOK   Brooks, Van Wyck. The Dream of Arcadia;
       American Writers and Artists in Italy,
       1760-1915. New York: Dutton, 1958.
       LC58-9597L.

BUC   Buckland, Charles E. Dictionary of Indian
       Biography. 1906. Reprint. Detroit: Gale,
       1968. LC68-23140.

BURG   Burgess, Gelett, ed. My Maiden Effort;
       Being the Personal Confessions of Well-
       known American Authors as to Their
       Literary Beginnings. Garden City, N.Y.:
       Pub. for the Authors' League of America
       by Doubleday, Page, 1921. LC21-20070.

BURK   Burke, William J. and Will D. Howe. American
       Authors and Books, 1640 to the Present Day.
       3d ed. New York: Crown, [c1972]. LC168332.

BURNT   Burnett, Whit, ed. This Is My Best. New
       York: Dial, 1942. LC42-36346.
          Also pub. as: America's 93 Greatest
       Living Authors Present This Is My Best.

CAS   Cassell's Encyclopaedia of World Literature.
       Rev. ed. 3 vols. New York: Morrow, [1973].
       LC73-10405.

CDME   Columbia Dictionary of Modern European
       Literature. 2d ed. New York: Columbia
       Univ. Press, 1980. LC80-17082.

CEL   Celebrity Register. International Celebrity
       Register. New York: Harper and Row, 1959.
       LC59-15865.

CEL2   _____. New York: Simon and Schuster, 1963.
       LC SC80-131.

CHA   Chambers, Robert. Chamber's Cyclopaedia of
       English Literature. Vol. 3, 19th--20th
       Century. Philadelphia: Lippincott, 1938.
       LC A40-2600.

CHABI   Chamber's Biographical Dictionary. Rev. ed.
       New York: St. Martin's, [1969, c1968].
       LC76-85529.

CHU   Church, Richard. _British Authors; a Twentieth Century Gallery_. Freeport, N.Y.: Books for Libraries, [1970]. LC79822.

CLARI   Balch, Emily. _Innocent Abroad_. 1931. Reprint. Westport, Conn.: Greenwood, 1975. LC74-2796.

CLARS   Clarke, Isabel C. _Six Portraits_. Reprint. Freeport, N.Y.: Books for Libraries, [1967]. LC67-26725.

CLE   Cleeve, Brian T. _Dictionary of Irish Writers. Vol. 1, Fiction, Novelists, Playwrights ... Writers in English_. Cork: Mercier, [1967]. LC71-14995R.

COLSA   Colby, Vineta. _The Singular Anomaly; Women Novelists of the Nineteenth Century_. New York: New York Univ. Press, 1970. LC70-92522.

CON   _Contemporary Authors: A Bio-Bibliographical Guide to Current Writers in Fiction...._ Vols. 45-108. Detroit: Gale, 1967-. LC62-52046.

CON-N   _____. _New Series...._ Vols. 1-. Detroit: Gale, 1962-. LC81-640179.

CON-P   _____. _Permanent Series_ ..., edited by Clare D. Kinsman. 2 vols. Detroit: Gale, c1975-78. LC75-13539.

CON-R   _____. _Revised Series_. Vols. 1-44. Detroit: Gale, 1967-. LC67-9634R.

CONO   Vinson, James. _Contemporary Novelists_. New York: St. Martin's, [1972]. LC75-189694.

CONW   Conley, Philip M., ed. _West Virginia Encyclopedia_. Charleston, W.Va.: West Virginia Pub. Co., 1929. LC30-14201.

COOPA   Cooper, Page. <u>Authors</u> <u>and</u> <u>Others</u>. 1927.
Reprint. Freeport, N.Y.: Books for
Libraries, [1970]. LC70-107689.

COOPE   Cooper, Frederic T. <u>Some</u> <u>English</u> <u>Tellers;</u>
<u>a</u> <u>Book</u> <u>of</u> <u>the</u> <u>Younger</u> <u>Novelists</u>. 1912.
Reprint. Freeport, N.Y.: Books for
Libraries, [1968]. LC68-54341.

COR   Corkran, Henriette. <u>Celebrities</u> <u>and</u> <u>I.</u>
London: Hutchinson, 1902. OCLC 3561395.

COU   Courtney, William L. <u>The</u> <u>Feminine</u> <u>Note</u> <u>in</u>
<u>Fiction</u>. 1904. Reprint. Norwood, Pa.:
Norwood editions, 1977. LC77-25172.

COY   Coyle, William, ed. <u>Ohio</u> <u>Authors</u> <u>and</u> <u>Their</u>
<u>Books:</u> <u>Biographical</u> <u>Data</u> <u>and</u> <u>Selective</u>
<u>Bibliographies</u> <u>for</u> <u>Ohio</u> <u>Authors,</u> <u>Native</u>
<u>and</u> <u>Resident,</u> <u>1796-1950</u>. Cleveland:
World, [1962]. LC62-7594.

CRO   Crone, John S. <u>A</u> <u>Concise</u> <u>Dictionary</u> <u>of</u>
<u>Irish</u> <u>Biography</u>. Rev. ed. 1937. Reprint.
Nendeln/Liechtenstein: Kraus, 1970.
OCLC 756325.

CROS   Crosland, Margaret. <u>Women</u> <u>of</u> <u>Iron</u> <u>and</u>
<u>Velvet,</u> <u>and</u> <u>the</u> <u>Books</u> <u>They</u> <u>Wrote</u> <u>in</u>
<u>France</u>. London: Constable, 1976.
LC77-359824.

CUR   <u>Current</u> <u>Biography</u> <u>Yearbook</u>. New York:
Wilson, 1940-. LC40-27432.

DAB   <u>Dictionary</u> <u>of</u> <u>American</u> <u>Biography</u>. 10 vols.
1928-37. Reprint. New York: Scribner,
1946?-1958. LC60-2195.

DAB-S   _____. <u>Supplement</u>. vols. 1-7. New York:
Scribner, 1944-1981.

DANB   <u>Dictionary</u> <u>of</u> <u>American</u> <u>Negro</u> <u>Biography,</u>
edited by Rayford W. Logan and Michael R.
Winston. New York: Norton, c1982.
LC81-9629.

DAW   Dawson, Lawrence H. <u>Nicknames</u> and <u>Pseud-</u>
       <u>onymns, Including Sobriquets</u> <u>of Persons</u>
       <u>in History, Literature, and the Arts</u>....
       1908. Reprint. Detroit: Gale, 1974.
       LC73-164216.

DELL   Dell, Floyd. <u>Women</u> as <u>Word Builders;</u>
       <u>Studies in Modern Feminism</u>. 1913.
       Reprint. Westport, Conn.: Hyperion,
       1976. LC75-21810.

DIL   <u>Dictionary of Irish Literature</u>. Westport,
       Conn.: Greenwood, 1979. LC78-20021.

DIX   Dixon, Ella H. <u>"As I Knew Them"; Sketches</u>
       <u>of People I Have Met on the Way</u>. London:
       Hutchinson, [1930]. OCLC 408431.

DNB   <u>Dictionary of National Biography</u>. 22 vols.
       London: Oxford Univ. Press, 1921-22.
       LC36-29738.

DNB-S   _____. <u>Supplement</u>. Vols. 1-7. London:
       Oxford Univ. Press, 1963-64, c1921-22.
          Supp. 1--1901-11   Supp. 2--1912-21
          Supp. 3--1922-30   Supp. 4--1931-40
          Supp. 5--1941-50   Supp. 6--1951-60
          Supp. 7--1961-70

DNZ   Scholefield, Guy H. <u>A Dictionary</u> of <u>New</u>
       <u>Zealand Biography</u>. 2 vols. Wellington,
       New Zealand: Dept. of Internal Affairs,
       1940. LC41-1230.

DODD   Dodd, Loring H. <u>Celebrities</u> at <u>Our</u>
       <u>Hearthside</u>. Boston: Dresser, Chapman &
       Grimes. [1959]. LC59-14846.

DOY   Doyle, Brian. <u>The Who's Who of Children's</u>
       <u>Literature</u>. New York: Schocken Books,
       [1968]. LC68-28904.

DR   <u>Dramatists</u>, edited by James Vinson. New
       York: St. Martin's, 1979. LC78-78303.
       Also published as: Vol. 3 of <u>Great</u>
       <u>Writers of the English Language</u>.

KEY

DSAB   Dictionary of South African Biography.
3 vols. [Pretoria]: Nasional Boekhandel
Bpk. for National Council for Social
Research, Dept. of Higher Education.
[1968-]. LC67-29091.

DUC   Duclaux, Agnes M. Twentieth Century French
Writers: (Reviews and Reminiscences).
1920. Reprint. Freeport, N.Y.: Books for
Libraries, [1969]. LC67-22089.

DUN   Dunaway, Philip and Mel Evans. A Treasury
of the World's Great Diaries. Garden City,
N.Y.: Doubleday, [1957]. LC57-9502.

EDW   Edwards, Matilda B. Six Life Studies of
Famous Women. 1880. Reprint. Freeport,
N.Y.: Books for Libraries, [1972].
LC73-39701.

EMD   Encyclopedia of Mystery and Detection. New
York: McGraw-Hill, c1976. LC75-31645.

ENZ   An Encyclopaedia of New Zealand. 3 vols.
Wellington, N.Z.: R.E. Owen, Govt.
Printer, 1966. LC67-4443.

FARR   Farrar, John C., ed. The Literary Spotlight.
1924. Reprint. Freeport, N.Y.: Books for
Libraries, 1970. LC70-117789.

FLE   Encyclopedia of World Literature in the
20th Century. 4 vols. New York:
F. Ungar, [1967-75]. LC67-13615R.

FUL   Fuller, Muriel, ed. More Junior Authors.
New York: Wilson, 1963. LC63-11816.

FUR   Furniss, Harry. Some Victorian Women, Good,
Bad, and Indifferent. New York: Dodd,
Mead, 1923. LC24-539.

GAR   Garland, Henry and Mary Garland. The Oxford
Companion to German Literature. Oxford
[Eng.]: Clarendon, 1976. LC76-367443.

GARRA   Garraty, John A. <u>Encyclopedia</u> of American
         <u>Biography.</u> New York: Harper, [1974].
         LC74-1807.

GARV   Garvin, John W. <u>Canadian</u> <u>Poets</u> <u>and</u> <u>Poetry.</u>
         New York: Stokes, [c1916]. LC17-10982.

GOW   Gowen, Herbert H. <u>A</u> <u>History</u> <u>of</u> <u>Indian</u>
         <u>Literature</u> <u>from</u> <u>Vedic</u> <u>Times</u> <u>to</u> <u>the</u>
         <u>Present</u> <u>Day.</u> New York and London:
         D. Appleton, 1931. LC31-29760.

GRE   Green-Armytage, A.J. <u>Maids</u> <u>of</u> <u>Honor....</u>
         Edinburgh: W. Blackwood, 1906. LC76-369032.

GRET   Green, Roger L. <u>Tellers</u> <u>of</u> <u>Tales;</u> an
         <u>Account</u> <u>of</u> <u>Children's</u> <u>Favourite</u> <u>Authors</u>
         <u>from</u> <u>1839</u> <u>to</u> <u>the</u> <u>Present</u> <u>Day, Their</u> <u>Books</u>
         <u>and</u> <u>How</u> <u>They</u> <u>Came</u> <u>to</u> <u>Write</u> Them.... New,
         enl. ed. Leicester, Eng.: E. Ward,
         [1953]. LC54-8455.

GRETB   _____. <u>Tellers</u> <u>of</u> <u>tales;</u> <u>British</u> <u>Authors</u>
         <u>of</u> <u>Children's</u> <u>Books</u> <u>from</u> <u>1800</u> <u>to</u> <u>1964.</u>
         Rev. ed. New York: F. Watts, [1965].
         LC65-12428.

GUS   Gustafson, Alrik. <u>A</u> <u>History</u> <u>of</u> <u>Swedish</u>
         <u>Literature.</u> Minneapolis: Univ. of
         Minnesota Press, [1961]. LC61-7722.

HAL   Halsey, Francis W., ed. <u>Women</u> <u>Authors</u> <u>of</u>
         <u>Our</u> <u>Day</u> <u>in</u> <u>Their</u> <u>Homes;</u> <u>Personal</u>
         <u>Descriptions</u> <u>and</u> <u>Interviews.</u> New York:
         J. Pott, 1903. LC03-7776.

HAMM   Hammerton, John A., ed. <u>Concise</u> <u>Universal</u>
         <u>Biography:</u> <u>a</u> <u>Dictionary</u> <u>of</u> <u>the</u> <u>Famous</u> <u>Men</u>
         <u>and</u> <u>Women</u> <u>of</u> <u>All</u> <u>Countries</u> <u>and</u> <u>All</u>
         <u>Times....</u> 2 vols. 1934-35. Reprint.
         Detroit: Gale, 1975. LC74-31444.

HAN   Hansson, Laura M. <u>Modern</u> <u>Women.</u> London:
         J. Lane, Boston: Roberts, 1896. LC01-977.

HAOXA   Hart, James D. <u>The</u> <u>Oxford</u> <u>Companion</u> <u>to</u>
         <u>American</u> <u>Literature.</u> 4th ed. New York:
         Oxford Univ. Press, 1965. LC65-22796.

HAOXE Harvey, Paul. The Oxford Companion to
English Literature. 4th ed. Oxford,
Clarendon, 1967. LC67-111134.

HAOXF Harvey, Paul and J.E. Heseltine, eds. The
Oxford Companion to French Literature.
Oxford: Clarendon, 1959. LC59-2367.

HAR Hargreaves-Mawdsley, W.N. Everyman's
Dictionary of European Writers. London:
Dent; New York: E.P. Dutton, 1968.
LC68-59559.

HARKF Harkins, Edward F. Famous Authors (Women).
1901. Reprint. Gale: Detroit, 1976.
LC73-173098.
  Also pub. as: Little Pilgrimages Among
the Women Who Have Written Famous
Books. Boston: L.C. Page, 1902.

HAY Haycraft, Howard. Murder for Pleasure: the
Life and Times of the Detective Story.
Enl. ed. New York: Biblo and Tannen,
1968, [c1941]. LC68-25809R.

HEN Henry, Stuart O. French Essays and Profiles.
New York: E.P. Dutton, [c1921]. LC21-12884R.

HIG Higginson, Alexander H. British and
American Sporting Authors, Their Writings
and Biographies. Berryville, Va.: Blue
Ridge Press, 1949. LC agr50-20.

HINA Hind, Charles L. Authors and I. 1921.
Reprint. Freeport, N.Y.: Books for
Libraries, [1968]. LC68-54351.

HIND _____. More Authors and I. 1922.
Reprint. Freeport, N.Y.: Books for
Libraries, [1969]. LC69-17576.

HINK Hinkel, Edgar J. and Wm. F. McCann, eds.
Biographies of California Authors and
Indexes of California Literature. 2 vols.
Oakland, Calif.: Alameda County Library,
1942. LC42-21715.

HO   Hoehn, Matthew, ed. <u>Catholic Authors;
          Contemporary Biographical Sketches.</u>
          [Newark, N.J.]: St. Mary's Abbey, 1952.
          LC48-2039.

HOE   _____. <u>Catholic Authors: Contemporary
          Biographical Sketches, 1930-1947.</u>
          [Newark, N.J.]: St. Mary's Abbey, 1948.
          LC48-2039.

HOL   Holmes, Urban T. <u>The French Novel in
          English Translation.</u> Chapel Hill:
          [Univ. of North Carolina Press], 1930.
          LC30-18665.

HUB   Hubbard, Elbert. <u>Little Journeys to the
          Homes of Famous People.</u> 1897. Reprint.
          New York: G.P. Putnam's Sons, [1924].
          LC25-13780.

HUN   Hunt, Rockwell D. <u>California's Stately Hall
          of Fame.</u> Stockton, Calif.: College of the
          Pacific, 1950. LC50-1660.

INN   Innis, Mary Q. <u>The Clear Spirit: Twenty
          Canadian Women and Their Times.</u> [Toronto]:
          Pub. for the Canadian Federation of
          University Women by the Univ. of Toronto
          Press, [1966]. LC66-31236.

JES   Jessup, Josephine L. <u>The Faith of Our
          Feminists; a Study in the Novels of Edith
          Wharton, Ellen Glasgow, Willa Cather.</u> New
          York: Biblo and Tannen, 1965. LC65-23482.
            First pub. 1950.

JO   Joint Committee on North Carolina Literature
          and Bibliography of the North Carolina
          English Teachers Association and the
          North Carolina Library Association. <u>North
          Carolina Authors: A Selective Handbook.</u>
          Chapel Hill: Univ. of North Carolina
          Library, 1952. LC53-62227R.

JOHDB Johnson, Rossiter. <u>A Dictionary of
          Biographies of Authors Represented in the
          Authors Digest Series.</u> 1927. Reprint.
          Detroit: Gale, 1974. LC71-167011.

JOHH Johannsen, Albert. The House of Beadle and Adams and Its Dime and Nickel Novels; the Story of a Vanished Literature. Vol. 2, The Authors and Their Novels. Norman: Univ. of Oklahoma Press, [1950]. LC50-8158R.

JOHH2 _____. The House of Beadle and Adams.... Vol. 3, Supplement, Addenda, Corrigenda. Norman: Univ. of Oklahoma Press, c1962. LC50-8158.

JONE Jones, Anna G. Tommorow Is Another Day: the Woman Writer in the South, 1859-1936. Baton Rouge: Louisiana State Univ. Press, c1981. LC80-29123.

JONES Jones, Joseph J. and Johanna Jones. Authors and Areas of Australia. Austin, Tex.: Steck-Vaughn, [1970]. LC74-120140.

KIL Kilmer, Joyce, comp. Literature in the Making, by Some of Its Makers. 1917. Reprint. Port Washington, N.Y.: Kennikat, 1968. LC68-26251.

KNIB Knight, Lucian L. Biographical Dictionary of Southern Authors. 1929. Reprint. Detroit: Gale, 1978. LC75-26631. Originally published as: Biographical Dictionary of Authors. Vol. 15, Library of Southern Literature.

KRO Kronenberger, Louis. Atlantic Brief Lives; a Biographical Companion to the Arts. Boston: Little, Brown, 1975, c1971. LC73-154960.

KU Kulkin, Mary-Ellen. Her Way: Biographies of Women for Young People. Chicago: American Library Association, 1976. LC76-25861.

KUAA Kunitz, Stanley J. and Howard Haycraft, eds. American Authors, 1600-1900; a Biographical Dictionary of American Literature. New York: Wilson, 1938. LC38-27938.

KUAT   Kunitz, Stanley J., Howard Haycraft and Wilbur C. Hadden, eds. Authors Today and Yesterday. New York: Wilson, 1933. LC33-27467.

KUBA   Kunitz, Stanley J. and Howard Haycraft, eds. British Authors of the Nineteenth Century. New York: Wilson, 1936. LC36-28581.

KUE   Kunitz, Stanley J. and Vineta Colby, eds. European Authors, 1000-1900; A Biographical Dictionary of European Literature. New York: Wilson, 1967. LC67-13870.

KUJ1   Kunitz, Stanley J. and Howard Haycraft, eds. Junior Book of Authors, an Introduction to the Lives of Writers and Illustrators for Younger Readers, from Lewis Carroll and Louisa Alcott to the Present Day. New York: Wilson, 1934. LC34-36776.

KUJ2   _____. The Junior Book of Authors. 2nd ed. New York: Wilson, 1951. LC51-13057.

KUL   Kunitz, Stanley, J., ed. Living Authors; a Book of Biographies. New York: Wilson, 1932. LC34-922.

KUT   Kunitz, Stanley J. and Howard Haycraft, eds. Twentieth Century Authors: a Biographical Dictionary of Modern Literature. New York: Wilson, 1942. LC43-51003.

KUTS   Kunitz, Stanley J. and Vineta Colby, eds. Twentieth Century Authors. First Supplement. New York: Wilson, 1955. LC43-51003.

LAS   Laski, Marghanita. Mrs. Ewing, Mrs. Molesworth, and Mrs. Hodgson Burnett. 1950. Reprint. Norwood, Pa.: Norwood Editions, 1977. LC77-16574.

LAU   Lauterbach, Edward S. and W. Eugene Davis. The Transitional Age; British Literature, 1880-1920. Troy, N.Y.: Whitson, 1973. LC72-87110.

KEY

LES   Lesbian Lives: Biographies of Women from the
          Ladder, edited by Barbara Grier and
          Coletta Reid. Baltimore: Diana, c1976.
          LC76-53806.

LIB   Library of Southern Literature. 17 vols.
          1909-23. Reprint. New York: Johnson
          Reprint Corp., [1970]. LC77-134264.
             Vol. 15--has title: Biographical
             Dictionary of Authors, by L.L. Knight
             (Indexed as KNIB).
LIB-S   Vol. 17--Supplement.

LOGG   Loggins, Vernon. I Hear America: ...
          Literature in the United States Since
          1900. 1937. Reprint. New York: Biblo
          and Tannen, 1967. LC67-18431.

LOGGN   _____. The Negro Author, His Development
          in America. New York: Columbia Univ.
          Press, 1931. LC31-32222.

LOGP   Logan, Mary S. The Part Taken by Women in
          American History. 1912. Reprint. New
          York: Arno, 1972. LC72-2613.

MAG   Magill, Frank N., Dayton Kohler, and T.F.
          Tilghman. Cyclopedia of World Authors.
          Rev. ed. 3 vols. Englewood Cliffs, N.J.:
          Salem Press, [1974]. LC74-174980.
             Original title: Masterplots Cyclopedia
             of World Authors.

MAGN   Magnus, Laurie. A Dictionary of European
          Literature. London: G. Routledge; New
          York: E.P. Dutton, 1926. LC26-7949.

MAJ   Majors, Monroe A. Noted Negro Women, Their
          Triumphs and Activities. Freeport, N.Y.:
          Books for Libraries, 1971, [c1893].
          LC73-138341.

MAN   Manly, John M. and Edith Rickert.
          Contemporary American Literature....
          New York: Harcourt, c1929. LC29-14937.

MANBL   _____. Contemporary British Literature; Outlines for Study, Indexes, Bibliographies. Rev. ed. New York: Harcourt, Brace, [c1928]. LC28-28542.

MAO   Manley, Seon and Susan Belcher. O, Those Extraordinary Women! Or the Joys of Literary Lib. Philadelphia: Chilton Book: [1972]. LC72-8061.

MAR   Marable, Mary H. and Elaine Boylan. A Handbook of Oklahoma Writers. Norman: Univ. of Oklahoma Press, 1939. LC39-27387.

MARB   Marble, Annie R. The Noble Prize Winners in Literature: 1901-1931. 1932. Reprint. Freeport, N.Y.: Books for Libraries, [1969]. LC70-84324.

MARBS   _____. A Study of the Modern Novel, British and American, Since 1900. New York: D. Appleton, 1928. LC28-25757.

MARL   Marlow, Joan. The Great Women. New York: A&W Publishers, c1979. LC79-65342.

MAT   Matlow, Myron. Modern World Drama; an Encyclopedia. New York: Dutton, 1972. LC71-185032.

MCC   McCabe, Joseph. A Biographical Dictionary of Modern Rationalists. London: Watts, 1920. LC21-3429.

MCCNP   McClintock, Marshall. The Nobel Prize Treasury. Garden City, N.Y.: Doubleday, 1948. LC48-7018.

MCR   McGraw-Hill Encyclopedia of Russia and the Soviet Union. New York: McGraw-Hill, [1961]. LC61-18169.

MCW   The McGraw-Hill Encyclopedia of World Biography; an International Reference Work. New York: McGraw-Hill, [1973]. LC70-37402.

MDCB   The Macmillan Dictionary of Canadian
        Biography. 4th ed. Toronto: Macmillan of
        Canada, c1978. LC79-308717.
            Earlier editions published as The
            Dictionary of Canadian Biography.

MDWB   The Macmillan Dictionary of Women's
        Biography, comp. and ed. by Jennifer S.
        Uglow. [London]: Macmillan Reference
        Books, 1982. OCLC 9188646.

MIA   Miller, Edmund M. Australian Literature
        from Its Beginnings to 1935; a Descriptive
        and Bibliographical Survey of Books by
        Australian Authors ... with Subsidiary
        Entries to 1938. Melbourne: Melbourne
        Univ. Press, 1940. OCLC 3020808.

MIAU   _____. Australian Literature, a
        Bibliography to 1938, Extended to 1950.
        Rev. ed. Sydney: Angus & Robertson,
        [1956]. LCa57-6327.

MICA   Millett, Fred B. Contemporary American
        Authors; a Critical Survey and 219
        Bio-bibliographies. New York: Harcourt,
        Brace, 1940. LC40-27229.

MICB   _____. Contemporary British Literature;
        a Critical Survey and 232 Author-
        bibliographies. 3d ed. New York:
        Harcourt, Brace, 1935. LC35-18933R.

MIG   Mighels, Ella S. The Story of the Files; a
        Review of California Writers and
        Literature. [San Francisco: Cooperative
        Printing Co.], c1893. LC1-5456.

MOB   Modern British Dramatists, 1900-1945,
        edited by Stanley Weintraub. 2 vols.
        Detroit: Gale, 1982. LC81-19234.

MOCL   Modern Commonwealth Literature. New York:
        Unger, 1977. LC75-35425.

MON   Monroe, Nellie E. The Novel and Society; a
Critical Study of the Modern Novel. 1941.
Reprint. Port Washington, N.Y.: Kennikat,
[1965]. LC65-27127.

MOO   Moore, Virginia. Distinguished Women
Writers. 1934. Reprint. Port Washington,
N.Y.: Kennikat, [1968]. LC68-26245.

MOR   Morgan, Henry J., ed. The Canadian Men and
Women of the Time. Toronto: W. Briggs,
1898.

MOR2   _____. The Canadian Men and Women of the
Time. 2nd ed. Toronto: Briggs, 1912.
OCLC 4818506.

MORG   Morgan, H. Wayne. Writers in Transition.
Hill and Wang, [1963]. LC63-8190.

MORGA   Morgan, Henry J. Types of Canadian Women
and of Women Who Are or Have Been
Connected with Canada. Vol. 1. Toronto:
Briggs, 1903. LC6-10811.

MYE   Myers, Robin. A Dictionary of Literature
in the English Language, from Chaucer to
1940. 2 vols. Oxford: Pergamon, [1970].
LC68-18529R.

NAW   Notable American Women, 1607-1950: a
Biographical Dictionary. 3 vols.
Cambridge, Mass.: Belknap Press of Harvard
Univ. Press, 1971. LC76-152274.

NAWM   Notable American Woman: the Modern Period: a
Biographical Dictionary. Cambridge,
Mass.: Belknap Press of Harvard Univ.
Press, 1980. LC80-18402.

NBI   National Bibliography of Indian Literature,
1901-1953. 4 vols. New Delhi: Sahitya
Akademi, [1962-74]. LC sa63-1991R.

NCAB   The National Cyclopedia of American
Biography.... Vols. 1-58 and A-M.
Clifton, N.J.: White, 1893-1979.
LC21-21756R.

KEY

NCH   The New Century Handbook of English
Literature. Rev. ed. New York:
Appleton-Century-Crofts, [1967].
LC67-12396.

NO   The Novel to 1900. New York: St. Martin's,
c1980. LC80-22573.

NOV   Novels and Novelists: a Guide to the World
of Fiction. London: Windward, 1980.
LC80-501056.

NPW   Novelists and Prose Writers. New York:
St. Martin's, 1979. LC78-78302.
Also published as: Vol. 2 of Great
Writers of the English Language, edited
by James Vinson. LC80-454948R.

OBIT1   Obituaries from the Times, 1951-1960 ...,
compiled by Frank C. Roberts. Westport,
Conn.: Meckler, c1979. LC79-12743.

OBIT2   Obituaries from the Times, 1961-1970 ...,
compiled by Frank C. Roberts. Reading,
Eng.: Newspaper Archive Developments Ltd.,
c1975. LC76-362909R.

OBIT3   Obituaries from the Times, 1971-1975 ...,
compiled by Frank C. Roberts. Westport,
Conn.: Meckler, 1978. LC77-22500.

OBRIR   O'Brien, John A., ed. The Road to Damascus;
the Spiritual Pilgrimage of Fifteen
Converts to Catholicism. Garden City,
N.Y.: Doubleday, 1949. LC49-9069.

ODP   O'Donoghue, D.J. The Poets of Ireland; a
Biographical and Bibliographical Dictionary of Irish Writers of English Verse.
1912. Reprint. Detroit: Gale, 1968.
LC68-30622.

OP   Opfell, Olga S. The Lady Laureates: Women
Who Have Won the Nobel Prize. Metuchen,
N.J.: Scarecrow, 1978. LC78-15995.

ORG   Orgain, Kate A. Southern Authors in Poetry
        and Prose. New York: Neale, 1908.
        LC08-23871.

OV   Overton, Grant M. The Women Who Make Our
        Novels. New York: Moffat, Yard, 1918.
        LC19-1643.

OV2   _____. The Women Who Make Our Novels.
        1928. Reprint. Freeport, N.Y.: Books for
        Libraries, [1967]. LC67-23257.

OVA   _____. Authors of the Day. New York:
        G.H. Doran, [c1924]. LC24-23739.
                "Consists of the chapters solely
                devoted to individual authors in the
                author's When Winter Comes to Main
                Street and American Nights
                Entertainment."

OVAM   _____. American Night's Entertainment.
        1923. Reprint. Freeport, N.Y.: Books for
        Libraries, [1973]. LC73-4635.

OVEWH   _____. When Winter Comes to Main Street.
        1922. Reprint. Freeport, N.Y.: Books for
        Libraries, [1972]. LC72-37798.

OXF   Oxford and Asquith, Margot A., ed.
        Myself When Young, by Famous Women of
        To-day. 2d ed. London: F. Muller,
        [1938]. LC39-63.

PAC   Pacifici, Sergio. The Modern Italian Novel.
        Vol. 2. Carbondale: Southern Illinois
        Univ. Press, [1967-79]. LC75-156786.

PAP   Papashvily, Helen W. All the Happy
        Endings. New York: Harper, [1956].
        LC55-8029.

PARR   Parry, Benita. Delusions and Discoveries;
        Studies on India in the British
        Imagination, 1880-1930. Berkeley, Univ.
        of California Press, [1972]. LC70-186786.

PEA   Penguin Companion to American Literature.
       New York: McGraw-Hill, [1971].
       LC70-158062.

PEE   Penguin Companion to English Literature.
       New York: McGraw-Hill, [1971]. LC77-158061.

PEEU   Penguin Companion to European Literature.
       New York: McGraw-Hill, [1971, c1969].
       LC74-158063.

PENN   Penn, I. Garland. The Afro-American Press
       and Its Editors. 1891. Reprint. New
       York: Arno, 1969. LC69-18574.

PHIS   Phelps, Ruth S. Italian Silhouettes.
       1924. Reprint. Freeport, N.Y.: Books
       for Libraries, [1968]. LC68-55853.

POW   Powell, Lawrence C. California Classics;
       the Creative Literature of the Golden
       State. Los Angeles: W. Ritchie, [1971].
       LC75-149085.

PRE   Preston, Wheeler. American Biographies.
       1940. Reprint. Detroit: Gale, 1974.
       LC73-10407.

RA   The Reader's Advisor; a Layman's Guide to
       Literature. 12th ed. Vol. 1, The Best
       in American and British ... Literary
       Biography.... New York: Bowker, 1974.

RCW   The Reader's Companion to World Literature.
       2d ed. New York: New American Library,
       [1973]. LC73-173311.

REA   The Reader's Encyclopedia of American
       Literature. New York: Crowell, [1962].
       LC62-16546.

REAW   The Reader's Encyclopedia of the American
       West. New York: Crowell, 1977.
       LC76-17236.

RHO   Rhodenizer, Vernon B. A Handbook of
       Canadian Literature. Ottawa, Can.:
       Graphic Pub., 1930. OCLC 2834502.

RIC   Richardson, Kenneth R. Twentieth Century
        Writing: a Reader's Guide to Contemporary
        Literature. London, New York: Newnes
        Books, 1969. LC70-431735.

RICDA   Richards, Robert F. Concise Dictionary of
        American Literature. New York:
        Philosophical Library, [1955]. LC55-14278.

RICEW   Richey, Elinor. Eminent Women of the West.
        Berkeley, Calif.: Howell-North Books,
        c1975. LC75-26293.

RICK   Richey, Ish. Kentucky Literature, 1784-1963.
        Tompkinsville, Ky.: Printed by Monroe
        County Press, 1963. LC64-3008.

RICMI   Richards, Carmen N. and Genevieve R. Breen,
        eds. Minnesota Writes; a Collection of
        Autobiographical Stories by Minnesota
        Prose Writers. Minneapolis, Minn.: Lund,
        1945. LC45-10025.

RIEG   Riegel, Robert E. American Feminists.
        1963. Reprint. Westport, Conn.:
        Greenwood, 1980. LC80-13163.

ROBI   Robinson, Wilhelmena S. Historical Negro
        Biographies. [2d ed]. New York:
        Publishers Co., [1968]. LC68-2920.

ROCK   Rock, James. Who Goes There: a Biblio-
        graphic Dictionary. Bloomington, Ind.:
        J.A. Rock, 1979. LC79-125345.

ROD   Roderick, Colin A. 20 Australian Novelists.
        Sydney: Angus & Robertson, 1947. LC48-23206.

ROS   Rosenthal, Eric. Encyclopedia of Southern
        Africa. 6th ed. London, New York:
        Warne, 1973. LC73-75028.

ROSE   _____. Southern Africa Dictionary of
        National Biography. London: Warne,
        [1966]. LC66-15690.

ROSS   Ross, Ishbel. Ladies of the Press. 1936.
        Reprint. New York: Arno, 1974. LC74-3972.

RUB   Rubin, Louis D. A Bibliographical Guide to the Study of Southern Literature. Baton Rouge: Louisiana State Univ. Press, [1969]. LC69-17627.

RULE   Rule, Jane. Lesbanian Images. Garden City, N.Y.: Doubleday, 1975. LC74-18829.

RUSB   Rush, Theressa G., Carol F. Myers, and Esther S. Arata. Black American Writers Past and Present: A Biographical and Bibliographical Dictionary. 2 vols. Metuchen, N.J.: Scarecrow, 1975. LC74-28400.

RUT   Rutherford, Mildred L. The South in History and Literature; a Hand-book of Southern Authors, from the Settlement of Jamestown, 1607, to Living Writers. [Atlanta, Ga.: Franklin-Turner, 1907]. LC07-25153.

SAV   Savage, Candace S. Foremothers: Personalities and Issues from the History of Women in Saskatchewan. [1975]. LC77-374402.

SCHM   Schmidt, Minna M. 400 Outstanding Women of the World. Chicago: the Author, 1933. LC33-18770.

SCHW   Schweikert, Harry C., ed. Short Stories. Englarged ed. New York: Harcourt, Brace, 1934. LC34-2345.

SEN   Sen, Siba P. Dictionary of National Biography. 4 vols. Calcutta: Institute of Historical Studies, 1972-1974. LC72-906859.

SER   Serle, Percival. Dictionary of Australian Biography. 2 vols. Sydney: Angus and Robertson, [1949]. LC49-6289.

SEYS   Seymour-Smith, Martin. Who's Who in Twentieth-Century Literature. New York: Holt, Rinehart and Winston, c1976. LC75-21470.

SHA   Sharp, Robert F. A Dictionary of English
        Authors, Biographical and
        Bibliographical.... Rev. ed. 1904.
        Reprint. Detroit: Gale, 1978. LC75-35577.

SHA-AP   _____. Appendix.

SHO   Showalter, Elaine. A Literature of Their
        Own: British Women Novelists from Bronte
        to Lessing. Princeton, N.J.: Princeton
        Univ. Press, c1977. LC76-3018.

SOME   Something About the Author. Vols. 1-.
        Detroit: Gale, 1971-. LC72-27107.

SOU   Southern Writers: a Biographical Dictionary,
        edited by Robert Bain, Joseph M. Flora,
        and Louis D. Rubin, Jr. Baton Rouge:
        Louisiana State Univ. Press, c1979, 1980.
        LC78-25899.

ST   Stahl, John M. Growing with the West; the
        Story of a Busy, Quiet Life. New York:
        Longmans, Green, 1930. LC30-10795.

STA   Standard Encyclopaedia of Southern Africa.
        12 vols. [Cape Town]: NASOU, [1970-1976].
        LC79-113594R.

STOD   Stoddard, Hope. Famous American Women.
        New York: Crowell, [1970]. LC73-87158.

STOK   Stokes, Sewell. Pilloried. New York:
        D. Appleton, 1929. LC29-6163.

STOXC   Story, Noah. The Oxford Companion to
        Canadian History and Literature. Toronto:
        Oxford Univ. Press, 1967. LC67-31959.

STOXC2 Toye, William. Supplement to the Oxford
        Companion to Canadian History and
        Literature. Toronto: Oxford Univ.
        Press, 1973. LC74-180951.

SY   Sylvestre, Guy, Brandon Conron, and Carl F.
        Klinck, eds. Canadian Writers: a
        Biographical Dictionary. Toronto:
        Ryerson, [1964]. LC65-3315.

TAV   Taves, Isabella. Successful Women and How
        They Attained Success. New York:
        E.P. Dutton, 1943. LC43-2956.

THE   These Modern Women: Autobiographical Essays
        from the Twenties. Old Westbury, N.Y.:
        Feminist Press, c1978. LC78-8750.

THOI   Thompson, Donald E. Indiana Authors and
        Their Books, 1917-1966. Crawfordsville,
        Ind.: Wabash College, 1974. LC74-178019.
        "A continuation of Indiana Authors
        and Their Books, 1816-1916, and
        containing additional names from
        the earlier period".

THOMC   Thomas, Clara. Canadian Novelists,
        1920-1945. 1946. Reprint. [Folcroft,
        Pa.]: Folcroft, 1970. LC72-194072.

TIT   Titus, William A. Wisconsin Writers;
        Sketches and Studies. Detroit: Gale,
        1974. LC74-4303.

TWCB   The Twentieth Century Biographical Dictio-
        nary of Notable Americans, edited by
        Rossiter Johnson and John H. Brown. 10
        vols. 1904. Reprint. Detroit: Gale,
        1968. LC58-19657.
        "Corrected edition of a work previously
        published under the titles: The Cyclo-
        paedia of American Biography 1897-1903,
        and Lamb's Biographical Dictionary of
        the United States, 1900-1903."

TWCC   Twentieth-Century Crime and Mystery Writers,
        edited by John M. Reilly. New York: St.
        Martin's. c1980. LC79-92844.

TWCR   Twentieth-Century Romance and Gothic
        Writers, edited by Kay Mussell. Detroit:
        Gale, c1982. LC82-15577.

TWCW   Twentieth-Century Western Writers, edited by
        James Vinson. Detroit: Gale, c1982.
        LC83-128541.

TYNAN   Tynan, Katharine. <u>Memories</u>. London:
        E. Nash & Grayson, [1924]. LC24-16027.

VDW   Van Doren, Charles L. <u>Webster's American</u>
        <u>Biographies</u>. Springfield, Mass.:
        G.&C. Merriam, [1974]. LC74-6341.

VIC   <u>Victorian Novelists After 1885</u>, edited by
        Ira B. Nadel and William E. Fredeman.
        Vol. 18, <u>Dictionary of Literary Biography</u>.
        Detroit: Gale, 1983. LC82-24200.

VIT   Vittorini, Domenico. <u>The Modern Italian</u>
        <u>Novel</u>. 1930. Reprint. New York: Russell
        & Russell, [1967]. LC66-27195.

WAG   Wagenknecht, Edward C., ed. <u>When I Was a</u>
        <u>Child; an Anthology</u>. New York:
        E.P. Dutton, 1946. LC46-11816.

WAGCA   _____. <u>Cavalcade of the American Novel,</u>
        <u>from the Birth of the Nation to the</u>
        <u>Middle of the Twentieth Century</u>. New
        York: Holt, [1952]. LC52-7022L.

WAGCE   _____. <u>Cavalcade of the English Novel</u>.
        New York: Holt, [1954]. LC54-2094L.

WAR   Warfel, Harry R. <u>American Novelists of</u>
        <u>Today</u>. Westport, Conn.: Greenwood,
        [1972, c1951]. LC72-599.

WARBD   Warner, Charles D., ed. <u>Biographical</u>
        <u>Dictionary and Synopsis of Books,</u>
        <u>Ancient and Modern</u>. 1902. Reprint.
        Detroit: Gale, 1965. LC66-4326.

WARD   <u>Our Famous Women: an Authorized Record of</u>
        <u>the Lives and Deeds of Distinguished</u>
        <u>American Women of Our Times ...</u>,
        edited by Elizabeth S. Ward. 1883.
        Reprint. Freeport, N.Y.: Books for
        Libraries, [1975]. LC73-1192.

WARLC   Ward, A.C. <u>Longman Companion to Twentieth</u>
        <u>Century Literature</u>. Harlow: Longman,
        1970. LC76-554609.

WEBB   Webb, Mary G. and Edna L. Webb. Famous
      Living Americans. Greencastle, Ind.:
      C. Webb, 1915. LC15-82.

WEBS   Webster's Biographical Dictionary.
      Springfield, Mass.: Merriam, c1980.
      LC79-23607.

WELL   Wellington, Amy. Women Have Told; Studies
      in the Feminist Tradition. Boston:
      Little, Brown, 1930. LC30-5739.

WENW   Webster's New World Companion to English
      and American Literature. New York: World,
      1973. LC72-12788.

WILA   Willard, Frances E. and Mary A. Livermore,
      eds. American Women: Fifteen Hundred
      Biographies with over 1,400 Portraits;
      a Comprehensive Encyclopedia of the Lives
      and Achievements of American Women During
      the Nineteenth Century. Rev. ed. 1897.
      Reprint. Gale, 1973. LC73-7985.
      First pub. in 1893 as A Woman of the
      Century. Another rev. ed. pub. in 1901
      as Portraits and Biographies of
      Prominent American Women.

WIN   Winslow, Helen M. Literary Boston of
      To-day. Boston: L.C. Page, 1903 [1902].
      LC02-20654.

WOMA   Women of Achievement; Biographies and
      Portraits of Outstanding American Women.
      New York: House of Field, [1940].
      LC43-12862.

WOWWA   Woman's Who's Who of America; a Biographical
      Dictionary of Contemporary Women of the
      United States and Canada, 1914-1915,
      edited by John W. Leonard. [c1914].
      Reprint. Detroit: Gale, 1976. LC74-6280.

WWLA   Who's Who Among Living Authors of Older
Nations, Covering the Literary Activities
of Living Authors and Writers of All
Countries of the World Except the United
States of America, Canada ..., edited by
Alberta C. Lawrence. Rev. ed.
1928. Reprint. Detroit: Gale, 1966.
LC28-28492.

WWNA   Who Was Who Among North American Authors,
1921-1939. 2 Vols. Detroit: Gale, c1976.
LC76-23548.
    Originally pub. as: Who's Who Among
    North American Authors, Volumes 1-7,
    1921-1939.

WWW   Who Was Who.... Vols. 1-6. London: A.&C.
Black, 1897-. LC20-14622R.

WWWA   Who Was Who in America.... Vols. 1-6.
Chicago: Marquis, 1967-. LC43-3789R.

WWWA-H   . Historical volume. Chicago:
Marquis, 1963. LC43-3789.

WWWE   Who Was Who Among English and European
Authors, 1931-1949. 3 vols. Detroit:
Gale, c1978. LC77-280.
    Based on entries which first appeared in
    The Author's and Writer's Who's Who &
    Reference Guide.... and in Who's Who
    Among Living Authors of Older Nations....
    A considerable number of U.S. authors
    are included.

WWWL   Who Was Who in Literature, 1906-1934.
2 vols. Detroit: Gale, c1979. LC78-25583.

WWWT   Who Was Who in the Theatre, 1912-1976: a
Biographical Dictionary of Actors,
Actresses, ... of the English-speaking
Theatre. 4 vols. Gale, c1978.
LC78-9634R.
    Compiled from Who's Who in the
    Theatre, Volumes 1-15, 1912-1972.

KEY

WYN   Wynn, William T., ed. <u>Southern</u> <u>Literature;</u>
       <u>Selections</u> <u>and</u> <u>Biographies.</u> New York:
       Prentice-Hall, 1932. LC32-11480.

YES   <u>Yesterday's</u> <u>Authors</u> <u>of</u> <u>Books</u> <u>for</u> Children:
       <u>Facts</u> <u>and</u> <u>Pictures</u> about <u>Authors</u> and
       <u>Illustrators</u> <u>of</u> <u>Books</u> <u>for</u> <u>Young</u> People ...,
       edited by Anne Commire. 2 vols. Detroit:
       Gale, c1977-. LC76-17501.

BIBLIOGRAPHY

Adams, Oscar F. A Dictionary of American Authors. 5th ed. 1904. Reprint. Detroit: Gale, 1969. LC68-21751.

Adams, William D. Dictionary of English Literature; Being a Comprehensive Guide to English Authors and Their Works. 2d ed. [188-?]. Reprint. Detroit: Gale, 1966. LC66-25162.

American Autobiography, 1945-1980: a Bibliography, edited by Mary L. Briscoe. Madison, Wis.: Univ. of Wisconsin Press, 1982. LC82-70547.

Author Biographies Master Index.... 2 vols. Detroit: Gale, 1975. LC76-27212.

Baker, Ernest A. A Guide to the Best Fiction, English and American, Including Translations from Foreign Languages. New and enl. ed. New York: Macmillan, 1932. LC32-27253.

Baker, Ernest A. A Guide to the Best Fiction in English. New ed. enl. and rev. London: G. Routledge, 1913. LC13-16912.

Biography and Genealogy Master Index ..., edited by Miranda C. Herbert and Barbara McNeil. 2d ed. 8 vols. Detroit: Gale, c1980. LC81-106706.

Biography Index. Vol. 1-. New York: H.W. Wilson, 1946-. LC47-6532R.

Burns, James A. New Zealand Novels and Novelists, 1861-1979: an Annotated Bibliography. Exeter, N.H.: Heinemann, 1981. LC81-161535.

Campbell, Dorothy W. Index to Black American Writers in Collective Biographies. Littleton, Colo.: Libraries Unlimited, 1983. LC82-14940.

Coombs, Richard E. Authors: Critical and Biographical References. Metuchen, N.J.: Scarecrow, 1971. LC73-167644.

Dargan, Marion. Guide to American Biography. Albuquerque: Univ. of New Mexico Press, 1949. LC49-48559.

BIBLIOGRAPHY

Fairbanks, Carol and Eugene A. Engeldinger. Black
American Fiction: a Bibliography. Metuchen,
N.J.: Scarecrow, 1978. LC78-1351.

Goodrich, Madge V. A Bibliography of Michigan
Authors. Richmond: Richmond Press, 1928.
LC28-16054.

Grimes, Janet and Diva Daims. Novels in English by
Women, 1891-1920: a Preliminary Checklist. New
York: Garland, 1981. LC79-7911.

Halkett, Samuel and John Laing. Dictionary
of Anonymous and Pseudonymous English
Literature. 9 vols. Edinburgh: Oliver
and Boyd, 1926-[62]. LC27-704.

Harris, Mark and R. Glenn Wright. Index to
Birthplaces of United Kingdom Authors.
Boston: G.K. Hall, c1979. LC79-17765.

Havlice, Patricia P. Index to Literary
Biography. 2 vols. Metuchen, N.J.:
Scarecrow, 1975. LC74-8315.

Hefling, Helen and Jessie W. Dyde. Index
to Contemporary Biography and Criticism.
2d ed. Boston: Gregg, 1972. LC72-10260.

Historical Biographical Dictionaries Master
Index.... Detroit: Gale, 1980.
LC80-10719.

Hymanson, Albert M. A Dictionary of Universal
Biography of All Ages and of All Peoples.
2d ed. London: Routledge and K. Paul, [1951].
LC51-6367.

International Index to Periodicals 1907/15-43/46.
Vols. 1-10. New York: H.W. Wilson: 1915-1947.
LC17-4969R.

Ireland, Norma O. Index to Women of the
World from Ancient to Modern Times; Biographies
and Portraits. Westwood, Mass.: Faxon, 1970.
LC75-120841.

BIBLIOGRAPHY

Kaplan, Louis. A Bibliography of American
   Autobiographies. Madison: Univ. of
   Wisconsin Press, 1961. LC61-5499.

Light, Beth and Veronica Strong-Boag. True
   Daughters of the North: Canadian Women's History:
   an Annotated Bibliography. Toronto: OISE Press,
   1980. LC80-504559.

Literary Criticism and Authors' Biographies: an
   Annotated Index, compiled by Alison P. Seidel.
   Metuchen, N.J.: Scarecrow, 1978. LC78-11857.

Lofts, William O. and D.J. Adley. The Men
   Behind Boys' Fiction. London: H. Baker,
   1970. LC70-564587.

McCormick, Eric H. New Zealand Literature,
   A Survey. London: Oxford Univ. Press,
   1959. LC59-2038.

Matthews, William. British Autobiographies; an
   Annotated Bibliography of British Autobiographies
   Published or Written Before 1951. Berkeley: Univ.
   of California Press, 1955. LC55-13593.

_____. Canadian Diaries and Autobiographies.
   Berkeley: Univ. of California, 1950. LC50-62732.

Mellown, Elgin W. A Descriptive Catalogue of the
   Bibliographies of 20th Century British Writers.
   Troy, N.Y.: Whitston, 1972. LC79-183301.

The New Cambridge Bibliography of English
   Literature. Vols. 3-4, 1800-1950. Cambridge
   [Eng.]: Univ. Press, 1969-1972. LC69-10199R.

New York Times Obituaries Index. 2 vols. New
   York: New York Times, 1970-1980. LC72-113422R.

Newman, Richard and R. Glenn Wright. Index
   to Birthplaces of American Authors. Boston:
   G.K. Hall, c1979. LC79-1244.

Nineteenth Century Readers' Guide to Periodical
   Literature, 1890-1899, with Supplementary
   Indexing, 1900-1922. 2 vols. New York: H.W.
   Wilson, 1944. LC a44-5439.

BIBLIOGRAPHY

O'Neill, Edward H. Biography by Americans,
    1658-1936; a Subject Bibliography. Philadelphia:
    Univ. of Pennsylvania Press, 1939. LC39-30813.

The Oxford History of Australian Literature,
    edited by Leonie Kramer. New York: Oxford Univ.
    Press, 1981. LC81-162174.

Readers' Guide to Periodical Literature.
    Vols. 1-15. New York: H.W. Wilson, 1905-1947.
    LC6-8232R.

Riches, Phyllis M., comp. An Analytical
    Bibliography of Universal Collected Biography
    Comprising Books Published in the English Tongue
    in Great Britain and Ireland, America and the
    British Dominions. 1934. Reprint. [New York:
    Johnson Reprint, 1973]. LC73-1215.

Stineman, Esther. Women's Studies: a Recommended
    Core Bibliography. Littleton, Colo.: Libraries
    Unlimited, 1979. LC79-13679.

Stonehill, Charles A., Andrew Block, and H.
    Winthrop Stonehill. Anonyma and Pseudonyma.
    2d ed. 4 vols. 1926-27. Reprint. New York:
    Milford House, 1969. LC68-8311.

Temple, Ruth Z. Twentieth Century British
    Literature; a Reference Guide and Bibliography.
    New York: Ungar, [1968]. LC67-13618.

The Times. London. Palmer's Index to the Times
    Newspaper, 1790-1940/41. New York: Kraus Reprint,
    1965-66. LC12-25874.

Vrana, Stan A. Interviews and Conversations with
    20th-Century Authors Writing in English: an
    Index. Metuchen, N.J.: Scarecrow, 1982.
    LC82-3275.

Wallace, William S. A Dictionary of North American
    Authors Deceased Before 1950. Detroit: Gale,
    1968, 1951. LC68-19955.

BIBLIOGRAPHY

atters, Reginald E. and Inglis F. Bell, comps. On Canadian Literature, 1806-1960; a Check List of Articles, Books, and Theses on English-Canadian Literature, Its Authors, and Language. [Toronto]: Univ. of Toronto Press, [1966]. LC66-1582.

Whiteman, Maxwell. A Century of Fiction by American Negroes, 1853-1952; a Descriptive Bibliography. Philadelphia: 1955. LC55-10876.

Woodress, James L. American Fiction, 1900-1950. Detroit: Gale, [1974]. LC73-17501.

Wright, Glenn. Author Bibliography of English Language Fiction in the Library of Congress through 1950. 8 vols. Boston: G.K. Hall, 1973. LC74-188840.

Women Novelists
1891–1920

A.L.O.E., pseud. (A Lady of England). See TUCKER, CHARLOTTE MARIE.

Abbott, Avery. See ABBOTT, MABEL AVERY (RUNDELL).

Abbott, Eleanor Hallowell. See COBURN, ELEANOR HALLOWELL (ABBOTT).

Abbott, Helen Raymond. See BEALS, HELEN RAYMOND (ABBOTT).

ABBOTT, JANE LUDLOW (DRAKE). 1881-1962. U.S.

Biography
AWO   WAR   WWWA-6

Obituary
NY TIMES (15 Dec 1962), 14:6.

ABBOTT, MABEL AVERY (RUNDELL). U.S.
        Avery Abbott

Biography
WWNA   WOWWA

ACKLAND, EMILY ANNA. b.1859.
        Hon. Lady Ackland

Biography
WWWL

Ackland, Hon. Lady.   See ACKLAND, EMILY ANNA.

Adair, Cecil, pseud.   See GREEN, EVELYN EVERETT-.

Adams, Mary, pseud.   See WARD, ELIZABETH STUART
    (PHELPS).

Adams, Mrs. Leith.   See LAFFAN, BERTHA JANE
    (GRUNDY) LEITH ADAMS.

ADDISON, JULIA DE WOLF (GIBBS). b.1866. U.S.

Biography
    ALY APP AWO BURK WEBS WOWWA WWNA WWWA-4

AGRESTI,   OLIVIA   FRANCES   MADOX   (ROSSETTI).
    1875-1960. Italy.
            Isabel Meredith, pseud.

Obituary
    TIMES (LONDON) (16 Nov 1960), 15:3.

AIKEN, EDNAH (ROBINSON). b.1872. U.S.

Biography
    BURK HINK WWWA-5

AKINS, ZOE. 1886-1958. U.S.

Biography
    APP AWO AWW BERE BURK DAB-S6 DIC HAOXA
    KUT MAN MAT MICA MYE REA RICDA WEBS WOWWA
    WWWA-3 WWWE

Obituary
    NY TIMES (30 Oct 1958), 31:1.
    TIMES (LONDON) (31 Oct 1958), 13:5.

AKUNIAN, ILSE (LEVIEN). 1852-1908. Germany.
　　　Ilse Frapan, pseud.

　　　　　　　Biography
　WARBD　WEBS

Albanesi, E. Maria.　See　ALBANESI, EFFIE ADELAIDE
　MARIA.

ALBANESI, EFFIE ADELAIDE MARIA. 1866-1936. England.
　　　E. Maria Albanesi
　　　Madame Albanesi
　　　Maria Albanesi
　　　Effie Adelaide Rowlands, pseud.

　　　　　　　Biography
　HAMM　WARLC　TWCR　WWWL

　　　　　　　Obituary
　TIMES (LONDON) (17 Oct 1936), 14:3.

Albanesi, Madame. See　ALBANESI, EFFIE ADELAIDE
　MARIA.

Albanesi, Maria.　See ALBANESI, EFFIE ADELAIDE
　MARIA.

Alcock, D.　See　ALCOCK, DEBORAH.

ALCOCK, DEBORAH. 1835-1913. England.
　　　D. Alcock

　　　　　　　Biography
　WWWL

ALDEN, CYNTHIA MAY (WESTOVER). 1862-1931. U.S.
　　　Cynthia M. Westover

　　　　　　　Biography
　APP　BICA　DAB-S1　NCAB-22　WILA　WOWWA　WWWA-1

ALDEN, ISABELLA (MACDONALD). 1841-1930. U.S.
       Mrs. G.R. Alden
       Pansy, pseud.

Autobiography
MEMORIES OF YESTERDAYS, edited by Grace
   Livingston Hill. Philadelphia: J.B.
   Lippincott, 1931. LC31-32946.

Biography
ALY APP AWW BD BOLS BURK COY DAB-S1 HAOXA
LOGP NAW NCAB-10 PAP TWCB WARBD WARLC WILA
WOWWA WWWA-1 YES-2

Obituary
PUBLISHERS WEEKLY 118 (16 Aug 1930), 600-601.

Alden, Mrs. G.R. See ALDEN, ISABELLA (MACDONALD).

ALDINGTON, MAY.
      Mrs. A.E. Aldington

Biography
WWWL

Aldington, Mrs. A.E. See ALDINGTON, MAY.

ALDIS, MARY (REYNOLDS). 1872-1949. U.S.

Biography
BURK WEBS WWWA-2

Aldon, Adair, pseud. See MEIGS, CORNELIA LYNDE.

ALDRICH, ANNE REEVE. 1866-1892. U.S.

Biography
BURK NCAB-4 WARBD WILA WWWA-H

ALDRICH, CLARA CHAPLINE (THOMAS). d.1967. U.S.
Darragh Aldrich, pseud.

Biography
AWO   BURK   THOI   WWNA   WWWA-4   WWWE

Aldrich, Darragh, pseud.   See ALDRICH, CLARA
CHAPLINE (THOMAS).

Aldrich, Dr. (Mrs.) F.L.S.   See ALDRICH, FLORA L.
(SOUTHARD).

ALDRICH, FLORA L. (SOUTHARD). 1859-1921. U.S.
Dr. (Mrs.) F.L.S. Aldrich

Biography
WILA

Aleramo, Sibilla, pseud.   See FACCIO, RINA
(COTTINO).

ALEXANDER, ELEANOR JANE. d.1939. Ireland.

Biography
BRI   WWLA   WWWE   WWWL

Obituary
TIMES (LONDON) (6 June 1939), 16:5; memorial
service (8 June 1939), 21:4.

ALEXANDER, GRACE CAROLINE. b.1872. U.S.

Biography
BAN   WOWWA   WWWA-5

ALEXANDER, MIRIAM. Ireland.
m. Stokes

Biography
BRI

Alexander, Mrs., pseud. See HECTOR, ANNIE (FRENCH).

ALLEN, EMMA SARAH (GAGE). b.1859. U.S.

Biography
BAN   HINK

Allston, Margaret, pseud. See BERGENGREN, ANNA (FARQUHAR).

ALLYN, EUNICE ELOISAE GIBBS. U.S.

Biography
WILA

ALMA-TADEMA, LAURENCE, MISS. d.1940. England.

Biography
WWWE   WWWL

Obituary
TIMES (LONDON) (21 Mar 1940), 11:5.

Almirall, N.   See ALMIRALL, NINA LOUISE.

ALMIRALL, NINA LOUISE. b.1877. U.S.
        N. Almirall

Biography
COY

Amber, Miles, pseud. See SICKERT, ELLEN MELICENT (COBDEN).

AMES, ELEANOR MARIA (EASTERBROOK). 1831-1908. U.S.
        Eleanor Kirk, pseud.

Biography
BURK   ROCK   WARBD   WILA

ANDERSON, ADA (WOODRUFF). b.1860. U.S.

Biography
APP   BURK   WOWWA   WWWA-4

ANDERSON, STELLA (BENSON). 1892-1933. England.
     Stella Benson

Biography
BERE   BRO   CHA   DNB-5   HAMM   KUL   KUT   MARBS
MICB   MYE   NCH   NOV   NPW   PEE   RIC   ROCK   SEYS
SHO   TWCR   WARLC   WEBS   WWWL

Bedell, R. Meredith.   STELLA BENSON.   Boston:
   Twayne, c1983. LC82-23223.

Bottome, Phyllis.   STELLA BENSON.   San Francisco:
   [Grabhorn], 1934. LCa35-792.
      15 pages

Roberts, Richard E.   PORTRAIT OF STELLA BENSON.
   London: Macmillan, 1939. LC40-2411.

Obituary
NY TIMES (8 Dec 1933), 23:3.
PUBLISHERS WEEKLY 124 (16 Dec 1933), 2083.
TIMES (LONDON) (8 Dec 1933), 9:3; (13 Dec), 9:3;
   (15 Dec), 19:2.

Andrews, Annulet.   See OHL, MAUDE ANNULET
   (ANDREWS).

ANDREWS, MARY RAYMOND (SHIPMAN). 1865?-1936. U.S.

Biography
BERE   BURK   KUJ1   KUT   MAN   NAW   WEBS   WWNA   WWWA-1

ANETHAN, ELEANOR MARY (HAGGARD) D'. 1860-1935.
   England.

Autobiography
FOURTEEN YEARS OF DIPLOMATIC LIFE IN JAPAN;
   LEAVES FROM THE DIARY OF BARONESS ALBERT
   D'ANETHAN.... London: S. Paul, [1912].

LC12-23677.
Covers the years 1893--1906.

Biography
WWLA   WWWE   WWWL

Obituary
TIMES (LONDON) (21 Nov 1935), 19:7.

ANGELLOTTI, MARION POLK. b.1887. U.S.

Biography
ALY   BURK   WWNA

Anglo-Australian, pseud. See HAY, AGNES GRANT
(GOSSE).

ANNESLEY, MAUDE GERTRUDE (WEBSTER-WEDDERBURN).
d.1930. England.
       m. (1)Haddon   (2)Rider   (3)Brownlow

Biography
WWWL

Obituary
TIMES (LONDON) (7 Nov 1930), 16:5.

ANSTRUTHER, EVA ISBELLA HENRIETTA. 1869-1935.
England.

Biography
WWWL

ANTHONY, GERALDINE W. d.1912. U.S.

Obituary
NY TIMES (21 Oct 1912), 11:6.

Antrobus, C.L. See ANTROBUS, CLARA LOUISA.

ANTROBUS, CLARA LOUISA (ROGERS). 1846-1919.
England.
      C.L. Antrobus

Biography
BEL

Obituary
TIMES (LONDON) (12 Feb 1919), 13:4.

Antrobus, Suzanne. See ROBINSON, SUZANNE (ANTROBUS).

APLINGTON, KATE ADELE (SMITH). b.1859. U.S.

Biography
BAR WOWWA

ARMFIELD, ANNE CONSTANCE (SMEDLEY). 1881-1941.
England.
      Mrs. Maxwell Armfield
      Constance Smedley
      X., pseud.

Autobiography
CRUSADERS; THE REMINISCENCES OF CONSTANCE SMEDLEY
(MRS. MAXWELL ARMFIELD). London: Duckworth,
1929. LC30-20276.

Biography
HAMM MDWB WWWE WWWL

Obituary
CUR-1941.
NY TIMES (13 Mar 1941), 21:5.
PUBLISHERS WEEKLY 139 (5 Apr 1941), 1467.
SCHOOL AND SOCIETY 53 (22 Mar 1941), 367.
WILSON 15 (May 1941), 710.

Armfield, Mrs. Maxwell. See Armfield, Anne Constance (Smedley).

ARMSTRONG, ANNE AUDUBON (WETZELL). 1872-1958. U.S.

Biography

AWO   WWNA   WWWA-3

McClellan, D.   "Personal Reminiscence."   In THIS
    DAY AND TIME, by Anne W. Armstrong.
    pp. ix-xvil. Johnson City: Research Advisory
    Council, East Tennessee State Univ., [1970,
    c1930]. LC76-627812.

Obituary

NY TIMES (18 Mar 1958), 29:3.

Armstrong, Elisa.   See BENGOUGH, ELISA (ARMSTRONG).

ARNOLD, ADELAIDE VICTORIA (ENGLAND). England.
        Mrs. J.O. Arnold

Biography

WWWL

Arnold, Birch, pseud.   See   BARTLETT, ALICE ELINOR
    (BOWEN).

Arnold, Mrs. J.O.   See   ARNOLD,   ADELAIDE VICTORIA
    (ENGLAND).

ARTHUR, MARY LUCY. d.1919. Ireland.
        George David Gilbert, pseud.

Obituary

TIMES (LONDON) (17 Sept 1919), 13:2.

Ashford, Daisy.   See   ASHFORD, MARGARET MARY.

ASHFORD, MARGARET MARY. 1881-1972. England.
        Daisy Ashford
        m. Devlin

12

ASHFORD

Biography
BERE   BRO   DOY   LAU   MYE   NCH   PEE   SOME-10
WARLC   WEBS

Obituary
CON-33--36R.
NY TIMES (18 Jan 1972), 34:1.
OBIT3, 25.
PUBLISHERS WEEKLY 201 (28 Feb 1972), 52-3.
TIMES (LONDON) (17 Jan 1972), 12:7; photo, 1:1.
WASHINGTON POST (21 Jan 1972).

ASHTON, HELEN ROSALINE. 1891-1958. England.
    m. Jordan

Biography
BERE   KUAT   MYE   NCH   WARLC   WEBS   WWWE

Obituary
BRITISH MEDICAL JOURNAL #5088 (12 July 1958), 110.
ILLUS LONDON NEWS 233 (12 July 1958), 77.
TIMES (LONDON) (3 July 1958), 14:2.
WILSON 33 (Nov 1958), 198.

ASHTON, WINIFRED. 1888-1965. England.
    Clemence Dane, pseud.

Biography
ADC   BERE   BRO   CHA   CHABI   DR   EMD   HAMM   KUL
KUT   KUTS   MANBL MARBS MICB   MOB   MYE   NCH   RIC
ROCK   SHO   TWCC   WARLC WEBS   WWLA WWWA-4 WWWE
WWWL   WWWT

Obituary
CON-93--96.
ILLUS LONDON NEWS 246 (3 Apr 1965), 25.
NY TIMES (29 Mar 1965), 33:2.
NEWSWEEK 65 (12 Apr 1965), 76.
PUBLISHERS WEEKLY 187 (12 Apr 1965), 45.
OBIT2, 185-6.
TIMES (LONDON) (29 Mar 1965), 33:2.

Athene, pseud. See HARRIS, MISS S.M.

ATHERTON, GERTRUDE FRANKLIN (HORN). 1857-1948. U.S.

Autobiography
ADVENTURES OF A NOVELIST. New York: Liveright, [c1932]. LC32-26332.

Biography
ADE AMN APP ASH AWO AWW BD BERE BIN BRO
BURG BURK CAS CHA CHABI CON-104 COR COU
CUR-1940 DAB-S4 HAL HAOXA HAOXE HARKF KUL
KUT LOGP MAN MARBS MICA MIG MYE NAW
NCAB-36 NOV NPW OV OV2 PEA POW RA REA
REAW RIC RICDA RICEW SHA TWCB TWCW WARBD
WARLC WEBS WOWWA WWNA WWWA-2 WWWE WWWL

Hamilton, Cosmo. PEOPLE WORTH TALKING ABOUT.
   pp. 87-95. Freeport, N.Y.: Books for
   Libraries, [1970], 1933. LC79-107706.

McClure, Charlotte S. GERTRUDE ATHERTON.
   Boston: Twayne, 1979. LC78-14208.

Obituary
CUR-1948.
NY TIMES (15 June 1948), 27:1.
NEWSWEEK 31 (28 June 1948), 65.
PUBLISHERS WEEKLY 153 (26 June 1948), 2639.
TIME 51 (21 June 1948), 95.
TIMES (LONDON) (15 June 1948), 4:2; (16 June),
   6:4.
WILSON 23 (Sept 1948), 10.

ATKINSON, ELEANOR (STACKHOUSE). 1863-1942. U.S.

Biography
AWO BAN BURK KUJ1 KUT WOWWA WWNA WWWA-2

Obituary
CUR-1943.
NY TIMES (11 Nov 1942), 25:3.

AUDOUX, MARGUERITE. 1863-1937. France.

Biography
BENN CROS HAMM HAOXF WARLC

Obituary
NY TIMES (3 Feb 1937), 24:1.
PUBLISHERS WEEKLY 131 (20 Mar 1937), 1330.
TIMES (LONDON) (4 Feb 1937), 9:6.

Augusta, Clara, pseud.   See   JONES,   CLARA AUGUSTA.

AUSTIN, JANE (GOODWIN). 1831-1894. U.S.

Biography
APP   AWW   BD   BURK   DAB-S1   HAOXA   JOHDB   KUAA
KUJ1   NCAB-6   REA   TWCB   WARBD   WILA

AUSTIN, MARTHA WADDILL. U.S.

Biography
KNIB

AUSTIN, MARY (HUNTER). 1868-1934. U.S.
         Gordon Stairs, pseud.

Autobiography
EARTH HORIZON, AUTOBIOGRAPHY.   Boston: Houghton
   Mifflin, 1932. LC32-31314.

LITERARY AMERICA, 1903-1934: THE MARY AUSTIN
   LETTERS, edited by T.M. Pearce.   Westport,
   Conn.: Greenwood, 1979. LC78-67914.

Biography
ADE   ALY   AMN   AWW   BICA   BODCA   BURG   BURK
DAB-S1 HAMM   HAOXA   HUN   KUL   KUT   LOGP   MAN
MARBS   MICA   MYE   NAW   OV   OV2   POW   PRE   REA
REAW   RICDA   ROCK   THE   TWCW   VDW   WAG   WAGCA
WEBS   WOWWA   WWWA-1   WWWL

Dillon, Richard H.   HUMBUGS AND HEROES; A GALLERY
   OF CALIFORNIA PIONEERS.   pp. 5-8.   Garden City,
   N.Y.: Doubleday, 1970.   LC70-89100.

Doyle, Helen M.   MARY AUSTIN, WOMAN OF GENIUS.
   New York: Gotham House, [c1939]. LC39-29445.

Fink, Augusta. I-MARY; A BIOGRAPHY OF MARY
   AUSTIN. Tucson, Ariz.: Univ. of Arizona Press,
   c1983. LC82-21807.

Gaer, Joseph, ed. MARY AUSTIN, BIBLIOGRAPHY AND
   BIOGRAPHICAL DATA. [California Literary
   Research Project], [1934]. LC35-27522.

Lyday, Jo W. MARY AUSTIN; THE SOUTHWEST WORKS.
   Austin, Tex.: Steck-Vaughn Co., [1968].
   LC68-22978.

Pearce, Thomas M. THE BELOVED HOUSE. Caldwell,
   Id.: Caxton Printers, 1940. LC40-10617.

_____. MARY HUNTER AUSTIN. New York: Twayne,
   [1966, c1965]. LC65-24245.

Sante Fe, N.M. Laboratory of Anthropology. MARY
   AUSTIN, A MEMORIAL, edited by Willard
   Houghland. Santa Fe., N.M.: Laboratory of
   Anthropology, 1944. LC45-2255.
      "14 testimonials contributed by writers,
      neighbors and friends."

Obituary

COMMONWEAL 20 (24 Aug 1934), 408.
NEWSWEEK 4 (25 Aug 1934), 30.
PUBLISHERS WEEKLY 126 (18 Aug 1934), 494.
SURVEY 70 (Sept 1934), 289.

AYRES, DAISY (FITZHUGH).

Biography

KNIB

AYRES, RUBY MILDRED. 1883-1955. England.
         m. Pocock

Biography

HAMM   NCH   RIC   TWCR   WARLC   WEBS   WWWE   WWWL

Obituary

NY TIMES (15 Nov 1955), 29:1.
OBIT1, 34.
TIMES (LONDON) (15 Nov 1955), 11:3.

BABCOCK, BERNIE (SMADE). 1868-1962. U.S.

Biography
ALY   AWO   COY   KNIB   LIB-17   WOWWA   WWNA   WWWA-5
WWWE   WWWL   WYN

Obituary
NY TIMES (15 June 1962), 27:4.

BABCOCK, WINNIFRED (EATON). b.1879. U.S./Canada.
m. (1)Babcock   (2)Reeve
Winnifred Reeve
Onoto Watanna, pseud.

Biography
BURK   THOMC   WEBS   WWWL

BACKUS, EMMA HENRIETTE (SCHERMEYER). b.1876. U.S.
Mrs. Henry Backus

Biography
COY   WOWWA   WWNA

Backus, Mrs. Henry.   See   BACKUS, EMMA HENRIETTE
(SCHERMEYER).

Bacon, Edward, pseud.   See   BACON, MARY D.

BACON, JOSEPHINE DODGE (DASKAM). 1876-1961. U.S.
Josephine Daskam
Josephine Dodge Daskam
Ingraham Lovell, pseud.

Biography
APP   AWO   BURG   BURK   CON-97--100   KUT   MAN   MARBS
WARBD   WEBS   WOWWA   WWWA-5   WWWE

Obituary
NY TIMES (31 July 1961), 19:2.
PUBLISHERS WEEKLY 180 (28 Aug 1961), 264.

BACON, MARY D. b.1866. U.S.
            Edward Bacon, pseud.

Biography
  BURK   WOWWA   WWWA-5

Bagnold, Enid.   See   JONES, ENID (BAGNOLD).

BAILEY, ALICE (WARD). 1857-1922. U.S.
            A.B. Ward

Biography
  WOWWA   WWNA   WWWA-4

BAILEY, EDITH LAWRENCE (BLACK). b.1870. U.S.
            Edith Lawrence, pseud.

Biography
  WOWWA

BAILEY, IRENE TEMPLE. 1880-1953. U.S.
            Temple Bailey

Biography
  AWO   AWW   BURK   DAB-S5   KUT   MARBS   OV2   REA
  WEBS   WWNA   WWWA-3

Obituary
  NY TIMES (8 July 1953), 27:3.
  NEWSWEEK 42 (20 July 1953), 64.
  PUBLISHERS WEEKLY 164 (18 July 1953), 195.
  TIME 62 (20 July 1953), 71.
  WILSON 28 (Sept 1953), 28.

BAILEY, MAY HELEN MARION   (EDGINTON). 1883-1957.
  England.
            H.M. Edginton
            May Edginton

Biography
  WWWE   WWWL

Bailey, Temple. See BAILEY, IRENE TEMPLE.

BAILLIE-SAUNDERS, MARGARET ELSIE (CROTHER).
1873-1949. England.

Biography

WWWE WWWL

Obituary
NY TIMES (25 Apr 1949), 23:2.
TIMES (LONDON) (25 Apr 1949), 7:4.
WILSON 23 (June 1949), 746.

BAIN, CHARLOTTE PIPER.

Biography
Bain, Francis W. "About My Mother." In AN ECHO
OF THE SPHERES: RESCUED FROM OBLIVION, edited
by F.W. Bain. pp.xix-xlv. London: Methuen,
1919. LC21-144.

Baines, Minnie Willis. See MILLER, MINNIE (WILLIS)
BAINES-.

BAIRD, JEAN KATHERINE. 1872-1918. U.S.

Biography

WOWWA WWWA-1

Baker, Amy J. See CRAWFORD, AMY JOSEPHINE
(BAKER).

BAKER, ETTA IVA (ANTHONY). U.S.

Biography
ALY AWO BURK WWNA

BAKER, JOSEPHINE R. (TURCK). d.1942. U.S.

Biography
ALY WOWWA WWWA-2

BALBACH, JULIA ANNA NENNINGER. b.1852. U.S.

Biography
NCAB-17   WOWWA

BALLARD, EVA CLODFELTER. U.S.

Biography
BAN

BAMFORD, MARY ELLEN. b.1857. U.S.

Biography
WOWWA   WWNA   WWWA-5

Bancroft, Lady. See BANCROFT, MARIE EFFIE (WILSON).

BANCROFT, MARIE EFFIE (WILSON). 1839-1921. England.
Lady Bancroft

Autobiography
THE BANCROFTS: RECOLLECTIONS OF SIXTY YEARS, by
Marie Bancroft and Squire Bancroft. New York:
B. Blom, [1969], 1909. LC70-87117.

MR. AND MRS. BANCROFT ON AND OFF THE STAGE.
WRITTEN BY THEMSELVES. 7th ed. London:
Bentley, 1889. LC12-29873.
Biography through 1885.

Biography
WEBS   WWWT

Obituary
NY TIMES (23 May 1921), 13:6.
TIMES (LONDON) (23 May 1921), 12:4.

BANKS, ELIZABETH L. 1870-1938. U.S.

Autobiography
THE AUTOBIOGRAPHY OF A NEWSPAPER GIRL. London:
Methuen, 1902. LC2-23850.

BANKS

THE REMAKING OF AN AMERICAN. New York:
   Doubleday, Doran, 1928. LC28-8746.

Biography
BURK   HAMM   ROSS   WOWWA   WWWA-1   WWWL

Obituary
NY TIMES (19 July 1938), 22:5.

BANKS, ISABELLA (VARLEY). 1821-1897. England.
   Mrs. G. Linnaeus Banks

Biography
BEL   BOASE-4   HAMM   NCH   SHO   WEBS

Burney, Edward L. MRS. G. LINNAEUS BANKS, AUTHOR
   OF THE MANCHESTER MAN, ETC. Manchester: E.J.
   Morten, 1969. LC72-184123.

Obituary
TIMES (LONDON) (6 May 1897), 6:6.

Banks, Mrs. G. Linnaeus.   See BANKS, ISABELLA
   (VARLEY).

BANNING, MARGARET (CULKIN). 1891-1982. U.S.

Biography
AWO   AWW   BICA   BOOCA   BURK   CON-N4   HAOXA   KUT
OV2   REA   RICMI   WAR   WEBS   WWNA   WWWE

Obituary
AB BOOKMAN'S WEEKLY (15 Feb 1982).
CHICAGO TRIBUNE (7 Jan 1982).
CON-105.
CUR-1982.
NY TIMES (6 Jan 1981), II 15:4.
PUBLISHERS WEEKLY 221 (22 Jan 1982), 18.
TIME 119 (18 Jan 1982), 89.

Barbara, pseud.   See   WRIGHT, MABEL (OSGOOD).

BARBER, MARGARET FAIRLESS. 1869-1901. England.
        Michael Fairless, pseud.
        All her books were posthumously published.

<u>Biography</u>
  BRO   HIND   KUT   MYE   SHO   WARLC

Dowson, Mary E. "A Biographical Note." In THE
   COMPLETE WORKS OF MICHAEL FAIRLESS. pp. 7-14.
   New York: E.P. Dutton, [c1932]. LC32-32271.

Dowson, Mary E. and A.M. Haggard. MICHAEL
   FAIRLESS; HER LIFE AND WRITINGS. London:
   Duckworth, 1913. LCa13-2059.

Barbour, A.M. See BARBOUR, ANNA MAY.

Barbour, A. Maynard. See BARBOUR, ANNA MAY.

BARBOUR, ANNA MAY. 1856-1941. U.S.
        A.M. Barbour
        A. Maynard Barbour

<u>Biography</u>
  BURK   WOWWA   WWNA   WWWA-1

BARCLAY, EDITH NOEL (DANIELL). b.1872. England.
        Mrs. Hubert Barclay

<u>Biography</u>
WWWE

BARCLAY, FLORENCE LOUISA (CHARLESWORTH). 1862-1921.
England.

<u>Biography</u>
  BERE   BRO   HAMM   KUT   MYE   NCH   RIC   ROCK   TWCR
  WARLC   WEBS

THE LIFE OF FLORENCE L. BARCLAY: A STUDY IN
   PERSONALITY, by one of her daughters. New
   York: Putnam's, 1921. LC22-26236.

BARCLAY

Obituary
NY TIMES (11 Mar 1921), 15:4.
TIMES (LONDON) (11 Mar 1921), 13:5.

Barclay, Mrs. Hubert. See BARCLAY, EDITH NOEL
(DANIELL).

Barcynska, Countess, pseud. See EVANS, MARGUERITE
FLORENCE HELENE (JERVIS) BARCLAY.

Barcynska, Countess Helene, pseud. See EVANS,
MARGUERITE FLORENCE HELENE (JERVIS) BARCLAY.

BARKER, ELLEN (BLACKMAR) MAXWELL. 1853?-1938. U.S.
Ellen Blackmar Maxwell

Biography
WOWWA   WWWA-5

Obituary
NY TIMES (22 Dec 1938), 21:5.

BARKER, ELSA. 1869-1954. U.S.

Biography
ALY   BURK   WWNA   WWWA-3

Obituary
NY TIMES (26 Aug 1954), 27:5.

Barker, Helen Manchester (Gates) Granville-. See
GRANVILLE-BARKER, HELEN MANCHESTER(GATES).

BARLOW, JANE. 1860-1917. Ireland.

Biography
BD   BOY   BRI   CHA   CHABI   CLE   CRO   DIL   KNIB
KUT   MCC   MYE   NCH   ODP   SHA   TYNAN   WEBS

Obituary
BOOKMAN (LONDON) 52 (June 1917), 78.
NY TIMES (20 Apr 1917), 13:6.

BARNES, ANNIE MARIA. b.1857. U.S.

Biography

BURK   KNIB   RUT   WILA   WOWWA   WWWA-4

BARNES, DJUNA (CHAPPELL). 1892-1982. U.S.

Biography

AMN   AMWRP   AWO   AWW   BERE   BURK   CAS   CHABI
CON-11--12R   CONO   FLE   HAOXA   KUT   MDWB   MYE
PEA   RA   REA   RIC   WARLC

Scott, James B. DJUNA BARNES. Boston:
   Twayne, c1976. LC75-45214.

Obituary

CHICAGO TRIBUNE (21 June 1982).
CON-107.
NY TIMES (20 June 1982), 32:3.
NEWSWEEK 100 (5 Sept 1982), 79.
PUBLISHERS WEEKLY 222 (2 July 1982), 23.
TIMES (LONDON) (21 June 1982), 12:6.
WASHINGTON POST (21 June 1982).

Bibliography

Messerli, Douglas. DJUNA BARNES: A BIBLIOGRAPHY.
   [Rhinebeck, N.Y.]: D. Lewis, 1975. LC75-43407.

BARNETT, EVELYN SCOTT (SNEAD). d.1921. U.S.

Biography

KNIB   WOWWA   WWWA-1

BARNUM, FRANCES COURTENAY (BAYLOR). 1848-1920. U.S.
   Frances Courtenay Baylor

Biography

APP   AWW   BD   BURK   DAB-S1   HAOXA   JOHDB   KUAA
LIB   NCAB-1   RUT   SOU   TWCB   WARBD   WILA   WWWA-H
WWWA-4

BARR, AMELIA EDITH (HUDDLESTON). 1831-1919. U.S.

Autobiography
ALL THE DAYS OF MY LIFE. New York: Arno, 1980,
[c1913]. LC79-8772.

THREE SCORE AND TEN; A BOOK FOR THE AGED. New
York: D. Appleton, 1915. LC15-25826.

Biography
ADE APP AWW BD BERE BURK DAB HAL HAMM
HAOXA HARKF JOHDB LIB LOGP MYE NAW NCAB-4
OV PRE REA RUT TWCB WARBD WEBS WOWWA
WWWA-1 WWWL

"A Successful Novelist: Fame After Fifty." In
HOW THEY SUCCEEDED; LIFE STORIES OF SUCCESSFUL
MEN TOLD BY THEMSELVES, by Orison S. Marden.
pp. 304-13. Boston: Lothrop, [1901]. LC01-31758.

Obituary
NY TIMES (12 Mar 1919), 11:3.
TIMES (LONDON) (12 Mar 1919), 10:2.

BARRETT, LILLIAN (FOSTER). 1884-1963. U.S.

Biography
AWO BURK NCAB-A WWNA WWWA-4

BARRINGTON, EMILIE ISABEL (WILSON). 1842-1933.
England.

Biography
HAMM

Obituary
TIMES (LONDON) (11 Mar 1933), 12:2.

Barrow, E.N. See BARROW, ELIZABETH N.

BARROW, ELIZABETH N. b.1869. U.S.
E.N. Barrow

Biography
WOWWA   WWWA-5

**BARSTOW, EMMA MAGDALENA ROSALIA MARIA JOSEFA
BARBARA ORCZY.** 1865-1947. England.
Baroness Orczy
Baroness Emmuska Orczy

Autobiography
LINKS IN THE CHAIN OF LIFE. New York:
Hutchinson, [1947]. LCa48-3833.

Biography
BERE BRO CHABI CON-104 EMD HAY KUT MYE
NCH NOV RIC ROCK TWCC TWCR WARLC WEBS
WWLA WWWE WWWL WWWT

Obituary
NY TIMES (13 Nov 1947), 27:4.
NEWSWEEK 30 (24 Nov 1947), 47.
PUBLISHERS WEEKLY 152 (29 Nov 1947), 2479.
TIME 50 (24 Nov, 1947), 100.
TIMES (LONDON) (13 Nov 1947), 7:4.
WILSON 22 (Jan 1948), 354.

BARTLETT, ALICE ELINOR (BOWEN). 1848-1920. U.S.
Birch Arnold, pseud.

Biography
BURK COY LOGP ROCK WILA WOWWA WWWA-4

Bartlett, Lucy Re. See RE, LUCY (BARTLETT).

BARTLEY, NALBRO ISADORAH. b.1888. U.S.
m. Clark

Biography
AWO BURK HINK OV2

BASH, BERTHA (RUNKLE). 1879-1958. U.S.
Bertha Runkle

Biography
ALY AWO BICA BURK HAL HARKF LOGP TWCB
WARBD WEBS WOWWA WWNA

BASSETT, SARA WARE. b.1872. U.S.

Biography
AWO BICA CUR-1956 WAR WWWA-5

BATES, EMILY KATHARINE (RUSLING). b.1884. U.S.

Autobiography
SEEN AND UNSEEN. Folcroft, Pa.: Folcroft, 1975.
LC75-32535R.
Personal record of psychic experiences.

Biography
WOWWA

BATES, MARGRET HOLMES (ERNSPERGER). 1844-1927. U.S.
Margaret Holmes
Margret Holmes

Biography
ALY BAN BURK COY NCAB-10 WILA WOWWA WWWA-4

BATES, SYLVIA (CHATFIELD). U.S.

Biography
AWO BURK WAR

BAUDER, EMMA POW (SMITH). 1848-1901. U.S.
Emma Pow Smith

Biography
HINK WILA WWNA

BAXTER, LUCY E. (BARNES). 1837-1902. England.
Leader Scott, pseud.

27

Biography
DNB-S2

Obituary
TIMES (LONDON) (27 Nov 1902), 11:2.

Baylor, Frances Courtenay. See BARNUM, FRANCES
COURTENAY (BAYLOR).

BAYLY, ADA ELLEN. 1857-1903. England.
Edna Lyall, pseud.

Biography
BD BLA BRI BRO CHA DNB-S2 HAOXE JOHDB MYE
NCH SHA SHO WARBD WARLC WEBS

Escreet, Jesse M. THE LIFE OF EDNA LYALL (ADA
ELLEN BAYLY). New York: Longmans, Green, 1904.
OCLC 168984.

Obituary
NY TIMES (10 Feb 1903), 9:7.
TIMES (LONDON) (10 Feb 1903), 8:5.

BAYNTON, BARBARA JANE (LAWRENCE). 1862?-1929.
Australia.
Lady Headley
m. (1)Frater (2)Baynton
(3)Alanson-Winn

Biography
AUDB-7 CHA MIAU SER WWW-3

"Introduction." In BARBARA BAYNTON, edited by
Sally Krimmer and Alan Lawson. pp. ix-xxxiii.
St. Lucia, Q.: Univ. of Queensland Press, 1980.
LC80-513908.

Bazan, Emilia Pardo. See PARDO BAZAN, EMILIA.

Beach, Mrs. William Hicks. See HICKS BEACH, SUSAN
EMILY (CHRISTIAN).

Beach, Susan Emily (Christian) Hicks. See HICKS
BEACH, SUSAN EMILY (CHRISTIAN).

BEAL, MARY LOUISE (BARNES). b.1844. U.S.

Biography

WOWWA   WWWA-4

BEALE, ANNE. d.1900. England.

Obituary
TIMES (LONDON) (20 Apr 1900), 7:6.

BEALE, MARIA PARKER (TAYLOR). b.1849. U.S.

Biography
KNIB   WOWWA   WWWA-4

BEALS, HELEN RAYMOND (ABBOTT). b.1888. U.S.
Helen Raymond Abbott

Biography
AWO   BURK   WWNA

BECKLEY, ZOE. d.1961. U.S.

Biography
WWWA-4

Obituary
NY TIMES (15 Jan 1961), 86:6.

Beckman, Mrs. William. See BECKMAN, NELLIE (SIMS).

BECKMAN, NELLIE (SIMS). d.1936. U.S.
Mrs. William Beckman

Biography
WOWWA

29

BEDDOW, ELIZABETH RUSSELL. b.1860. U.S.
Mrs. Charles P. Beddow

KNIB   WOWWA   Biography

Beddow, Mrs. Charles P.   See   BEDDOW, ELIZABETH
RUSSELL.

BEDFORD, RUTH. Australia.

MIAU   Biography

BEHRENS, BERTHA. 1850-1912. Germany.
W. Heimburg, pseud.

GAR   WARBD   Biography

BELDEN, JESSIE PERRY (VAN ZILE). 1857-1910. U.S.

WWWA-1   Biography

BELL, EVA MARY (HAMILTON). b.1878. England.
John Travers, pseud.

WWWE   WWWL   Biography

BELL,   FLORENCE   EVELEEN   ELEANORE   (OLLIFFE).
1851-1930.   England.
Lady Bell
Mrs. Hugh Bell

HAMM   WWWL   Biography

                   Obituary
TIMES (LONDON) (15 May 1930), 14:2-3.

Bell, Lady.   See   BELL, FLORENCE EVELEEN ELEANORE
(OLLIFFE).

Bell, Lilian. See BOGUE, LILIAN LIDA (BELL).

Bell, Lilian Lida. See BOGUE, LILIAN LIDA (BELL).

Bell, Mrs. Hugh.   See   BELL, FLORENCE EVELEEN
ELEANORE (OLLIFFE).

BELL, PEARL DOLES. d.1968. U.S.
    m. Ruben

                    Biography
AWO   BURK   WWNA

                    Obituary
NY TIMES (13 Mar 1968), 53:5.

BELLINGER, MARTHA IDELL (FLETCHER). b.1870. U.S.

                    Biography
WOWWA   WWWA-5

Belloc, Marie Adelaide.   See LOWNDES, MARIE
ADELAIDE (BELLOC).

Belloc-Lowndes, Marie Adelaide. See LOWNDES, MARIE
ADELAIDE (BELLOC).

BELSER, SUSAN (MISHLER). b.1862. U.S.

                    Biography
WOWWA

BENGOUGH, ELISA (ARMSTRONG). B.1877?. U.S.
    Elisa Armstrong

                    Biography
WWWA-1

31

Benson, M.E.   See   BENSON, MARY ELEANOR.

BENSON, MARY ELEANOR. 1863-1890. England.
           M.E. Benson

                        Biography
       BOASE-4

Benson, Stella.   See   ANDERSON, STELLA (BENSON).

Bentzon, Th., pseud.   See   BLANC, MARIE THERESE (DE
   SOLMS).

Beresford, Max, pseud.   See   HAMILTON, ANNIE E.
   (HOLDSWORTH) LEE.

BERGENGREN, ANNA (FARQUHAR). b.1865. U.S.
       Margaret Allston, pseud.
       Anna Farquhar

                        Biography
       BAN   HARKF   LOGP   NCAB-14   WIN   WOWWA

Betham-Edwards, Matilda.   See   EDWARDS, MATILDA
   BARBARA BETHAM-.

Bevans, Neile, pseud.   See   Van Slingerland, Nellie
   Bingham.

Bewicke, A.E.N.   See   LITTLE, ALICIA HELEN NEVA
   (BEWICKE).

BIANCHI, MARTHA GILBERT (DICKINSON). 1866-1943.
   U.S.

                        Biography
       AWO

                        32

BIANCHI

Phi Delta Gamma. Zeta Chapter, Columbia Univ.
GUESTS IN EDEN: EMILY DICKINSON, MARTHA
DICKINSON BIANCHI. New York: Phi Delta Gamma,
1946. LC47-15105.

Obituary
NY TIMES (22 Dec 1943), 23:4.
PUBLISHERS WEEKLY 145 (29 Jan 1944), 504.
WILSON 18 (Feb 1944), 422.

BIANCO, MARGERY (WILLIAMS). 1880-1944. U.S.
Margery Williams

Biography
AWW   BURK   DOY   KUJ1   KUJ2   KUL   NAW   NCH
SOME-15   WEBS   WWWA-6

Moore, Annie C. and Bertha M. Miller, eds.
WRITING AND CRITICISM, A BOOK FOR MARGERY
BIANCO. Boston: Horn Book, 1951. LC51-5594.

Obituary
NY TIMES (5 Sept 1944), 19:6.
PUBLISHERS WEEKLY 146 (23 Sept 1944), 1254.

BIBBINS, RUTHELLA BERNARD (MORY). 1865-1942. U.S.

Biography
WOWWA

Obituary
NY TIMES (26 May 1942), 21:6.

BIGELOW, EDITH EVELYN (JAFFRAY). 1861-1932. U.S.
Mrs. Poultney Bigelow

Biography
WWWA-4

Obituary
NY TIMES (4 May 1939), 23:1.

Bigelow, Marguerite Ogden.   See WILKINSON,
MARGUERITE OGDEN (BIGELOW).

Bigelow, Mrs. Poultney. See BIGELOW, EDITH EVELYN
(JAFFRAY).

BINNIE-CLARK, GEORGINA. Canada.

Autobiography
WHEAT AND WOMAN, with an introduction by Susan
  Jackel. Toronto; Buffalo: Univ. of Toronto
  Press, c1979. LC80-463250.

Biography
STOXC

BIRCHENOUGH, MABEL CHARLOTTE (BRADLEY). 1860-1936.
England.

Obituary
TIMES (LONDON) (23 July 1936), 18:4; tribute
  (27 July), 17:4.

BIRD, MARY (PAGE). b.1866. U.S.
          Neil Christison, pseud.

Biography
KNIB

BIRKHEAD, ALICE. England.

Biography
WWWL

BIRRELL, OLIVE MARY. 1848-1926. England.

Obituary
TIMES (LONDON) (17 Feb 1926), 16:3.

Bisland, Elizabeth. See WETMORE, ELIZABETH
(BISLAND).

BLACK, **MARGARET HORTON (POTTER).** 1881-1911. U.S.
Margaret Potter
Margaret Horton Potter
Robert Dolly Williams, pseud.

Biography
BURK   TWCA   WWWA-1

BLACK, **MARGARET (SHAFER).** 1859-1913. U.S.
Mrs. T.F. Black

Biography
COY

Black, Mrs. T.F. See BLACK, MARGARET (SHAFER).

BLACKALL, **EMILY (LUCAS).** 1836-1900. U.S.

Biography
BAN   WILA

BLAIR, **ELIZA (NELSON).** 1859-1907. U.S.

Biography
WWWA-1

BLAKE, **EMILY (CALVIN).** b.1882. U.S.

Biography
BURK   WWNA   WWWA-3

BLAKE, **KATHARINE EVANS.** b.1859. U.S.

Biography
WWNA

BLANC, **MARIE THERESE (DE SOLMS).** 1840-1907. France.
Th. Bentzon, pseud.

Biography
BD   JOHDB   WARBD

35

BLANC

Blaze de Bury, Yetta. FRENCH LITERATURE OF
  TO-DAY; A STUDY OF THE PRINCIPAL ROMANCERS AND
  ESSAYISTS. pp. 239-62. Port Washington, N.Y.:
  Kennikat, [1969]. LC68-8223.

BLANCHARD, AMY ELLA. 1856-1926. U.S.

Biography
KNIB   WARBD   WOWWA   WWWA-1

Blanco White, Amber (Reeves). See   WHITE, AMBER
  (REEVES) BLANCO.

BLAND, EDITH (NESBIT). 1858-1924. England.
      m. (1)Bland   (2)Tucker
      E. Nesbit

Autobiography
LONG AGO WHEN I WAS YOUNG, [by] E. Nesbit.
  London: Macdonald and Jane's, 1974.
  LC75-318608.

Biography
ASH   BRO   CAS   CHABI   DNB-4   DOY   FUL   GRET
GRETB   HAOXE   KRO   KUAT   KUJ1   KUT   LAU   MYE   NCH
PEE   ROCK   SHO   WARLC   WEBS   WWW-2   WWWL   YES-1

Bell, Anthea. E. NESBIT. New York: H.Z. Walck,
  1964. LC64-20835.

Moore, Doris L. E. NESBIT; A BIOGRAPHY. Rev.
  Philadelphia: Chilton Books, [1966].
  LC66-27601.

Streatfeild, Noel. MAGIC AND THE MAGICIAN: E.
  NESBIT AND HER CHILDREN'S BOOKS. New York:
  Abelard Schuman, [c1958]. LC62-17795.

Obituary
LITERARY REVIEW 4 (24 May 1924), 129.
OUTLOOK 137 (28 May 1924), 129.
TIMES (LONDON) (5 May 1924), 16:5; tribute
  (9 May), 11:3.

BLODGETT, MABEL LOUISE (FULLER). 1869-1959. U.S.

<u>Biography</u>
ALY   BURK   NCAB-A   WOWWA   WWWA-3

BLOEDE, GERTRUDE. 1845-1905. U.S.
      Stuart Sterne, pseud.

<u>Biography</u>
BURK   DAB-S1   NCAB-10   WARBD   WILA   WWWA-1

BLOUNT, MELESINA MARY. England.
      Mrs. George Norman, pseud.

<u>Biography</u>
BOOCA-2   WWWL

BLUE, KATE LILLY. U.S.

<u>Biography</u>
KNIB

BLUNDELL, MARY E. (SWEETMAN). 1857-1930. Ireland.
      Mrs. Francis Blundell
      Mrs. Francis
      M.E. Francis, pseud.

<u>Autobiography</u>
THE THINGS OF A CHILD, by M.E. Francis [pseud.].
  London: W. Collins Sons, [c1918]. LC A19-103.
    Childhood in Ireland.

<u>Biography</u>
BRI   CLE   CRO   WARLC   WWWL   WWWT

<u>Obituary</u>
TIMES (LONDON) (11 Mar 1930), 18:2; tribute
  (15 Mar), 17:2.

Blundell, Mrs. Francis. See BLUNDELL, MARY   E.
(SWEETMAN).

BOGGS, SARA ELISABETH (SIEGRIST). b.1843. U.S.

Biography

WWWA-3

BOGUE, LILIAN LIDA (BELL). 1867-1929. U.S.
Lilian Lida Bell
Lilian Bell

Biography

HARKF   LOGP   NCAB-14   WEBS

BOHAN, ELIZABETH BAKER. 1849-c.1942. U.S.

Biography

WILA   WOWWA

Bohl De Faber, Cecilia. See   DE FABER, CECILIA
FRANCISCA JOSEFA BOHL.

BOILEAU, ETHEL MARY (YOUNG). 1882?-1942. England.

Biography

BRO   KUT   WWWE

Obituary

CUR-1942.
TIMES (LONDON) (17 Jan 1942), 2:3.

BONE, FLORENCE. England.

Biography

WWWL

BONE, GERTRUDE HELENA (DODD). b.1876. England.

Biography

WARLC

BONNER, GERALDINE. 1870-1930. U.S.

Biography
ALY   NCAB-12   WWNA   WOWWA   WWWA-1

BOOTH, EMMA (SCARR). 1835-1927. U.S.

Biography
COY   WILA

BOOTH, MAUD BALLINGTON (CHARLESWORTH). 1865-1948.
U.S.
    M.E. Charlesworth, pseud.

Biography
AWO   NCAB-14,38   NCH   WEBB   WOWWA   WWWA-2

Welty, Susan E.   LOOK UP AND HOPE! THE MOTTO OF
    THE VOLUNTEER PRISON LEAGUE; THE LIFE OF MAUD
    BALLINGTON BOOTH.   New York: T. Nelson,
    [1961].   LC61-12423.

Borden, Mary.   See SPEARS, MARY (BORDEN) TURNER.

BOREL, MARGUERITE (APPELL). b.1883. France.
    Camille Marbo, pseud.

Biography
ROCK

BOSANQUET, THEODORA. England.

Biography
WWWE

BOSHER, KATE LEE (LANGLEY). 1865-1932. U.S.
    Kate Cairns, pseud.

Biography
BURK   KNIB   LIB-17   SOU   WOWWA   WWWA-1

Obituary
PUBLISHERS WEEKLY 122 (6 Aug 1932), 425.

BOTELER, MATTIE M. 1859-1929. U.S.

Biography
COY

BOTTOME, PHYLLIS. 1884-1963. England.
m. Forbes-Dennis

Autobiography
THE CHALLENGE. London: Faber and Faber.
[1952]. LC52-67332.

THE GOAL. London: Faber and Faber, c1962.
OCLC 2586945.

SEARCH FOR A SOUL. [FRAGMENT OF AN AUTOBIOGRAPHY].
New York: Reynal & Hitchcock, [1948]. LC48-8431.

Biography
BERE   BRO   KUL   KUT   MYE   NCH   PEE   RIC   WARLC
WEBS   WWWE   WWWL

Obituary
CON-93--96.
ILLUS LONDON NEWS 243 (31 Aug 1963), 318.
NY TIMES (23 Aug 1963), 25:1; (24 Aug), 19:2.
OBIT2, 86-7.
PUBLISHERS WEEKLY 184 (9 Sept 1963), 47.
TIME 82 (9 Sept 1963), 39.
TIMES (LONDON) (23 Aug 1963), 10:3.

BOUCICAULT, RUTH BALDWIN (HOLT). U.S.

Biography
WWWA-5

BOULGER,   THEODORA   (HAVERS). 1847-1889.   England.
Theo Gift, pseud.

Biography
ASH   WWWL

BOUVE, PAULINE CARRINGTON (RUST). d.1928. U.S.

Biography
WOWWA   WWWA-1

Bouvet, Marguerite. See Bouvet, Marie Marguerite.

BOUVET, MARIE MARGUERITE. 1865-1915. U.S.
Marguerite Bouvet

Biography
BURK   DAB-Sl   KUAA   WARBD   WOWWA   WWWA-1

Obituary
NY TIMES (3 June 1915), 11:5

Bowen, M.   See LONG, GABRIELLE MARGARET VERE (CAMPBELL) COSTANZO.

Bowen, Marjorie, pseud.   See LONG, GABRIELLE MARGARET VERE (CAMPBELL) COSTANZO.

Bower, B.M., pseud.   See SINCLAIR, BERTHA (MUZZY).

BOWLES, EVELYN MAY (CLOWES) WIEHE. 1877-1942. England.
Eleanor Mordaunt, pseud.
Elenor Mordaunt, pseud.
Elinor Mordaunt, pseud.

Autobiography
SINABADA, [by] Elinor Mordaunt. New York: Greystone, 1938. LC38-5785.

Biography
BRO   HAMM   KUAT   KUT   MIA   MYE   NCH   SER   WARLC
WEBS   WWLA

Obituary
TIMES (LONDON) (27 June 1942), 6:6.

BOWLES, JANET BYFIELD (PAYNE). d.1948. U.S.

Biography
BAN

Boyce, Neith. See HAPGOOD, NEITH BOYCE.

BOYD, MARY STUART (KIRKWOOD). b.1860. England.
Paxton Holgar, pseud.

Biography
WWLA   WWWE   WWWL

Obituary
TIMES (LONDON) (31 July 1937), 17:3.

BOYLAN, GRACE (DUFFIE) GELDERT. 1862-1935. U.S.

Biography
BURK   WOWWA   WWWA-1

Boyle, C. Nina. See BOYLE, CONSTANCE ANTONINA.

BOYLE, CONSTANCE ANTONINA. b.1865. England.
C. Nina Boyle

Biography
WWWE   WWWL

BOYLE, VIRGINIA (FRAZER). 1863-1938. U.S.

Biography
ALY   AWO   BICA   BURG   BURK   CON-93--96   LIB
NCAB-13   WARBD   WOWWA   WWNA   WWWA-1

BOYNTON, HELEN (MASON). b.1841. U.S.
Helene Hall, pseud.

Biography
BICA

BRABY, MAUD (CHURTON). England.

Biography
WWWL

Braddon, M.E.   See MAXWELL, MARY ELIZABETH (BRADDON).

Braddon, Miss M.E. See MAXWELL, MARY ELIZABETH (BRADDON).

BRADLEY, MARY WILHELMINA (HASTINGS). U.S.

Biography
ALY   AWO   BURK   WWNA   WWWE

BRADSHAW, ANNIE. England.

Biography
WWWL

BRAINERD, ELEANOR (HOYT). 1868-1942. U.S.
      Eleanor Hoyt

Biography
BURK   WOWWA   WWWA-2

Obituary
NY TIMES (19 Mar 1942), 21:2.

Brainerd, Thomas H., pseud.   See JARBOE, MARY HALSEY (THOMAS).

BRAMSTON, MARY. 1841-1912. England.

Obituary
TIMES (LONDON) (10 Feb 1912), 11:5.

BRANCH, MARY LYDIA (BOLLES). 1840-1922. U.S.

Biography
ALY   APP   NCAB-21   TWCB   WOWWA   WWWA-1

BRAZELTON, ETHEL MAUDE (COLSON). U.S.
  Ethel Maude Colson

Biography
AWO   WWNA

Breitenbach, Louise M.   See   CLANCY, LOUISE MARKS
  (BREITENBACH).

Brent of Bin Bin, pseud.   See   FRANKLIN, STELLA
  MARIA SARAH MILES.

BREWER, ESTELLE HEMPSTEAD MANNING. b.1882. U.S.

Biography
WOWWA

BRIGHT, FLORENCE KATHARINE. England.

Biography
WWWE   WWWL

**BRIGHT, MARY CHAVELITA (DUNNE) MELVILLE CLAIRMONTE
GOLDRING.** 1860-1945. Australia.
  George Egerton, pseud.

Autobiography
A LEAF FROM THE YELLOW BOOK; THE CORRESPONDENCE
OF GEORGE EGERTON, edited by Terence de Vere
White.   London: Richards, 1958. LC59-19988.

Biography
BRO   CHA   HAN   KUT   WARLC   WEBS   WWWL   WWWT

Briscoe, Margaret Sutton.   See   HOPKINS, MARGARET
  SUTTON (BRISCOE).

BRODHEAD, EVA WILDER (MCGLASSON). 1870-1915. U.S.
        Eva Wilder Mcglasson

<u>Biography</u>
.BURK   KNIB   RICK   WARBD

Brooke, Alison, pseud.   See   MASON, CAROLINE
(ATWATER).

Brooke, E.F.   See   BROOKE, EMMA FRANCES.

BROOKE, EMMA FRANCES. d.1926. England.
        E.F. Brooke

<u>Biography</u>
WWWL

Brooke, Magdalen, pseud.   See   CAPES, HARRIET MARY
(MOTHER MARY REGINALD).

BROOKS, AMY. d.1931. U.S.
        m. Loomis

<u>Biography</u>
ALY   BURK   WOWWA   WWNA

Broster, D.K.   See   BROSTER, DOROTHY KATHLEEN.

BROSTER, DOROTHY KATHLEEN. 1877/78-1950. England.
        D.K. Broster

<u>Biography</u>
BRIT   KUJl   KUJ2   MYE   RIC   ROCK   TWCR   WWLA
WWWE   WWWL

<u>Obituary</u>
NY TIMES (11 Feb 1950), 15:4.
TIMES (LONDON) (10 Feb 1950), 9:5.
WILSON 24 (Apr 1950), 554.

BROUGHTON, RHODA. 1840-1920. England.

Biography
ASH BD BEL BLA BRO CHA CHABI DAB-S3 HAMM
HAOXE JOHDB JOHH KNIB KUBA MYE NCH SHA
SHO VIC WAGCE WARLC WEBS

Obituary
Arnold, E.M. "Rhoda Broughton As I Knew Her."
  FORTNIGHTLY REVIEW (LONDON). 114 (Aug 1920),
  262-78.
NY TIMES (7 June 1920), 15:2.
TIMES (LONDON) (7 June 1920), 17:2.

BROWN, ALICE. 1857-1948. U.S.
        Martin Redfield, pseud.

Biography
ADE AWO AWW BRO HAOXA KUAT KUT MAN MARBS
NAW NCAB-15 OV OV2 REA TWCB WAGCA WEBS
WIN WWWA-2

Macmillan Co., New York. ALICE BROWN. New York:
  [Macmillan, n.d.]. OCLC 184161.

Walker, Dorothea. ALICE BROWN. New York:
  Twayne, [1974]. LC73-17019.

Obituary
NY TIMES (22 June 1948), 25:2.
WILSON 23 (Sept 1948), 10.

Brown, Anna Robeson. See BURR, ANNA ROBESON
  (BROWN).

Brown, Caroline, pseud. See KROUT, CAROLINE
  VIRGINIA.

BROWN, DEMETRA (VAKA). 1877-1946. U.S.
        Mrs. Kenneth Brown
        Demetra Vaka

Biography
AWO BURK KNIB OV OV2 WOWWA WWNA WWWA-2

BROWN

NY TIMES (19 Dec 1946), 29:3.
WILSON 21 (Feb 1947), 400.

BROWN, EDNA ADELAIDE. 1875-1944. U.S.

Biography
AWO   BURK   KUJ1   KUJ2   WWNA   WWWA-2

BROWN, HELEN DAWES. 1857-1941. U.S.

Biography
BURK   WOWWA   WWNA   WWWA-1

Obituary
CUR-1941.
NY TIMES (7 Sept 1941), 51:5.
PUBLISHERS WEEKLY 140 (4 Oct 1941), 1391.
SCHOOL AND SOCIETY 54: (13 Sept 1941), 190.

BROWN, KATHARINE HOLLAND. 1876-1931. U.S.

Biography
NCAB-29   WOWWA   WWWA-1

BROWN, LILIAN, KATE ROWLAND. 1863-1959. England.
        Rowland Grey, pseud.

Biography
WWWE   WWWL

Brown, Mrs. Kenneth.   See   BROWN, DEMETRA (VAKA).

BROWNE, ALICE (HARRIMAN). 1861-1925. U.S.
        Alice Harriman
        John Ryce, pseud.

Obituary
NY TIMES (25 Dec 1925), 17:4.

Browne, Cynthia Stockley.   See   STOCKLEY, CYNTHIA.

47

BROWNELL, ANNA GERTRUDE (HALL). 1863-1961. U.S.
Gertrude Hall.

Biography
BURK   ROCK   WARBD   WOWWA   WWWA-4

Obituary
NY TIMES (1 Mar 1961), 33:4.

BRUCE, ANDASIA KIMBROUGH. b.1868. U.S.
Mrs. William Liddell Bruce

Biography
WARBD

Bruce, Mrs. William Liddell. See   BRUCE, ANDASIA
KIMBROUGH.

BRUERE, MARTHA S. (BENSLEY). b.1879. U.S.

Biography
WOWWA

BRYAN, ELLA HOWARD. b.1872. U.S.

Biography
NCAB-13   WARBD   WOWWA

BRYAN, EMMA LYON. U.S.

Biography
WARBD

BRYANT, ANNA (BURNHAM). b.1860. U.S.

Biography
WWWA-5

Bryant, Marguerite.   See   MUNN, MARGUERITE (BRYANT).

Bryher, W., pseud. See ELLERMAN, ANNIE WINIFRED.

Bryher, Winifred. See ELLERMAN, ANNIE WINIFRED.

BUCHAN, ANNA. d.1948. Scotland.
O. Douglas, pseud.

Autobiography
FAREWELL TO PRIORSFORD; A BOOK BY AND ABOUT ANNA
BUCHAN (O. DOUGLAS). London: Hodder and
Stoughton, [1950]. LC51-4548.

UNFORGETTABLE, UNFORGOTTEN. London: Hodder &
Stoughton, [1945]. LC46-253.

Biography
BRO CHA MYE WWWE

Obituary
NY TIMES (25 Nov 1948), 31:1.
TIMES (LONDON) (25 Nov 1948), 7:5.

BUCK, MARY K. b.1849. U.S.
Mrs. M.K. Buck

Biography
WILA

Buck, Mrs. M.K. See BUCK, MARY K.

Buckrose, J.E., pseud. See JAMESON, ANNIE EDITH
(FOSTER).

BUDGETT, FRANCES ELIZABETH JANES. 1873-1928. U.S.
Elizabeth Dejeans, pseud.

Biography
BURK COY KNIB WWNA

BUEL

BUEL, ELIZABETH CYNTHIA (BARNEY). 1868-1943. U.S.

Biography
NCAB-32   WOWWA

BUERSTENBINDER, ELISABETH. 1838-1918. Germany.
E. Werner, pseud.

Biography
GAR   ROCK   WEBS

BUGG, LELIA HARDIN. U.S.

Biography
WOWWA   WWWA-5

BURHANS, VIOLA. b.1892. U.S.

Biography
WWNA

Burnett, Frances Hodgson. See TOWNESEND, FRANCES ELIZA (HODGSON) BURNETT.

Burnett, Ivy Compton-. See COMPTON-BURNETT, IVY.

BURNHAM, CLARA LOUISE (ROOT). 1854-1927. U.S.

Biography
ALY   AWW   BD   BURK   DAB   NCAB-9,21   OV   OV2
ST   WARBD   WILA   WOWWA   WWNA   WWWA-1

Obituary
NY TIMES (22 June 1927), 27:5.

BURR, AMELIA JOSEPHINE. 1878-1966. U.S.
m. Elmore
Biography
AWO   BURK   WEBS

50

BURR, ANNA ROBESON (BROWN). 1873-1941. U.S.
  Anna Robeson Brown

      Biography
 BURK KUT WOWWA WWNA WWWA-1

Burr, Jane, pseud. See WINSLOW, ROSE GUGGENHEIM.

BURT, KATHARINE (NEWLIN). 1882-1977. U.S.

      Biography
 AWO BURK JO KUT REA TWCR WAR WEBS WWNA

BURTON, ALMA HOLMAN. b.1855. U.S.

      Biography
 BAN

BUSH, BERTHA EVANGELINE. b.1866. U.S.

      Biography
WOWWA

BUTLER, ELIZABETH SOUTHERDEN (THOMPSON). 1851-1933.
 England.

     Autobiography
 AN AUTOBIOGRAPHY. London: Constable, 1923.
  LC23-26235.

      Biography
 DNB-S5

      Obituary
 CHRISTIAN CENTURY 50 (25 Oct 1933), 1345.
 FORTNIGHTLY 140 (Nov 1933), 618-9.

BYNG, EVELYN (MORETON) BYNG. 1870-1949. England.
    full name Marie Evelyn
    Mrs. Julian Byng
    Lady Byng of Vimy

BYNG

Autobiography

UP THE STREAM OF TIME, by Viscountess Byng of
  Vimy. Toronto: Macmillan of Canada, 1945.
  LC46-16423.

Obituary

NY TIMES (22 June 1949), 31:5.
TIMES (LONDON) (22 June 1949), 4:5; (23 June),
  7:5.

Caballero, Fernan, pseud.   See   DE FABER, CECILIA
FRANCISCA JOSEFA BOHL.

CABELL, ISA (CARRINGTON). b.1860. U.S.

Biography
WARBD   WOWWA   WWWA-4

CADELL, JESSIE. 1844-1884. Scotland.

Biography
BOASE   BUC   DNB

Obituary
TIMES (LONDON) (27 June 1884), 10:5.

CAFFYN, KATHLEEN MANNINGTON (HUNT). 1855?-1926.
England.
    Mrs. Mannington Caffyn
    Iota, pseud.

Biography
CHA   MIA   MIAU

Caffyn, Mrs. Mannington.   See CAFFYN, KATHLEEN
MANNINGTON (HUNT).

CAIRD, ALICE MONA (ALISON). 1858-1932. England.
    Mona Caird

Biography
HAMM   KUBA   SHO

Obituary
TIMES (LONDON) (5 Feb 1932), 14:5.

Caird, Mona.   See   CAIRD, ALICE MONA (ALISON).

Cairns, Kate, pseud. See BOSHER, KATE LEE (LANGLEY).

CALDWELL, WILLIE WALKER. b.1860. U.S.

Biography

KNIB WOWWA

CALHOUN, ALICE J. U.S.

Biography

KNIB

CALLAHAN, DORIS EGERTON (JONES). Australia.
        D. Egerton Jones

Biography

MIAU

Cambridge, Ada. See CROSS, ADA (CAMBRIDGE).

Cameron, E. Lovett. See CAMERON, EMILY (SHARP).

CAMERON, EMILY (SHARP). d.1921. England.
        E. Lovett Cameron
        Mrs. Emily Lovett Cameron
        Mrs. H. Lovett Cameron
        Mrs. Lovett Cameron

Biography

BLA

Obituary
TIMES (LONDON) (9 Aug 1921), 11:2.

Cameron, Margaret. See KILVERT, MARGARET (CAMERON) LEWIS.

Cameron, Mrs. Emily Lovett. See CAMERON, EMILY (SHARP).

Cameron, Mrs. H. Lovett. See CAMERON, EMILY (SHARP).

Cameron, Mrs. Lovett. See CAMERON, EMILY (SHARP).

CAMPBELL, DAISY RHODES. 1845-1927. U.S.

Biography
ALY   BAR   WWNA   WWWA-6

CAMPBELL, HARRIETTE (RUSSELL). 1883-1950. U.S.

Biography
WWWE

Obituary
NY TIMES (29 July 1950), 13:5.

CAMPBELL, HELEN (STUART). 1839-1918. U.S.

Biography
APP   AWW   BD   BURK   NCAB-9   TWCB   WARBD   WILA
WOWWA   WWWA-4

Canadienne, pseud. See HUNT, ANNA REBECCA (GALE).

CANDEE, HELEN (CHURCHILL) HUNGERFORD. 1858/61-1949. U.S.

Biography
BICA   WOWWA   WWNA   WWWA-2

Canfield, Dorthy. See FISHER, DOROTHEA FRANCES (CANFIELD).

Canuck, Janey, pseud. See MURPHY, EMILY (FERGUSON).

CAPES, HARRIET MARY (MOTHER MARY REGINALD). b.1849.
England.
> Magdalen Brooke, pseud.

Biography
WWWE

CAREY, ROSA NOUCHETTE. 1840-1909. England.
> Le Voleur, pseud.

Biography
BD   BLA   DNB-2   HAMM   NCH   SHO   WARLC   WEBS   WWWL

Obituary
NY TIMES (20 July 1909), 7:6.
TIMES (LONDON) (20 July 1909), 13:3.

Carleton, S. pseud.   See   JONES, SUSAN   CARLETON.

Carleton-Milecete, joint pseud. of SUSAN CARLETON
JONES and HELEN MILECETE.

CARR, ALICE VANSITTART (STRETTEL). 1850-1927.
England.
> Mrs. Comyns Carr

Autobiography
MRS. J. COMYNS CARR'S REMINISCENCES, edited by
Eve Adam. 2d ed. London: Hutchinson, [1926?].
OCLC 2672644.

Obituary
TIMES (LONDON) (13 Oct 1927), 1:1; (18 Oct) 21:3.

Carr, M.E.   See   CARR, MILDRED EMILY.

CARR, MILDRED EMILY. b.1877. England.
> M.E. Carr
> Ward Copley

Biography
WWWE

CARR, SARAH (PRATT). b.1850. U.S.

Biography
WOWWA   WWWA-4

Carruth, Frances Weston. See PRINDLE, FRANCES
    WESTON (CARRUTH).

CARSON, NORMA (BRIGHT). b.1883. U.S.

Biography
WOWWA   WWNA

CARSWELL,   CATHERINE   ROXBURGH   (MACFARLANE).
    1879-1946. Scotland.
    m. (1)Jackson--annulled

Autobiography
LYING AWAKE; AN UNFINISHED AUTOBIOGRAPHY AND
OTHER POSTHUMOUS PAPERS, edited by John
Carswell. London: Secker & Warburg, 1950.
LC51-19841.

Biography
BERE   BRO   HAMM   KUAT   KUT   NCH   PEE   WARLC   WEBS
WWWE   WWW-4

Obituary
TIMES (LONDON) (22 Feb 1946), 8:5.

CASE, FRANCES POWELL. U.S.
    Frances Powell, pseud.

Biography
BURK   WOWWA

Casey, Sadie Katherine. See MAYNARD, SARA
    KATHERINE (CASEY).

Castelar, Isabella, pseud. See WINTER, ELIZABETH
    (CAMPBELL).

57

CASTLE, AGNES (SWEETMAN). d.1922. England.
Mrs. Egerton Castle

Biography
NCH   WARLC   WEBS   WWW1

Obituary
TIMES (LONDON) (22 May 1922), 11:3.

Castle, Mrs. Egerton.   See   CASTLE,   AGNES
(SWEETMAN).

CASTLEMAN, VIRGINIA CARTER. b.1864. U.S.

Biography
ALY   BURK   KNIB   WOWWA   WWNA   WWWA-3

CATHER, WILLA SIBERT. 1873-1947. U.S.

Autobiography
WILLA CATHER IN EUROPE; HER OWN STORY OF THE
FIRST JOURNEY.   New York: Knopf, 1956.
LC56-10906.

Biography
AMN   APP   AUC   AW   AWO   AWW   BERE   BOYS   BRO
BURK   BURNT   CAS   CHA   CHABI   CON-104   DAB-S4
FLE   GARRA   HAMM   HAOXA   HAOXE   JES   JOHDB   KRO
KU   KUJ1   KUL   KUT   LES   LOGG   MAG   MAN   MARBS
MCW   MDWB   MICA   MON   MORG   MYE   NAW   NCAB-44
NOV   NPW   OV   OV2   PEA   RA   RCW   REA   REAW   RIC
RICDA   RULE   SEYS   STOD   STOXC   TWCW   VDW   WAGCA
WARLC   WEBS   WENW   WOWWA   WWNA   WWWA-2

Bailey, Helen M.   40 AMERICAN BIOGRAPHIES.
pp. 189-94.   New York: Harcourt, Brace & World,
[1964].   LC64-56614.
juvenile literature

Bennett, Mildred R.   THE WORLD OF WILLA CATHER.
New ed.   Lincoln: Univ. of Nebraska Press,
1961.   LC61-7235.

Bonham, Barbara. WILLA CATHER. Philadelphia:
Chilton, [1970]. LC76-111603.
juvenile literature

Brown, Edward K. WILLA CATHER, A CRITICAL
BIOGRAPHY. New York: Avon, 1980, c1953.
LC52-12204.

Brown, Marion W. and Ruth Crone. ONLY ONE POINT
OF THE COMPASS: WILLA CATHER IN THE NORTHEAST.
[Danbury, Ct.]: Archer, c1980. LC80-11384.

_____. WILLA CATHER, THE WOMAN AND HER WORKS.
New York: Scribner, [1970].
juvenile literature

Bryne, Kathleen D. and Richard C. Snyder.
CHRYSALIS, WILLA CATHER IN PITTSBURGH, 1896-
1906. Pittsburgh: Historical Society of
Western Pennsylvania, c1980. LC80-80284.

Edel, Leon. "Homage to Willa Cather." In THE
ART OF WILLA CATHER, edited by Bernice Slote
and Virginia Faulkner. pp. 185-204. Lincoln:
Dept. of English, Univ. of Nebraska-Lincoln,
[1974]. LC74-78479.

Gerber, Philip L. WILLA CATHER. Boston: Twayne,
[1975]. LC75-2287.

Gray, Dorothy. WOMEN OF THE WEST. pp. 147-58.
Millbrae, Calif.: Les Femmes, c1976.
LC75-28773.

Hardesty, Nancy. GREAT WOMEN OF FAITH: THE
STRENGTH AND INFLUENCE OF CHRISTIAN WOMEN.
pp. 41-44. Grand Rapids, Mich.: Baker Book
House, c1980. LC80-65440.

"Introduction." In WRITINGS FROM WILLA CATHER'S
CAMPUS YEARS, edited by James R. Shively.
pp. 11-27. [Lincoln]: Univ. of Nebraska Press,
[1950]. LC50-6537.

Johnson, John R. REPRESENTATIVE NEBRASKANS.
pp. 34-40. Lincoln, Neb.: Johnsen, [1954].
LC54-3445.

Knopf, Alfred A. "Miss Cather." In THE ART OF WILLA CATHER, edited by Bernice Slote and Virginia Faulkner. pp. 205-224. Lincoln: Dept. of English, Univ. of Nebraska-Lincoln, [1974]. LC74-78479.

Knopf (Alfred A.) Inc., New York. WILLA CATHER; A BIOGRAPHICAL SKETCH, AN ENGLISH OPINION.... New York: Knopf, [1927]. LC27-12839R.
    16 pages

Lewis, Edith. WILLA CATHER LIVING: A PERSONAL RECORD. Lincoln: Univ. of Nebraska Press, [1976] c1953. LC76-17551.

McFarland, Dorothy T. WILLA CATHER. pp. 1-18. New York: Ungar, [1972]. LC74-190351.

Rapin, Rene. WILLA CATHER. New York: R.M. McBride, 1930. LC30-30426.

Robinson, Phyllis. C. WILLA, THE LIFE OF WILLA CATHER. Garden City, N.Y.: Doubleday, 1983. LC82-46017.

Sergeant, Elizabeth S. WILLA CATHER, A MEMOIR. [Lincoln]: Univ. of Nebraska Press, [1963]. LC63-3155.
    Covers 1910-1931

SIXTEEN MODERN AMERICAN AUTHORS; A SURVEY OF RESEARCH AND CRITICISM, edited by Jackson R. Bryer. pp. 29-73. Rev. ed. New York: Norton, [1973]. LC73-979.
    First edition title: FIFTEEN MODERN AMERICAN AUTHORS.

Van Ghent, Dorothy B. WILLA CATHER. Minneapolis: Univ. of Minnesota Press, [1964]. LC64-63341.

Vermorcken, Elizabeth M. THESE TOO WERE HERE; LOUISE HOMER AND WILLA CATHER. pp. 45-62. Univ. of Pittsburgh Press, [c1950]. OCLC 6472484.

CATHER

WILLA CATHER: A PICTORIAL MEMOIR. Photos. by
Lucia Woods et al. Text by Bernice Slote.
Lincoln: Univ. of Nebraska Press, [c1973].
LC72-91511.

Woodress, James L. WILLA CATHER: HER LIFE AND
ART. Lincoln: Univ. of Nebraska Press, 1982,
c1970. LC82-7041.

Obituary
NY TIMES (25 Apr 1947), 21:1.
NEWSWEEK 29 (5 May 1947), 54.
PUBLLISHERS WEEKLY 151 (10 May 1947), 2439.
TIME 49 (5 May 1947), 81.
TIMES (LONDON) (26 Apr 1947), 7:5.
WILSON 21 (June 1947), 702.

Bibliography
Lathrop, JoAnna. WILLA CATHER: A CHECKLIST OF
HER PUBLISHED WRITING. Lincoln: Univ. of
Nebraska Press, [1975]. LC74-82561.

CATHERWOOD, MARY (HARTWELL). 1847-1902. U.S.

Biography
APP AWW BAR BD BURK COY DAB HAOXA JOHDB
KUAA KUJ1 MYE NAW NCAB-9 PRE REA ST TWCB
WAGCA WARBD WILA WWWA-1

Wilson, Milton L. BIOGRAPHY OF MARY HARTWELL
CATHERWOOD. Newark, O.: American Tribune
Printery, 1904. OCLC 4170763.

Obituary
NY TIMES (27 Dec 1902), 9:5.

CAVENDISH, PAULINE BRADFORD (MACKIE) HOPKINS.
1873-1956. U.S.
Mrs. Herbert Mueller Hopkins
Pauline Bradford Mackie

Biography
BURK COY HARKF LOGP WARBD WOWWA WWNA

Obituary
NY TIMES (22 May 1956), 33:1.

CHALMERS, MARGARETT REBECCA (PIPER). b.1879. U.S.
    Margaret R. Piper

Biography
ALY BURK WOWWA WWWA-6

CHAMPION DE CRESPIGNY, ROSE (KEY). 1860-1935.
England.
    Mrs. Philip Champion de Crespigny

Autobiography
THIS WORLD AND BEYOND. London, Toronto: Cassell,
[1934]. LC34-32144.
"Autobiographical reminiscences, mainly of
spiritualistic experiences."

Biography
HAMM WWLA WWWL

BIOGRAPHICAL DICTIONARY OF PARAPSYCHOLOGY.
1964-66, edited by Helene Pleasants. p. 78.
New York: Garrett, [1964]. LC64-4288.

Obituary
TIMES (LONDON) (12 Feb 1935), 1:1; (18 Feb),
19:1.

CHAMPNEY, ELIZABETH (WILLIAMS). 1850-1922. U.S.

Biography
BD BURK COY KNIB NCAB-11 TWCB WILA WOWWA
WWWA-1

Obituary
NY TIMES (14 Oct 1922), 13:5.

CHANDLER, IZORA CECILIA. d.1906. U.S.

Biography
WWWA-1

Obituary
NY TIMES (26 Aug 1906), 9:6.

62

Channon, E.M.   See   CHANNON, ETHEL MARY.

CHANNON, ETHEL MARY. b.1875. England.
   E.M. Channon
   Mrs. Francis Channon

WWWE   Biography

Channon, Mrs. Francis.   See   CHANNON, ETHEL MARY.

CHANT, LAURA ORMISTON (DIBBIN). 1848-1923. England.
   Mrs. Ormiston Chant

KNIB   Biography

           Obituary
NY TIMES (17 Feb 1923), 13:4.
TIMES (LONDON) (17 Feb 1923), 12:3.

Chant, Mrs. Ormiston.   See   CHANT, LAURA ORMISTON
(DIBBIN).

CHAPEAU, ELLEN CHAZAL. b.1844. U.S.

           Biography
   WARBD   WWWA-4

CHAPIN, ANNA ALICE. 1880-1920. U.S.

           Biography
   BURK   WOWWA   WWWA-1

           Obituary
NY TIMES (27 Feb 1920), 13:4.

CHAPMAN, KATHARINE (HOPKINS). 1872-1930. U.S.

           Biography
   KNIB   WOWWA   WWWA-5

CHARLES, FRANCES ASA. b.1872. U.S.

Biography
BURK   HINK   WOWWA   WWWA-5

Charlesworth,   M.E.,   pseud.   See   BOOTH,   MAUD
BALLINGTON (CHARLESWORTH).

CHARNWOOD, DOROTHEA MARY ROBY (THORPE) BENSON.
1876-1942. England.
Lady Charnwood

Autobiography
"Personal Memories." In CALL BACK YESTERDAY; A
BOOK OF OLD LETTERS CHOSEN FROM HER COLLECTION
WITH SOME MEMORIES OF HER OWN..., by Lady
Charnwood. pp. 294-314. [London]: Eyre and
Spottiswoode, 1937. OCLC 1304775.

Obituary
TIMES (LONDON) (22 Apr 1942), 7:5.

Chartres,   A.   Vivanti.   See   CHARTRES,   ANITA
(VIVANTI).

CHARTRES, ANITA (VIVANTI). 1868-1942. England.
A. Vivanti Chartres
Annie Chartres

Biography
CDME   WEBS   WWWL

Obituary
NY TIMES (26 Feb 1942), 19:5.

Chartes,   Annie.   See   CHARTRES,   ANITA   (VIVANTI).

Chase, Beatrice, pseud.   See PARR, OLIVE KATHARINE.

CHASE, JESSIE (ANDERSON). 1865-1949. U.S.

Biography
BURK   COY   WOWWA   WWNA   WWWA-5

CHAUNDLER, CHRISTINE. b.1887.   England.

Biography
CON-P2   DOY   SOME-1

CHAVANNE, LOVEAU DE. b.1861.   U.S.

Biography
WWWA-4

CHEEVER, HARRIET ANNA. fl.1890-1911.   U.S.

Biography
BURK   WWWA-1

Cher, Marie, pseud.   See   SCHERR, MARIE.

CHESSON, NORA (HOPPER). 1871-1906.   Ireland.

Biography
DIL   NCH

Obituary
TIMES (LONDON) (21 Apr 1906), 8:4.

Chester, Eliza, pseud.   See   PAINE, HARRIET ELIZA.

CHESTERTON, ADA ELIZABETH (JONES). 1886-1962.
England.
     John Keith Prothero, pseud.

Biography
NCH   WEBS   WWWE

CHESTERTON

Obituary
OBIT2, 137.
TIMES (LONDON) (23 Jan 1962), 14:1; (25 Jan), 12:5.

Chetwynd, Hon. Mrs. Henry. See CHETWYND, JULIA
BOSVILLE (DAVIDSON).

CHETWYND, JULIA BOSVILLE (DAVIDSON). 1818/19-1901.
England.
Hon. Mrs. Henry Chetwynd

Biography
BLA

Obituary
TIMES (LONDON) (8 June 1901), 11:6.

CHILDS, ELEANOR STUART (PATTERSON). 1876-1920. U.S.
Eleanor Stuart, pseud.

Biography
BURK   WWWA-1

CHILES, ROSA PENDLETON. b.1866. U.S.

Biography
AWO   NCAB-D   WWNA

Chipperfield, Robert Orr, pseud. See OSTRANDER,
ISABEL EGENTON.

CHISHOLM, BELLE V. b.1843. U.S.

Biography
COY

Cholmondeley, Alice, pseud. See RUSSELL, MARY
ANNETTE (BEAUCHAMP) ARNIM RUSSELL.

CHOLMONDELEY, MARY. 1859-1925. England.

Autobiography
UNDER ONE ROOF: A FAMILY RECORD. London:
J. Murray, 1918. LC A19-805.

Biography
BD BRO CHA HAMM JOHDB KUT MYE NCH SHO
WARLC WEBS

Crisp, Jane. MARY CHOLMONDELEY 1859-1925: A
BIBLIOGRAPHY. St. Lucia [Australia]: Dept. of
English, Univ. of Queensland, [1981?].
OCLC 9137245.

Lubbock, Percy. MARY CHOLMONDELEY; A SKETCH FROM
MEMORY. London: J. Cape, [1928]. LC28-17803.

Obituary
NY TIMES (16 July 1925), 9:3.
TIMES (LONDON) (17 July 1925), 19:4.

CHOPIN, KATE (O'FLAHERTY). 1851-1904. U.S.

Biography
AML AMR AWW BD BERE BURK CAS CON-104 DAB
HAOXA JONE KIR KUAA LIB MDWB MYE NAW
NCAB-25 NOV PEA REA RICDA RUB SOU VDW
WWWA-1

Rankin, Daniel S. KATE CHOPIN AND HER CREOLE
STORIES. Philadelphia, 1932. LC32-30396.

Seyersted, Per. KATE CHOPIN. A CRITICAL
BIOGRAPHY. Baton Rouge: Louisiana State
Univ. Press, 1969. LC77-88740R.

Obituary
BOSTON EVENING TRANSCRIPT (26 Aug 1904), 5.
ST. LOUIS DAILY GLOBE-DEMOCRAT (22 Aug 1904), 13.
ST. LOUIS MIRROR (25 Aug 1904), XIV 1.
ST. LOUIS POST-DISPATCH (22 Aug 1904), 1.

Bibliography
Springer, Marlene. EDITH WHARTON AND KATE
CHOPIN: A REFERENCE GUIDE. Boston: G.K. Hall,
c1976. LC76-1831.

Christie, Agatha. See MALLOWAN, AGATHA MARY CLARISSA (MILLER) CHRISTIE.

Christison, Neil, pseud. See BIRD, MARY (PAGE).

CHURCH, VIRGINIA WOODSON (FRAME). b.1880. U.S.

Biography
WOWWA

CHURCHILL, LIDA ABBIE. b.1859. U.S.

Biography
WILA   WOWWA   WWWA-5

CLANCY, LOUISE MARKS (BREITENBACH). U.S.
Louise M. Breitenbach

Biography
AWO   WWNA

Clare, Austin, pseud. See JAMES, WILHELMINA MARTHA.

CLARE, CORA ESTELLA BENNETT (STEPHENSON). b.1872. U.S.
Cora Bennett Stephenson

Biography
BAN

Clare, Kathleen, pseud. See McCHESNEY, DORA GREENWALL.

CLARK, FELICIA (BUTTZ). 1862-1931. U.S.

Biography
BURK   WWWA-4

CLARK

Obituary
CHRISTIAN CENTURY 48 (21 Mar 1931), 422.
PUBLISHERS WEEKLY 119 (28 Mar 1931), 1694.

Clark, Georginia Binnie. See BINNIE-CLARK, GEORGINA.

CLARK, IMOGEN. d.1936. U.S.

Biography
BURK   WARBD   WOWWA   WWNA   WWWA-1

Clark, Kate (Upson). See CLARK, KATHARINE PICKENS (UPSON).

CLARK, KATHARINE PICKENS (UPSON). 1851-1935. U.S.
Kate Upson Clark

Biography
ALY   APP   BURK   NCAB-30   WOWWA   WWNA   WWWA-1

Obituary
NY TIMES (18 Feb 1935), 15:3.
PUBLISHERS WEEKLY 127 (2 Mar 1935), 970.

Clark, S.C. See CLARK, SUSIE CHAMPNEY.

CLARK, SUSIE CHAMPNEY. b.1856. U.S.
S.C. Clark
Deborah Morrison, pseud.

Biography
WOWWA

Clarke, I. See CLARKE, ISABEL CONSTANCE.

CLARKE, IDA CLYDE (GALLAGHER). 1878-1956. U.S.

Biography
AWO   WWNA   WWWA-3

CLARKE, ISABEL CONSTANCE. d.1951. England.
I. Clarke

Biography
BOOCA-3   WWWE   WWWL

CLARKE, REBECCA SOPHIA. 1833-1906. U.S.
Sophie May, pseud.

Biography
APP AWW BURK DAB KUAA NAW NCAB-8 TWCB
WARBD WEBS WILA WWWA-1

CLARKE, VIOLET. 1879-1909. Australia.
full name Constance Violet

Biography
MIAU

CLEARY, KATE (MACPHELIM). b.1863. U.S.

Biography
WILA

Cleeve, Lucas, pseud. See KINGSCOTE, ADELINE
GEORGINA ISABELLA (WOLFF).

CLEGHORN, SARAH NORCLIFFE. 1876-1959. U.S.

Autobiography
THREESCORE: THE AUTOBIOGRAPHY OF SARAH N.
CLEGHORN, introduction by Robert Frost. New
York: H. Smith & R. Haas, 1936. LC36-7642.

Biography
AWO AWW BURK DAB-S6 KUT NCAB-45 REA WEBS
WOWWA WWNA WWWA-3

Obituary
NY TIMES (5 Apr 1959), 86:3.

CLEMENT, ELLIS (MEREDITH). b.1865. U.S.
    Ellis Meredith

Biography
AWO   WOWWA   WWNA

CLERKE, ELLEN MARY. 1840-1906. Ireland.

Biography
CLE   CRO   DNB-2   ODP

Huggins, Margaret L. AGNES MARY CLERKE, AND
  ELLEN MARY CLERKE; AN APPRECIATION. Printed
  for private circulation. 1907. LC15-21204.

**CLIFFORD, ELIZABETH LYDIA ROSABELLE (BONHAM) DE LA
PASTURE.** 1866-1945. England.
    Lady Clifford
    Mrs. Henry De La Pasture

Biography
HAMM MARBS SHO WARLC WEBS WWWE WWWT

Obituary
TIMES (LONDON) (1 Nov 1945), 6:4.

Clifford, Josephine. See McCRACKIN, JOSEPHINE
(WOEMPNER) CLIFFORD.

Clifford, Lady. See CLIFFORD, ELIZABETH LYDIA
ROSABELLE (BONHAM) DE LA PASTURE.

CLIFFORD, LUCY (LANE). 1854-1929. England.
    Mrs. W.K. Clifford
    full name Sophia Lucy Lane Clifford

Biography
BERE CHA COR HAMM KUT NCH WARLC WEBS

Obituary
TIMES (LONDON) (22 Apr 1929), 16:3; tribute
  (23 Apr), 9:3.

Clifford, Mrs. W.K. See CLIFFORD, LUCY (LANE).

CLUETT, ISABEL MAUDE (PEACOCKE). b.1881. New
  Zealand.
        Isabel Maud Peacocke

Biography
WWWE

Clyde, Constance. See McADAM, CONSTANCE.

Cobden, Ellen Melicent. See SICKERT, ELLEN
  MELICENT (COBDEN).

COBURN, ELEANOR HALLOWELL (ABBOTT). b.1872. U.S.
      Eleanor Hallowell Abbott

Autobiography
BEING LITTLE IN CAMBRIDGE WHEN EVERYONE ELSE WAS
  BIG, by Eleanor Hallowell Abbott. New York:
  D. Appleton-Century, 1936. LC36-20358.

Biography
AWO AWW BRO BURK DAB-S6 HAOXA KUT LOGP OV
OV2 REA WAG WOWWA WWNA WWWL

COCKE, SARAH JOHNSON. b.1865. U.S.

Biography
KNIB WOWWA

COHEN, ROSE (GALLUP). b.1880. U.S.

Autobiography
OUT OF THE SHADOW. [New York: J.S. Ozer, 1971],
  1918. LC77-145475.

COHN, CLARA (VIEBIG). 1860-1952. Germany.
      Clara Viebig

Biography
CDME   CHABI   KUAT   WEBS

Obituary
NY TIMES (6 Aug 1952), 21:2.
TIMES (LONDON) (9 Aug 1952), 6:6; tribute (22 Aug
   1952), 6:5.
WILSON 27 (Oct 1952), 108.

COLBURN, FRONA EUNICE WAIT (SMITH). 1859-1946. U.S.
     Frona Eunice Wait, pseud.

HINK
Biography

COLE, SOPHIE. 1862-1947. England.

Obituary
NY TIMES (13 Feb 1947), 23:2.
TIMES (LONDON) (12 Feb 1947), 6:5.
WILSON 21 (Apr 1947), 572.

Coleridge, M.E.   See   COLERIDGE,   MARY   ELIZABETH.

COLERIDGE, MARY ELIZABETH. 1861-1907. England.
     M.E. Coleridge

Autobiography
GATHERED LEAVES FROM THE PROSE OF MARY E.
   COLERIDGE, WITH A MEMOIR, by Edith Sichel.
   Freeport, N.Y.: Books for Libraries, [1971],
   1910. LC70-169545.
   "Memoir," pp. 1-44.
   "Collection of Passages from Letters and
     Diaries," pp. 217-78.

Biography
BRO   CHA   DNB-2   HAOXE   KUBA   MYE   NCH   SHO
WARLC   WEBS

Obituary
TIMES (LONDON) (28 Aug 1907), 8:3.

Colette, pseud. See DE JOUVENAL, SIDONIE GABRIELLE (COLETTE) GATHER-VILLARS.

COLLIN, GRACE LATHROP. U.S.

Biography
WOWWA

Collins, E. Burke, pseud. See SHARKEY, EMMA AUGUSTA (BROWN).

Collins, Mabel. See COOK, MABEL (COLLINS).

Colmore, G., pseud. See WEAVER, BAILLE GERTRUDE RENTON (COLMORE).

Colson, Ethel Maude. See BRAZELTON, ETHEL MAUDE (COLSON).

COLTHARP, JEANNETTE DOWNES. U.S.

Biography
KNIB

COMER, CORNELIA ATWOOD (PRATT). d.1929. U.S.
     Cornelia Atwood Pratt

Biography
BURK COY WOWWA

COMFORT, BESSIE (MARCHANT). 1862-1941. England.
     Mrs. J.A. Comfort
     Bessie Marchant

Biography
DOY YES-2

Comfort, Mrs. J.A. See COMFORT, BESSIE (MARCHANT).

COMMANDER, LYDIA KINGSMILL. U.S.
     m. Casson
<u>Biography</u>
WOWWA

COMPTON-BURNETT, IVY. 1892-1969. England.

<u>Biography</u>
BERE BRO CAS CHABI CON-N4 FLE HAOXE KUTS
MDWB MYE NCH NOV NPW PEE RA RIC RULE
SEYS SHO WARLC WENW WWWA-5

Baldanza, Frank. IVY COMPTON-BURNETT. New York:
  Twayne, [1964]. LC64-8325.

Burkhart, Charles. HERMAN AND NANCY AND IVY:
  THREE LIVES IN ART. London: Gollancs, 1977.
  LC79-314280.

Dick, Kay. IVY AND STEVIE: IVY COMPTON-BURNETT
  AND STEVIE SMITH: CONVERSATIONS AND REFLECTIONS.
  London: Duckworth, 1971. LC71-878156.

Greig, Cicely. IVY COMPTON-BURNETT: A MEMOIR.
  London: Garnstone, 1972. LC72-169394.

Grylls, Rosalie G. I. COMPTON-BURNETT.
  [Harlow, Eng.]: Published for the British
  Council by Longman Group, [1971]. LC74-859329.
    Replaces work by P. Johnson published in
      1951. 30 pages.

"Ivy Compton-Burnett Issue." In TWENTIETH CENTURY
  LITERATURE, edited by Charles Burkhart.
  Hempstead, N.Y.: Hofstra Univ. Press, 1979.
  OCLC 8005855.
    Also pub. as: Vol. 25 (Summer 1979).

Sprigge, Elizabeth. THE LIFE OF IVY COMPTON-
  BURNETT. New York: G. Braziller, [1973].
  LC72-96072.

Spurling, Hilary. IVY WHEN YOUNG; THE EARLY LIFE
  OF I. COMPTON-BURNETT. London: Gollancz, 1974.
  LC74-174604.

COMPTON-BURNETT

Obituary
ANTIQUARIAN BOOKMAN (15 Sept 1969).
CON-25--28R.
NY TIMES (28 Aug 1969), 36:2.
NEWSWEEK 74 (8 Sept 1969), 62.
OBIT2, 160-61.
PUBLISHERS WEEKLY (15 Sept 1969).
TIME 94 (5 Sept 1969), 84.
TIMES (LONDON) (28 Aug 1969), 10:2.

COMSTOCK, ANNA (BOTTSFORD). 1854-1930. U.S.
Marian Lee, pseud.

Autobiography
THE COMSTOCKS OF CORNELL: JOHN HENRY COMSTOCK
AND ANNA BOTSFORD COMSTOCK; AN AUTOBIOGRAPHY,
edited by Glenn W. Herrick and Ruby G. Smith.
New York: Comstock Publishing Associates,
[1953]. LC53-13083.

Biography
AWW   NAW   NCAB-11,22   PRE   TWCB   WEBS   WOWWA
WWNA   WWWA-1

Obituary
NATURE MAGAZINE 16 (Oct 1930), 207.

COMSTOCK, HARRIET THERESA (SMITH). b.1860. U.S.

Biography
ALY   AWO   BURK   OV   OV2   WOWWA   WWNA   WWWA-5

COMSTOCK, SARAH. d.1960. U.S.

Biography
AWO   BURK   WOWWA   WWWA-3

Obituary
NY TIMES (24 Jan 1960), 88:2.
WILSON 34 (Apr 1960), 552.

CONKLIN, JENNIE MARIA (DRINKWATER). 1841-1900. U.S.
Jennie M. Drinkwater

Biography
BURK   DAB   WWWA-1

CONQUEST, JOAN. 1888?-1941. England.
    m. (1)Martin-Nicholson (2)Cooke

Autobiography
STRANGE BEDS. LIFE STORY OF LOVE, THRILLS AND
ADVENTURES. London: Jarrolds, 1937. LC37-5865.

Biography
ROCK   WWWE   WWWL

Obituary
NY TIMES (24 Oct 1941), 23:5.
TIMES (LONDON) (24 Oct 1941), 4:3; (28 Oct), 7:5.

CONVERSE, FLORENCE. b.1871. U.S.

Biography
AWO BURK KNIB NCAB-13 WEBS WOWWA WWNA
WWWA-6 WWWE WWWL

CONWAY, KATHERINE ELEANOR. 1853-1927. U.S.

Biography
AWW BRI BURK ODP TWCB WARBD WILA WIN
WWWA-1

Obituary
CATHOLIC WORLD 124 (Feb 1927), 698-9.
Driscoll, A.S. "In Memoriam." CATHOLIC WORLD
126 (Feb 1928), 481-7.

CONYERS, DOROTHEA (SMYTH). 1873-1949. Ireland.

Biography
CLE WWWL

COOK, MABEL (COLLINS). 1851-1927. England.
    Mabel Collins

Biography
ROCK WWWL

COOKE, GRACE (MACGOWAN). b.1863. U.S.

Biography
BURK   COY   KNIB   LOGP   WOWWA   WWWA-4

COOKE, JANE GROSVENOR. U.S.

Biography
WOWWA

COOKE, MAJORIE BENTON. 1876-1920. U.S.

Biography
BAN   OV   WOWWA   WWWA-1

Obituary
NY TIMES (27 Apr 1920), 9:3.

COOLEY, WINNIFRED (HARPER). U.S.

Biography
AWO   THOI   WOWWA   WWNA

COOLIDGE, ASENATH CARVER. b.1830. U.S.

Biography
WOWWA

COOLIDGE, EMMA DOWNING. 1884-1968. U.S.

Biography
WWWA-4

Coolidge, Susan, pseud. See WOOLSEY, SARAH CHAUNCEY.

COOPER, ELIZABETH (HUNT). 1877-1945. U.S.

Biography
AWO   BURK   WWNA   WWWA-5

CORBETT, ELIZABETH (FRANCES). 1887-1981. U.S.

Autobiography
OUT AT THE SOLDIERS' HOME, A MEMORY BOOK. New
York: D. Appleton-Century, 1941. LC41-4568.

Biography
AWO BURK CON-N2 KUT NAW REA TIT WAR WWNA
WWWE WWWL

Obituary
CON-102.
NY TIMES (31 Jan 1981), 11:6.

Corelli, Marie, pseud. See MACKAY, MARY.

CORKRAN, HENRIETTE. d.1911. England.

Autobiography
CELEBRITIES AND I. London: Hutchinson, 1902.
OCLC 3561395.

ODDITIES, OTHERS, AND I. London: Hutchinson,
1904. NUC.

CORNELIUS, MARY ANN (MANN). 1827-1918. U.S.

Biography
WILA WOWWA WWWA-1

CORNELIUS, OLIVIA SMITH. b.1882. U.S.

Biography
WOWWA

Corson, Geoffrey, pseud. See SHOLL, ANNA MACCLURE.

CORY, MATILDA WINIFRED MURIEL (GRAHAM).
c.1875-1950. England.
Winifred Graham Cory
Winifred Graham

CORY

Autobiography
THAT REMINDS ME---. 2 vols. New York:
Skeffington, [1945-47]. LC46-2600R.
Vol. 2 title: OBSERVATIONS, CASUAL AND
INTIMATE. LCa48-3211.

I INTRODUCE, BEING THE COMPANION VOLUME OF THAT
REMINDS ME, AND OBSERVATIONS; THE TRINITY OF
AN AUTOBIOGRAPHY. New York: Skeffington,
[1948]. LC49-24783.

Biography
HAMM   ROCK   WWLA   WWWL

Obituary
NY TIMES (6 Feb 1950), 25:6.
TIMES (LONDON) (6 Feb 1950), 8:5.

CORY, VIVIAN. England.
Victoria Cross, pseud.

Biography
ROCK   STOK

Cory, Winifred Graham. See   CORY, MATILDA WINIFRED
MURIEL (GRAHAM).

COSTELLO, FANNY KEMBLE (JOHNSON). 1868-1950. U.S.
Fanny Kemble Johnson

Biography
CONW

Turner, Ella M., ed.   STORIES AND VERSE OF WEST
VIRGINIA. p. 309.   Richwood, W. Va.: Comstock,
1974. LC78-111733.

Cotes, Everard. See COTES, SARA JEANNETTE (DUNCAN).

Cotes, Mrs. Everard.   See   COTES,   SARA JEANNETTE
(DUNCAN).

COTES, SARA JEANNETTE (DUNCAN). 1862?-1922. Canada.
  Everard Cotes
  Mrs. Everard Cotes
  Sara Jeannette Duncan
  Sarah Jeannette Duncan

Biography
BD CHA MDCB MOR MOR2 MORGA MYE NCH RHO
SCHM STOXC SY WARBD WEBS WILA

Tausky, Thomas E. SARA JEANNETTE DUNCAN:
  NOVELIST OF EMPIRE. Port Credit, Ont.: P.D.
  Meany, 1980. LC80-487736.

COUVREUR, JESSIE CATHERINE (HUYBERS). 1848-1897.
  Australia.
  Tasma, pseud.

Biography
AUDB BEI BEL BOASE-4 CHA MIA MIAU MYE SER

COVEY, ELIZABETH (ROCKFORD). b.1873. Canada.
  Elizabeth Fremantle, pseud.

Biography
MOR2

COX, ANNE. England.
  Annabel Gray, pseud.

Biography
ROCK WWWL

COX, MARIAN (METCALF). b.1882 U.S.

Autobiography
Cox, Marian M. THE SPINX WORE AN ORCHID;
  MEMOIRS OF MARIAN COX. New York: Vantage,
  [1967]. LC66-29965.

Coxon, Mrs. Sidney. See COXON, MURIEL (HINE).

COXON, MURIEL (HINE). England.
Mrs. Sidney Coxon
Muriel Hine.

Biography
ROCK   WWWL

Craddock, Charles Egbert, pseud.   See   MURFREE,
MARY NOAILLES.

CRAIG, KATHERINE LEE. b.1862. U.S.

Biography
WWNA

CRAIGIE, PEARL MARY TERESA (RICHARDS). 1867-1906.
England.
John Oliver Hobbes, pseud.

Autobiography
THE LIFE OF JOHN OLIVER HOBBES TOLD IN HER
CORRESPONDENCE WITH NUMEROUS FRIENDS.
2d ed. New York: Dutton, 1911. OCLC 2167746.
Includes a biographical sketch by her father.

Biography
APPS AWW BD BEL BERE BRO BURK CHA CLARS
COLSA COU DNB-2 FUR HAL HAMM HAOXE HARKF
HINA KUBA LAU LOGP MYE NCAB-10 PRE SHA
SHO WAGCE WARBD WARLC WEBS WWWL

Maison, Margaret M. JOHN OLIVER HOBBES: HER LIFE
AND WORK. London: The Eighteen Nineties
Society, 1976. LC78-319635.

Weintraub, Stanley. THE LONDON YANKEES:
PORTRAITS OF AMERICAN WRITERS AND ARTISTS IN
ENGLAND, 1894-1914. pp. 57-83. New York:
Harcourt Brace Jovanovich, c1979. LC78-22276.

Obituary
NY TIMES (14 Aug 1906), 7:1.
TIMES (LONDON) (15 Aug 1906), 7:5.

Craik, Georgiana M. See MAY, GEORGIANA MARION
(CRAIK).

CRAM, MILDRED. b.1889. U.S.
m. McDowell

Biography
CON-49--52

CRANSTON, RUTH. d.1956. U.S.
Anne Warwick, pseud.

Biography
ROCK

Obituary
NY TIMES (Apr 4 1956), 29:3.

CRAWFORD, AMY JOSEPHINE (BAKER). b.1895. England.
Amy J. Baker
Mrs. Maynard Crawford

Biography
WWWE   WWWL

Crawford, Mrs. Maynard. See CRAWFORD, AMY
JOSEPHINE (BAKER).

Creed, Mrs. J. Percy. See LEYLAND, MARIE LOUISE
(MACK) CREED.

CREED, SIBYL MARY. d.1926. England.

Obituary
TIMES (LONDON) (12 Aug 1926), 13:2; tribute (13
Aug), 12:3.

CREEVEY, CAROLINE ALATHEA (STICKNEY). 1843-1920.
U.S.

Autobiography
A DAUGHTER OF THE PURITANS, AN AUTOBIOGRAPHY.
New York: G.P. Putnam's Sons, 1916. LC17-6643.

Biography
NCAB-30   WWWA-1

CRIM, MARTHA JANE. U.S.
Matt Crim

Biography
KNIB

Crim, Matt. See CRIM, MARTHA JANE.

CROAL, FRANCES A.
Frances Hammond, pseud.

Biography
WWWL

Croker, B.M. See CROKER, BITHIA MARY (SHEPPARD).

CROKER, BITHIA MARY (SHEPPARD). d.1920. Ireland.
B.M. Croker

Biography
BLAP   BRI   CLE   PARR   WARBD

Obituary
TIMES (LONDON) (22 Oct 1920), 13:5.

Cromartie, Countess of. See MACKENZIE, SIBELL
LILIAN (BLUNT).

Cromarty, Deas, pseud. See WATSON, ELIZABETH
SOPHIA (FLETCHER).

CROMMELIN, MARIA HENRIETTA DE LA CHEROIS. d.1934.
Ireland.
     May Crommelin, pseud.

                    Biography
  BD BLA BRI CLE

Crommelin, May, pseud.   See CROMMELIN, MARIA
  HENRIETTA DE LA CHEROIS.

CROSBIE, MARY. England.

                    Biography
  BRI

CROSS, ADA (CAMBRIDGE). 1844-1926. Australia.
     Ada Cambridge

                 Autobiography
  THIRTY YEARS IN AUSTRALIA, by Ada Cambridge.
  London: Methuen, 1903. LC09-32411.

                    Biography
  AUDB BD BEI CHA JOHDB KUBA MIA MYE SER
  SHO WEBS WWWL

Cross, Victoria, pseud. See Cory, Vivian.

CROTTIE, JULIA M. b.1853. Ireland.

                    Biography
  BRI

CROW, LOUISA. d.1894. England.

                    Biography
  BOASE-4

CROW, MARTHA (FOOTE). 1854-1924. U.S.

Biography
NCAB-22 TWCB WEBS WOWWA WWWA-1

CROWELL, KATHARINE RONEY. 1854-1926. U.S.

Biography
WWA-1

CROWLEY, MARY CATHERINE. d.1920. U.S.

Biography
BURK ODP WOWWA WWWA-1

CROWNFIELD, GERTRUDE FREDERICA. 1867-1945. U.S.

Biography
AWO BURK COY KUJ1 KUJ2 WA WWNA WWWA-2

Obituary
CUR-1945.
NY TIMES (3 June 1945), 32:2.
PUBLISHERS WEEKLY 148 (18 Aug 1945), 610.

CROWNINSHIELD, MARY (BRADFORD). 1854-1913. U.S.
Mrs. Schuyler Crowninshield

Biography
BURK LOGP ROCK WARBD WOWWA WWWA-1

Crowninshield, Mrs. Schuyler. See CROWNINSHIELD,
MARY (BRADFORD).

CRUGER, JULIA GRINNELL (STORROW). d.1920. U.S.
m. (1)Cruger (2)Chance
Julien Gordon, pseud.

Biography
APP AWW BD BURK ROCK TWCB WARBD WWWA-1

CRUGER

Obituary
NY TIMES (13 July 1920), 11:4.

CRUGER, MARY. 1834-1908. U.S.

Biography
WILA   WWWA-1

Obituary
NY TIMES (20 Nov 1908), 9:3.

CUDLIP, ANNIE HALL (THOMAS). 1838-1918. England.
Mrs. Pender Cudlip
Annie Thomas

Biography
JOHH

Cudlip, Mrs. Pender.   See CUDLIP, ANNIE HALL
(THOMAS).

CULTER, MARY NANTZ (MACCRAE). b.1858. U.S.

Biography
BAN   WWNA   WWWA-4   WWWL

Cummings, G.D.   See CUMMINS, GERALDINE DOROTHY.

CUMMINS, GERALDINE DOROTHY. 1890-1960.   Ireland.
G.D. Cummins

Biography
CLE   CON-P1   WWWE   WWWL

CURLEWIS, ETHEL SYBIL (TURNER). 1872-1958.
Australia.
Ethel Sybil Turner
sister of Lilian Turner Thompson

Biography
MIA   MIAU   WWWL

CURLEWIS

Obituary
NY TIMES (9 Apr 1958), 33:1.
TIMES (LONDON) (9 Apr 1958), 11:4.
WILSON 32 (June 1958), 692.

Curtois, M.A.   See   CURTOIS, MARGARET ANNE.

CURTOIS, MARGARET ANNE. d.1932. England.
M.A. Curtois

Obituary
TIMES (LONDON) (15 Sept 1932), 14:2.

CURTIS, ALICE (TURNER). 1860-1958. U.S.
Mrs. Irving Curtis

Biography
AWO   BURK   WWNA   WWWA-1

CURTIS, ISABEL (GORDON). 1863-1915. U.S.

Biography
WOWWA   WWNA   WWWA-1

Curtis, Mrs. Irving.   See   CURTIS, ALICE (TURNER).

CUTHELL, EDITH E.

Biography
WWWL

CUTTING, MARY STEWART (DOUBLEDAY). 1851-1924. U.S.

Biography
BURG   BURK   WOWWA   WWWA-1

Obituary
NY TIMES (11 Aug 1924), 13:5.

DABNEY, JULIA PARKER. b.1850. U.S.

Biography
TWCB   WOWWA   WWWA-4

DAFFAN, KATIE. U.S.

Biography
BARN   BURK   KNIB   NCAB-A   WOWWA

DAGGETT, MABEL ANNA (POTTER). 1871-1927. U.S.

Biography
ALY   WOWWA   WWNA   WWWA-1

DAGGETT, MARY (STEWART). 1856-1922. U.S.
    Mrs. Charles Stewart Daggett

Biography
ALY   BURK   COY   NCAB-9

Daggett, Mrs. Charles Stewart.   See   DAGGETT, MARY
(STEWART).

DAHLGREN, SARAH MADELEINE (VINTON) GODDARD.
1825-1898. U.S.

Biography
COY   DAB   KUAA   LOGP   NCAB-22   ROCK   WWWA-H

DALE, ALICE MARY. Australia.

Biography
MIAU

Dale, Darley, pseud.   See   STEELE, FRANCESCA MARIA.

DALLAS, MARY (KYLE). 1830-1897. U.S.

BURK   Biography

DALLYN, VIOLA (MEYNELL). 1886-1956. England.
    Viola Meynell

Biography
BRO   HINA   HOE   KUT   MANBL   MICB   MYE   NCH   SHO
WARLC   WEBS   WWW-5

Obituary
TIMES (LONDON) (29 Oct 1956), 14:2; (6 Nov), 13:4.

D'Alpens, Marquesa, pseud.   See   WILLIAMSON, ALICE
MURIEL (LIVINGSTON).

Dalrymple, Leona.   See   WILSON, LEONA   (DALRYMPLE).

DANA, OLIVE ELIZA. b.1859. U.S.

WILA   Biography

Dane, Clement, pseud.   See   ASHTON, WINIFRED.

D'Anetham, Eleanora Mary (Haggard).   See   ANETHAN,
ELEANORA MARY (HAGGARD) D'.

DANIELS, CORA LINN (MORRISON). b.1852. U.S.

WILA   WWWA-4   Biography

D'APERY, HELEN (BURRELL) GIBSON. 1842-1915. U.S.
    Olive Harper, pseud.

Biography
NCAB-5   ROCK

D'APERY

Obituary
NY TIMES (4 May 1915), 15:5.

Daring, Hope, pseud. See Johnson, Anna.

Darmesteter, Madame James. See DUCLAUX, AGNES MARY
FRANCES (ROBINSON) DARMESTETER.

DASHWOOD, EDMEE ELIZABETH MONICA (DE LA PASTURE).
1890-1943. England.
    E.M. Delafield, pseud.

Biography
BERE BRO CHA CHABI HAMM KUL KUT MANBL
MARBS MICB MYE NCH TWCR WARLC WEBS WWLA
WWWE WWWL WWWT

Obituary
CUR-1944.
NY TIMES (3 Dec 1943), 23:3.
PUBLISHERS WEEKLY 144 (11 Dec 1943), 2184.
TIMES (LONDON) (3 Dec 1943), 7:4.
WILSON 18 (Feb 1944), 422.

Daskam, Josephine. See BACON, JOSEPHINE DODGE
(DASKAM).

Daskam, Josephine Dodge. See BACON, JOSEPHINE
DODGE (DASKAM).

Daskein, Mrs. See DASKEIN, TARELLA (QUINN).

Daskein, T. Quinn. See DASKEIN, TARELLA(QUINN).

DASKEIN, TARELLA (QUINN). Australia.
    Mrs. Daskein
    T. Quinn Daskein
    Tarella Quinn

Biography

MIA

DAULTON, AGNES WARNER (MACCLELLAND). 1867-1944.
U.S.

Biography
AWO   BURK   COY   WOWWA   WWNA   WWWA-2

Obituary
NY TIMES (6 June 1944), 17:6.

DAVIESS, MARIA (THOMPSON). 1872-1924. U.S.

Autobiography
SEVEN TIMES SEVEN: AN AUTOBIOGRAPHY. New
    York: Arno, 1980 [c1924]. LC79-8786.

Biography
BICA   BURK   DAB   LIB-17   WWWA-1

Obituary
NY TIMES (4 Sept 1924), 19:5.

DAVIS, EDITH (SMITH). 1859-1917. U.S.

Biography
WOWWA   WWWA-1

DAVIS, HARRIET RIDDLE. 1849-1938. U.S.

Biography
COY

Noel, Francis R. "Biographical Sketch of Henry
    Edgar Davis and Harriet Riddle Davis." In
    COLUMBIA HISTORICAL SOCIETY. RECORDS. Vol.44-45.
    pp. 37-53. Washington, D.C.: 1944. LC A45-2218.

Davis, M.E.M. See DAVIS, MARY EVELYN (MOORE).

DAVIS

DAVIS, MARY EVELYN (MOORE). 1852-1909. U.S.
M.E.M. Davis

Biography
AWW BURK DAB KUAA LIB NCAB-10 WARBD WWWA-1

DAVIS, NORAH. b.1878. U.S.

Biography
BURK WOWWA WWWA-6

DAVIS, REBECCA BLAINE (HARDING). 1831-1910. U.S.

Biography
ADE AML APP AWO AWW BD BERE BURK CON-104
DAB HAL HAOXA JOHDB KUAA MCW MDWB MYE NAW
NCAB-8 NOV NPW PRE REA SOU TWCB WAGCA
WARBD WEBS WWWA-1

Olsen, Tillie. "A Biographical Interpretation."
In LIFE IN THE IRON MILLS ..., by Rebecca H.
Davis. pp. 69-174. [New York]: Feminist
Press, 1972. LC72-8880.

Langford, Gerald. THE RICHARD HARDING DAVIS
YEARS; A BIOGRAPHY OF A MOTHER AND SON. New
York: Holt, Rinehart and Winston, [1961].
LC61-5801.

DAVIS, VARINA ANNE JEFFERSON. 1864-1898. U.S.
Daughter of Varina Howell and Jefferson
Davis

Biography
APP-S AWO BURK DAB LIB NCAB-23 PRE TWCB
WARBD WEBS WILA WWNA WWWA-H

Ferrell, Chiles C. "THE DAUGHTER OF THE
CONFEDERACY"; HER LIFE, CHARACTER AND
WRITINGS. [Oxford? Miss., 1899]. LC07-21482.

Obituary
"Daughter of the Confederacy." HARPER'S WEEKLY
42 (1 Oct 1898), 974.
NY TIMES (19 Sept 1898), 4:6.

Dawson-Scott, C.A. See SCOTT, CATHARINE AMY DAWSON.

Deamer, Dulcie, pseud. See GOLDIE, MARY ELIZABETH KATHLEEN DULCIE (DEAMER).

Dean, Mrs. Andrew, pseud. See SIDGWICK, CECILY (ULLMANN).

DEAN, S. ELLA (WOOD). b.1871. U.S.

WOWWA   Biography

DEAN, SARA. b.1870. U.S.

                Biography
HINK WOWWA WWWA-5

Dearborn, Laura, pseud. See PICTON, NINA.

DEARMER, JESSIE MABEL (WHITE). 1872-1915. England.
        Mrs. Percy Dearmer

WWWL   Biography

                Obituary
TIMES (LONDON) (13 July 1915), 5:3.

Dearmer, Mrs. Percy. See DEARMER, JESSIE MABEL (WHITE).

DEASE, ALICE. b.1875?. Ireland.
        m. Chichester

CLE   Biography

94

DE BATHE, EMILIE CHARLOTTE (LE BRETON) LANGTRY.
1853-1929. England.
Lillie Langtry

Autobiography
THE DAYS I KNEW, by Lillie Langtry. New York:
Arno, [1982], 1925. LC79-8067.

Biography
APP BERE CHABI FLE HAMM MDWB NCH WEBS
WWWA-2,4 WWWT

Birkett, Jeremy and John Richardson. LILLIE
LANGTRY, HER LIFE IN WORDS AND PICTURES.
New York: Sterling, 1979. LC80-511144.

Brough, James. THE PRINCE AND THE LILY. New
York: Ballantine Books, 1976. LC74-79684.

Gerson, Noel B. BECAUSE I LOVED HIM; THE LIFE
AND LOVES OF LILLIE LANGTRY. New York:
Morrow, 1971. LC70-151901.

Porter, Haywood T. LILLIE LANGTRY; THE "JERSEY
LILY". St. Helier: Jersey, the Museum, 1973.
LC73-167710.

Rather, Lois. TWO LILIES IN AMERICA: LILLIAN
RUSSELL AND LILLIE LANGTRY. Oakland, Calif.:
Rather, 1973. LC74-154264.

Sichel, Pierre. THE JERSEY LILY; THE STORY OF
THE FABULOUS MRS. LANGTRY. Englewood Cliffs,
N.J.: Prentice-Hall, [1958]. LC58-11744.

De Chavanne, Loveau. See CHAVANNE, LOVEAU DE.

De Coulevain, Helene Favre. See FAVRE DE
COULEVAIN, HELENE.

De Coulevain, Pierre, pseud. See FAVRE DE
COULEVAIN, HELENE.

De Crespigny, Rose Champion. See CHAMPION DE
CRESPIGNY, ROSE (KEY).

DE FABER, CECILIA FRANCISCA JOSEFA BOHL. 1796-1877.
Spain.
Fernan Caballero, pseud.
Name also appears as Bohl de Faber
m. (1)Planells (2)Del Arco (3)De Ayala

Biography
BD BERE CAS EDW HAR KUE MAGN MDWB PEE
WARBD WEBS

"Fernan Caballero." In SIX LIFE STUDIES OF
FAMOUS WOMEN, by Matilda Betham-Edwards.
pp. 1-40. Freeport, N.Y.: Books for Libraries,
[1972], 1880. LC73-39701.

Hespelt, Ernest H. FERNAN CABALLERO, A STUDY OF
HER LIFE AND LETTERS. Ithaca, N.Y.: [1925?].

Klibbe, Lawrence H. FERNAN CABALLERO. New York:
Twayne, [1973]. LC72-4655.

Newmark, Maxim. DICTIONARY OF SPANISH LITERATURE.
pp. 120-1. New York: Philosophical Library,
[1956]. LC56-13978.

THE OXFORD COMPANION TO SPANISH LITERATURE,
edited by Philip Ward. pp. 69-70. Oxford
[Eng.]: Clarendon, 1978. LC78-325227.

Obituary
TIMES (LONDON) (19 Apr 1877), 8:2.

Dehan, Richard, pseud. See GRAVES, CLOTILDE INEZ
MARY.

De Jan, Mrs. Henry. See DE JAN, WINIFRED LEWELLIN
(JAMES).

DE JAN, WINIFRED LEWELLIN (JAMES). 1876-1941.
Australia.
Mrs. Henry De Jan
Winifred James

DE JAN

Autobiography
OUT OF THE SHADOWS, by Winifred James....
London: Chapman and Hall, 1924. LC24-11995.

Biography
HAMM   MIA   MIAU   SER   WWWE

De Janville, Sybille Gabrielle. See   MARTEL   DE
JANVILLE, SYBILLE GABRIELLE MARIE ANTOINETTE
(DE RIQUETTI DE MIRABEAU).

Dejeans, Elizabeth, pseud.   See   BUDGETT, FRANCES
ELIZABETH JANES.

DE JOUVENAL,   SIDONIE   GABRIELLE   (COLETTE)
GAUTHER-VILLARS. 1873-1954. France.
        m. (1)Gauther-Villars   (2)De Jouvenal
        (3)Goudeket
        Colette, pseud.
        Colette Willy, pseud.

Autobiography
THE BLUE LANTERN, by Colette, translated by
Roger Senhouse. Westport, Conn.: Greenwood,
[1972, c1963]. LC72-178781.

EARTHLY PARADISE; AN AUTOBIOGRAPHY, DRAWN FROM
HER LIFETIME WRITINGS, by Robert Phelps,
translated by Herma Briffault et al. New York:
Farrar, Straus & Giroux, 1966. LC65-23837.

THE EVENING STAR: RECOLLECTIONS, translated by
David Le Vay. New York: Bobbs-Merrill, 1973.
LC73-11793.

JOURNEY FOR MYSELF: SELFISH MEMORIES, by Colette,
translated by David Le Vay. London: Owen,
1971. LC77-859343.

LETTERS FROM COLETTE, selected and translated by
Robert Phelps. New York: Farrar, Straus,
Giroux, c1980. LC80-20680.

LOOKING BACKWARDS, by Colette, translated by
David Le Vay. Introduction by Maurice
Goudeket. Bloomington: Indiana Univ. Press,
1975. LC74-2905.

PLACES, translated by David Le Vay. Foreword by
Margaret Crosland. Indianapolis: Bobbs-Merrill,
[1971]. LC70-163017R.

Biography
BERE   CAS   CHABI   CON-104   CROS   DUC   FLE   HAOXE
HAOXF HAR   HOL   KRO   KUAT   KUT   KUTS   LES   MAG
MCW   MDWB   NOV   PEE   RIC   RULE   SEYS   WARLC   WEBS

Benet, Mary K. WRITERS IN LOVE. pp. 187-251.
New York: Macmillan, c1977. LC76-25560.

Cocteau, Jean. MY CONTEMPORARIES, edited and
introduced by Margaret Crosland. Philadelphia:
Chilton, [1968]. LC68-31695R.

Cottrell, Robert D. COLETTE. New York: F.
Ungar, [1974]. LC73-84598.

Crosland, Margaret. COLETTE--THE DIFFICULTY OF
LOVING: A BIOGRAPHY. Indianapolis: Bobbs-
Merrill, [1974?], c1973. LC73-1741.

_____. COLETTE, A PROVINCIAL IN PARIS. New
York: British Book Centre, [1954]. LC54-4607L.
Pub. in Eng. as: MADAME COLETTE: A PROVINCIAL
IN PARIS. 1953.

Davies, Margaret B. COLETTE. New York: Grove,
[1961]. LC61-12357.

Goudeket, Maurice. CLOSE TO COLETTE; AN INTIMATE
PORTRAIT OF A WOMAN OF GENIUS. Westport,
Conn.: Greenwood, [1972, c1957]. LC70-178786.

_____. THE DELIGHTS OF GROWING OLD, translated
by Patrick O'Brian. New York: Farrar, Straus
and Giroux, [1966]. LC66-14150.

Highet, Gilbert. TALENTS AND GENIUSES.
pp. 75-83. New York: Meridian, [1959, c1957].
LC59-12911.

Marks, Elaine. COLETTE. New Brunswick, N.J.: Rutgers Univ. Press, [1960]. LC60-9694L.

Mitchell, Yvonne. COLETTE: A TASTE FOR LIFE. London: Weidenfeld and Nicolson, c1975. LC75-329704.

Phelps, Robert. BELLES SAISONS: A COLETTE SCRAPBOOK. New York: Farrar, Straus and Giroux, c1978. LC78-6944.

Sarde, Michele. COLETTE: FREE AND FETTERED, translated by Richard Miller. New York: Morrow, 1980. LC79-24978.

Stansbury, Milton H. FRENCH NOVELISTS OF TODAY. pp. 101-19. Philadelphia: Univ. of Pennsylvania Press, 1935. LC35-20871.

Stewart, Joan H. COLETTE. Boston: Twayne, c1983. LC82-17475.

Obituary
ILLUS LONDON NEWS 225 (14 Aug 1954), 271.
NY TIMES (4 Aug 1954), 21:4; (8 Aug), 85:3.
NEWSWEEK 44 (16 Aug 1954), 60.
OBIT1, 158-9.
PUBLISHERS WEEKLY 166 (14 Aug 1954), 624-5.
TIME 64 (16 Aug 1954), 94.
TIMES (LONDON) (4 Aug 1954), 9:1; (10 Aug), 8:6.
WILSON 29 (Oct 1954), 104.

DE KOVAN, ANNE (FARWELL). 1860-1953. U.S.

Biography
APP   AWO   BICA   BURK   NCAB-16,48   WOWWA   WWNA

Obituary
MUSICAL AMERICA 73 (1 Apr 1953), 26.
NY TIMES (13 Jan 1953), 27:3.
NEWSWEEK 41 (26 Jan 1953), 73.
WILSON 27 (Mar 1953), 476.

Delafield, E.M., pseud. See DASHWOOD, EDMEE ELIZABETH MONICA (DE LA PASTURE.)

DELAMARE, HENRIETTE EUGENIE. 1858-1937. U.S.

Biography

WWNA

DELAND, ELLEN DOUGLAS. 1860-1923. U.S.

Biography

TWCB   WARBD   WOWWA   WWWA-1

DELAND, MARGARET WADE (CAMPBELL). 1857-1945. U.S.

Autobiography

GOLDEN YESTERDAYS. New York: Harper & Bros.,
[c1941]. LC41-22156.

IF THIS BE I, AS I SUPPOSE IT BE. New York:
D. Appleton-Century, 1935. LC35-27401.

Biography

ADE AML APP AWO AWW BD BERE BURK CHA
CHABI DAB-S3 HAL HAOXA JOHDB KUL KUT LOGP
MAN MARBS MYE NAW NCAB-3,33 NPW OV OV2
REA TWCB WAGCA WARBD WARLC WEBS WILA WIN
WOWWA WWNA WWWA-2 WWWL

Gilder, Jeannette L., ed. AUTHORS AT HOME;
PERSONAL AND BIOGRAPHICAL SKETCHES OF WELL-
KNOWN AMERICAN WRITERS. pp. 357-67. New York:
A. Wessels, 1902. LC2-25430.

Obituary

CUR-1945.
NY TIMES (14 Jan 1945), 40:1.
PUBLISHERS WEEKLY 147 (3 Feb 1945), 649.
TIME 45 (22 Jan 1945), 68.

DELANO, EDITH (BERNARD). 1875-1946. U.S.

Biography

BURG   BURK   WEBS   WWNA   WWWA-2

Obituary

NY TIMES (9 Sept 1946), 9:2.
WILSON 21 (Nov 1946), 202.

De La Pasture, Mrs. Henry. See CLIFFORD, ELIZABETH
LYDIA ROSABELLE (BONHAM) DE LA PASTURE.

DE LA RAMEE, MARIE LOUISE. 1840-1908. England.
Ouida, pseud.

Biography
ADE   BD   BEL   BRO   CAS   CHA   CHABI   DNB-2   FUR
HAMM HAOXE JOHDB JOHH KUBA KUJ1 MAG   MAGN
MCC   MDWB MYE   NCH   NO   NOV   NPW   PEE   SHA   SHO
SMITH SOME-20 VIC WAGCE WARBD WARLC WEBS
WWWL

Bigland, Eileen. OUIDA, THE PASSIONATE
VICTORIAN. New York: Duell, Sloan and Pearce,
1951. LC51-10422.

THE BRITISH ECCENTRIC, edited by Harriet
Bridgeman and Elizabeth Drury. pp. 88-97.
New York: C.N. Potter, 1976, c1975. LC75-41406.

Ffrench, Yvonne. OUIDA, A STUDY IN OSTENTATION.
London: Cobden-Sanderson, [1938]. LC38-22849.

Huntington, Henry G. MEMORIES: PERSONAGES,
PEOPLE, PLACES. pp. 190-296. London:
Constable, 1911. OCLC 5199456.

Lee, Elizabeth. OUIDA: A MEMOIR. London:
T.F. Unwin, [1914]. LC15-2872.

Smith-Dampier, John L. EAST ANGLIAN WORTHIES.
p. 65. Oxford: B. Blackwell, 1949. LC49-26023.

Stirling, Monica. THE FINE AND THE WICKED; THE
LIFE AND TIMES OF OUIDA. New York: Coward-
McCann, [1958]. LC58-6285.

DE LASZOWSKA, JANE EMILY (GERARD). 1849-1903.
Scotland.
        Madame De Laszowska
        E. Gerard
        Emily Gerard

Biography
BLAP   WWWL

De Laszowska, Madame. See DE LASZOWSKA, JANE EMILY (GERARD).

Deledda, Grazia. See MADESANI, GRAZIA COSIMA (DELEDDA).

DELL, ETHEL MARY. 1881-1939. England.
m. Savage

Biography
BERE BRO CHABI DNB-S5 HAMM NCH RIC SAT-15
SHO TWCR WEBS WWWE

Dell, Penelope. NETTIE AND SISSIE: THE BIOGRAPHY OF ETHEL M. DELL AND HER SISTER ELLA. London: Hamilton, 1977. LC77-377388.

Obituary
NY TIMES (18 Sept 1939), 19:6.
PUBLISHERS WEEKLY 136 (23 Sept 1929), 1268.
TIMES (LONDON) (19 Sept 1939), 8:7.

De Longgarde, Dorothea (Gerard). See LONGARD DE LONGGARDE, DOROTHEA (GERARD).

De Longgarde, Madame Longard. See LONGARD DE LONGGARDE, DOROTHEA (GERARD) LONGARD.

De Meissner, Sophie (Radford). See MEISSNER, SOPHIE (RADFORD) DE.

DEMPSTER, CHARLOTTE LOUISA HAWKINS. 1835-1913. Scotland.

Biography
WARBD

Obituary
TIMES (LONDON) (15 May 1913), 9:4.

DENISON, MARY (ANDREWS). 1826-1911. U.S.

Biography
APP AWW BURK JOHH JOHH2 NAW NCAB-19 TWCB
WARBD WWWA-1

Obituary
TIMES (LONDON) (18 Oct 1911), 11:4.

Dennen, G.A. See DENNEN, GRACE ATHERTON.

DENNEN, GRACE ATHERTON. 1874-1927. U.S.
      G.A. Dennen

Biography
WOWWA WWNA

De Savallo, Dona Teresa. See WILLIAMSON, ALICE
MURIEL (LIVINGSTON).

DE SELINCOURT, ANNE DOUGLAS (SEDGWICK). 1873-1935.
England.
      Mrs. Basil De Selincourt
      Anne Douglas Sedgwick

Autobiography
ANNE DOUGLAS SEDGWICK; A PORTRAIT IN LETTERS,
chosen and edited by Basil de Selincourt.
Boston: Houghton Mifflin, 1936. LC36-22210.

A CHILDHOOD IN BRITTANY EIGHTY YEARS AGO, by Anne
Douglas Sedgwick. New York: Century, 1919.
LC19-14551.

Biography
AWW BRO BURK CHABI DAB-S1 HAMM HAOXA KUL
KUT KUTS MAN MARBS MICA MYE NAW OV2 REA
RICDA WEBS WWW-3 WWWA-1 WWWL

Forbes, Esther. ANNE DOUGLAS SEDGWICK. AN
INTERVIEW. Boston: Houghton Mifflin, 1927.
16 pages.

DE SELINCOURT

Obituary

"Irreplaceable Voice." COMMONWEAL 22 (2 Aug 1935), 336.

Lunt, S.A. PUBLISHERS WEEKLY 128 (27 July 1935), 225.

TIMES (LONDON) (22 July 1935), 14:2.

WILSON 10 (Sept 1935), 8.

DE SELINCOURT, IRENE RUTHERFORD (MCLEOD). b.1891. England.

Irene Rutherford Mcleod

Biography

MANBL NCH WEBS

De Selincourt, Mrs. Basil. See DE SELINCOURT, ANNE DOUGLAS (SEDWICK).

Devereux, M. See WATSON, MARY (DEVEREUX).

Devereux, Mary. See WATSON, MARY (DEVEREUX).

Devi, Srimati Svarna Kumari. See GHOSAL, SRIMATI SVARNA KUMARI DEVI.

Devoore, Ann. See WALDEN, ANN BREVOORT (EDDY).

Dewing, E.B. See KAUP, ELIZABETH BARTOL (DEWING).

DE WITT, JULIA A. WOODHULL, d.1906. U.S.

Biography

WWWA-1

DICKENS, MARY ANGELA (EVANS). 1838-1896. England.

Biography

WARBD

DICKINSON, MARY (LOWE). 1839-1914. U.S.

WOWWA   WWWA-1   Biography

Dickson, Miss S. O'H.   See   DICKSON, SALLIE O'HEAR.

DICKSON, SALLIE O'HEAR. d.1916. U.S.
            Miss S. O'H. Dickson

                          Biography
KNIB

DIEHL, ALICE (MANGOLD). 1844-1912. England.
          Mrs. A.M. Diehl

                    Autobiography
MUSICAL MEMORIES, by A.M. Diehl.   London:
    R. Bentley, 1897. LC06-3677.

THE TRUE STORY OF MY LIFE; AN AUTOBIOGRAPHY BY
ALICE M. DIEHL, NOVELIST-WRITER-MUSICIAN.
New York: J. Lane, 1908. LC09-30626.

                          Biography
WWWL

Diehl, Mrs. A.M.   See   DIEHL, ALICE (MANGOLD).

DIEUDONNE, FLORENCE LUCINDA (CARPENTER). b.1850.
U.S.

                          Biography
WILA

DILLON, MARY C. (JOHNSON). d.1923. U.S.

                          Biography
WOWWA   WWWA-1

Dillon, Mrs. G.F.   See TURNBULL, DORA AMY (ELLES) DILLON.

DIVER, KATHERINE HELEN MAUD (MARSHALL). 1867-1945. England.
Maud Diver

Biography
BRO HAMM KUT MARBS PARR RIC ROCK SHO TWCR
WARLC WWLA WWW-4 WWWE WWWL

Obituary
NY TIMES (11 Nov 1945), 42:2.
TIMES (LONDON) (17 Oct 1945), 7:5.
WILSON 20 (Jan 1946), 328.

Diver, Maud.   See DIVER, KATHERINE HELEN MAUD (MARSHALL).

DIX, BEULAH MARIE. b.1876. U.S.
m. Flebbe

Biography
AWW BURK KUJ1 KUJ2 LOGP REA WEBS WIN
WOWWA WWWT

Scott, Evelyn F. HOLLYWOOD WHEN SILENTS WERE GOLDEN. New York: McGraw-Hill, [1972]. LC72-37361.

Dix, Dorothy, pseud.   See GILMER,   ELIZABETH (MERIWETHER).

DIXIE, FLORENCE CAROLINE (DOUGLAS). 1857-1905. England.

Biography
ADE DNB-2 HAMM

Obituary
TIMES (LONDON) (8 Nov 1905), 9:6.

DIXON, ELLA NORA HEPWORTH. d.1932. England.
Margaret Wynman, pseud.

Biography
WWLA WWWE

DOBBIN, GERTRUDE (PAGE). 1873-1922. England.
Rhodesia.
Gertrude Page

Biography
BRI ROS ROSE STA

Rasmussen, R. Kent. HISTORICAL DICTIONARY OF
RHODESIA/ZIMBABWE. pp. 243-4. Metuchen, N.J.:
Scarecrow, 1979. LC78-23671.

Obituary
NY TIMES (2 Apr 1922), 29:3.
TIMES (LONDON) (3 Apr 1922), 5:3.

DODD, ANNA BOWMAN (BLAKE). 1855-1929. U.S.

Biography
WARBD WILA WWWA-2

DODD, CATHERINE ISABEL. 1860-1932. England.

Biography
WWLA WWWE

Wilson, Edith C. CATHERINE ISABELLA DODD, 1860-
1932. A MEMORIAL SKETCH. London: Sidgwick and
Jackson, 1936. LC36-32055.

Obituary
TIMES (LONDON) (16 Nov 1932), 16:4; tribute
(18 Nov), 16:4.

Dodge, Mary Thurston, pseud. See LE FEUVRE, AMY.

Don-Carlos, Cooke. See DON-CARLOS, LOUISA COOKE.

DON-CARLOS, LOUISA (COOKE). b.1874. U.S.
    Cooke Don-Carlos

               Biography
  WOWWA WWNA

DONNELL, ANNIE (HAMILTON). 1862-1943. U.S.

             Biography
  ALY WOWWA WWNA WWWA-3

DONNELLY, ELEANOR CECILIA. 1838-1917. U.S.

              Biography
  APP BURK DAB NCAB-2 TWCB WILA WWWA-1

              Obituary
  NY TIMES (2 May 1917), 11:5.
  Schwertner, Thomas M. "Eleanor Donnelly - the
  Singer of Pure Religion." CATHOLIC WORLD 105
  (June 1917), 352-60.

DONWORTH, GRACE. d.1945. U.S.

             Biography
  WOWWA WWWA-2

Dorman, C.T. See DORMAN, CAROLINE TROTTI.

DORMAN, CAROLINE TROTTI. b.1853. U.S.
    C.T. Dorman

DORR, JULIA CAROLINE (RIPLEY), 1825-1913. U.S.

             Biography
  APP AWW BD BURK DAB KNIB KUAA NCAB-6 PRE
  TWCB WARBD WEBS WOWWA WWWA-1

Doubleday, Roman, pseud. See LONG, LILY AUGUSTA.

Dougall, L.   See DOUGALL, LILY.

DOUGALL, LILY. 1858-1923. Canada.
         L. Dougall

              Biography
  CHA   MOR   MOR2   MDCB   MORGA   STOXC   WOWWA   WWWL

DOUGLAS, AMANDA MINNIE. 1837-1916. U.S.

              Biography
  APP   AWW   BD   BURK   DAB   KUAA   NCAB-2   PAP   TWCB
  WARLC   WEBS   WILA   WOWWA   WWWA-1

              Obituary
  NY TIMES (19 July 1916), 9:5.

Douglas, Julia, pseud.   See EVERETT, MRS. H.D.

Douglas, Katharine Waldo.   See   FEDDEN, KATHARINE
  WALDO DOUGLAS.

Douglas, O., pseud.   See BUCHAN, ANNA.

Douglas, Theo, pseud.   See EVERETT, MRS. H.D.

Dowdall, Hon. Mrs.   See DOWDALL, MARY FRANCES
  HARRIET (BORTHWICK).

DOWDALL, MARY FRANCES   HARRIET   (BORTHWICK).
  1876-1939. England.
         Hon. Mrs. Dowdall

              Biography
  WWLA   WWWE   WWWL

              Obituary
  TIMES (LONDON) (20 May 1939), 14:2.

Dowie, Menie Muriel. See FITZGERALD, MENIE MURIEL (DOWIE) NORMAN.

Downs, Mrs. George Sheldon. See DOWNS, SARAH ELIZABETH (FORBUSH).

Downs, Mrs. Georgie Sheldon. See DOWNS, SARAH ELIZABETH (FORBUSH).

DOWNS, SARAH ELIZABETH (FORBUSH). b.1843. U.S.
Mrs. George Sheldon Downs
Mrs. Georgie Sheldon Downs
Mrs. Georgie Sheldon, pseud.

Biography
BURK   LOGP   WOWWA   WWWA-4

DOYLE, MARTHA CLAIRE (MACGOWAN). b.1868/69. U.S.
Martha James, pseud.

Biography
BURK   LOGP   WWWA-5

DRAGOUMIS, JULIA D. (PASPATI). b.1858. England.

Biography
WWLA   WWWE

DRAKE, JEANIE. U.S.

Biography
KNIB   WOWWA

Drinkwater, Jennie M. See CONKLIN, JENNIE MARIE (DRINKWATER).

DRISCOLL, CLARA. 1881-1945. U.S.
m. Sevier--divorced and through court
order resumed her maiden name

Biography
BURK   WWWA-2

Obituary
NY TIMES (19 July 1945), 23:6.

Dromgoole, Will Allen.   See DROMGOOLE, WILLIAM
ALLEN.

DROMGOOLE, WILLIAM ALLEN. 1860-1934. U.S.
    Will Allen Dromgoole

Biography
BURK   DAB-Sl   LIB   NCAB-8   RUT   TWCB   WARBD
WOWWA   WWNA   WWWA-1   WYN

DROWER,   ETHEL   STEFANA   (STEVENS). 1879-1972.
England.
    Ethel Stefana Stephens
    E.S. Stevens

Biography
AWWW   CON-Pl   WWWE   WWWL

Obituary
TIMES (LONDON) (31 Jan 1972), 14:8.

Drum, Blossom.   See   OLIPHANT, BLOSSOM DRUM.

DU BOIS,   CONSTANCE GODDARD. 1855-1911. U.S.

Biography
BURK   COY

DUBOIS,   MARY CONSTANCE. 1879-1959. U.S.

Biography
ALY   AWO   BURK   WOMA   WOWWA   WWWA-3

Obituary
NY TIMES (21 July 1959), 92:7.

111

Duchess, The, pseud.   See   HUNGERFORD, MARGARET
    WOLFE   (HAMILTON).

DUCLAUX, AGNES MARY FRANCES (ROBINSON) DARMESTETER.
    1857-1944. England.
        Madame James Darmesteter
        Mary Duclaux

                    Biography
    CHABI COR HAMM LAU MCC WEBS WWLA WWWE

Duclaux, Mary. See DUCLAUX, AGNES MARY.

DUDENEY, ALICE (WHITTIER). 1866-1945. England.
    Mrs. H. Dudeney
    Mrs. Henry Dudeney

                Biography
    COOPE NCH WEBS WWWE

                Obituary
    TIMES (LONDON) (23 Nov 1945), 8:5.

Dudeney, Mrs. H. See DUDENEY, ALICE (WHITTIER).

Dudeney, Mrs. Henry.   See DUDENEY, ALICE
    (WHITTIER).

DUER, CAROLINE KING. 1865-1956. U.S.

                Autobiography
    "White Is Made of Many Colors." In THIS I
        BELIEVE: THE LIVING PHILOSOPHIES OF ONE HUNDRED
        THOUGHTFUL MEN AND WOMEN ..., compiled by
        Edward R. Murrow. pp.45-46. New York: Simon
        and Schuster, 1952. LC52-14364.

                Biography
    BICA WOWWA WWWA-3

                Obituary
    NY TIMES (23 Jan 1956), 25:2.
    WILSON 30 (Mar 1956), 502.

DUGANNE, PHYLLIS. b.1899. U.S.
        m. (1)Parker (2)Given

        Biography
AWO

DUGGAN, JANIE PRICHARD. b.1899. U.S.

        Biography
AWO KNIB

DUMOND, ANNIE (HAMILTON) NELLES. b.1837. U.S.

        Autobiography
ANNIE NELLES; OR, THE LIFE OF A BOOK AGENT. AN
AUTOBIOGRAPHY. Cincinnati: The Author, 1868.
LC17-19638.

        Biography
KNIB

Duncan, Frances. See MANNING, FRANCES DUNCAN.

Duncan, Sara Jeannette. See COTES, SARA JEANNETTE
(DUNCAN).

Duncan, Sarah Jeannette. See COTES, SARA JEANNETTE
(DUNCAN).

DUNIWAY, ABIGAIL JANE (SCOTT). 1834-1915. U.S.

        Autobiography
PATH BREAKING; AN AUTOBIOGRAPHICAL HISTORY OF THE
EQUAL SUFFRAGE MOVEMENT IN PACIFIC COAST
STATES. 2d ed. New York: Schocken, [1971].
LC79-162285.

        Biography
AWW BURK DAB KUAA PRE REAW WILA WWWA-4

113

Johnson, Jalmar. BUILDERS OF THE NORTHWEST.
pp. 151-69. New York: Dodd, Mead, [c1963].
LC63-11086.

Morrison, Dorothy N. LADIES WERE NOT EXPECTED:
ABIGAIL SCOTT DUNIWAY AND WOMEN'S RIGHTS.
New York: Atheneum, 1977. LC77-2969R.

Moynihan, Ruth B. REBEL FOR RIGHTS, ABIGAIL
SCOTT DUNIWAY. New Haven: Yale Univ. Press,
1983. LC83-1142.

Reifert, Gail and Eugene M. Dermody. WOMEN WHO
FOUGHT: AN AMERICAN HISTORY. pp. 193-7.
Norwalk, Calif.: Dermody, c1978. LC78-106358.

Obituary
NY TIMES (12 Oct 1915), 11:5.

DUNN, MARTHA (BAKER). 1848-1915. U.S.

Biography
WOWWA   WWWA-4

Obituary
NY TIMES (24 July 1915), 9:7.

DURAND, ALICE MARIE CELESTE (FLEURY). 1842-1902.
France.
          Henri Greville, pseud.

Biography
CHABI   HAR   JOHDB   WEBS

Ticknor, Caroline. GLIMPSES OF AUTHORS.
pp. 181-91. Freeport, N.Y.: Books for
Libraries, [1972, c1922]. LC70-167429.

Obituary
NY TIMES (27 May 1902), 9:4.
TIMES (LONDON) (27 May 1902), 10:2.

Durham, Julian, pseud.   See HENSHAW, JULIA WILMOTTE
(HENDERSON).

114

DURLEY, ELLA HAMILTON. U.S.

Biography
WILA   WOWWA

DURYEA, NINA LARREY (SMITH). 1874-1951. U.S.

Biography
AWO   BICA   BURK   WWWA-3

Obituary
NY TIMES (3 Nov 1951), 17:1.

DWYER, VERA GLADYS. Australia.
m. Coldham-Fussel

Biography
MIAU   WWWE

DYAR, MURIEL CAMPBELL. b.1876. U.S.

Biography
COY

DYE, EVA (EMERY). 1855-1947. U.S.

Biography
ALY   AWO   BIN   HINK   NCAB-13   REAW   WOWWA   WWNA
WWWA-3

Earle, Victoria. See MATTHEWS, VICTORIA (EARLE).

EASTMAN, REBECCA LANE (HOOPER). 1877-1937. U.S.

Biography
WOWWA   WWWA-5

Obituary
NY TIMES (20 June 1937), II 6:8.

EATON, ISABEL GRAHAM. b.1845. U.S.

Biography
WOWWA

EBNER VON ESCHENBACH, MARIE. 1830-1916. Austria.
Marie Von Ebner-Eschenbach
Marie Von Ebner Eschenbach

Biography
ADE BD CAS FLE GAR HAMM HAR KUE MDWB
PEEU SCHM WARBD WEBS WWWL

O'Connor, Eileen M. MARIE EBNER. [London]:
C. Palmer, [1928]. NUC.

Ungar, Frederick, comp. HANDBOOK OF AUSTRIAN
LITERATURE. pp. 75-79. New York: F. Ungar,
[1973]. LC71-125969.

Obituary
NY TIMES (15 Mar 1916), 11:6.

Ebner-Eschenbach, Marie Von. See EBNER VON
ESCHENBACH, MARIE.

ECCLES, CHARLOTTE O'CONOR. d.1911. Ireland.
Hal Godfrey, pseud.

Biography
BEL   ODP   ROCK   WWWL

Edginton, H.M.   See   BAILEY, MAY HELEN MARION
(EDGINTON).

Edgington, May.   See   BAILEY, MAY HELEN MARION
(EDGINTON).

Edwardes, Annie.   See   EDWARDS, ANNIE.

EDWARDS, ANNIE. 1873-1896. England.
Annie Edwardes

Biography
BD   BOASE-5

EDWARDS, LOUISE BETTS. 1873-1928. U.S.

Biography
WALD   WWWA-1

Edwards, M. Betham.   See   EDWARDS, MATILDA BARBARA
BETHAM-.

EDWARDS, MATILDA BARBARA BETHAM-. 1836-1919.
England.
Matilda Betham-Edwards
M. Betham Edwards

Autobiography
REMINISCENCES, by M. Betham-Edwards. London:
G. Redway, 1898. LC3-13846.

Biography
BD   BLA   CHA   CHABI   DNB-3   EDW   HAMM   KUBA   NCH
WARBD   WARLC   WEBS

Grand, Sarah. "Personal Sketch." In MID-
VICTORIAN MEMORIES, by Matilda Betham-Edwards.
pp. vii-lxvi. London: J. Murray, 1919.
LC20-6149.

Obituary
TIMES (LONDON) (7 Jan 1919), 11:4.

Egerton, George, pseud. See BRIGHT, MARY CHAVELITA
(DUNNE) MELVILLE CLAIRMONTE GOLDING.

Eliot, Annie, pseud. See TRUMBULL, ANNIE ELIOT.

**ELISABETH, QUEEN CONSORT OF CHARLES I, KING OF
RUMANIA.** 1843-1916. Rumania.
maiden name Pauline Elizabeth Ottilia
Louisa
Queen of Rumania
Carmen Sylva, pseud.

Autobiography
LETTERS AND POEMS OF QUEEN ELISABETH (CARMEN
SYLVA). Boston: Bibliophile Society, 1920.
LC21-592.

Biography
ADE BD CHABI GAR HAMM HAR KUE MAGN MDWB
ROCK SCHM TWCR WARBD WARLC WEBS

Burgoyne, Elizabeth. CARMEN SYLVA: QUEEN AND
WOMAN. London: Eyre and Spottiswoode, 1941.
LC41-19600.

Kelly, John. "Carmen Sylvia, Poetess and Queen."
In LOUISA OF PRUSSIA, AND OTHER SKETCHES.
pp. 164-92. [London]: Religious Tract Society,
1888. OCLC 5633628.

[Macchetta, Blanche R.] ELISABETH OF ROUMANIA; A
STUDY.... London: Chapman and Hall, 1891. NUC.

"Queen Elizabeth of Roumania." In THE SOVEREIGN
LADIES OF EUROPE, edited by Marie Bothmer.
pp. 341-68. London: Hutchinson, 1899.
LC06-39435.

ELISABETH

Vacarescu, Elena. KINGS AND QUEENS I HAVE KNOWN.
pp. 1-47. New York: Harper & Bros., 1904.
LC04-27140.

Viaud, Julien. CARMEN SYLVA, AND SKETCHES FROM
THE ORIENT, translated by Fred Rothwell. New
York: Macmillan, 1912. LC12-28467.

Obituary
NY TIMES (3 Mar 1916), 11:1.
OUTLOOK 112 (15 Mar 1916), 598; portrait, 612.
"Tribute to Carmen Sylvia." REVIEW OF REVIEWS
53 (May 1916), 606-7.

Elizabeth, pseud. See RUSSELL, MARY ANNETTE
(BEAUCHAMP) ARNIM RUSSELL.

ELLERMAN, ANNIE WINIFRED. 1894-1983. England.
    W. Bryher, pseud.
    Winifred Bryher
    name legally changed to Bryher
    m. (1)McAlmon (2)MacPherson

Autobiography
THE DAYS OF MARS: A MEMOIR, 1940-1946, by
Bryher. London: Calder and Boyars, 1972.
LC73-163586.

THE HEART TO ARTEMIS; A WRITER'S MEMOIRS, by
Winifred Bryher. New York: Harcourt, Brace
and World, [1962]. LC62-13519R.

Biography
BERE CON-104 CONO KUTS RA SHO WARLC

Beach, Sylvia. SHAKESPEARE AND COMPANY.
pp. 99-103. Lincoln: Univ. of Nebraska Press,
1980, c1959. LC79-26571.

Obituary
CON-108.
NY TIMES (1 Feb 1983), IV 23:1.
PUBLISHERS WEEKLY 223 (25 Feb 1983), 27.

120

ELLIOTT

Elliott, L. Elwyn. See JOYCE, LILIAN ELWYN (ELLIOTT).

ELLIOTT, MAUD (HOWE). 1854-1948. U.S.

Autobiography
THREE GENERATIONS. Boston: Little, Brown, 1923. LC23-15949.

Biography
ALY AWO AWW BD BURK HAOXA NAW NCAB-36 REA
TWCB WARBD WEBS WILA WOWWA WWNA WWWA-2

Obituary
NY TIMES (20 Mar 1948), 13:1.

ELLIOTT, SARAH (BARNWELL). 1848-1928. U.S.

Biography
AWW BD BURK DAB HAOXA KUAA LIB NAW NCAB-21
RICDA RUT SOU WARBD WOWWA WWWA-1

ELLIOTT, SUMNER (LOCKE). 1881-1908. Australia.
full name Helene Sumner Locke Elliott
Sumner Locke

Biography
MIA MIAU

ELLIS, EDITH MARY OLDHAM (LEES). 1861-1916.
England.
Mrs. Havelock Ellis

Biography
Goldberg, Isaac. HAVELOCK ELLIS; A BIOGRAPHICAL AND CRITICAL SURVEY WITH A SUPPLEMENTARY CHAPTER ON EDITH ELLIS. New York: Simon & Schuster, 1926. LC26-9698.

Obituary
NY TIMES (3 Oct 1916), 11:4.

Ellis, Mrs. Havelock. See ELLIS, EDITH MARY OLDHAM
(LEES).

ELLISON, EDITH NICHOLL (BRADLEY). U.S.

Autobiography
THE DESERT AND THE ROSE. Boston: Cornhill,
[c1921]. LC21-15190R.

EMERY, FLORENCE (FARR). 1873-1917. England.
Florence Farr

Biography
BEL   WWWL   WWWT

Johnson, Josephine. FLORENCE FARR: BERNARD
SHAW'S "NEW WOMAN". Totowa, N.J.: Rowan
and Littlefield, 1975. LC75-329754.

Obituary
TIMES (LONDON) (14 July 1917), 3:4.

EMERY, SARAH ANNA. 1821-1907. U.S.

Biography
WWWA-1

**ERSKINE, ANGELA SELINA BLANCHE (FORBES) SAINT
CLAIR-.** b.1876.
Lady Angela St.Clair-Erskine
Lady Angela Forbes

Autobiography
MEMORIES AND BASE DETAILS, by Lady Angela Forbes.
2d ed. London: Hutchinson, [1921]. LC23-4340.

FORE AND AFT. London: Jarrolds, 1932. OCLC 2461591.

ERSKINE, BEATRICE CAROLINE (STRONG). England.

Biography
WWWE

ERSKINE, EMMA (PAYNE). 1854-1924. U.S.
Payne Erskine, pseud.

Biography
WOWWA   WWWA-1

Erskine, Lady Angela St. Clair.   See   ERSKINE,
ANGELA SELINA BLANCHE ST. CLAIR.

Erskine, Payne, pseud.   See   ERSKINE, EMMA (PAYNE).

Eschenbach, Marie Von Ebner.   See   EBNER   VON
ESCHENBACH,   MARIE.

Esler, E. Rentoul.   See   ESLER, ERMINDA (RENTOUL).

ESLER, ERMINDA (RENTOUL). d.1924.   Ireland.
E. Rentoul Esler

Biography
BRI   CLE

ESTABROOK, ALMA (MARTIN). U.S.

Biography
WOWWA

EUSTIS, EDITH LIVINGSTON (MORTON). 1874-1964. U.S.

Obituary
NY TIMES (14 Nov 1964), 29:4.

EVANS, ELIZABETH EDSON (GIBSON). 1832-1911. U.S.

Biography
APP   BURK   NCAB-9   TWCB   WARBD

Obituary
NY TIMES (15 Sept 1911), 9:6.

EVANS, FLORENCE (WILKINSON). U.S.
Florence Wilkinson

Biography
BURK   WOWWA   WWNA

EVANS, MARGUERITE FLORENCE HELENE (JERVIS) BARCLAY.
1894-1964. England.
m. (1)Barclay (2) Evans
Countess Barcynska, pseud.
Countess Helene Barcynska, pseud.
Oliver Sandys, pseud.

Autobiography
FULL AND FRANK, THE PRIVATE LIFE OF A WOMAN
NOVELIST, by Oliver Sandys. London: Hurst and
Blackett, [1941]. LC42-12447.

Biography
NCH   ROCK   TWCR   WEBS   WWWE   WWWL

Everest, Hope, pseud.   See   JAMES, WILHELMINA
MARTHA.

EVERETT, MRS. H.D. U.S.
Julia Douglas, pseud.
Theo Douglas, pseud.

Biography
WWWL

Everett-Green, Evelyn. See GREEN, EVELYN EVERETT.

Ewell, A.M. See EWELL, ALICE MAUDE.

EWELL, ALICE MAUDE. 1860-1946. U.S.
A.M. Ewell
Elizabeth Godstowe, pseud.

Biography
KNIB

EWING, JULIANA HORATIA (GATTY). 1841-1885. England.

Autobiography
"Mrs. Ewing's Letters [1867-1869]." In LEAVES
FROM JULIANA HORATIA EWING'S "CANADA HOME", by
Elizabeth S. Tucker. pp. 85-143. Boston:
Robert Brothers, 1896. LC6-36158.

Biography
BD BOASE BRO CAS DOY GRET GRETB HAMM
HAOXA KUBA KUJ1 LAS MYE NCH SOME-16 WARBD
WEBS

Avery, Gillian. MRS. EWING. New York: H.Z.
Walck, [1964, c1961]. LC64-20838.

Eden, Horatia K. JULIANA HORATIA EWING AND HER
BOOKS. Detroit: Gale, 1969, 1896. LC71-77001.

Maxwell, Christabel W. MRS. GATTY AND MRS.
EWING. London: Constable, [1949]. LC49-6574.

Obituary
TIMES (LONDON) (16 May 1885), 10:5.

Eyster, Nellie Blessing. See EYSTER, PENELOPE ANNA
MARGARETTA (BLESSING).

EYSTER, PENELOPE ANNA MARGARETTA (BLESSING).
1831?-1922. U.S.
Nellie Blessing Eyster

Biography
APP BD BURK KNIB NCAB-10 TWCB WARBD WILA
WOWWA WWWA-4

F., L., pseud. See HAWKER, MORWENNA PAULINE.

F., M., pseud. See FISHER, MARY.

Faber, Christine, pseud. See SMITH, MARY E.

FACCIO, RINA (COTTINO). 1876-1960. Italy.
    Sibilla Aleramo, pseud.

Biography
CAS   CDME   COL   MDWB   PAC   PHIS   VIT

Drake, William. CONTEMPORARY EUROPEAN WRITERS.
    pp. 80-86. Freeport, N.Y.: Books for
    Libraries, [1967]. LC67-26734R.

Obituary
TIMES (LONDON) (14 Jan 1960), 17:1.

FAHNESTOCK,   HARRIETTE   ZEPHINE   (HUMPHREY).
    1874-1956. U.S.
        Zephine Humphrey

Biography
AWO   BURK

Obituary
NY TIMES (16 Nov 1956), 27:4.

FAIRBRIDGE, DOROTHEA. 1862?-1931. South Africa.

Biography
DSAB   MYE   ROSE

FAIRFIELD, CICILY ISABEL. 1892-1983. England.
    m. Andrews
    Rebecca West, pseud.

127

FAIRFIELD

Autobiography
"Goodness Doesn't Just Happen." In THIS I
BELIEVE: THE LIVING PHILOSOPHIES OF ONE HUNDRED
THOUGHTFUL MEN AND WOMEN ..., compiled by
Edward R. Murrow. pp. 187-8. New York: Simon
and Schuster, 1952. LC52-14364.

Biography
ADC   BEATG   BERE   BRO   CEL   CHABI   CHU   CON-7--8R
CUR-1968   FLE   HAMM   KUL   KUT   MAG   MANBL   MARBS
MDWB   MICB   MYE   NCH   NOV   NPW   OV   OVA   OVEWH
PEE   RA   RIC   SEYS   SHO   STOK   WARLC   WEBS   WELL
WWLA   WWWE   WWWL

British Broadcasting Corp. WRITERS ON
THEMSELVES. pp. 8-16. [London: 1964].
LC67-1196.

Deakin, Motley F. REBECCA WEST. Boston:
Twayne, 1980. LC79-27601.

Ray, Gordon N. H.G. WELLS AND REBECCA WEST.
New Haven: Yale Univ. Press, 1974. LC74-77990.

Obituary
CUR 44 (May 1983), 47.
MACLEANS 96 (28 Mar 1983), 4.
NATIONAL REVIEW 35 (15 Apr 1983), 421.
NY TIMES (16 Mar 1983), II 7:1-5.
NEW YORKER 59 (28 Mar 1983), 104.
NEWSWEEK 101 (28 Mar 1983), 60.
TIME 121 (28 Mar 1983), 45.

Fairless, Michael, pseud. See BARBER, MARGARET
FAIRLESS.

Falconer, Lanoe, pseud. See HAWKER, MORWENNA
PAULINE.

FALL, ANNA CHRISTY. b.1855. U.S.

Biography
WILA

128

FANE, FRANCES GORDON. b.1867. U.S.

Biography

WOWWA   WWWA-4

FARJEON, ELEANOR. 1881-1965. England.

Autobiography

PORTRAIT OF A FAMILY.... New York: Stokes, 1936.
LC36-27048.
Also pub. as: A NURSERY IN THE NINETIES.
LC60-2714.

Biography

CAS CHABI CON-P1 DOY KU KUJ1 KUJ2 KUT MYE
NCH RIC SOME-2 WARLC WEBS

Blakelock, Denys. ELEANOR; PORTRAIT OF A
FARJEON. London: Gollancz, 1966. LC66-73758.

Colwell, Eileen H. ELEANOR FARJEON. New York:
H.Z. Walck, [1962, c1961]. LC 62-13176.

Obituary

LIBRARY ASSOCIATION RECORD 67 (July 1965), 248.
LIBRARY JOURNAL 90 (15 Sept 1965), 3715.
NY TIMES (6 June 1965), 84:6.
OBIT2, 260.
PUBLISHERS WEEKLY 187 (21 June 1965), 80.
TIMES (LONDON) (7 June 1965), 10:5.

Farmer, Lydia Hoyt. See Painter, Lydia (Hoyt)
Farmer.

Farningham, Marianne, pseud. See HEARN, MARY ANN.

Farquhar, Anna. See BERGENGREN, ANNA (FARQUHAR).

Farr, Florence. See EMERY, FLORENCE (FARR).

FAULDING, GERTRUDE MINNIE. b.1875. England.

WWWE
Biography

FAVERSHAM, JULIE (OPP). 1873-1921. U.S.

WEBS
Biography

FAVRE DE COULEVAIN, HELENE. 1871-1913. France.
Pierre De Coulevain, pseud.

Biography
Whale, Winifred S. FRENCH NOVELISTS OF TO-DAY.
(FIRST SERIES). pp. 85-123. Freeport, N.Y.:
Books for Libraries, [1968, 1914]. LC68-20338.

Obituary
TIMES (LONDON) (25 Aug 1913), 9:3.

FEARING, LILIAN BLANCHE. 1863-1901. U.S.
Raymond Russell, pseud.

BURK WILA
Biography

FEDDEN, KATHARINE WALDO DOUGLAS. d.1939. U.S.
Katharine Waldo Douglas
Mrs. Romilly Fedden

ALY BURK WWNA
Biography

Fedden, Mrs. Romilly. See FEDDEN, KATHARINE WALDO
DOUGLAS.

FEE, MARY HELEN. b.1864. U.S.

HINK
Biography

FELKIN, ELLEN THORNEYCROFT (FOWLER). 1860-1929.
England.
    Hon. Mrs. Alfred Felkin
    Mrs. Alfred Laurence Felkin
    Mrs. Felkins
    Ellen Thorneycroft Fowler

                Biography
CHA DNB-4 JOHDB NCH SHA SHO WARBD WEBS
WWLA WWW-3 WWWE

                Obituary
TIMES (LONDON) (24 June 1929), 20:2.

Felkin, Hon. Mrs. Alfred. See FELKIN, ELLEN
THORNEYCROFT (FOWLER).

Felkin, Mrs. Alfred Laurence. See FELKIN, ELLEN
THORNEYCROFT (FOWLER).

Felkins, Mrs. See FELKIN, ELLEN THORNEYCROFT
(FOWLER).

FENOLLOSA, MARY (MCNEIL). c.1865-1954. U.S.
    Sidney McCall, pseud.

                Biography
BURG BURK LIB WARBD WOWWA WWNA WWWA-3

                Obituary
NY TIMES (13 Jan 1954), 31:4.
WILSON 28 (Mar 1954), 526.

FERBER, EDNA. 1887-1968. U.S.
               Autobiography
A KIND OF MAGIC. Garden City, N.Y.:
    Doubleday, [c1963]. LC63-18030.
      Sequel to A PECULIAR TREASURE. Covers 1939
    to 1963.

A PECULIAR TREASURE; [AUTOBIOGRAPHY]. Garden
City, N.Y.: Doubleday, 1960. LC60-8865.

FERBER

Biography
AML APP-S AWO AWW BERE BRO BURG BURK BURNT
CEL CEL2 CHA CHABI CON-7--8R DODD FARR FLE
HAMM HAOXA KUL KUT MAN MARBS MAT MCW MICA
MYE NAWM NCAB-C NOV NPW OV OV2 PEA REA
REAW RIC RICDA SOME-7 TIT TWCR TWCW VDW
WAGCA WAR WEBS WWNA WWWA-5 WWWE WWWT

Dickinson, Rogers. EDNA FERBER; A BIOGRAPHICAL
SKETCH WITH A BIBLIOGRAPHY. Garden City, N.Y.:
Doubleday, Doran & Co., [c1925]. LC30-29145.

Gilbert, Julie G. FERBER, A BIOGRAPHY. Garden
City, N.Y.: Doubleday, 1978. LC76-57512.

Levitan, Tina N. JEWS IN AMERICAN LIFE.
pp. 204-7. New York: Hebrew Pub. Co., [1969].
LC68-31729.

St. Johns, Adela R. SOME ARE BORN GREAT.
pp. 102-92. Garden City, N.Y. Doubleday, 1974.
LC74-7636.

Obituary
ANTIQUARIAN BOOKMAN (6-13 May 1968).
BOOKS ABROAD (Spring 1969).
CON-25--28R.
NY TIMES (17 Apr 1968), 1:2; (19 Apr), 47:2.
NEWSWEEK 71 (29 Apr 1968), 62.
OBIT2, 262-3.
PUBLISHERS WEEKLY 193 (29 Apr 1968), 61.
TIME 91 (26 Apr 1968), 90.
TIMES (LONDON) (17 Apr 1968), 12:7.
WASHINGTON POST (17 Apr 1968).

Ferguson, Emily. See MURPHY, EMILY (FERGUSON).

FERGUSON, EMMA (HENRY). 1840-1905. U.S.

Biography
KNIB WWWA-1

FESSENDEN, LAURA CANFIELD SPENCER (DAYTON). d.1924.
U.S.

Biography
BURK WOWWA WWWA-3

FIELD, ISOBEL (OSBOURNE) STRONG. 1858-1953. U.S.
Isobel Strong, pseud.

Autobiography
THIS LIFE I'VE LOVED. New York: Longmans, Green,
1937. LC37-27188.

Biography
BAN WOWWA

Obituary
NY TIMES (28 June 1953), 60:6.
OBIT1, 247.
TIMES (LONDON) (29 June 1953), 10:7.
WILSON 28 (Sept 1953), 28.

FIELD, LOUISE FRANCES (STORY). b.1856. England.

Biography
BURK WOWWA

FIELD, MARY HANNAH (BACON). 1833-1912. U.S.

Biography
HINK

FINDLATER, JANE HELEN. 1866-1946. Scotland.

Biography
HAMM NCH WARLC WWLA WWWE

Mackenzie, Eileen. THE FINDLATER SISTERS;
LITERATURE AND FRIENDSHIP. [London]:
J. Murray, [1964]. LC65-83572.

FINDLATER, MARY. 1865-1963. Scotland.

Biography
WARLC   WWLA   WWWE

Brown, Janet E. THE SAGA OF ELSIE DINSMORE; A
STUDY IN NINETEENTH CENTURY SENSIBILITY.
pp. 79-82. [Buffalo, 1945]. LC46-5319.

Mackenzie, Eileen. THE FINDLATER SISTERS...
[London]: J. Murray, [1964]. LC65-83572.

Obituary
TIMES (LONDON) (26 Nov 1963), 21:6.

FINLEY, MARTHA (FARGUHARSON). 1828-1909. U.S.

Biography
AML   APP   AWW   BAN   BURK   COY   DAB   DOY   HAOXA
KNIB NAW   NCAB-11 PAP   REA   RICDA   TWCB   WARD
WEBS WILA WWWA-1

Obituary
NY TIMES (31 Jan 1909), 11:6.

FISHER, DOROTHEA FRANCES (CANFIELD). 1879-1958.
U.S.
　　　Dorothea Canfield
　　　Dorothy Canfield Fisher

Biography
AMN   APP-S   AWO   AWW   BERE   BURK   BURNT   CHA
DAB-S6   HAOXA   JOHDB   KU   KUJ1   KUL   KUT   MAN
MARBS   MICA   MYE   NAWM   NCAB-18,44   NOV   OV   OV2
REA   RICDA   SCHW   VDW   WAGCA   WAR   WARLC   WEBS
WOMA   WOWWA   WWNA   WWWA-3   WWWL   YES-1

Fisher, Dorothea F. AMERICAN PORTRAITS.
pp. 146-8. New York: Holt, [1946]. LC47-1029.

Washington, Ida H. DOROTHY CANFIELD FISHER: A
BIOGRAPHY. Shelburne, Vt.: New England Press,
c1982. LC81-83287.

Yates, Elizabeth. THE LADY FROM VERMONT; DOROTHY
CANFIELD FISHER'S LIFE AND WORLD. Brattleboro,
Vt.: Greene Press, [1971]. LC74-148629.

Obituary
NY TIMES (10 Nov 1958), 29:4; tribute (14 Nov),
26:5.
NEWSWEEK 52 (17 Nov 1958), 85.
PUBLISHERS WEEKLY 174 (17 Nov 1958), 32.
SATURDAY REVIEW 41 (29 Nov 1958), 13-14.
TIME 72 (17 Nov 1958), 98.
TIMES (LONDON) (10 Nov 1958), 15:4.
WILSON 33 (Jan 1959), 328.

Fisher, Dorothy Canfield. See FISHER, DOROTHEA
FRANCES CANFIELD.

FISHER, MARY. b.1858. U.S.
F., M., pseud.

Biography
AWO   HINK   TWCB   WWNA   WWWA-4

FISHER, SOPHIE. England.

Biography
BURK

Fitch, A.H. See FITCH, ABIGAIL HETZEL.

FITCH, ABIGAIL HETZEL. d.1938. U.S.
A.H. Fitch

Obituary
NY TIMES (17 Sept 1938), 17:4.

FITZGERALD, MENIE MURIEL (DOWIE) NORMAN. 1866-1945.
England.
Menie Muriel Dowie

Biography
BD   SHO   WWWE

135

FITZGERALD

Obituary
TIMES (LONDON) (2 Apr 1945), 6:5.

FITZPATRICK, KATHLEEN. b.1872. Ireland.

Biography
BRI

FLANDRAU, GRACE C. (HODGSON). d.1971. U.S.

Biography
AWO   BURK   WWNA   WWWA-5

Fleming, George, pseud.   See FLETCHER, JULIA
CONSTANCE.

FLEMING, MAY AGNES (EARLY). 1840-1880. Canada.
27 of the 42 novels she wrote were
published posthumously.

Biography
MDCB(3d ed.)   MORGA   STOXC   WARBD

FLEMING, SARAH LEE BROWN. U.S.

Biography
MAR

Flemming,Harford, pseud.   See McCLELLAN, HARRIET
(HARE).

FLETCHER, JULIA CONSTANCE. 1858-1938. U.S.
George Fleming, pseud.

Biography
BD   BURK   NCAB-13   SHA-AP   TWCB   WARBD   WEBS
WWWA-4

FLEWELLYN, JULIA (COLLITON). b.1850. Canada.

MOR
Biography

FLINT, ANNIE AUSTIN. 1866-1949. U.S.

Biography
BICA   WOWWA

Obituary
NY TIMES (16 Dec 1949), 31:3.

FONDA, MARY ALICE (IVES) SEYMOUR. 1837-1892. U.S.
Octavia Hensel, pseud.

Biography
WILA

FOOTE, MARY (HALLOCK). 1847-1938. U.S.

Autobiography
A VICTORIAN GENTLEWOMAN IN THE FAR WEST; THE
REMINISCENCES OF MARY HALLOCK FOOTE, edited
by Rodman W. Paul. San Marino, Calif.:
Huntington Library, 1972. LC72-86535.

Biography
AML AWW BD   BURK HAOXA NAW   NCAB-6 REA REAW
TWCB WARBD WEBS WILA WOWWA WWNA WWWA-1

Johnson, Lee Ann. MARY HALLOCK FOOTE. Boston:
Twayne, 1980. LC79-24294.

Maguire, James H. MARY HALLOCK FOOTE. Boise,
Idaho: Boise State College, 1972. LC72-619586.

Taft, Robert. ARTISTS AND ILLUSTRATORS OF THE
OLD WEST, 1850-1900. pp. 172-5. New York:
Scribner, 1953. LC53-7577.

FORBES

FORBES, HELEN EMILY (CRAVEN). b.1874.

Biography
WWWL

Forbes, Lady Angela. See ERSKINE, ANGELA SELINA BLANCHE (FORBES) SAINT CLAIR-.

FORD, MARY HANFORD (FINNEY). b.1856. U.S.

Biography
WWWA-4

Forget-Me-Not, pseud. See KELLEY, EMMA DUNHAM.

FORRESTER, IZOLA LOUISE. b.1878. U.S.

Biography
BURK   WOWWA

Forsslund, Louise, pseud. See FOSTER, MARY LOUISE.

Forsslund, M. Louise, pseud. See FOSTER, MARY LOUISE.

Fortescue, Will, pseud. See MCCHESNEY, DORA GREENWALL.

FOSTER, EDNA ABIGAIL. d.1945. U.S.

Biography
BURK   LOGP   WOWWA   WWWA-2

Obituary
NY TIMES (12 July 1945), 11:4.

Foster, M. Louise, pseud. See FOSTER, MARY LOUISE.

FOSTER, MABEL GRAU. b.1869. U.S.

<u>Biography</u>
WOWWA   WWWA-5

FOSTER, MARY LOUISE. 1873-1910. U.S.
Louise Forsslund, pseud.
M. Louise Forsslund, pseud.
M. Louise Foster, pseud.

<u>Biography</u>
WOWWA

FOSTER, THEODOSIA MARIA (TOLL). 1838-1923. U.S.
Faye Huntington, pseud.

<u>Biography</u>
BURK   TWCB   WOWWA   WWWA-3,4

FOTHERGILL, JESSIE. 1851-1891. England.

<u>Biography</u>
BLA   BOASE-5   DNB-S1   JOHDB   NCH   SHO   WARBD
WEBS

Crisp, Jane, comp. JESSIE FOTHERGILL, 1851-1891:
A BIBLIOGRAPHY. St. Lucia, Australia: Dept. of
English, Univ. of Queensland, c1980.
LC81-160116.

<u>Obituary</u>
ATHENAEUM 98 (1 Aug 1891), 161.
CRITIC 19, n.s. 16 (29 Aug 1891), 106.
ILLUS LONDON NEWS 99 (8 Aug 1891), 167.
TIMES (LONDON) (31 July 1891), 9:6.

Fowler, Edith Henrietta. See HAMILTON,   EDITH
HENRIETTA (FOWLER).

Fowler, Ellen   Thorneycroft. See FELKIN,   ELLEN
THORNEYCROFT (FOWLER).

Fox, David, pseud. See OSTRANDER, ISABEL EGENTON.

FOX, MARION INEZ DOUGLAS (WARD). b.1885. England.
Marion Fox, pseud.

Biography
WWLA   WWWE

Francis, M.E., pseud. See BLUNDELL, MARY E.
(SWEETMAN).

Francis, Mrs. See BLUNDELL, MARY E. (SWEETMAN).

FRANKAU, JULIA (DAVIS). 1864-1916. Ireland.

Biography
BRI CLE COOPE CRO HAMM ROCK WARBD WWWL

Obituary
NY TIMES (18 Mar 1916), 11:3.
TIMES (LONDON) (18 Mar 1916), 11:2.

Franklin, Miles. See FRANKLIN, STELLA MARIA SARAH
MILES.

FRANKLIN, STELLA MARIA SARAH MILES. 1879-1954.
Australia.
Brent of Bin Bin, pseud.
Miles Franklin

Autobiography
CHILDHOOD AT BRINDABELLA: MY FIRST TEN YEARS.
Sydney: Angus and Robertson, 1974. LC77-370443.

Biography
CAS CON-104 JONES MCW MDWB MIA MIAU MYE
RIC

Barnard, Marjorie F. MILES FRANKLIN. New York:
Twayne, [1967]. LC66-29182.

FRANKLIN

Coleman, Verna. MILES FRANKLIN IN AMERICA: HER
UNKNOWN (BRILLANT) CAREER. London: Angus &
Robertson, 1981. LC82-123206.

Mathew, Ray. MILES FRANKLIN. Melbourne:
Lansdowne, [1963]. LC64-3561.
37 pages

Frapan, Ilse, pseud. See AKUNIAN, ILSE (LEVIEN).

FRASER, AGNES MAUDE. 1859-1944. England.
Frances MacNab, pseud.

Biography
STOXC   WWLA   WWWE   WWWL

FRASER, MARY (CRAWFORD). 1851-1922. England.
Mrs. Hugh Fraser

Biography
ADE   LOGP   WARBD   WEBS

Fraser, Mrs. Hugh. See FRASER, MARY (CRAWFORD).

FREEMAN, MARY ELEANOR (WILKINS). 1852-1930. U.S.
Mary E. Wilkins

Biography
ADE   ALY   AML   AMR   ASH   AWW   BD   BERE   BURG
BURK   CAS   CHA   CON-106   COU   DAB   HAL   HAOXA
HAOXE   HARKF   KUAT   KUT   LOGP   MAN   MYE   NAW
NCAB-9   NOV   NPW   OV   PEA   PRE   REA   RICDA
SHA-AP   VDW   WARBD   WARLC   WEBS   WILA   WOWWA
WWWA-1

Foster, Edward. MARY E. WILKINS FREEMAN. New
York: Hendricks House, 1956. LC56-4024.

Westbrook, Perry D. MARY WILKINS FREEMAN. New
York: Twayne, [1967]. LC67-24763.

Obituary
PUBLISHERS WEEKLY 117 (22 Mar 1930), 1685.

141

Fremantle, Elizabeth, pseud. See COVEY, ELIZABETH (ROCKFORD).

FRENCH, ALICE. 1850-1934. U.S.
  Octave Thanet, pseud.

Biography
ALY APP APP-S AWW BD BERE BURK DAB-S1
HAMM HAOXA HARKF KUAA LES LIB LOGP MAN
NAW NCAB-10,25 PRE REA ROCK TWCB WARBD
WARLC WEBS WILA WWWA-1

McMichael, George L. JOURNEY TO OBSCURITY; THE
LIFE OF OCTAVE THANET. Lincoln: Univ. of
Nebraska Press, [1965]. LC64-19852.

Obituary
PUBLISHERS WEEKLY 125 (27 Jan 1934), 406.

FRENCH, ANNE RICHMOND (WARNER). 1869-1913. U.S.
  Anne Warner

Biography
BURK DAB WEBS WWWA-1

Obituary
NY TIMES (4 Feb 1913), 11:5.

FRENCH, LILLIE HAMILTON. 1854-1939. U.S.

Biography
BURK WOWWA WWWA-4

Obituary
NY TIMES (5 June 1939), 17:2.

FRENCH, MINNIE REID. U.S.

Biography
CONW

FROOKS, DOROTHY. b.1899. U.S.

Autobiography
LADY LAWYER. New York: R. Speller, [1975].
LC74-8881.

Biography
AWO CON-57--60

FROTHINGHAM, EUGENIA BROOKS. b.1874. U.S.

Autobiography
YOUTH AND I. Boston: Houghton Mifflin, 1938.
LC38-33701.

Biography
BICA BURK WOWWA WWWA-5

FRY, SHEILA KAYE (SMITH). 1887-1956. England.
Sheila Kaye-Smith

Autobiography
THREE WAYS HOME. New York: Harper, 1937.
LC37-28779.

Biography
ADC AWW BERE BOOCA-4 BRO CHABI HAMM KUL
KUT KUTS LAU MAG MANBL MARBS MICB MYE NCH
PEE RIC SHO WAGCE WARLC WEBS WWWA-3 WWWL

Stern, Gladys B. AND DID HE STOP AND SPEAK TO
YOU? pp. 74-92. Chicago: H. Regnery, 1958.
LC58-11699.

Walker, Dorothea. SHEILA KAYE-SMITH. Boston:
Twayne, 1980. LC79-16671.

Obituary
ILLUS LONDON NEWS 228 (21 Jan 1956), 82.
NY TIMES (16 Jan 1956), 21:1.
NEWSWEEK 47 (21 Jan 1956), 71.
OBIT1, 404-5.
PUBLISHERS WEEKLY 169 (4 Feb 1956), 754.
TIME 67 (23 Jan 1956), 91.
TIMES (LONDON) (16 Jan 1956), 12:3.
WILSON 30 (Mar 1956), 502.

FRY, SUSANNA MARGARET DAVIDSON. 1841-1920. U.S.

Biography
COY

FULLER, ANNA. 1853-1916. U.S.

Biography
TWCB   WARBD   WIN   WOWWA   WWWA-1

Obituary
NY TIMES (21 July 1916), 9:8.

FULLER, CAROLINE MACOMBER. b.1873. U.S.

Biography
ALY   AWO   KNIB   WOWWA   WWNA   WWWA-5

FURMAN, LUCY S. 1870-1958. U.S.

Biography
AWO   BURK   MARBS   RICK   WWNA   WWWA-3

Obituary
NY TIMES (26 Aug 1958), 29:4.

FURSDON, MRS. F.R.M. b.1878.

Biography
WWWL

FUTRELLE, MAY (PEEL). b.1876. U.S.

Biography
WWWA-5

GALE, ZONA. 1874-1938. U.S.
m. Breese

Biography
ALY AMN AWW BERE BRO BURK CON-105 DAB-S2
DODD FARR HAMM HAOXA KUL KUT MAN MARBS
MAT MICA MYE NAW NCAB-30 OV OV2 OVAM PEA
PRE REA RIC RICDA TIT WAGCA WARLC WEBS
WOWWA WWNA WWWA-1 WWWT

Derleth, August W. STILL SMALL VOICE; THE
BIOGRAPHY OF ZONE GALE.... New York: D.
Appleton-Century, 1940. LC40-27781.

Simonson, Harold P. ZONA GALE. New York:
Twayne, [1962]. LC62-13672L.

State Historical Society of Wisconsin.
DICTIONARY OF WISCONSIN BIOGRAPHY. p. 140.
Madison, 1960. LC63-043.

Obituary
LIBRARY JOURNAL 64 (15 Jan 1939), 70.
NATION 148 (7 Jan 1939), 23.
NEWSWEEK 13 (9 Jan 1939), 2+.
NY TIMES (28 Dec 1938), 21:1.
PUBLISHERS WEEKLY 135 (7 Jan 1939), 40.
WILSON 13 (Feb 1939), 356.

GARDENER, HELEN HAMILTON (CHENOWETH). 1853-1925.
U.S.

Biography
ALY AWW BURK COY DAB NCAB-9 WEBS WOWWA
WWWA-1

Obituary
WOMAN CITIZEN n.s. 10 (Sept 1925), 23-4.

GARDINER, RUTH (KIMBALL). 1872-1924. U.S.

Obituary
NY TIMES (23 Nov 1924), 7:1.

GARDNER, CELIA EMMELINE. b.1844. U.S.

Biography
WWWA-4

GARNETT, MARTHA (ROSCOE). 1869-1946. England.
Mrs. R.S. Garnett

Obituary
TIMES (LONDON) (12 Aug 1946), 7:5.

Garnett, Mrs. R.S. See GARNETT, MARTHA (ROSCOE).

Garrett, Edward, pseud. See MAYO, ISABELLA
(FYVIE).

Garrison, Adele, pseud. See WHITE, NANA (SPRINGER).

GATES, ELEANOR. 1875-1951. U.S.
full name Mary Eleanor
m. (1)Tully (2)Moore

Biography
AWO AWW BURG BURK NCAB-15 REA WEBS WOWWA
WWNA WWWA-3 WWWT

Obituary
NY TIMES (8 Mar 1951), 29:5.

Gaunt, Mary. See MILLER, MARY ELIZA BAKEWELL
(GAUNT).

**GAY, MARIE FRANCOISE SOPHIE (NICHAULT DE
LAVALETTE).** 1776-1852. France.
Sophie Gay

Biography
BD HAOXF WARBD WEBS

GAY, MAUDE (CLARK). 1876-1952. U.S.

Biography
WOWWA   WWWA-3

Gay, Sophie.   See GAY, MARIE FRANCOISE SOPHIE
(NICHAULT DE LAVALETTE).

Gerard, D.   See LONGARD   DE LONGGARDE, DOROTHEA
(GERARD).

Gerard, Dorothea.   See   LONGARD   DE LONGGARDE,
DOROTHEA (GERARD).

Gerard, E.   See DE LASZOWSKA, JANE EMILY (GERARD).

Gerard, Emily.   See   DE LASZOWSKA, JANE EMILY
(GERARD).

GERARD, LOUISE. 1878-1970. England.

Obituary
TIMES (LONDON) (6 Nov 1970), 12:8.

GEROULD, KATHARINE (FULLERTON). 1879-1944. U.S.

Biography
AWO   AWW   BURG   BURK   HAOXA   KUT   MAN   MICA   MYE
NAW   REA   WEBS   WOWWA   WWWA-2

Obituary
TIME 44 (7 Aug 1944), 82.
WILSON 19 (Sept 1944), 8.

GERRY, MARGARITA (SPALDING). 1870-1939. U.S.

Biography
BURK   WWWA-5

147

GERSTENBERG

GERSTENBERG, ALICE. b.1885. U.S.

Biography
ALY AWO AWW BURK PRE ST WEBS WOWWA WWNA

GESTEFELD, URSULA NEWELL, REV. 1845-1921. U.S.

Biography
AWW WOWWA WWWA-1

Obituary
NY TIMES (25 Oct 1921), 17:5.

Ghosal, Mrs. See GHOSAL, SRIMATI SVARNA KUMARI
DEVI.

GHOSAL, SRIMATI SVARNA KUMARI DEVI. 1857-1932.
India.
     Srimati Svarna Kumari Devi
     Mrs. Ghosal

HAMM   Biography

GIBERNE, AGNES. 1845-1939. England.

Biography
HAMM WWLA WWWE

Obituary
NY TIMES (22 Aug 1939), 19:4.
TIMES (LONDON) (22 Aug 1939), 12:5.

GIELOW, MARTHA (SAWYER). 1854?-1933. U.S.

Biography
WARBD WOWWA WWWA-1

Gift, Theo, pseud. See BOULGER, THEODORA (HAVERS).

148

Gilbert, George David, pseud. See ARTHUR, MARY LUCY.

Gilbert, Lady. See GILBERT, ROSA (MULHOLLAND).

GILBERT, ROSA (MULHOLLAND). 1841-1921. Ireland.
Lady Gilbert
Rosa Mulholland

Biography
BOY BRI CLE CRO DIL ODP TYNAN

Obituary
NY TIMES (27 Apr 1921), 17:4.
TIMES (LONDON) (26 Apr 1921), 7:5.

GILCHRIST, ANNIE (SOMERS). fl.1884-1906. U.S.

Biography
AWW BURK

GILCHRIST, BETH BRADFORD. 1879-1957. U.S.

Biography
AWO BURK NCAB-47 WOWWA WWNA WWWA-3

GILCHRIST, ROSETTA LUCE. 1851-1921. U.S.

Biography
COY WILA

GILDER, JEANNETTE LEONARD. 1849-1916. U.S.

Biography
AWW BURK DAB HAL LOGP NAW NCAB-8 PRE TWCB
WARBD WEBS WILA WOWWA WWWA-1

Obituary
NY TIMES (18 Jan 1916), 11:3.

GILLMORE

Gillmore, Inez Haynes. See IRWIN, INEZ (HAYNES) GILLMORE.

GILMAN, CHARLOTTE (PERKINS) STETSON. 1860-1935. U.S.
Charlotte Perkins Stetson

Autobiography
THE LIVING OF CHARLOTTE PERKINS GILMAN: AN AUTOBIOGRAPHY. New York: Harper & Row, 1975, c1935. LC75-324195.

Biography
ADE ALY APP-S AWW BURK CON-106 DAB-S1 DELL
LOGP MARL MCC MDWB NCAB-13 PRE TWCB WARBD
WEBS WELL WOWWA WWNA WWWA-1

Hedges, Elaine R. "Afterword." In THE YELLOW WALLPAPER, by Charlotte Gilman. pp. 37-63. [New York]: Feminist Press, 1973. LC73-5795.

Hill, Mary A. CHARLOTTE PERKINS GILMAN: THE MAKING OF A RADICAL FEMINIST, 1860-1896. Philadelphia: Temple Univ. Press, 1980. LC79-22395.

Obituary
PUBLISHERS WEEKLY 128 (24 Aug 1935), 514.

GILMAN, DOROTHY FOSTER. b.1891. U.S.

Biography
BURK

GILMER, ELIZABETH (MERIWETHER). 1861/70-1951. U.S.
Dorothy Dix, pseud.

Biography
AWW BERE BURK CUR-1940 DAB-S5 HAOXA REA ROSS
WARBD WEBS WOWWA WWNA WWWA-5

Carnegie, Dale. "Dorothy Dix." In BIOGRAPHICAL ROUNDUP.... pp. 181-6. Freeport, N.Y.: Books for Libraries Press, [1970, c1944]. LC77-117764.

Deutsch, Herman B. "Dorothy Dix Talks." In POST
BIOGRAPHIES OF FAMOUS JOURNALISTS, edited by
John E. Drewry. pp. 29-47. Athens: Univ. of
Georgia Press, 1942. LC43-64.

Kane, Harnett T. DEAR DOROTHY DIX; THE STORY OF
A COMPASSIONATE WOMAN. Garden City, N.Y.:
Doubleday, 1952. LC52-11003.

Obituary
CUR-1952.
NY TIMES (17 Dec 1951), 31:1.

GIRARDOT, MARION REID. U.S.

Biography
BOYA

GLASGOW, ELLEN ANDERSON GHOLSON. 1874-1945. U.S.

Autobiography
LETTERS, compiled and edited by Blair Rouse.
New York: Harcourt, Brace, [1958]. LC58-5473.

THE WOMAN WITHIN. New York: Hill and Wang,
1980, c1954. LC79-28704.

Biography
ADE   AMN   AMR   AW   AWO   AWW   BERE   BRO   BURK
BURNT   CAS   CHA   CLARI   CON-104   COOPA   DAB-S3
FLE   HAMM   HAOXA   HAOXE   HARKF   JES   JOHDB   JONE
KIL   KRO   KUL   KUT   KUTS   LIB   LOGG   LOGP   MAG
MAN   MARBS   MCW   MDWB   MICA   MON   MORG   MYE   NAW
NCAB-13,35   NOV   NPW   OV   OV2   PEA   RA   REA   RIC
RICDA   RUB   RUT   SOU   VDW   WAGCA   WARBD   WARLC
WEBS   WELL   WENW   WOWWA   WWNA   WWWA-2   WWWE   WYN

Auchincloss, Louis. ELLEN GLASGOW. Minneapolis:
Univ. of Minnesota Press, [1964]. LC64-63338.

ELLEN GLASGOW: CENTENNIAL ESSAYS, edited by M.
Thomas Inge. pp. 25-64. Charlottesville: Univ.
Press of Virginia, 1976. LC75-15976.

Godbold, E. Stanly. ELLEN GLASGOW AND THE WOMAN
WITHIN. Baton Rouge: Louisiana State Univ.
Press, [1972]. LC71-165068.

Richards, Marion K. ELLEN GLASGOW'S DEVELOPMENT
AS A NOVELIST. The Hague: Mouton, 1971.
LC70-110957.

Rouse, Blair. ELLEN GLASGOW. New York: Twayne,
[c1962]. LC62-16821.

Thiebaux, Marcelle. ELLEN GLASGOW. New York:
F. Ungar, c1982. LC81-70128.

Obituary
CUR-1946.
NY TIMES (22 Nov 1945), 34-35.
PUBLISHERS WEEKLY 148 (1 Dec 1945), 2248.
TIME 46 (3 Dec 1945), 72.
TIMES (LONDON) (22 Nov 1945), 4:6; (23 Nov), 8:4.
WILSON 20 (Jan 1946), 328.

Bibliography
Kelly, William W. ELLEN GLASGOW, A BIBLIOGRAPHY.
Charlottesville: Univ. Press of Virginia,
[1964]. LC64-4758.

Glaspell, Susan. See MATSON, SUSAN KEATING
(GLASPELL) COOK.

GLENTWORTH, MARGEURITE LINTON. 1881-1956. U.S.

Biography
WOWWA

Obituary
NY TIMES (4 Sept 1956), 30:2.

GLYN, ELINOR CLAYTON (SUTHERLAND). 1864-1943.
England.

Autobiography
ROMANTIC ADVENTURE; BEING THE AUTOBIOGRAPHY OF
ELINOR GLYN. New York: E.P. Dutton, 1937.
LC37-1320.

Biography
BENN   BRO   HAMM   KUT   RIC   SHO   TWCR   WEBS   WWW-4

Glyn, Anthony G.   ELINOR GLYN: A BIOGRAPHY.
Rev. ed.   London: Hutchinson, 1968.
LC68-142748.

Obituary
CUR-1943.
NY TIMES (24 Sept 1943), 23:1.
PUBLISHERS WEEKLY 144 (2 Oct 1943), 1349.
TIME 42 (4 Oct 1943), 74.
TIMES (LONDON) (24 Sept 1943), 7:4.
WILSON 18 (Nov 1943), 206.

GLYNN, KATE A.   U.S.
        Ike, pseud.

                    Biography
WWNA

Godfrey, Hal, pseud.   See   ECCLES,   CHARLOTTE
O'CONOR.

Godstowe, Elizabeth, pseud.   See   EWELL,   ALICE
MAUDE.

Goetchius, Marie Louise, pseud.   See   HALE,   MARICE
RUTLEDGE (GIBSON).

GOLDIE, MARY ELIZABETH KATHLEEN DULCIE (DEAMER).
b.1890.   Australia.
        Dulcie Deamer

                    Biography
MIA   MIAU   MYE   **WWWL**

Goodloe, A. Carter.   See   GOODLOE,   ABBE   CARTER.

GOODLOE, ABBE CARTER. b.1867. U.S.
    A. Carter Goodloe
    Carter Goodloe

              Biography
  AWO BURK LIB WOWWA

Goodloe, Carter. See GOODLOE, ABBE CARTER.

GOODWIN, MAUD (WILDER). 1856-1935. U.S.

             Biography
  AWW BURK REA TWCB WARBD WOWWA WWWA-1

             Obituary
  PUBLISHERS WEEKLY 127 (23 Feb 1935), 890.

GORDON, HELEN (VAN METRE) VAN ANDERSON. b.1859.
U.S.
    Helen Van Anderson

             Biography
  BD WARBD

Gordon, Julien, pseud. See CRUGER, JULIE GRINNELL
(STORROW).

Gorst, Mrs. Harold E. See GORST, NINA CECILIA
FRANCESCA (KENNEDY).

GORST, NINA CECILIA FRANCESCA (KENNEDY). 1869-1926.
England.
      Mrs. Harold E. Gorst

          Autobiography
  THE NIGHT IS FAR SPENT. 1919. WWWL.

             Biography
  WWWL

             Obituary
  TIMES (LONDON) (21 Oct 1926), 9:2.

GOULD, ELIZABETH LINCOLN. 1873-1914. U.S.

Biography
LOGP   WOWWA   WWWA-1

GOULD, ELIZABETH PORTER. 1848-1906. U.S.

Biography
WILA

GOWING, EMILIA AYLMER (BLAKE). 1846-1905. Ireland.

Biography
ODP

Graham, Winifred.   See CORY, MATILDA WINIFRED
MURIEL (GRAHAM.)

Grand, Madame Sarah, pseud. See MCFALL, FRANCES
ELIZABETH (CLARKE).

Grand, Sarah, pseud.   See MCFALL, FRANCES
ELIZABETH (CLARKE).

Grant, Douglas, pseud. See OSTRANDER, ISABEL
EGENTON.

GRANT, ETHEL (WATTS) MUMFORD. 1878-1940. U.S.
Ethel Watts Mumford

Biography
ALY AWO BURG BURK REA WEBS WWNA WWWA-1

Obituary
CUR-1940.
NY TIMES (3 May 1940), 21:6.

GRANVILLE-BARKER, HELEN MANCHESTER (GATES). d.1950.
U.S.
   m. (1)Huntington (2)Granville-Barker
   Helen Huntington, pseud.

                    Biography
   BURK   WEBS   WWWT

Pearson, Hesketh. THE PILGRIM DAUGHTERS.
   London: Heinemann, [1961]. OCLC 1311585.
   Pub. also as THE MARRYING AMERICANS.

               Obituary
NY TIMES (18 Feb 1950), 15:2.

GRAVES, CLOTILDE INEZ MARY. 1863-1932. Ireland.
   Richard Dehan, pseud.

                    Biography
   ASH   CHA   CLE   CRO   DSAB-3   HAMM   NCH   ODP   OVEWH
   ROCK   STA   WARLC   WEBS   WWLA   WWW-3   WWWE   WWWL
   WWWT

                 Obituary
PUBLISHERS WEEKLY 122 (17 Dec 1932), 2254.
TIMES (LONDON) (5 Dec 1932), 17:4; tribute
   (12 Dec), 17:4.

Gray, Annabel, pseud. See COX, ANNE.

GRAY, ANNIE JOSLYN. U.S.
       Joslyn Gray

                     Biography
   BURK   WWNA   WWWA-5

GRAY, CHARLOTTE ELVIRA. 1873-1938. U.S.

                     Biography
   ALY   WWWA-1

Gray, Joslyn. See GRAY, ANNIE JOSLYN.

Gray, Maxwell, pseud. See TUTTIETT, MARY GLEED.

Green, Anna Katharine. See ROHLFS, ANNA KATHARINE
(GREEN).

Green, E. Everett. See GREEN, EVELYN EVERETT-.

GREEN, EVELYN EVERETT-. 1856-1932. England.
    Cecil Adair, pseud.
    Edward Everett-Green
    E. Everett Green
    E. Ward, pseud.

Biography
DOY HAMM LOF WWWL

Obituary
TIMES (LONDON) (25 Apr 1932), 7:7; (26 Apr),
    18:3; tribute (29 Apr), 19:2.

GREENE, AELLA. 1838-1903. U.S.

Biography
WARBD WWWA-1

Greene, Belle C. See GREENE, ISABEL CATHERINE
(COLTON).

GREENE, FRANCES NIMMO. 1850-1921. U.S.

Biography
LIB-17

GREENE, ISABEL CATHERINE (COLTON). b.1842/44. U.S.
    Belle C. Greene

Biography
WILA WWWA-4

GREENE, SARAH PRATT (MACLEAN). 1856-1935. U.S.

Biography
LOGP NAW NCAB-13 PRE TWCB WEBS WOWWA WWWA-1

GREENLEAF, SUE. U.S.

Biography
WOWWA

GREGG, HILDA CAROLINE. 1868-1933. England.
Sydney C. Grier, pseud.

Obituary
TIMES (LONDON) (26 June 1933), 16:5.

Gregory, Sacha, pseud. See HUTTEN ZUM STOLZENBERG,
BETSEY (RIDDLE).

GREVILLE, BEATRICE VIOLET (GRAHAM) GREVILLE.
1842-1932. England.

Autobiography
VIGNETTES OF MEMORY, by Lady Violet Greville.
London: Hutchinson, [1927]. LC28-2547.

Greville, Henri, pseud. See DURAND, ALICE MARIE
CELESTE (FLEURY).

Grey, Rowland, pseud. See BROWN, LILIAN KATE
ROWLAND.

Grier, Sydney C., pseud. See GREGG, HILDA
CAROLINE.

GRIFFITH, HELEN (SHERMAN). 1873-1961. U.S.

Biography
BURK WWNA WWWA-4 WWWE

Obituary
NY TIMES (15 July 1961), 19:6.

GRIMSHAW, BEATRICE ETHEL. 1871-1953. Australia.

Autobiography
ISLES OF ADVENTURE; FROM JAVA TO NEW CALEDONIA
BUT PRINCIPALLY PAPUA. Boston: Houghton
Mifflin, 1931. LC31-4761.

Biography
BRI   BRO   CLE   HAMM   MDWB   MIA   MIAU   WARLC   WWLA
WWWE

Obituary
NY TIMES (1 July 1953), 29:5.
OBIT1, 313.
TIMES (LONDON) (1 July 1953), 8:5.
WILSON 28 (Sept 1953), 28.

GRIMWOOD, ETHEL SAINT CLAIR. England.

Autobiography
MY THREE YEARS IN MANIPUR.   Delhi: Vivek Pub.
House, 1975, 1891. OCLC 3489409.

GRINNELL, ELIZABETH (PRATT). 1851-1935. U.S.

Biography
WWWA-1

GRISSOM, IRENE (WELCH). b.1873. U.S.

Biography
WWNA   WWWA-5

GRISWOLD, HATTIE (TYNG). 1840-1909. U.S.

Biography
APP   BD   NCAB-10   TIT   TWCB   WARBD   WILA   WWWA-1

GRISWOLD, LATTA. 1876-1931. U.S.

BURK   COY   NCAB-25   Biography
                       WWNA   WWWA-1

GROSS, MYRA GERALDINE. b.1872. U.S.

ALY   WOWWA   WWWA-6   Biography

GROSSMAN, EDITH HOWITT (SEARLE). 1863-1931. New
Zealand.

MYE   NPW   Biography

GUNN, JEANNIE (TAYLOR). 1870-1960/61. Australia.
      Mrs. Aeneas Gunn

MIA   MAIU   Biography

Gunn, Mrs. Aeneas. See GUNN, JEANNIE (TAYLOR).

GUYTON, EMMA JANE (WORBOISE). 1825-1887. England.
        Emma Jane Worboise

DNB   Biography

Gyp, pseud.   See MARTEL DE JANVILLE, SYBILLE
   GABRIELLE   MARIE   ANTOINETTE   (DE RIQUETTI DE
   MIRABEAU).

H., A.K., pseud. See HOPKINS, ALICE (KIMBALL).

HACK, ELIZABETH JANE (MILLER). 1878-1961. U.S.
     Mrs. Oren S. Hack

                 Biography
     BAN BURK WOWWA WWWA-4

                 Obituary
     NY TIMES (20 Aug 1961), 86:3.

Hack, Mrs. Oren S. See HACK, ELIZABETH JANE
     (MILLER).

Hahn, Countess Hahn. See HAHN-HAHN, IDA MARIE
     LUISE SOPHIE FREDERIKE GUSTAVA VON.

Hahn, Ida Marie. See HAHN-HAHN, IDA MARIE
     LUISE SOPHIE FREDERIKE GUSTAVA VON.

**HAHN-HAHN, IDA MARIE LUISE SOPHIE FREDERIKE
GUSTAVA VON.** 1805-1880. Germany.
     Countess Hahn Hahn
     Ida Marie Hahn

                 Biography
     BD CHABI GAR WARBD WEBS

                 Obituary
     TIMES (LONDON) (15 Jan 1880), 10:4.

HAINES, ALICE CALHOUN. U.S.
     m. Baskin

                 Biography
     WWNA

161

HALE, ANNE GARDNER. 1823-1914. U.S.

Biography
WWWA-1

HALE, BEATRICE (FORBES-ROBERTSON). b.1883. U.S.

Biography
AWO   WWNA   WWWE   WWWT

HALE, LOUISE (CLOSSER). 1872-1933. U.S.

Biography
BURK   DAB-1   HAOXA   KUJ1   PRE   REA   WARBD   WWWA-1

Obituary
Benet, W.R.   SAT REVIEW OF LIT 10 (5 Aug 1933), 33.

HALE, MARICE RUTLEDGE (GIBSON). b.1884. U.S.
      Marie Louise Goetchius, pseud.
      Marice Rutledge
      Marie Louise Van Saanen, pseud.

Biography
BURK

HALE, SARAH ALICE. b.1856. U.S.

Biography
KNIB

HALL, AMANDA BENJAMIN. b.1890. U.S.

Biography
BURK   REA   WWNA

Hall, Eliza Calvert, pseud.   See OBENCHAIN, ELIZA
CAROLINE (CALVERT).

Hall, Gertrude.   See BROWNELL, ANNA   GERTRUDE
(HALL).

Hall, Helene, pseud. See BOYNTON, HELEN (MASON).

HALL, RUTH. b.1858. U.S.

Biography

BURK   WARBD   WOWWA   WWNA   WWWA-4

HALL, VIOLETTE. U.S.

Biography

WOWWA   WWNA

HALSTED, LENORA B. U.S.

Biography

WOWWA

HAMILTON, ANNIE E. (HOLDSWORTH) LEE. England.
Max Beresford, pseud.
Mrs. Lee Hamilton
Annie E. Holdsworth

Biography

BD

HAMILTON, CATHERINE JANE. England.

Biography

BRI   WWWL

HAMILTON, CICELY MARY. 1875?-1952. England.
Registered at birth as Cecily Mary Hammill
but adopted the name of Cecily Hamilton.

Autobiography

LIFE ERRANT. London: Dent, [1935]. LC36-3119.

Biography

HAMM   MOB   WWW-5   WWWE   WWWL   WWWT

Obituary
ILLUS LONDON NEWS 221 (13 Dec 1952), 1000.
OBIT1, 328.
TIMES (LONDON) (8 Dec 1952), 10:4; tribute
(12 Dec), 10:6.

HAMILTON, EDITH HENRIETTA (FOWLER). 1865-1963.
England.
Edith Henrietta Fowler
Hon. Mrs. Robert Hamilton

Biography
CON-77--80   LES   SOME-20

Obituary
CUR-1963.
NY TIMES (1 June 1963), 21:4; tribute (16 June),
IV 10:6.
TIMES (LONDON) (3 June 1963), 10:5.

Hamilton, Hon. Mrs. Robert.   See HAMILTON, EDITH
HENRIETTA (FOWLER).

HAMILTON, KATE WATERMAN. 1841-1934. U.S.

Biography
APP   AWW   NCAB-4   TWCB   WOWWA   WWWA-5

HAMILTON, LILLIAS.
Dr. Lillias Hamilton

Biography
BD   WWWL

Hamilton, M., pseud.   See LUCK, MARY CHURCHILL
(SPOTTISWOODE-ASHE).

HAMILTON, MARY AGNES (ADAMSON). 1884-1962. England.

Autobiography
REMEMBERING MY GOOD FRIENDS.   London: J. Cape,
[1944]. LC45-1704.

UP-HILL ALL THE WAY; A THIRD CHEER FOR DEMOCRACY.
London: Cape, [1953]. LC54-38985.

Biography
BRO   HAMM   KUT   WARLC   WWW-6   WWWL

Obituary
NY TIMES (12 Feb 1966), 25:2-3.
OBIT2, 339.
TIMES (LONDON) (11 Feb 1966), 18:4.

Hamilton, Mrs. Lee.   See HAMILTON, ANNIE E.
(HOLDSWORTH) LEE.

Hamlet, Edith.   See LYTTLETON, EDITH SOPHY
(BALFOUR).

Hammond, Frances, pseud.   See CROAL, FRANCES A.

Hammond, L.H.   See HAMMOND, LILY (HARDY).

HAMMOND, LILY (HARDY). 1859-1925. U.S.
L.H. Hammond

Biography
ALY

HANCOCK, ELIZABETH HAZLEWOOD. 1871-1915. U.S.

Biography
KNIB   WWWA-1

HAPGOOD, NEITH (BOYCE). 1872-1951. U.S.
Neith Boyce

Biography
BAN   BURK   WEBS   WOWWA   WWWA-3   WWWL

Obituary
NY TIMES (3 Dec 1951), 31:6.
WILSON 26 (Feb 1952), 428.

HARBERT, ELIZABETH MORRISSON (BOYNTON). 1845-1925.
U.S.

Biography
BAN   WILA   WOWWA   WWWA-1

Harding, D.C.F.   See   HARDING, DOLORES CHARLOTTE
FREDERICA.

HARDING, DOLORES CHARLOTTE FREDERICA. b.1888.
England.
        D.C.F. Harding

Biography
WWWL

HARDY, IZA DUFFUS. d.1922. England.

Biography
BLA   WARBD

Obituary
TIMES (LONDON) (31 Aug 1922), 9:2.

HARDY, ROBINA FORRESTER. d.1891. Scotland.

Biography
BOASE-5

Obituary
ILLUS LONDON NEWS (22 Aug 1891), 258.
TIMES (LONDON) (18 Aug 1891), 7:6.

HARGROVE, ETHEL C.

Biography
WWWL

Harker, L. Allen.   See   HARKER, LIZZIE ALLEN
(WATSON).

HARKER, LIZZIE ALLEN (WATSON). 1863-1933. England.
L. Allen Harker
Mrs. L. Allen Harker

Biography
BRO HAMM KUT WWWE WWWL

Obituary
NY TIMES (15 Apr 1933), 13:6.
TIMES (LONDON) (15 Apr 1933), 12:4.

Harker, Mrs. L. Allen. See HARKER, LIZZIE ALLEN
(WATSON).

Harland, Marion, pseud. See TERHUNE, MARY VIRGINIA
(HAWES).

HARPER, CARRIE ANNA. d.1918. U.S.

Biography
WOWWA WWWA-1

HARPER, FRANCES ELLEN (WATKINS). 1825-1911. U.S.

Biography
AWW BURK DANB LOGGN MAJ NAW PENN RUSB

Brawley, Benjamin G., ed. EARLY NEGRO AMERICAN
WRITERS; SELECTIONS WITH BIOGRAPHICAL AND
CRITICAL INTRODUCTIONS. pp. 290-2. Chapel
Hill: Univ. of North Carolina Press, c1935.
LC35-7296.

_____. THE NEGRO GENIUS; A NEW APPRAISAL OF THE
ACHIEVEMENT OF THE AMERICAN NEGRO IN LITERATURE
AND THE FINE ARTS. pp. 116-20. New York:
Biblo and Tannen, 1966,c1937. LC66-17517.

Dannett, Sylvia G. PROFILES OF NEGRO WOMANHOOD.
pp. 102-9. Vol. 1. Yonkers, N.Y.: Educational
Heritage, [1964-66]. LC64-25013R.

Davis, John P., ed. THE AMERICAN NEGRO REFERENCE
BOOK. pp. 854-6. Englewood Cliffs, N.J.:

Prentice-Hall, [1966]. LC65-12919.

THE NEGRO ALMANAC: A REFERENCE WORK ON THE AFRO-AMERICAN, compiled and edited by Harry A. Ploski and James Williams. pp. 985. 4th ed. New York: Wiley, 1983. LC82-17469.

Page, James A. SELECTED BLACK AMERICAN AUTHORS: AN ILLUSTRATED BIO-BIBLIOGRAPHY. p. 115. Boston: G.K. Hall, 1977. LC77-16009.

Still, William. "Introduction." In IOLA LEROY; OR, SHADOWS UPLIFTED, by Frances E. Harper. pp. 1-3. New York: AMS, [1971], 1893. LC76-153097.

Whiteman, Maxwell. "Introduction." In POEMS ON MISCELLANEOUS SUBJECTS, by Frances E. Harper, n.p. [Philadelphia, Pa.: Rhistoric, 1969]. LC78-77078.
    Reprint of the 1857 edition, with a new introduction.

Harper, Olive, pseud. See D'APERY, HELEN (BURRELL) GIBSON.

HARRADEN, BEATRICE. 1864-1936. England.

Biography
BD   BERE   BRO   CHA   DNB-5   HAMM   KUT   NCH   RIC
SHO   WARBD   WARLC   WEBS   WWLA   WWWE   WWWL

Obituary
NY TIMES (6 May 1936), 23:3.
TIMES (LONDON) (6 May 1936), 18:3; tribute (7 May), 21:1.

Harriman, Alice. See BROWNE, ALICE (HARRIMAN).

HARRIOTT, CLARA MORRIS. 1848?-1925. U.S.
    Clara Morris

HARRIOTT

Autobiography
THE LIFE OF A STAR & CO. New York: McClure,
Phillips, 1906. LC06-16284.

LIFE ON THE STAGE; MY PERSONAL EXPERIENCES AND
RECOLLECTIONS, by Clara Morris. New York:
McClure, Phillips, 1901. LC1-26550.

Biography
APP AWW BURK COY DAB NAW NCAB-11 PRE TWCB
WARBD WEBS WILA WOWWA WWWA-1 WWWT

Obituary
NY TIMES (22 Nov 1925), 9:1.

HARRIS, CORRA MAY (WHITE). 1869-1935. U.S.

Autobiography
AS A WOMAN THINKS. Boston: Houghton Mifflin,
1925. LC25-20051.

THE HAPPY PILGRIMAGE. Boston: Houghton Mifflin,
1927. LC27-19555.

MY BOOK AND HEART. Boston: Houghton Mifflin,
1924. LC24-8389.

Biography
AWW LIB-17 MARBS NAW NCAB-26 OV OV2 SOU
WEBS WWWA-1 WYN

Talmadge, John E. CORRA HARRIS, LADY OF PURPOSE.
Athens: Univ. of Georgia Press, [1968].
LC68-28362.

Obituary
Moncrief, A.J., Jr. CHRISTIAN CENTURY 52 (13
Mar 1935), 350.
NEWSWEEK 5 (16 Feb 1935), 16.
PUBLISHERS WEEKLY 127 (23 Feb 1935), 890.

HARRIS, FRANCES ALLEN. U.S.
Biography
KNIB

HARRIS

HARRIS, LINNIE SARAH. b.1868. U.S.

Biography
WOWWA

HARRIS, MIRIAM (COLES). 1834-1925. U.S.

Biography
ALY APP AWW BURK DAB KUAA NCAB-11 TWCB
WARBD WOWWA WWWA-4

HARRIS, MISS S.M. Ireland.
    Athene, pseud.

Biography
BRI

HARRISON, CONSTANCE (CARY). 1843-1920. U.S.
    Mrs. Burton Harrison

Biography
APP APP-S AWW BAS BD BURK CHA DAB HAOXA
HARKF JOHDB KUAA LIB LOGP NAW NCAB-4 PRE
REA RICDA RUT SOU WARBD WEBS WILA WWWA-1

Obituary
NY TIMES (22 Nov 1920), 15:2.

HARRISON, EDITH (OGDEN). d.1955. U.S.

Autobiography
"STRANGE TO SAY-"; RECOLLECTIONS OF PERSONS AND
    EVENTS IN NEW ORLEANS AND CHICAGO. Chicago:
    A. Kroch, 1949. LC49-4230.

Biography
AWO BURK HINK KNIB LOGP WOWWA WWNA WWWA-3

HARRISON, ELLANETTA. U.S.

Biography
KNIB

170

HARRISON, IDA (WITHERS). 185-1927. U.S.

Biography
WOWWA   WWNA   WWWA-1

HARRISON, MARY SAINT LEGER (KINGSLEY). 1852-1931.
England.
Lucas Malet, pseud.

Biography
BD   CHA   CHABI   COU   DNB-5   FUR   HAL   KUT   NCBEL-3
NCH   ROCK   SHA-A   WARLC   WEBS   WWLA   WWWE

Obituary
CATHOLIC WORLD 134 (Dec 1931), 365.
PUBLISHERS WEEKLY 120 (14 Nov 1931), 2235.
TIMES (LONDON) (29 Oct 1931), 14:4.

Harrison, Mrs. Burton.   See   HARRISON, CONSTANCE
(CARY).

Harrison, S.F.   See   HARRISON,   SUSIE   FRANCES
(RILEY).

Harrison, S. Frances.   See   HARRISON, SUSIE FRANCES
(RILEY).

HARRISON, SUSIE FRANCES (RILEY). 1859-1935. Canada.
        S.F. Harrison
        S. Frances Harrison
        Seranus, pseud.

Biography
APP   GARV   MDCB   MOR   MOR2   MYE   ODP   STOXC
WOWWA   WWNA

HARROD, FRANCES (FORBES-ROBERTSON). 1866-1956.
England.
        Frances Forbes Robertson

Biography
WWWE

171

Obituary
TIMES (LONDON) (25 May 1956), 13:3.

HART, ELIZABETH. b.1883. Ireland.

Biography
BRI

HART, FRANCES NEWBOLD (NOYES). 1890-1943. U.S.
Frances Newbold Noyes

Biography
AWW BURK EMD HAOXA KUT MARS REA WARLC
WEBS WWNA WWWA-2

Obituary
NY TIMES (26 Oct 1943), 23:3.
PUBLISHERS WEEKLY 144 (6 Nov 1943), 1800.
WILSON 18 (Dec 1943), 303.

HARWOOD, FRYNIWYD TENNYSON (JESSE). 1889-1958.
England.
F. Tennyson Jesse
Fryniwyd Tennyson Jesse
Fryn Tennyson-Jesse [WWWL]
Beamish Tinker, pseud.

Biography
BERE BRO CHABI EMD HAMM KUT MANBL MICB
NCH WARLC WEBS WWW-5 WWWL WWWT

Obituary
NY TIMES (7 Aug 1958), 25:3.
OBIT1, 390.
TIMES (LONDON) (7 Aug 1958), 8:5; tribute
(12 Aug), 8:4.

HASKELL, HELEN (EGGLESTON). b.1871. U.S.

Biography
AWO BURK KUJ1 KUJ2 WOMA WWWA-5

HASLETT, HARRIET HOLMES. b.1866. U.S.

HINK
Biography

Hastings, Elizabeth, pseud. See SHERWOOD, MARGARET POLLOCK.

HATCH, MARY ROXANNA (PLATT). 1848-1935. U.S.

Biography
AWW BURK WILA WWNA

Haverfield, E.L. See HAVERFIELD, ELEANOR LUISA.

HAVERFIELD, ELEANOR LUISA. b.1870.
E.L. Haverfield

WWWL
Biography

HAWEIS, MARY ELIZA (JOY). 1852-1898. England.

Biography
BOASE-5 WEBS

Obituary
ILLUS LONDON NEWS (3 Dec 1898), 821.
TIMES (LONDON) (29 Nov 1898), 6:5.

Hawker, Mary Elizabeth. See HAWKER, MORWENNA PAULINE.

HAWKER, MORWENNA PAULINE. 1848-1908. England.
L.F., pseud.
Lanoe Falconer, pseud.
Mary Elizabeth Hawker

Biography
DNB-2 ROCK SHO WARBD

173

Phillipps, Evelyn M. LANOE FALCONER. London:
Nisbet, 1915. OCLC 2607222.

Obituary
TIMES (LONDON) (20 June 1908), 15:6.

Hawthorne, Hildegarde. See OSKISON, HILDEGARDE
(HAWTHORNE).

HAY, AGNES GRANT (GOSSE). Australia.
Anglo-Australian, pseud.

Biography
MIA   MIAU

Headley, Lady. See BAYNTON, BARBARA   JANE
(LAWRENCE).

HEARN, MARY ANN. 1834-1909. England.
Marianne Farningham, pseud.

Autobiography
A WORKING WOMAN'S LIFE; AN AUTOBIOGRAPHY, by
Marianne Farningham. London: Clarke, [1907?].
OCLC 3647578.

Biography
BEL   DNB-2   ROCK

HECTOR, ANNIE (FRENCH). 1825-1902. Ireland.
Mrs. Alexander, pseud.

Biography
BD   BEL   BLA   BOY   CLE   CRO   DNB-S2   HAMM   JOHDB
NCH   SHO   WARBD   WARLC   WEBS

Heimburg, W., pseud. See BEHRENS, BERTHA.

HENNIKER, FLORENCE ELLEN HUNGERFORD (MILNES).
d.1923. England.

Biography
WWWL

Henry-Ruffin, Margaret. See RUFFIN, MARGARET
ELLEN (HENRY).

Hensel, Octavia, pseud. See FONDA, MARY ALICE
(IVES) SEYMOUR.

Henshaw, J.W. See HENSHAW, JULIA WILMOTTE
(HENDERSON).

HENSHAW, JULIA WILMOTTE (HENDERSON). 1869-1937.
Canada.
Julian Durham, pseud.
J.W. Henshaw

Biography
MDCB   MOR2   STOXC   WOWWA   WWNA

Obituary
NY TIMES (21 Nov 1937), II 9:3.

HERBERT, AGNES. England.

Biography
WWLA   WWWE

HERBERT, ALICE. b.1867. England.

Biography
WWWL

HERBERTSON, AGNES GROZIER. England.

Biography
WWWE

HERBERTSON, JESSIE LECKIE. England.

Biography
WWWE

HERRICK, CHRISTINE (TERHUNE). 1859-1944. U.S.

Biography
ALY AWO NCAB-8,2 TWCB WARBD WILA WOWWA
WWWA-2

Herrick, Huldah, pseud. See OBER, SARAH ENDICOTT.

HERRING, FRANCES ELIZABETH (CLARKE). 1851-1916.
Canada.

Biography
MOR2 WOWWA

**HEYKING, ELIZABETH AUGUSTE LUISE HELENE MELUSINE
MAXIMILIANE (VON FLEMMING) VON.** 1861-1925.
Germany.

Biography
GAR

Obituary
NY TIMES (6 Jan 1925), 25:5.

Hicks Beach, Mrs. William. See HICKS BEACH, SUSAN
EMILY (CHRSITIAN).

HICKS BEACH, SUSAN EMILY (CHRISTIAN). 1865/66-1958.
England.
       Mrs. William Hicks Beach
       name also appears as Hicks-Beach

Biography
WWWE WWWL

Obituary
TIMES (LONDON) (21 Nov 1958), 15:2.

HIGGINS

Higgins, Elizabeth. See SULLIVAN, ELIZABETH (HIGGINS).

HIGGINSON, ELLA (RHOADS). 1862-1940. U.S.

Biography
ALY AWW BURK TWCB WILA WOWWA WWWA-1 WWWE

Higginson, Mrs. S.J. See HIGGINSON, SARAH, JANE (HATFIELD).

HIGGINSON, SARAH JANE (HATTFIELD). 1840-1916. U.S.
Mrs. S.J. Higginson

Biography
WARBD

HILDYARD, IDA JANE (LEMON). b.1867. England.
Ida Lemon

Biography
WWWE

Hill, Grace Livingston. See LUTZ, GRACE (LIVINGSTON) HILL.

HILL, MARION. 1870-1918. U.S.

Biography
WOWWA WWWA-1

HILL, MILDRED. b.1878. England.

Biography
WWWL

177

HILLERN, WILHELMINE (BIRCH) VON. 1836-1916.
Germany.

Biography
BD   WARBD   WEBS

Hine, Muriel.   See   COXON, MURIEL (HINE).

HINKSON, KATHARINE (TYNAN). 1861-1931.   Ireland.
Mrs. Hinkson
Mrs. H.A. Hinkson
Katharine Tynan

Autobiography
LIFE IN THE OCCUPIED AREA, by Katharine Tynan.
London: Hutchinson: [1925]. LC25-8218.

MEMORIES, by Katharine Tynan. London: E. Nash
& Grayson, [1924]. LC24-16027.

THE MIDDLE YEARS, by Katharine Tynan. Boston:
Houghton Mifflin, 1917. OCLC 4151022.

TWENTY-FIVE YEARS: REMINISCENCES, by Katharine
Tynan. New York: Devin-Adair, [c1913].
LC14-1401.

THE WANDERING YEARS, by Katharine Tynan. Boston:
Houghton Mifflin, 1922. LC22-27472.

THE YEARS OF THE SHADOW, by Katharine Tynan.
Boston: Houghton Mifflin, 1919. LC19-27582.

Biography
BERE   BOY   BRI   BRO   CHA   CHABI   CLE   CON-104
CRO   DIL   DNB-5   HAMM   HOE   KUAT   KUT   LAU   MAN
MANL   MICB   MYE   NCH   ODP   RIC   SHA-A   SHO   WARLC
WEBS

Fallon, Ann C. KATHARINE TYNAN. Boston: Twayne,
1979. LC79-12331.

Rose, Marilyn G. KATHARINE TYNAN. Lewisburg,
[Pa.]: Bucknell Univ. Press, [1974].
LC71-126276R.

Obituary
BOOKMAN (LONDON) 80 (May 1931), 101-102.
CATHOLIC WORLD 133 (May 1931), 235.
CHRISTIAN CENTURY 48 (29 Apr 1931), 584.
PUBLISHERS WEEKLY 119 (11 Apr 1931), 1912.
TIMES (LONDON) (4 Apr 1931), 12:2.

Hinkson, Mrs. See HINKSON, KATHARINE (TYNAN).

Hinkson, Mrs. H. A. See HINKSON, KATHARINE
(TYNAN).

HITCHCOCK, MARY E. (HIGGINS). U.S.
Mrs. Roswell D. Hitchcock

Autobiography
TWO WOMEN IN THE KLONDIKE; THE STORY OF A JOURNEY
TO THE GOLD-FIELDS OF ALASKA. New York: G.P.
Putnam's Sons, 1899. LC99-2927R.

Biography
STOXC   WOWWA

Hitchcock, Mrs. Roswell D. See HITCHCOCK, MARY E.

Hobbes, John Oliver, pseud. See CRAIGIE, PEARL
MARY TERESA (RICHARDS).

HOBHOUSE, VIOLET (MACNEILL). 1864-1902. Ireland.

Biography
BRI   CLE

HOBSON, HARRIET MALONE. U.S.

Biography
BURK

HODGSON, GERALDINE EMMA. b.1865. England.

<u>Biography</u>
WWLA   WWWE   WWWL

HOLDEN, MARTHA EVERTS. 1844-1896. U.S.

<u>Biography</u>
BURK

HOLDING, ELISABETH (SANXAY). 1889-1955. U.S.

<u>Biography</u>
AWW   BURK   EMD   WEBS   WWNA   WWWA-3

<u>Obituary</u>
NY TIMES (9 Feb 1955), 27:2.
TIMES (LONDON) (16 Feb 1955), 10:5.

Holdsworth, Annie E.   See HAMILTON, ANNIE E.
(HOLDSWORTH) LEE.

HOLDSWORTH, GLADYS BRONWYN (STERN). 1890-1973.
England.
        G.B. Stern
        Christened Bertha, she did not care for
        the name and adopted the name of Browyn

<u>Autobiography</u>
ALL IN GOOD TIME, by Gladys Bronwyn Stern.   New
York: Sheed and Ward, [1954]. LC546146L.

ANOTHER PART OF THE FOREST, by G.B. Stern.   New
York: Macmillan, 1941. LC41-51830.

BENEFITS FORGOT, by Gladys Browyn Stern.   New
York: Macmillan, 1949. LC49-11683.

MONOGRAM, by G.B. Stern.   New York: Macmillan,
1936. LC36-27162.

A NAME TO CONJURE WITH, by Gladys Browyn Stern.
London: Collins, [1953]. LC53-29726.

THE WAY IT WORKED OUT. New York: Sheed and Ward,
[1957, c1956]. LC56-12816.

Biography
BRO KUL KUT MANBL MICB RIC SHO STOK WEBS
WWLA WWWE WWWL WWWT

O'Brien, John A. WHERE DWELLEST THOU? INTIMATE
PERSONAL STORIES OF TWELVE CONVERTS TO THE
CATHOLIC FAITH. pp. 66-75. New York: Gilbert,
[c1956]. LC56-6793.

Obituary
NY TIMES (20 Sept 1973), 55:3.
OBIT3, 508.
TIME 102 (1 Oct 1973), 79.
TIMES (LONDON) (20 Sept 1973), 20:8.

Holgar, Paxton, pseud. See BOYD, MARY STUART
(KIRKWOOD).

HOLLEY, MARIETTA. 1844-1926. U.S.
      Josiah Allen's Wife

Biography
ALY AMH AWW BD BERE BURK DAB HAOXA KUAA
LOGP NAW NCAB-9 PRE REA TWCB WARBD WEBS
WILA WOWWA WWWA-1

Obituary
OUTLOOK 142 (10 Mar 1926), 354.

Holme, Constance. See PUNCHARD, CONSTANCE (HOLME).

HOLMES, GEORGIANA (KLINGLE). U.S.
      George Klingle, pseud.

Biography
WILA

Holmes, Margaret. See BATES, MARGRET HOLMES
(ERNSPERGER).

Holmes, Margret.   See   BATES,   MARGRET   HOLMES
(ERNSPERGER).

HOLMES, MARY CAROLINE. 1859-1927. U.S.

Biography
WWWA-1

HOLMES, MARY JANE (HAWES). 1825-1907. U.S.

Biography
APP AWW BURK DAB HAOXA KNIB MYE NAW NCAB-8
PAP REA RICDA RICK TWCB WARBD WEBS WILA
WWWA-1

Obituary
NY TIMES (8 Oct 1907), 11:5.

HOLT, EMILY SARAH. b.1836. England.

Biography
BEL

HOOKER, FORRESTINE (COOPER). 1867-1932. U.S.

Biography
BURK KRO WWWA-1

Obituary
Murneek, A.E.   SCIENCE n.s. 70 (29 Nov 1932),
531.

HOOPES, MARY HOWARD (PETERSON). U.S.
Maud Howard Peterson, pseud.

Biography
WWNA

HOOVER, BESSIE RAY. b.1874. U.S.

Biography
WWWA-5

182

HOPE, FRANCES ESSEX THEODORA. England.
Essex Smith, pseud.

WWWE

Biography

Hope, Graham, pseud. See HOPE, JESSIE GRAHAM.

HOPE, JESSIE GRAHAM. d.1920. England.
Graham Hope, pseud.

Obituary
TIMES (LONDON) (6 May 1920), 18:5.

HOPKINS, ALICE (KIMBALL). b.1839. U.S.
A.K.H., pseud.

ROCK

Biography

HOPKINS, LOUISE VIRGINIA MARTIN-BURK. b.1860. U.S.

Biography
BURK   WOWWA   WWWA-4

HOPKINS, MARGARET SUTTON (BRISCOE). b.1864.   U.S.
Margaret Sutton Briscoe

Biography
BURK   KNIB   WARBD   WOWWA   WWNA   WWWA-4

Hopkins, Mrs. Herbert Mueller.   See CAVENDISH,
PAULINE BRADFORD (MACKIE) HOPKINS.

HOPKINS, PAULINE ELIZABETH. 1859-1930. U.S.

Biography
AWW   DANB   LOGGN

Shockley, Ann A. "Pauline Elizabeth Hopkins: a
Biographical Excursion into Obscurity." PHYLON
33 (Spring 1972), 22-26.

HOPKINS, UNA NIXSON. U.S.

WOWWA Biography

HOSKEN, ALICE CECIL (SEYMOUR). b.1877. England.
Coralie Stanton, pseud.

WWLA WWWE WWWL Biography

HOUGHTON, LOUISE (SEYMOUR). 1838-1920. U.S.

ALY WOWWA WWWA-1 Biography

HOUK, ELIZA PHILLIPS THRUSTON. 1833-1914. U.S.

COY WOWWA WWWA-1 Biography

HOUSTON, MARGARET BELL. d.1966. U.S.

AWO BARN BURK WWWA-4 Biography

HOUSTOUN, MATILDA CHARLOTTE (JESSE) FRASER.
1815?-1892. England.

BLA BOASE-5 Biography

Howard, Blanche Willis. See TEUFFEL, BLANCHE
WILLIS (HOWARD) VON.

HOWARTH, ANNA. South Africa.

Biography
STA

HOWLAND, FRANCES LOUISE (MORSE). 1855-1944. U.S.
Kenyon West, pseud.

Biography
ALY AWO BURK WOWWA WWNA WWWA-4

Hoyt, Eleanor. See BRAINERD, ELEANOR (HOYT).

HUESTON, ETHEL (POWELSON). b.1887. U.S.

Biography
BURK REA WAR

HULING, CAROLINE ALDEN. 1857-1941. U.S.

Biography
WWNA

Obituary
NY TIMES (12 Mar 1941), 21:4.

Hull, E.M. See HULL, EDITH MAUDE.

HULL, EDITH MAUDE. England.
E.M. Hull

Biography
BERE BRO KUT MYE NCH WARLC WEBS

Humphrey, Zephine. See FAHNESTOCK, HARRIETTE
ZEPHINE (HUMPHREY).

HUMPHREYS, ELIZA MARGARET J.(GOLLAN). 1860-1938.
Scotland.
   Mrs. Desmond Humphreys
   Rita, pseud.

Autobiography
RECOLLECTIONS OF A LITERARY LIFE, by "Rita" (Mrs.
Desmond Humphreys). London: A. Melrose,
[1936]. LC36-19817.

Biography
BRI   BRO   SHO   WWLA   WWWE   WWWL

Obituary
NY TIMES (4 Jan 1938), 23:1.
TIMES (LONDON) (4 Jan 1938), 14:3.
WILSON 12 (Feb 1938), 356.

HUMPHREYS, MARY GAY. 1889-1915. U.S.
   Henry Somerville, pseud.

Biography
COY   HOE

Obituary
NY TIMES (15 Oct 1915), 11:5.

Humphreys, Mrs. Desmond.   See HUMPHREYS, ELIZA
MARGARET J. (GOLLAN).

HUNGERFORD, MARGARET WOLFE (HAMILTON). 1855?-1897.
Ireland.
   The Duchess, pseud.
   Mrs. Hungerford

Biography
BEL   BLA   BOASE-5   BRI   CHA   CLE   CRO   DNB-1
KNIB   KUBA   NCH   SHO   WARBD   WEBS

Obituary
ILLUS LONDON NEWS (30 Jan 1897), 142.
NY TIMES (25 Jan 1897), 2:5.
TIMES (LONDON) (25 Jan 1897), 10:4.

Hungerford, Mrs. See HUNGERFORD, MARGARET WOLFE (HAMILTON).

HUNT, ANNA REBECCA (GALE). Canada.
Canadienne, pseud.

Biography
MOR2

HUNT, ISOBEL VIOLET. 1866-1942. England.
Violet Hunt

Autobiography
THE FLURRIED YEARS. [London]: Hurst & Blackett, [1926]. LC26-10935.

Biography
ADC BERE HAMM KUAT KUT KUTS NCH PEE SHO
WARLC WWW-4 WWWE WWWL

Goldring, Douglas. SOUTH LODGE; REMINISCENCES OF VIOLET HUNT, FORD MADOX FORD AND THE ENGLISH REVIEW CIRCLE. London: Constable, [1943]. LCa44-303.

Obituary
TIMES (LONDON) (19 Jan 1942), 6:4.

HUNT, MARGARET (RAINE). 1831-1912. England.
Mrs. Alfred W. Hunt

Obituary
TIMES (LONDON) (2 Nov 1912), 9:4.

Hunt, Mrs. Alfred W. See Hunt, Margaret (Raine).

Hunt, Violet. See HUNT, ISOBEL VIOLET.

Huntington, Faye, pseud. See FOSTER, THEODOSIA MARIA (TOLL).

187

Huntington, Helen, pseud. See GRANVILLE-BARKER, HELEN MANCHESTER (GATES).

HUNTLEY, FLORENCE (CHANCE). 1860-1912. U.S.

Biography
COY   LOGP   WILA   WWWA-1

HUSTON, ETHELYN LESLIE. b.1869. U.S.

Biography
WWNA

HUTCHINSON, EDITH STOTESBURY. b.1877. U.S.

Biography
WWWA-5

Hutten, Bettina Von. See   HUTTEN ZUM STOLZENBERG, BETSEY (RIDDLE) VON.

HUTTEN ZUM STOLZENBERG, BETSEY (RIDDLE) VON. 1874-1957. U.S.
        Gregory Sacha, pseud.
        Baroness Von Hutten
        Bettina Von Hutten
        Betsey (Riddle) Von Hutten Zum Stolzenberg

Biography
BURK   HAMM   OXF   TWCR   WEBS   WWWA-3   WWWE   WWWL

Obituary
NY TIMES (29 Jan 1957), 31:5.
OBIT1, 375.
TIMES (LONDON) (29 Jan 1957), 10:4.
WILSON 31 (Mar 1957), 505+.

HUZARD, ANTOINETTE (DE BERGEVIN). 1874-1953.
France.
    Colette Yver, pseud.

                    Biography
WEBS

HYLAND, M.E.F.
    Kythe Wylwynne, pseud.

                    Biography
WWWL

Ike, pseud. See GLYNN, KATE A.

INGELOW, JEAN. 1820-1897. England.

Autobiography
SOME RECOLLECTIONS OF JEAN INGELOW AND HER EARLY
FRIENDS. Port Washington, N.Y.: Kennikat,
[1972]. LC79-160761.

Biography
ADE BD BEL BLA BOASE-5 BRO CHA CHABI DNB-1
DOY GRE GRET GRETB HAMM HAOXE JOHDB KUBA
KUJ1 MAGN MYE NCH PEE SHA WARBD WEBS

O'Brien, Sophie R. UNSEEN FRIENDS. pp. 216-232.
New York: Longmans, Green, 1912. LC12-26015.

Peters, Maureen. JEAN INGELOW, VICTORIAN
POETESS. [Totowa, N.J.]: Rowman and
Littlefield, [1972]. LC72-194422R.

Stedman, Eustace A. AN APPRECIATION [OF JEAN
INGELOW, WITH EXTRACTS FROM HER WORKS AND A
PORTRAIT]. London: Chiswick, 1935. BMC.

Obituary
ATHENAEUM 110 (24 July 1897), 129.
CRITIC 31, n.s. 28 (24 July 1897), 48.
NY TIMES (21 July 1897), 5:2.
REVIEW OF REVIEWS 16 (Sept 1897), 360.
TIMES (LONDON) (21 July 1897), 8:3.

INGRAM, ELEANOR MARIE. 1886-1921. U.S.

Biography
WOWWA WWWA-1

Iota, pseud. See CAFFYN, KATHLEEN MANNINGTON
(HUNT).

IRELAND

IRELAND, MARY ELIZA (HAINES). b.1834. U.S.

Biography
WILA   WOWWA   WWWA-4

Iron, Ralph, pseud. See SCHREINER, OLIVE EMILIE
ALBERTINA (SCHREINER) CRONWRIGHT.

IRWIN, FLORENCE. 1869?-1956. U.S.

Biography
AWO   BURK   WWNA

Obituary
NY TIMES (28 Sept 1956), 27:1.

IRWIN, INEZ (HAYNES) GILLMORE. 1873-1970. U.S.
    Inez Haynes Gillmore.

Biography
AWO   AWW   BURK   CON-102   KUT   NAWM   NCAB-F   OV2
REA   ROCK   THE   WEBS   WOWWA   WWNA   WWWA-5   WWWE

"Ines Haynes Irwin." In GIRLS WHO DID; STORIES
OF REAL GIRLS AND THEIR CAREERS, by Helen J.
Ferris and Virginia Moore. pp. 77-90. New
York: E.P. Dutton, [c1927]. LC27-18604.
juvenile literature

Irwin, M.E.F. See MONSELL, MARGARET EMMA FAITH
(IRWIN).

Irwin, Margaret. See MONSELL, MARGARET EMMA FAITH
(IRWIN).

IRWIN, VIOLET MARY. b.1881. U.S.

Biography
AWO   BURK   REA   WWNA

IVES, SARAH NOBLE. b.1864. U.S.

Biography
BURK   WOWWA   WWNA   WWWA-5

JACKSON, GABRIELLE EMILIE (SNOW). b. 1861. U.S.

Biography

BURK   WOWWA   WWWA-4

JACKSON, MARGARET (DOYLE). b.1868. England.

Biography

BURK

Jacob, Mrs. Arthur.   See JACOB, VIOLET MARY AUGUSTA
FREDERICA (KENNEDY-ERSKINE).

JACOB, VIOLET MARY AUGUSTA FREDERICA (KENNEDY-
ERSKINE). 1863-1946. Scotland.
            Mrs. Arthur Jacob

Biography

BRO   CAS   CHABI   NCH   PEE

Obituary

TIMES (LONDON) (11 Sept 1946), 7:5; tribute
(26 Sept), 7:5.

JACOBI, MARY CORINNA (PUTNAM). 1842-1906. U.S.

Autobiography

LIFE AND LETTERS OF MARY PUTNAM JACOBI, edited
by Ruth Putnam. New York: G.P. Putnam's Sons,
1925. LC25-5667.

"Physician, Teacher, Author." In MARY PUTNAM
JACOBI, M.D., A PATHFINDER IN MEDICINE WITH
SELECTIONS FROM HER WRITINGS ..., edited by
the Women's Medical Assoc. of New York City.
pp. xiii-xxxii. New York: G.P. Putnam's Sons,
1925. LC25-6636.

JACOBI

Biography
ADE APP AWW DAB HAMM LOGP MDWB NCAB-8 PRE
RIEG TWCB WARBD WEBS WILA WWWA-1

Hume, Ruth F. GREAT WOMEN OF MEDICINE.
   pp. 173-217. New York: Random, [1964].
   LC64-20645.

Truax, Rhoda. THE DOCTORS JACOBI. Boston:
   Little, Brown, 1952. LC52-5014.

Obituary
NY TIMES (12 June 1906), 9:5.

JAMES, FLORENCE ALICE (PRICE). 1857-1929. England.
   Florence Warden, pseud.

Biography
SHA-A WARBD

Obituary
TIMES (LONDON) (14 Mar 1929), 21:3.

James, Martha, pseud. See DOYLE, MARTHA CLAIRE
(MACGOWAN).

JAMES, WILHELMINA MARTHA.
         Austin Clare, pseud.
         Hope Everest, pseud.

Biography
WWWL

James, Winifred. See DE JAN, WINIFRED LEWELLIN
(JAMES).

JAMESON, ANNIE EDITH (FOSTER). 1868-1931. England.
         J.E. Buckrose, pseud.

Biography
HAMM ROCK WWLA WWWE WWWL

JAMESON

Obituary
TIMES (LONDON) (11 Aug 1931), 12:2.

JAMESON, MARGARET STORM. b.1897. England.
    m. Chapman
    Storm Jameson

Autobiography
JOURNEY FROM THE NORTH: AUTOBIOGRAPHY OF STORM
JAMESON. London: Collins; Harvill P., 1969-.
LC71-442886.

NO TIME LIKE THE PRESENT. New York: A.A. Knopf,
1933. LC33-18504.

Biography
ADC BERE BRO CHABI CON-81--84 CONO HAMM
KUL KUT MANBL MARBS MICB MYE NCH PEE RIC
ROCK SHO WAGCE WARLC WEBS WWWE WWWL

Jameson, Storm. See JAMESON, MARGARET STORM.

JAMISON, CECILIA VIETS (DAKIN) HAMILTON.
1837?-1909. U.S.
    Mrs. C.V. Jamison

Biography
AWW BURK DAB KNIB KUAA WARBD WEBS

Jamison, Mrs. C.V. See JAMISON, CECILIA VIETS
(DAKIN) HAMILTON.

JANIS, ELSIE. 1890-1956. U.S.
    Bierbower real surname; Janis stage name

Autobiography
THE BIG SHOW; MY SIX MONTHS WITH THE AMERICAN
EXPEDITIONARY FORCES. New York: Cosmopolitan
Book Corp., 1919. LC19-15617.

SO FAR, SO GOOD! AN AUTOBIOGRAPHY. New York:
E.P. Dutton, 1932. LC32-4670.

Biography
COY DAB-S6 NCAB-A WEBS WOWWA WWWA-3 WWWT

Obituary
NY TIMES (28 Feb 1956), 1:2.
OBIT1, 387-8.
TIMES (LONDON) (29 Feb 1956), 11:2.

JANVIER, MARGARET THOMSON. 1845-1913. U.S.
Margaret Vandegrift, pseud.

Biography
AWW BURK DAB KNIB KUAA NCAB-12 WARBD WOWWA
WWWA-1

JARBOE, MARY HALSEY (THOMAS). 1842-1921. U.S.
Thomas H. Brainerd, pseud.

Biography
HINK

JAY, EDITH KATHARINE SPICER. d.1901. England.
E. Livingston Prescott, pseud.

Biography
BEL WWW-1

Jay, W.M.L., pseud.   See WOODRUFF, JULIA LOUISA
MATILDA (CURTISS).

JENKINS, HESTER DONALDSON. 1869-1941. U.S.

Biography
WOWWA WWNA

Obituary
NY TIMES (24 Apr 1941), 21:4.

JENNER, KATHERINE LEE (RAWLINGS). b.1853. England.
Mrs. Henry Jenner
Katherine Lee, pseud.

Biography
WWLA   WWWE   WWWL

Jenner, Mrs. Henry. See JENNER, KATHERINE LEE
(RAWLINGS).

JEPHSON, HARRIET JULIA (CAMPBELL). England.
Lady Jephson

Biography
WOWWA

Jephson, Lady.   See JEPHSON, HARRIET JULIA
(CAMPBELL).

Jesse, F. Tennyson.   See HARWOOD, FRYNIWYD TENNYSON
(JESSE).

JEWELL, LOUISE POND. 1867-1943. U.S.

Biography
BURK   COY   WWWA-2

JEWETT, SARAH ORNE. 1849-1909. U.S.

Autobiography
LETTERS OF SARAH ORNE JEWETT, edited by Annie
Fields. Boston: Houghton Mifflin, 1911.
LC11-26427.

LETTERS OF SARAH ORNE JEWETT NOW IN THE COLBY
COLLEGE LIBRARY, edited by Carl J. Weber.
Waterville: Colby College Press, 1947.
LC47-12323.

Biography
ADE AML AMR APP AUC AW AWW BD BERE BRO
BURK CAS CHA CON-108 DAB HAOXA HAOXE HARKF
JOHDB KRO KUAA KUJ1 LOGP MAG MCW MDWB MYE
NAW NCAB-1 NOV NPW PEA PRE REA RICDA
SOME-15 TWCB VDW WAGCA WARBD WEBS WENW
WILA WIN WWWA-1 WWWL

Cary, Richard. SARAH ORNE JEWETT. New York: Twayne, [c1962]. LC62-13673.

Donovan, Josephine. SARAH ORNE JEWETT. New York: F. Ungar, c1980. LC80-5334.

Frost, John E. SARAH ORNE JEWETT. Kittery Point, Maine: Gundalow Club, [c1960]. LC60-11676.

Howe, Helen H. THE GENTLE AMERICANS, 1864-1960: BIOGRAPHY OF A BREED. pp. 83-87, 92-94. Westport, Conn.: Greenwood, 1979, c1965. LC78-24027.

Howe, M.A. MEMORIES OF A HOSTESS; A CHRONICLE OF EMINENT FRIENDSHIPS DRAWN CHIEFLY FROM THE DIARIES OF MRS. JAMES T. FIELDS. pp. 281-305. Boston: Atlantic Monthly, [c1922]. LC22-19693.

_____. WHO LIVED HERE? A BAKER'S DOZEN OF HISTORIC NEW ENGLAND HOUSES AND THEIR OCCUPANTS. pp. 88-100. Boston: Little, Brown, 1952. LC52-5872.

Matthiessen, Francis O. SARAH ORNE JEWETT. Boston: Houghton Mifflin, 1929. LC29-9532.

Richards, Laura E. STEPPING WESTWARD. pp. 361-72. New York: D. Appleton, 1931. LC31-31652.

Spofford, Harriet E. A LITTLE BOOK OF FRIENDS. pp. 21-42. Boston: Little, Brown, 1916. LC16-19447.

Thorp, Margaret F. SARAH ORNE JEWETT. Minneapolis: Univ. of Minnesota Press, [1966]. LC66-64594.

Obituary
BOSTON EVENING TRANSCRIPT (25 June 1909), 5, 10.
NY TIMES (25 June 1909), 9:4.
OUTLOOK 92 (3 July 1909), 542-3.
STANDARD (CHICAGO) 56 (17 July 1909), 15.
TIMES (LONDON) (26 July 1909), 13:3.

JEWETT

Bibliography
Nagel, Gwen L. and James Nagel. SARAH ORNE
   JEWETT: A REFERENCE GUIDE. Boston: G.K. Hall,
   c1978. LC77-7392R.

Weber, Clara C. and Carl J. Weber. A
   BIBLIOGRAPHY OF THE PUBLISHED WRITINGS OF SARAH
   ORNE JEWETT. Waterville, Me.: Colby College
   Press, 1949. LC49-10893.

Jocelyn, Mrs. Robert.   See   RODEN, ADA MARIA
   (JENYNS) JOCELYN.

John, Alix, pseud.   See   JONES, ALICE.

JOHN, EUGENIE. 1825-1887. Germany.
         E. Marlitt, pseud.

                    Biography
   CAS   WARBD

JOHNSON, AMELIA E. b.1859. U.S.
         Mrs. A.E. Johnson

                    Biography
   MAJ   PENN   RUSB

JOHNSON, ANNA. 1860-1943. U.S.
         Hope Daring, pseud.

                    Biography
   ALY   AWW   BURK   WOWWA   WWWA-3

Johnson, Annie Fellows.   See   JOHNSTON, ANNIE
   (FELLOWS).

JOHNSON, ELIZABETH WINTHROP. b.1850. U.S.

                    Biography
   BURK   WOWWA   WWWA-4

199

Johnson, Fanny Kemble. See COSTELLO, FANNY KEMBLE
(JOHNSON).

JOHNSON, LILLIAN (HARTMAN). 1862?-1941. U.S.

Obituary
NY TIMES (12 Nov 1941), 24:2.

Johnson, Mrs. A.E. See JOHNSON, AMELIA E.

JOHNSON, VIRGINIA WALES. 1849-1916. U.S.

Biography
APP BURK DAB KUAA NCAB-13 TWCB WARBD WWWA-1

JOHNSTON, ANNIE (FELLOWS). 1863-1931. U.S.
Annie Fellows Johnson

Autobiography
THE LAND OF THE LITTLE COLONEL; REMINISCENCE AND
AUTOBIOGRAPHY. Boston: L.C. Page, [c1929].
LC29-20421.

Biography
BAN BURK DAB HAOXA KNIB KUJ1 KUT LIB-17
NAW NCAB-13 REA WEBS WOWWA WWWA-1

Boyer, Mary G., ed. ARIZONA IN LITERATURE; A
COLLECTION OF THE BEST WRITINGS OF ARIZONA
AUTHORS FROM EARLY SPANISH DAYS TO THE
PRESENT TIME. pp. 254-5. New York: Haskell
House, 1970. LC78-129967.

Obituary
PUBLISHERS WEEKLY 120 (10 Oct 1931), 1691.

JOHNSTON, GRACE LESLIE KEITH. Scotland.
Leslie Keith, pseud.

Biography
BD

JOHNSTON, MARY. 1870-1936. U.S.

Biography

ADE   AMN   AWW   BD   BERE   BURK   CHA   DAB-S2   FARR
HAL   HAMM   HAOXA   HARKF   JOHDB   JONE   KUL   KUT
LIB   LOGP   MAG   MAN   MARBS   NAW   NCAB-10,C   OV
OV2   PRE   REA   RICDA   RUB   RUT   SHA-A   SOU   TWCB
TWCR   WAGCA   WARBD   WARD   WARLC   WEBS   WOWWA
WWWA-1   WYN

Cella, C. Ronald. MARY JOHNSTON. Boston:
Twayne, 1981. LC80-27690.

Obituary

COMMONWEAL 24 (22 May 1936), 83.
NY TIMES (10 May 1936), II 9:1.
PUBLISHERS WEEKLY 129 (16 May 1936), 1958.
SAT REVIEW OF LIT 14 (23 May 1936), 8.
TIME 27 (18 May 1936), 53.

Bibliography

Longest, George C. THREE VIRGINIA WRITERS: MARY
JOHNSTON ...: A REFERENCE GUIDE. pp. 1-66.
Boston: G.K. Hall, c1978. LC77-9566R.

JONES, ALICE. 1853-1933. Canada.
        Alix John, pseud.

Biography

MDCB   MOR   MORGA   STOXC

JONES, ALICE ILGENFRITZ. d.1906. U.S.

Biography

MOR2   WARBD

JONES, CLARA AUGUSTA. 1839-1905. U.S.
        Clara Augusta, pseud.
        Hero Strong, pseud.
        Kate Thorn, pseud.

Biography

JOHH   JOHH2   ROCK

Jones, D. Egerton. See CALLAHAN, DORIS EGERTON (JONES).

Jones, E.B.C. See LUCAS, EMILY BEATRIX COURSOLLES (JONES).

JONES, ENID (BAGNOLD). 1889-1981. England.
Enid Bagnold

Autobiography
A DIARY WITHOUT DATES. New York: W. Morrow,
1935. LC35-27393.
Diary of work in hospital during World
War I written when she was 19.

ENID BAGNOLD'S AUTOBIOGRAPHY (FROM 1889).
London: Heinemann, 1969. LC75-457120R.

LETTERS TO FRANK HARRIS AND OTHER FRIENDS,
edited and with an introduction by R.P. Lister.
Andoversford [Eng].: Whittington Press, [1980].
LC80-508346.

Biography
BERE BRO CEL CON-N5 CUR-1964 DOY DR HAOXE
KUT LON MAT MYE NCH NOV RIC SHO
SOME-1,25 WEBS WWWE

Obituary
CON-103.
CUR-1981.
MACLEANS 94 (13 Apr 1981), 4.
NY TIMES (1 Apr 1981), IV 23:5.
NEWSWEEK 97 (13 Apr 1981), 80.
PUBLISHERS WEEKLY 219 (24 Apr 1981), 35.
TIME 117 (13 APR 1981), 85.
TIMES (LONDON) (1 APR 1981), 16:6.
WASHINGTON POST (3 Apr 1981).

JONES, MABEL (CRONISE). 1850-1920. U.S.

Biography
ALY COY WOWWA WWWA-1

Jones, S. Carlton.   See   JONES,   SUSAN   CARLETON.

JONES, SUSAN CARLETON. 1864-1926. U.S.
      S. Carleton, pseud.
      Carleton-Milecete. joint pseud. with
        Helen Milecete
      S. Carlton Jones

ROCK   Biography

JORDAN, ELIZABETH GARVER. 1867-1947. U.S.

              Autobiography
THREE ROUSING CHEERS. New York: D. Appleton-
   Century, 1938. LC38-27234.

                Biography
AWO   BICA   BOOCA-2   BURG   BURK   HAMM   LOGP   MARBS
NCAB-40   REA   ROSS   TIT   WEBS   WILA   WOWWA   WWNA
WWWA-2   WWWL

                Obituary
AMERICA 76 (8 Mar 1947), 620.
CATHOLIC WORLD 165 (Apr 1947), 83.
NY TIMES (25 Feb 1947), 25:1.
TIME 49 (10 Mar 1947), 94.
WILSON 21 (Apr 1947), 572+.

Jordan, Kate.   See   VERMILYE, KATE (JORDAN).

Josiah Allen's Wife.   See   HOLLEY, MARIETTA.

JOYCE, LILIAN ELWYN (ELLIOTT). b.1884. England.
      L. Elwyn Elliott

BURK   Biography

JUDAH, MARY JAMESON. 1851-1930. U.S.

BAN
<u>Biography</u>

JUSTICE, MAIBELLE HEICKS (MONROE). b.1871. U.S.

BAN
<u>Biography</u>

Katydid, pseud. See McKINNEY, KATE (SLAUGHTER).

KATZENBERGER, FRANCES ISABELLE. 1861-1938. U.S.

COY   Biography

KAUFFMAN, CATHERINE. 1859-1948. U.S.

COY   Biography

KAUFFMAN, RUTH (HAMMITT). d.1952. U.S.

AWW   BURK   WWWE   Biography

KAUP, ELIZABETH BARTOL (DEWING). b.1885. U.S.
        E.B. Dewing

BURK   WAR   Biography

Kaye-Smith, Sheila. See FRY, SHEILA (KAYE-SMITH).

KEATS, GWENDOLINE. d.1910. England.
        Zack, pseud.

BD   WARBD   Biography

Keays, H.A.   See KEAYS, HERSILIA A. MITCHELL
(COPP).

Keays, H.A. Mitchell.   See   KEAYS, HERSILIA A.
MITCHELL (COPP).

KEAYS, HERSILIA A. MITCHELL (COPP). 1861-1910?
U.S.
H.A. Keays
H.A. Mitchell Keays

Biography
WOWWA   WWWA-4

KEDDIE, HENRIETTA. 1827-1914. Scotland.
Sarah Tytler, pseud.

Biography
BD   WARBD   WWWL

Obituary
NY TIMES (10 Jan 1914), 9:5.
TIMES (LONDON) (9 Jan 1914), 9:4.

KEELER, LUCY ELLIOT. 1864-1930. U.S.

Biography
COY   WOWWA

Obituary
LIBRARIES 35 (May 1930), 199-200.

KEELING, ELSA D'ESTERRE. 1860-1935. Ireland.

Biography
ODP

Keith, Leslie, pseud.   See   JOHNSTON, GRACE LESLIE
KEITH.

Keith, Marian, pseud.   See   MACGREGOR, MARY ESTHER
(MILLER).

KELLEY, EMMA DUNHAM. U.S.
Forget-Me-Not, pseud.

Biography
RUSB

206

KELLEY, ETHEL MAY. b.1878. U.S.

ALY   WWNA
$\underline{\text{Biography}}$

KELLNER, ELISABETH WILLARD (BROOKS). d.1916. U.S.

WOWWA   WWWA-1
$\underline{\text{Biography}}$

KELLY, ELEANOR (MERCEIN). b.1880. U.S.

$\underline{\text{Biography}}$
AWO AWW BURK KUAT KUT OV RICK WEBS WWNA
WWWE

KELLY, FLORENCE (FINCH). 1858-1939. U.S.

$\underline{\text{Autobiography}}$
FLOWING STREAM; THE STORY OF FIFTY-SIX YEARS IN
AMERICAN NEWSPAPER LIFE. New York: E.P.
Dutton, 1939. LC39-27667.

$\underline{\text{Biography}}$
AWO BURK WOWWA WWNA WWWA-1

$\underline{\text{Obituary}}$
CUR-1940.
NY TIMES (18 Dec 1939), 23:3.
PUBLISHERS WEEKLY 136 (23 Dec 1939), 2259.

KELLY, JOAN COLLINGS (SUTHERLAND). 1890-1947.
England.
    Joan Sutherland, pseud.

$\underline{\text{Biography}}$
WWLA WWWE WWWL

$\underline{\text{Obituary}}$
TIMES (LONDON) (7 June 1947), 4:6.

KELLY, MYRA. 1850-1910. U.S.
   m. Macnaughton

Biography
AWW   BURK   DAB   NCAB-24   WEBS   WWWA-2

Obituary
NY TIMES (1 Apr 1910), 11:5.

KENEALY, ANNSLEY.

Biography
WWWL

KENEALY, ARABELLA. 1864-1938. England.

Biography
BD   HAMM   WWWE   WWWL

Obituary
TIMES (LONDON) (21 Nov 1938), 14:4.

KENNARD, MARY E. (LAING). 1850-1914. England.

Biography
BD   BLA

KENNEDY, SARA BEAUMONT (CANNON). d.1921. U.S.

Biography
ALY   BURK   KNIB   WOWWA   WWWA-1

KENNY, LOUISE M. (DUNNE) STACPOOLE. b.1885?
Ireland.

Biography
BRI   CLE   CRO   WWWL

KENT, NORA. b.1899. England.

Biography
AWWW   CON-Pl

KENTON, EDNA. 1876-1954. U.S.

Biography
WOWWA   WWWA-3

KENYON, CAMILLA EUGENIA (LIES). b.1876. U.S.

Biography
HINK

KERNAHAN, MARY JEAN HICKLING (GWYNNE) BETTANY.
1857-1941. England.
    m. (1)Bettany (2)Kernahan
    Mrs. Coulson Kernahan
    Identified as Jeannie Gwynne Bettany
    Kernahan in BMC.

Biography
FUR NCH WEBS WWLA WWWE WWWL

Obituary
NY TIMES (18 Jan 1941), 15:4.

Kernahan, Mrs. Coulson. See KERNAHAN, MARY JEAN
HICKLING (GWYNNE) BETTANY.

KERR, SOPHIE. 1880-1965. U.S.
    m. Underwood

Biography
BURK DAB-S7 KUT OV OV2 WAR WEBS WWNA
WWWA-4 WWWL

Obituary
NY TIMES (8 Feb 1965), 25:3.
PUBLISHERS WEEKLY 186 (1 Mar 1965), 52.

KETTLE, MARY ROSA STUART. d.1895. England.
Called herself Rosa MacKenzie-Kettle
assuming her mother's maiden name as
a Christian name.

Biography
BOASE-5 WARBD

Obituary
TIMES (LONDON) (23 Mar 1895), 12:3.

KEYES, FRANCES PARKINSON (WHEELER). 1885-1970. U.S.

Autobiography
ALL FLAGS FLYING; REMINISCENCES OF FRANCES
PARKINSON KEYES. New York: McGraw-Hill, [1972].
LC70-38971.

THE COST OF A BEST SELLER. New York: Messner,
[1950]. LC50-9958.

ROSES IN DECEMBER. Garden City, N.Y.: Doubleday,
1960. LC60-13740L.

Biography
AWO AWW BERE BICA BOOCA-5 BREI BRO BURK
CEL CEL2 CON-N7 KUT KUTS OBRIR PEA RIC
TWCR WAR WARLC WEBS WWNA WWWA-5

Obituary
ANTIQUARIAN BOOKMAN (20-27 July 1970).
CON-25--28R.
NY TIMES (4 July 1970), 21:2.
NEWSWEEK 76 (13 July 1970), 71.
PUBLISHERS WEEKLY 198 (27 July 1970), 52.
TIME 96 (13 July 1970), 64.
WASHINGTON POST (4 July 1970).

KIDD, BEATRICE ETHEL. b.1867.
Mark Winterton, pseud.

Biography
WWWE

KILVERT, MARGARET (CAMERON) LEWIS. 1867-1947. U.S.
Margaret Cameron

Biography
ALY AWO WEBS WOWWA WWNA

Obituary
NY TIMES (5 Feb 1947), 23:5.
WILSON 21 (Apr 1947), 572.

KING, GEORGIANA GODDARD. 1871-1939. U.S.

Biography
BURK WWNA

Obituary
NY TIMES (5 May 1939), 23:4.

KING, GRACE ELIZABETH. 1852-1932. U.S.

Autobiography
MEMORIES OF A SOUTHERN WOMAN OF LETTERS.
Freeport, N. Y.: Books for Libraries, [1971].
LC76-146863.

Biography
AMR AWW BAS BURK DAB HAOXA JONE KIR LIB
MAN MYE NAW NCAB-2 ORG RUB RUT SOU TWCB
WARBD WOWWA WWWA-1 WYN

Kirby, David K. GRACE KING. Boston: Twayne,
1980. LC79-17988.

Rand, Clayton. STARS IN THEIR EYES; DREAMERS AND
BUILDERS IN LOUISIANA. pp. 202-3. Gulfport,
Miss.: Dixie, 1953. LC54-266.

Obituary
Dart, Henry P. "Death of Grace King." LOUISIANA
HISTORICAL QUARTERLY 15 (Apr 1932), 330.
Faust, Marie E. "In Memoriam: Grace Kelly."
BOOKMAN 75 (Aug 1932), 360-1.
PUBLISHERS WEEKLY 121 (30 Jan 1932), 528.

KING

KING, MAUDE EGERTON (HINE). 1867-1927. England.

Obituary
TIMES (LONDON) (25 Apr 1927), 19:3.

KINGSBURY, SARA. 1876-1948. U.S.

Biography
BAN   COY

KINGSCOTE, ADELINE GEORGINA ISABELLA (WOLFF).
d.1908. England.
Lucas Cleeve, pseud.

Biography
WWWL

Obituary
TIMES (LONDON) (16 Sept 1908), 11:3.

KINGSLEY, FLORENCE (MORSE). 1859-1937. U.S.

Biography
ALY   BURK   COY   NCAB-11   WOWWA   WWWA-1

KINKAID, MARY HOLLAND (MACNEISH). 1861-1948. U.S.

Biography
SHO   WOWWA   WWNA   WWWA-2

Obituary
NY TIMES (21 Oct 1948), 27:3.

Kinkead, Eleanor Talbot.   See SHORT, ELEANOR TALBOT
(KINKEAD).

Kinkead, Nellie Talbot.   See   SHORT, ELEANOR TALBOT
(KINKEAD).

KIRK, DOLLY WILLIAMS. U.S.

WWWA-5

Biography

Kirk, Eleanor, pseud.   See   AMES, ELEANOR   MARIA
(EASTERBROOK).

KIRK, ELLEN WARNER (OLNEY). 1842-1928. U.S.

Biography
APP   AWW   BD   BURK   JOHBD   LOGP   NCAB-1   WARBD
WILA   WOWWA   WWWA-4

KIRKLAND, WINIFRED MARGARETTA. 1872-1943. U.S.
James Priceman, pseud.

Biography
ALY   AWO   BURK   JO   WOWWA   WWNA   WWWA-2

Obituary
CUR-1943.
NY TIMES (15 May 1943), 15:3.
WILSON 18 (Sept 1943), 8.

Kirschner, Aloysia.   See   KIRSCHNER, LULA.

KIRSCHNER, LULA. 1854-1934. Russia.
Ossip Schubin, pseud.
Aloysia Kirschner

Biography
GAR

Klingle, George, pseud.   See   HOLMES,   GEORGIANA
(KLINGLE).

KNAPP, ADELINE. 1860-1909. U.S.

Biography
WWWA-1

KNEELAND, CLARISSA ABIA. b.1878.

WWNA

Biography

KNIGHT, ADELE (FERGUSON). b.1867. U.S.

Biography
ALY AWO WWNA WWWA-4

KNOWLES, MABEL WINIFRED. 1875-1949. England.
Lester Lurgan, pseud.
May Wynne, pseud.

Biography
BRI ROCK TWCR WWLA WWWE

Obituary
NY TIMES (1 Dec 1949), 31:3.
TIMES (LONDON) (30 Nov 1949), 4:5; (5 Dec), 7:6.

KNOX, JANETTE HILL. b.1845. U.S.

Biography
WILA WOWWA

KOVALEVSKAIA, SOF'IA VASIL'EVNA (KORVIN-KRUKOVSKAIA). 1850-1891. Russia.
Sophia Kovalevsky

Autobiography
SONYA KOVALEVSKY; HER RECOLLECTIONS OF CHILDHOOD,
translated by Isabel F. Hapgood. With a
biography by Anna C. Leffler, translated by A.M.
Clive Bayley, and a biographical note by Lily
Wolffsohn. New York: Century, 1895. LC02-20573R.

A RUSSIAN CHILDHOOD, translated, edited and
introduced by Beatrice Stillman. New York:
Springer-Verlag, 1978. LC78-12955.

Biography
ADE CHABI HAMM HAN MARL MDWB SCHM WARBD
WEBS

214

Cajanello, Anna C. SONIA KOVALEVSKY, BIOGRAPHY
AND AUTOBIOGRAPHY. I. MEMOIR, by A.C. Leffler
.... II. REMINISCENCES OF CHILDHOOD, written by
herself, translated by Louise von Cossel. New
York: Macmillan, 1895. NUC.

Kennedy, Don H. LITTLE SPARROW: A PORTRAIT OF
SOPHIA KOVALEVSKY. Athens: Ohio Univ. Press,
c1983. LC82-12405.

Kovalevsky, Sophia. See KOVALEVSKAIA, SOF'IA
VASIL'EVNA (KORVIN-KRUKOVSKAIA).

KRAUSE, LYDA FARRINGTON. 1864-1939. U.S.

Biography
BURK   WOWWA   WWWA-1

Obituary
NY TIMES (1 Nov 1939), 23:5.

KROUT, CAROLINE VIRGINIA. 1853-1931. U.S.
Caroline Brown, pseud.

Biography
BAN   BURK   WOWWA

KURZ, ISOLDE. 1853-1944. Germany.

Biography
FLE

KYLE, RUBY BERYL. U.S.

Biography
KNIB

LADD, ANNA COLEMAN (WATTS). 1878-1939. U.S.

Biography
AWO   BURK   WEBS   WOWWA   WWNA   WWWA-1

Obituary
NY TIMES (4 June 1939), 8:8.

LAFFAN, BERTHA JANE (GRUNDY) LEITH ADAMS. d.1912.
England.
         Mrs. Leith Adams
         Mrs. R.S. De C. Laffan
         Mrs. R.S. De Courcy Laffan
         Bertha Jane (Grundy) Leith-Adams
         Mrs. Leith-Adams

                  Biography
BD   BLA   WWWL

                  Obituary
TIMES (LONDON) (7 Sept 1912), 9:5.

Laffan, Mrs. R.S. De C.   See   LAFFAN, BERTHA JANE
(GRUNDY) LEITH ADAMS.

Laffan, Mrs. R.S. De Courcy.   See   LAFFAN, BERTHA
JANE (GRUNDY) LEITH ADAMS.

LAGERLOF, SELMA OTTILIANA LOUISA. 1858-1940. Sweden.

                  Autobiography
THE DIARY OF SELMA LAGERLOF, translated by Velma
S. Howard. Millwood, N.Y.: Kraus, 1975, c1936.
LC74-20821.

MJARBACKA, translated by Velma S. Howard.
Detroit: Gale, 1974, 1926. LC70-167024.
Recollections of the author's youth.

                  217

MEMORIES OF MY CHILDHOOD: FURTHER YEARS AT
MJARBACKA, translated by Velma S. Howard.
Millwood, N.Y.: Kraus, 1975, c1934.
LC75-5996.

Biography
ADE BERE CAS CDME CHABI COL CON-108 COOPA
DOY FLE GUS HAMM HAR KUJ1 KUL KUT MAG
MARB MCCNP MCW MON OP PEEU RIC SEYS
SOME-15 WARLC WEBS WWLA WWWE

Berendsohn, Walter A. SELMA LAGERLOF; HER LIFE
AND WORK, translated by George F. Timpson.
Port Washington, N.Y.: Kennikat, [1968], 1931.
LC67-27576.

Budd, John, comp. EIGHT SCANDINAVIAN NOVELISTS:
CRITICISM AND REVIEWS IN ENGLISH. pp. 17-21.
Westport, Conn.: Greenwood, 1981. LC80-24895.

Gustafson, Alrik. A HISTORY OF SWEDISH
LITERATURE. pp. 305-16. Published for the
American-Scandinavian Foundation by the Univ.
of Minnesota Press, [1961]. LC61-7722.

Larsen. Hanna A. SELMA LAGERLOF. Millwood,
N.Y.: Kraus, 1975, c1936. LC74-20796.

Maule, Harry E. SELMA LAGERLOF; THE WOMAN, HER
WORK, HER MESSAGE, INCLUDING LIBERAL QUOTATION
FROM DR. LAGERLOF'S OWN AUTOBIOGRAPHICAL
WRITINGS AND FROM SOME OF HER CRITICS. Garden
City, N.Y.: Doubleday, Page, 1926. LC26-14537.

Moffat, Mary J. and Charlotte Painter, comps.
REVELATIONS: DIARIES OF WOMEN. pp. 314-24. New
York: Random, [1974]. LC74-8040.

Pace, Dixie A. VALIANT WOMEN. pp. 78-80. New
York:Vantage, [1972]. OCLC 1050350.

Vrieze, Folkerdina S. FACT AND FICTION IN THE
AUTOBIOGRAPHICAL WORKS OF SELMA LAGERLOF.
Assen, Netherlands: Van Gorcum, 1958.
LC62-2611.

Obituary

CUR-1940.
NY TIMES (17 Mar 1940), 49:1.
NEWSWEEK 15 (25 Mar 1940), 8.
PUBLISHERS WEEKLY 137 (23 Mar 1940), 1232.
SCHOOL AND SOCIETY 51 (23 Mar 1940), 379.
TIME 35 (25 Mar 1940) 71.
TIMES (LONDON) (18 Mar 1940), 10:3.

LAMB, MARY ELIZABETH (JORDAN). b.1839. U.S.

Biography

BAN   GRE   WOWWA

LA MOTTE, ELLEN NEWBOLD. 1873-1961. U.S.

Biography

AWO   WWWA-4

Obituary

NY TIMES (4 Mar 1961), 23:5.

Lancaster, G.B., pseud. See LYTTLETON, EDITH
JOAN.

LANDA, GERTRUDE (GORDON). d.1941. England.
full name Annie Gertrude

Obituary

TIMES (LONDON) (2 July 1941), 2:6.

LANE, ANNA (EICHBERG) KING. 1853-1927. U.S.
, Mrs. John Lane

Biography

WOWWA   WWWA-4

LANE, ELINOR (MACARTNEY). b.1864/73-1909. U.S.

Biography

BURK   LIB   WWWA-1

LANE

Obituary
NY TIMES (17 Mar 1909), 9:3.

Lane, Laura M. See LUFFMANN, LAURETTA MARIE
(LANE).

Lane, Mrs. John. See LANE, ANNA (EICHBERG) KING.

LANE, ROSE (WILDER). 1887-1968. U.S.

Autobiography
THE LADY AND THE TYCOON; LETTERS OF ROSE WILDER
LAND AND JASPER CRANE, edited by Roger L.
MacBride. Caldwell, Idaho: Caxton Printers,
1973. LC72-78366R.
Letters--1946-1966.

Biography
AWO AWW BURK CON-102 KUT NCAB-54 REA ROSS
SOME-28,29 WEBS WWNA WWWA-5

Obituary
NY TIMES (1 Nov 1968), 47:4.

LANGBRIDGE, ROSAMOND. b.1880. Ireland.

Biography
BRI CLE WWWE WWWL

Langtry, Lillie. See DE BATHE, EMILIE CHARLOTTE
(LANGTRY).

LANZA, CLARA (HAMMOND). 1859-1939. U.S.

Biography
BD WARBD WILA WWNA WWWA-4

Obituary
NY TIMES (15 July 1939), 15:6.

LAPAGE, GERTRUDE. b.1870. U.S.

Biography
WOWWA

LAPAUZE, JEANNE (LOISEAU). 1860-1921. France.
Daniel Leseur, pseud.

Biography
WARBD   WEBS

Obituary
NY TIMES (4 Jan 1921), 13:3.

LATIMER, MARY ELIZABETH (WORMELEY). 1822-1904. U.S.

Biography
AWW   BURK   DAB   KUAA   LOGP   NCAB-9   TWCB   WILA
WWWA-1

Obituary
NY TIMES (5 Jan 1904), 1:4.

LAUDER, MARIA ELSIE TURNER. Canada.

Biography
MOR

LAUGHLIN, CLARA ELIZABETH. 1873-1941. U.S.

Biography
ALY   AWO   BURK   WAG   WWNA

Obituary
CUR-1941.
PUBLISHERS WEEKLY 139 (15 Mar 1941), 1212.
TIME 37 (17 Mar 1941), 63.
WILSON 15 (Apr 1941), 614.

Laut, A.C.   See   LAUT, AGNES CHRISTINA.

221

LAUT, AGNES CHRISTINA. 1871-1936. Canada.
        A.C. Laut

Biography
AWW   BURK   KUJ1   KUJ2   MDCB   MOR2   MORGA   REA
STOXC   SY   THOMC   WEBS   WOWWA   WWNA   WWWA-1

Obituary
AMERICAN HISTORICAL REVIEW 42 (Jan 1937), 417.
TIMES (LONDON) (19 Nov 1936), 19:1.
WILSON 11 (Dec 1936), 234.

LAWLESS, EMILY. 1845-1913. Ireland.

Biography
BD   BERE   BRI   CHA   CLE   CRO   DIL   HAOXE   KUBA
MYE   NCH   ODP   SHO   WARBD   WEBS   WWW-1

Obituary
NY TIMES (24 Oct 1913), 11:5.
TIMES (LONDON) (23 Oct 1913), 11:4.

Lawrence, Albert, pseud. See   LAWRENCE, ALBERTA
ELIZA INEZ (CHAMBERLAIN).

LAWRENCE, ALBERTA ELIZA INEZ (CHAMBERLAIN). b.1875.
U.S.
        Albert Lawrence, pseud.

Biography
AWO   BURK   COY   WWNA

LAWRENCE, LOU. 1854-1932. U.S.

Biography
COY

Lawrence, Edith, pseud.   See BAILEY, EDITH LAWRENCE
(BLACK).

LAWSON, JESSIE (KERR). 1838-1917. Canada.
      Mrs. J. Kerr Lawson

Biography
MDCB

Lawson, Mrs. J. Kerr. See LAWSON, JESSIE (KERR).

LEA, FANNY HEASLIP. 1884-1955. U.S.
      m. Agee

Biography
AWO AWW BURK KUT NCAB-42 REA WEBS WWNA
WWWA-3

Obituary
NY TIMES (14 Jan 1955), 21:2.

LEAN, FLORENCE (MARRYAT) CHURCH. 1837-1899.
England.
      Florence Marryat

Biography
BLA BOASE-6 CHABI DNB-1 FUR JOHH NCH SHO
WARBD WEBS

Obituary
ILLUS LONDON NEWS (4 Nov 1899), 645; (16 Dec),
  890.
NY TIMES (28 Oct 1899), 7:2.
PUBLISHERS WEEKLY 56 (1899), 843.

LEBLANC, GEORGETTE. 1869-1941. France.

Autobiography
SOUVENIRS; MY LIFE WITH MAETERLINCK, translated
  by Janet Flanner. New York: E.P. Dutton,
  [c1932]. LC32-7384.

Obituary
NY TIMES (29 Oct 1941), 23:3.

LE BLOND, ELIZABETH ALICE FRANCES (HAWKINS-WHITSHED) BURNABY MAIN. 1860-1934. England.
>>>>Mrs. Aubrey Le Blond
>>>>Mrs. Main
>>>>m. (1)Burnaby (2)Main (3)Le Blond

>>>>>>Autobiography
DAY IN, DAY OUT. London: J. Lane, [1928].
>>OCLC 8957860.

>>>>>>Biography
MDWB WWLA WWWE WWWL

Le Blond, Mrs. Aubrey. See LE BLOND, ELIZABETH ALICE FRANCES (HAWKINS-WHITSHED) BURNABY MAIN.

LEE, ALICE LOUISE. 1868-1952. U.S.

>>>>>>Biography
ALY AWO BURK WOWWA WWWA-4

>>>>>>Obituary
NY TIMES (4 Apr 1952), 25:4.

LEE, HELENA (CRUMETT). b.1867. U.S.
>>>>Mrs. John Clarence Lee

>>>>>>Biography
WOWWA WWNA

LEE, JENNETTE BARBOUR (PERRY). 1860-1951. U.S.

>>>>>>Biography
BURK MAN MARBS NCAB-A WARBD WEBS

Lee, Katherine, pseud. See JENNER, KATHERINE LEE (RAWLINGS).

LEE, MARGARET. 1841-1914. U.S.

>>>>>>Biography
BURK NCAB-15 WOWWA WWWA-1

Lee, Marian, pseud. See COMSTOCK, ANNA (BOTSFORD).

LEE, MARY CATHERINE (JENKINS). d.1927. U.S.

Biography
WWNA   WWWA-5

LEE, MARY (CHAPPELL). 1849-1932. U.S.
Mrs. Frank Lee

Biography
COY   WWNA

Lee, Mrs. Frank. See LEE, MARY (CHAPPELL).

Lee, Mrs. John Clarence. See LEE, HELENA (CRUMETT).

LEE, SUSAN RICHMOND. England.
Curtis Yorke, pseud.

Biography
BD   WWWL

Lee, Vernon, pseud. See PAGET, VIOLET.

LE FEUVRE, AMY. d.1929. England.
Mary Thurston Dodge, pseud.

Obituary
TIMES (LONDON) (3 May 1929), 10:4.

LEIGHTON, MARIE FLORA BARBARA (CONNOR). d.1941.
England.

Biography
WARLC   WWLA   WWWE

Leighton, Clare. TEMPESTUOUS PETTICOAT; THE
STORY OF AN INVINCIBLE EDWARDIAN. New York:
Rinehart, 1947. LC47-30125R.

Obituary
TIMES (LONDON) (4 Feb 1941), 9:3.

Leith-Adams, Bertha Jane (Grundy). See LAFFAN,
BERTHA JANE (GRUNDY) LEITH ADAMS.

Leith-Adams, Mrs. See LAFFAN, BERTHA JANE (GRUNDY)
LEITH ADAMS.

Lemon, Ida. See HILDYARD, IDA JANE (LEMON).

Lemore, Clara. See ROBERTS, CLARA (LEMORE).

Lenore, pseud. See ROWLAND, K. ALICE.

LEONARD, MARY (FINLEY). b.1862. U.S.

Biography
ALY   BURK   KNIB   WOWWA   WWWA-4

LEONARD, MARY HALL. 1847-1921. U.S.

Biography
ALY   NCAB-20   WWWA-1

LEROY, AMELIE CLAIRE. b.1851. England.
Esme Stuart, pseud.

Biography
BD   WARBD

Leslie, Henrietta, pseud. See SCHUETZE, GLADYS
HENRIETTA (RAPHAEL).

Lesuer, Daniel, pseud. See LAPAUZE, JEANNE (LOUSEAU).

Letts, W.M. See LETTS, WINIFRED MABEL.

LETTS, WINIFRED MABEL. 1882-1972. England.
    m. Verschoyle
    W.M. Letts

Biography
BRI   WEBS   WWLA   WWWE   WWWL

LEVERSON, ADA. 1865-1933. England.

Biography
BERE   KUTS   MDWB   NPW   WARLC

Brown, John M. "Edwardian Spinx." In AS THEY
   APPEAR. pp. 11-17. Westport, Conn.: Greenwood,
   [1971, c1952]. LC71-138208.

Burkhart, Charles. ADA LEVERSON. New York:
   Twayne, 1973. LC72-13370.

Wyndham, Violet. THE SPHINX AND HER CIRCLE; A
   BIOGRAPHICAL SKETCH OF ADA LEVERSON, 1862-1933.
   [London]: A. Deutsch, [1963]. LC66-81961.

Obituary
TIMES (LONDON) (1 Sept 1933), 17:7.

Le Voleur, pseud. See CAREY, ROSA NOUCHETTE.

Lewald, Fanny. See STAHR, FANNY LEWALD.

LEWIS, HARRIET NEWELL (O'BRIEN). 1841-1878. U.S.

Biography
JOHH

LEYLAND, MARIE LOUISE (MACK) CREED. 1874-1935.
Australia.
     Mrs. J. Percy Creed
     Louise Mack

Autobiography
A WOMAN'S EXPERIENCE IN THE GREAT WAR, by Louise
Mack. London: T.F. Unwin, [1915]. LC A15-1289.

Biography
MIA   MIAU

LIBBEY, LAURA JEAN. 1862-1924. U.S.
     m. Stilwell

Biography
AWW BURG BURK NAW NCAB-19 PAP REA WEBS
WOWWA WWWA-1

LILJENCRANTZ, OTTILIA ADELINA. 1876-1910. U.S.

Biography
BURK WOWWA

LILLIE, LUCY CECIL (WHITE). 1855-1908? U.S.

Biography
BD BURK WARBD WWWA-1

LINCOLN, JEANIE THOMAS (GOULD). 1846-1921. U.S.

Biography
BURK LOGP TWCB WARBD WOWWA WWWA-1

LINCOLN, NATALIE SUMNER. 1881-1935. U.S.

Biography
BURK WEBS WOWWA WWNA WWWA-1

Obituary
PUBLISHERS WEEKLY 128 (14 Sept 1935), 832.

228

LINDSAY, CAROLINE BLANCHE ELIZABETH (FITZROY).
1844-1912. England.

Obituary
TIMES (LONDON) (15 Aug 1912), 7:5.

Linton, E. Lynn. See LINTON, ELIZABETH (LYNN).

Linton, Eliza. See LINTON, ELIZABETH (LYNN).

LINTON, ELIZABETH (LYNN). 1822-1898. England.
E. Lynn Linton
Eliza Linton
Mrs. Lynn Linton

Autobiography
MY LITERARY LIFE; with a prefatory note by Miss
Beatrice Harraden. London: Hodder and
Stoughton, 1899. LC03-440.

Biography
BD   BLA   BOASE-6   BRO   COLSA   COR   DNB-1   KUBA
MCC   MDWB   SHA   SHA-A   SHO   VIC   WEBS

Layard, George S. MRS. LYNN LINTON: HER LIFE,
LETTERS, AND OPINIONS. London: Methuen, 1901.
LC2-21166.

Sessions, Frederick. "A Successful Novelist--
Eliza Lynn Linton." In LITERARY CELEBRITIES OF
THE ENGLISH LAKE-DISTRICT. pp. 53-62. London:
E. Stock, 1905. OCLC 3960562.

Van Thal, Herbert M. ELIZA LYNN LINTON: THE GIRL
OF THE PERIOD: A BIOGRAPHY. Boston: Allen and
Unwin, 1979. LC78-41056.

Obituary
ATHENAEUM 112 (23 July 1898), 131-2.
ILLUS LONDON NEWS (23 July 1898), 121.
TIMES (LONDON) (16 July 1898), 12:4.

Linton, Mrs. Lynn. See LINTON, ELIZABETH (LYNN).

LIPPMANN, JULIA MATHILDE. 1864-1952. U.S.

Biography
ALY   AWO   BURK   TWCB   WOWWA   WWWA-3

LITCHFIELD, GRACE DENIO. 1849-1944. U.S.

Biography
ALY   AWO   BURG   BURK   NCAB-12,43   WARBD   WILA
WOWWA   WWNA   WWWA-2   WWWL

Obituary
NY TIMES (5 Dec 1944), 23:5.

LITTLE, ALICIA HELEN   NEVA (BEWICKE). 1845?-1926.
England.
        A.E.N. Bewicke
        Mrs. Archibald Little

Biography
FUR   WWWL

Obituary
TIMES (LONDON) (6 Aug 1926), 17:5.

Little, Frances, pseud.   See MACAULAY, FANNIE
(CALDWELL).

Little, M.   See LITTLE, MAUDE.

LITTLE, MAUDE. b.1890. England.
        M. Little

Biography
WWWL

Little, Mrs. Archibald.   See LITTLE, ALICIA HELEN
NEVA   (BEWICKE).

LOCKE, GLADYS EDSON. b.1887. U.S.

<u>Biography</u>

AWO   BURK   WWNA

Locke, Sumner.   See   ELLIOTT, SUMNER (LOCKE).

LOCKHART, CAROLINE. b.1875. U.S.

<u>Biography</u>

AWO   BURK   WWNA   WWWA-5

LODGE, HARRIET (NEWELL). b.1848. U.S.

<u>Biography</u>

BAN

LOGAN, BELLE V. 1864-1957. U.S.

<u>Biography</u>

COY

Lombardi, Cynthia.   See   LOMBARDI, GEORGINA   MARIE
(RICHMOND).

LOMBARDI, GEORGINA MARIE (RICHMOND). d.1942. U.S.
            Cynthia Lombardi

<u>Biography</u>

AWO   WWNA

LONG, FANNY F. 1859-1935. U.S.

<u>Biography</u>

COY

LONG, GABRIELLE MARGARET VERE (CAMPBELL) COSTANZO.
1888-1952. England.
            M. Bowen
            Marjorie Bowen, pseud.

231

Autobiography

THE DEBATE CONTINUES; BEING THE AUTOBIOGRAPHY OF
MARJORIE BOWEN, by Margaret Campbell. London:
Heinemann, [1939]. LC40-219.

Biography

ASH   BERE   BRO   HAMM   KUT   MYE   NCH   RIC   ROCK
TWCR   WAG   WAGCE   WARLC   WEBS   WWLA   WWWE   WWWL

Obituary

EUGENICS REVIEW 45 (Apr 1953), 14.
ILLUS LONDON NEWS 222 (3 Jan 1953), 7.
NY TIMES (27 Dec 1952), 9:5.
OBIT1, 90.
PUBLISHERS WEEKLY 163 (10 Jan 1953), 132.
TIME 61 (5 Jan 1953), 64.
TIMES (LONDON) (27 Dec 1952), 6:6; (1 Jan 1953),
    10:6.
WILSON 27 (Feb 1953), 420+.

LONG, LILY AUGUSTA. 1890-1927. U.S.
        Roman Doubleday, pseud.

Biography

ALY   WWWA-1

LONG, MAE VAN NORMAN. b.1870. U.S.

Biography

BURK   WWNA

LONGARD DE LONGGARDE, DOROTHEA (GERARD). 1855-1915.
Scotland.
        Madame Longarde De Longgarde
        D. Gerard
        Dorothea Gerard

Biography

BD   BLAP   WARBD

Obituary

TIMES (LONDON) (18 Nov 1915), 11:2.

LOOSE, KATHARINE RIEGEL. b.1877. U.S.
        Georg Schock, pseud.

Biography
AWO   WOWWA   WWNA   WWWA-5

LORIMER, NORMA OCTAVIA. b.1864. Scotland.

Biography
HAMM   WWLA   WWWE   WWWL

LOTHROP, HARRIET MULFORD (STONE). 1844-1924. U.S.
        Margaret Sidney, pseud.

Biography
AWW   BD   BERE   BURK   DAB   HAOXA   KUAA   LOGP   NAW
NCAB-8   SOME-20   TWCB   WARBD   WEBS   WOWWA   WWWA-1

LOUGHEAD, FLORA (HAINES) APPONYI. b.1855. U.S.

Biography
BURK   NCAB-11   WILA   WWNA   WWWA-4

LOUTHAN, HATTIE (HORNER). b.1865. U.S.

Biography
AWO   BAR   BURK   WOWWA   WWWA-5

LOVEJOY, MARY EVELYN WOOD. 1847-1928. U.S.

Biography
WOWWA

Lovell, Ingraham, pseud.   See BACON, JOSEPHINE
    DODGE (DASKAM).

LOWE, CORINNE MARTIN. 1882-1952. U.S.

Biography
ROSS

LOWENBERG, BETTIE (LILIENFELD). b.1845. U.S.
Mrs. I. Lowenberg

Biography
HINK   WOWWA

Lowenberg, Mrs. I. See LOWENBERG, BETTIE (LILIENFELD).

LOWNDES, MARIE ADELAIDE (BELLOC). 1868-1947.
England.
Marie Adelaide Belloc
Marie Adelaide Belloc-Lowndes
Mrs. Belloc Lowndes

Autobiography
"I, TOO, HAVE LIVED IN ARCADIA"; A RECORD OF LOVE
AND OF CHILDHOOD, by Mrs. Belloc Lowndes.
London: Macmillan, 1941. LCa42-191.

THE MERRY WIVES OF WESTMINSTER, by Mrs. Belloc
Lowndes. London: Macmillan, 1946. LC46-20314.

A PASSING WORLD. London: Macmillan, 1948.
LC49-4848.

WHERE LOVE AND FRIENDSHIP DWELT. New York: Dodd,
Mead, 1943. LC43-14633.

Biography
ASH   BERE   BRO   CHABI   CON-104   EMD   HAMM   HOE
KUAT   KUT   KUTS   MYE   NCH   RIC   SHO   TWCC   TWCR
WARLC   WEBS   WWWE   WWWL

Obituary
NY TIMES (15 Nov 1947), 17:1.
NEWSWEEK 30 (24 Nov 1947), 47.
PUBLISHERS WEEKLY 152 (6 Dec 1947), 2556.
TIME 50 (24 Nov 1947), 100.
TIMES (LONDON) (15 Nov 1947), 6:6; tribute
(20 Nov), 7:2,7.
WILSON 22 (Jan 1948), 354.

Lowndes, Mrs. Belloc.   See LOWNDES, MARIE ADELAIDE
(BELLOC).

LUCAS, EMILY BEATRIX COURSOLLES (JONES). 1893-1966.
England.
   E.B.C. Jones

       Biography
MICB WWLA WWWE

       Obituary
TIMES (LONDON) (5 July 1966), 14:6.

LUCK, MARY CHURCHILL (SPOTTISWOODE-ASHE).
fl.1895-1914. Ireland.
   M. Hamilton, pseud.

       Biography
BRI CLE

Luffmann, Laura Bogue. See LUFFMANN, LAURETTA
MARIE (LANE).

LUFFMANN, LAURETTA MARIE (LANE). 1846-1929.
Australia.
   Laura M. Lane
   Laura Bogue Luffmann

       Biography
MIA MIAU

Lurgan, Lester, pseud. See KNOWLES, MABEL
WINIFRED.

LUST, ADELINA (COHNFELDT). b.1860. U.S.

       Biography
WWWA-4

LUTES, DELLA (THOMPSON). d.1942. U.S.

COUNTRY SCHOOLMA'AM. Boston: Little, Brown,
 1941. LC41-51866.
  Reminiscences of the author's 16th year.

Biography

AWO   BURK   WWWA-2

Hilbert, Rachel M., ed. MICHIGAN AUTHORS.
    p. 42. Ann Arbor: Michigan Assoc. of School
    Librarians, 1960. LC60-16690.

Obituary

CUR-1942.
JOURNAL OF HOME ECONOMICS 34 (Oct 1942), 566.
NY TIMES (14 July 1942), 19:2.
PUBLISHERS WEEKLY 142 (25 July 1942), 245.
WILSON 17 (Sept 1942), 8.

LUTZ, GRACE (LIVINGSTON) HILL. 1865-1947. U.S.
        Grace Livingston Hill
        Mrs. Lutz

Biography

ALY   AWO   AWW   BURK   DAB-S4   KUT   NAW   NCAB-40
REA   TWCR   WOWWA   WWNA   WWWA-2   WWWE   WWWL   YES-2

Karr, Jean. GRACE LIVINGSTON HILL: HER STORY AND
    HER WRITING. Mattituck, N.Y.: Amereon, 1982,
    c1948. LC82-70025.

Obituary

NY TIMES (24 Feb 1947), 19.
NEWSWEEK 29 (3 Mar 1947), 47.
PUBLISHERS WEEKLY 151 (8 Mar 1947), 1498.
TIME 49 (3 Mar 1947), 96.
TIMES (LONDON) (24 Feb 1947), 4:3.
WILSON 21 (Apr 1947), 572.

Lutz, Helen Rowland. See ROWLAND, HELEN.

Lutz, Mrs. See LUTZ, GRACE (LIVINGSTON) HILL.

Lyall, David, pseud.
        See entries for Helen Buckingham
        (Mathers) Reeves and Annie S. (Swan) Smith
        both of whom used this pseud.

Lyall, Edna, pseud. See BAYLY, ADA ELLEN.

LYNCH, GERTRUDE. U.S.

Biography

BURG   WOWWA

LYNCH, HANNAH. c.1862-1904. England.

Biography

BRI

LYNCH, HARRIET LOUISE (HUSTED). 1864-1943. U.S.
     Mrs. Jerome Morley Lynch
     Marie Saint Felix, pseud.

Biography

AWO   BURK   WWNA

Obituary

NY TIMES (19 Sept 1943), 48:1.

Lynch, Lawrence L., pseud. See VAN DEVENTER, EMMA
MURDOCH.

Lynch, Mrs. Jerome Morley. See LYNCH, HARRIET
LOUISE (HUSTED).

LYND, SYLVIA (DRYHURST). 1888-1952. England.

Biography

MYE   NCH   WEBS   WWW-5

Obituary

TIMES (LONDON) (22 Feb 1952), 8:5; (8 Mar), 8:5.

LYNN, MARGARET. U.S.

Biography

BURK   WWNA

LYON, ANNA E. (PARKER). 1862/63-1937. U.S.
Mrs. Dore Lyon

Obituary
NY TIMES (2 May 1937), II 8:6.

Lyon, Mrs. Dore. See LYON, ANNA E. (PARKER).

LYTTLETON, EDITH JOAN. 1874-1945. New Zealand.
G.B. Lancaster, pseud.

Biography
MIA   MIAU   ROD   WEBS   WWWL

LYTTLETON, EDITH SOPHY (BALFOUR). 1865-1948.
England.
Edith Hamlet

Biography
MYE   NCH   WEBS   WWWT

Obituary
NY TIMES (3 Sept 1948), 19:5.
TIMES (LONDON) (3 Sept 1948), 7:5.

MABIE, LOUISE (KENNEDY). d.1957. U.S.

Biography
AWO   COY   HINK   WWWA-3

Obituary
NY TIMES (13 Nov 1957), 35:1.
WILSON 32 (Jan 1958), 329.

McADAM, CONSTANCE. New Zealand.
Constance Clyde.

Biography
MIA

MACARTHUR, RUTH ALBERTA (BROWN). b.1881. U.S.

Biography
AWO   BURK   WWNA   WWWA-6

MACAULAY, FANNIE (CALDWELL). 1863-1941. U.S.
Frances Little, pseud.

Biography
ALY   BURK   KNIB   WEBS   WWNA

Obituary
NY TIMES (8 Jan 1941), 19:5.

Macaulay, R. See Macaulay, Rose.

MACAULAY, ROSE. 1881-1958. England.
　　R. Macaulay

Autobiography
LAST LETTERS TO A FRIEND, 1952-1958, edited by
Constance Babington-Smith. New York: Atheneum,
1963. LC63-7792L.
Letters written to her cousin, Rev. John
Hamilton Cowper Johnson.

LETTERS TO A FRIEND, 1950-1952, edited by
Constance Babington-Smith. New York: Atheneum,
1962 [c1961]. LC62-7937L.
Letters written to Rev. Johnson.

LETTERS TO A SISTER, edited by Constance
Babington-Smith. New York: Atheneum, 1964.
LC64-18730.
Letters written to Jean Macaulay 1926--1958.

Biography
BERE　BRIT　BRO　CHA　CHABI　CON-104　FLE　HAMM
HAOXE　KUL　KUT　LAU　MANBL　MARBS　MDWB　MICB
MYE　NCH　NPW　PEE　RIC　SHO　WARLC　WEBS　WENW

Babington Smith, Constance. ROSE MACAULAY.
London: Collins, 1972. LC73-153062.

Bensen, Alice R. ROSE MACAULAY. New York:
Twayne, [c1969]. LC69-18507.

Obituary
ILLUS LONDON NEWS 233 (8 Nov 1958), 811.
NEW STATESMAN 56 (8 Nov 1958), 626.
NY TIMES (31 Oct 1958), 29:1.
NEWSWEEK 52 (10 Nov 1958), 66.
OBIT1, 458-9.
PUBLISHERS WEEKLY 174 (17 Nov 1958), 32.
SPECTATOR (LONDON) 201 (7 Nov 1958), 603.
TIME 72 (10 Nov 1958), 88.
TIMES (LONDON) (31 Oct 1958), 13:3; tributes
(4 Nov), 15:5; (7 Nov), 15:5.
WILSON 33 (Dec 1958), 265.

MACBETH, MADGE HAMILTON (LYONS). 1878-1965. Canada.

Autobiography
BOULEVARD CAREER. Toronto: Kingswood House,
1957. OCLC 3905587.

OVER MY SHOULDER. Toronto: Ryerson, [1953].
LC55-58254.

Biography
MDCB   STOXC   THOMC   WWNA

Obituary
NY TIMES (11 Oct 1965), 61:3.

McCAHAN, BELLE (TRAVERS). U.S.

Biography
WOWWA

McCall, Sidney, pseud. See   FENOLLOSA, MARY
(McNEIL).

McCARTER, MARGARET (HILL). 1860-1938. U.S.

Biography
ALY   BAN   BAR   BURK   WOWWA   WWNA   WWWA-1

Obituary
NY TIMES (1 Sept 1938), 23:3.

MACCARTHY, MARY (WARRE CORNISH). England.

Autobiography
A NINETEENTH-CENTURY CHILDHOOD. London:
H. Hamilton, [1948]. LC49-19714.

McCARTY, IDA HELEN DOUTHETT. b.1876. U.S.

Biography
BAR   COY

McCHESNEY, DORA GREENWALL. 1871-1912. U.S.
Kathleen Clare, pseud.
Will Fortescue, pseud.

Biography
WWWL

Obituary
NY TIMES (6 July 1912), 7:4.

McCHESNEY, ELIZABETH (STUDDIEFORD). 1841-1906. U.S.
L. Studdieford McChesney, pseud.

Biography
WWWA-1   WWWL

McChesney, L. Studdieford, pseud.   See   McCHESNEY,
ELIZABETH (STUDDIEFORD).

MACCHETTA, BLANCHE ROOSEVELT (TUCKER). 1853-1898.
U.S.
Blanche Roosevelt, pseud.

Biography
COY

Obituary
NY TIMES (11 Sept 1898), 7:6.

McCLELLAN, HARRIET (HARE). U.S.
Harford Flemming, pseud.
Mrs. George McClellan

McClellan, Mrs. George. See McCLELLAN, HARRIET
(HARE).

McClelland, M.G.   See   McCLELLAND, MARY GREENWAY.

McCLELLAND, MARY GREENWAY. 1853-1895. U.S.
    M.G. McClelland

Biography
BD   LIB   NCAB-2   ROCK   RUT   WARBD

McCLUNG, NELLIE LETITIA (MOONEY). 1873-1951.
Canada.

Autobiography
CLEARING IN THE WEST; MY OWN STORY.   New York:
   F.H. Revell, [c1936]. LC36-6980.

THE STREAM RUNS FAST; MY OWN STORY.   Toronto:
   T. Allen, 1965. LC68-127450.

TEA WITH THE QUEEN.   Vancouver: Intermedia,
   1980. LC80-486678.

Biography
AWO   MDCB   MOR2   STOXC   THOMC   SY   WOWWA   WWNA
WWWL

Benham, Mary L. NELLIE McCLUNG.   Don Mills,
   Ont.: Fitzhenry & Whiteside, c1975. LC78-320669.

Matheson, Gwen and V.E. Lang.   "Nellie McClung:
   Not a Nice Woman." In WOMEN IN THE CANADIAN
   MOSAIC, edited by Gwen Matheson, pp. 1-20.
   Toronto: P. Martin Associates, c1976.
   LC76-362564.

Savage, Candace S.   OUR NELL: A SCRAPBOOK
   BIOGRAPHY OF NELLIE L. McCLUNG.   Saskatoon:
   Western Producer Prairie Books, 1979.
   LC80-475293.

Wright, Helen K.   NELLIE McCLUNG AND WOMEN'S
   RIGHTS.   Agincourt, [Ont.]: Book Society of
   Canada, 1980. LC80-487241.

Obituary
NY TIMES (3 Sept 1951), 13:2.
WILSON 26 (Nov 1951), 202.

MACCONNELL, SARAH ASTON WARDER. 1869-1953. U.S.

Biography
BURK   COY

McCRACKIN,   JOSEPHINE   (WOEMPNER)   CLIFFORD.
1838-1920.   U.S.
Josephine Clifford

Biography
ALY   AWW   MIG   NAW   WOWWA   WWWA-1

McCULLOCH, CATHARINE GOUGER (WAUGH). 1862-1945. U.S.

Biography
BICA   NAW   WILA   WOWWA   WWWA-2

Obituary
NY TIMES (21 Apr 1945)

McCULLOUGH, MYRTLE (REED). 1874-1911. U.S.
Myrtle Reed

Biography
AWW   BURK   DAB   NAW   NCAB-15   REA   TWCB   WAGCA
WWNA   WWWA-1,2,5

Obituary
NY TIMES (20 Aug 1911), II 9:6.

MACDONALD,   LUCY   MAUD   (MONTGOMERY).   1874-1942.
Canada.
Lucy Maud Montgomery

Autobiography
THE ALPINE PATH: THE STORY OF MY CAREER, by L.M.
Montgomery. Don Mills, Ont.: Fitzhenry &
Whiteside, [1974?] c1917. LC75-312096.

THE GREEN GABLES LETTERS: FROM L.M. MONTGOMERY TO
EPHRAIM WEBER, 1905-1909, edited by Wilfred
Eggleston. Toronto: Ryerson, 1960. LC60-50636.

MY DEAR MR. M.: LETTERS TO G.B. MACMILLAN FROM
L.M. MONTGOMERY, edited by Francis W.P. Bolger
and Elizabeth R. Epperly. Toronto; New York:
McGraw-Hill Ryerson, 1980. LC80-155519.

Biography
AWO BERE BRO CHA GARV HAOXC INN KUJ1 KUT
MDCB MOR2 MYE NCH REA RHO RIC STOXC SY
THOMC TWCR WARLC WEBS WOWWA WWNA WWWE WWWL
YES-1

Bolger, Francis W. THE YEARS BEFORE "ANNE."
Prince Edward Island Heritage Foundation,
1974. LC75-326461.

Gillen, Mollie. LUCY MAUD MONTGOMERY. Don
Mills, Ont.: Fitzhenry & Whiteside, c1978.
LC79-305519.

------. THE WHEEL OF THINGS: A BIOGRAPHY OF L.M.
MONTGOMERY, AUTHOR OF ANNE OF GREEN GABLES.
Don Mills, Ont.: Fitzhenry & Whiteside, c1975.
LC76-353181R.

L.M. MONTGOMERY: AN ASSESSMENT, edited by John
R. Sorfleet. Guelph, Ont.: Canadian Children's
Press, c1976. LC79-301719.

Phelps, Arthur L. CANADIAN WRITERS. pp. 85-93.
Freeport, N.Y.: Books for Libraries, [1972,
c1951]. LC73-38030R.

Ridley, Hilda M. THE STORY OF L.M. MONTGOMERY.
London: G.G. Harrap, [1956]. LC65-28995.

Obituary
CUR-1942.
PUBLISHERS WEEKLY 141 (2 May 1942), 1675.
WILSON 16 (June 1942), 788.

McELROY, LUCY (CLEAVER). 1860-1901. U.S.

Biography
KNIB

McFadden, G.V. See McFADDEN, GERTRUDE VIOLET.

McFADDEN, GERTRUDE VIOLET. England.
G.V. McFadden

Biography

WWLA WWWE WWWL

McFALL, FRANCES ELIZABETH (CLARKE). 1862-1943.
Ireland.
Madame Sarah Grand, pseud.
Sarah Grand, pseud.

Biography

BD BLAP CHA CHABI HAOXE JOHDB KUT MDWB
MYE NCH SHA-A SHO WARBD WARLC WEBS WWWE

Huddleston, Joan, comp. SARAH GRAND ...: A
   BIBLIOGRAPHY. St. Lucia, Australia: Dept. of
   English, Univ. of Queensland, c1979. LC80-469587.

Obituary

CUR-1943.
NY TIMES (13 Mar 1943), 21:6.
PUBLISHERS WEEKLY 143 (29 May 1943), 2064.
TIMES (LONDON) (24 May 1943), 6:4.
WILSON 18 (Sept 1943), 8.

MACGILL, MARGARET (GIBBONS). England.
Mrs. Patrick MacGill

Biography

WWWL

MacGill, Mrs. Patrick. See MACGILL, MARGARET
   (GIBBONS).

McGlasson, Eva Wilder. See BRODHEAD, EVA WILDER
   (McGLASSON).

MACGOWAN, ALICE. 1858-1947. U.S.

Biography

BURK COY KNIB LOGP WOWWA WWWA-4

MACGREGOR, MARY ESTHER (MILLER). 1876-1961. Canada.
Marian Keith, pseud.

Biography
MOR2   RHO   STOXC   WOWWA

MACHAR, AGNES MAULE. 1837-1927. Canada.

Biography
MDCB   MOR   MOR2   MORGA   MYE   STOXC   WOWWA   WWWL

McILWRAITH, JEAN NEWTON. 1859-1938. Canada.

Biography
MDCB   MOR   MOR2   MYE   STOXC   WEBS   WOWWA   WWNA

Mack, Louise.   See   LEYLAND, MARIE LOUISE (MACK)
CREED.

MACKARNESS,   MATILDA   ANNE   (PLANCHE).   1826-1881.
England.

Biography
BOASE   DNB   WARBD

McKAY, ANNIE E.   U.S.
Mrs. Alfred Almond McKay

Biography
KNIB

MACKAY, HELEN GANSEVOORT (EDWARDS).   b.1876.   U.S.

Biography
BURK   WWWA-4,5

MACKAY,   ISABEL   ECCLESTONE   (MACPHERSON).   1875-1928.
Canada.

Biography
GARV   MDCB   MOR2   MYE   REA   STOXC   THOMC   WEBS
WOWWA   WWNA   WWWL

MACKAY, KATHERINE DYER. b.1878. U.S.

Biography
WOWWA

MACKAY, MARY. 1855-1924. England.
Marie Corelli, pseud.

Biography
ADE ASH BD BERE BLA BLAP BRO CHA DNB-4
FUR HAMM HAOXE KUT LAU LES NO NOV NPW
PEE RIC ROCK SHA-A SHO TWCR WAGCE WARBD
WARLC WEBS WWWL

Bigland, Eileen. MARIE CORELLI, THE WOMAN AND
THE LEGEND; A BIOGRAPHY. New York: Jarrolds,
[1953]. LC53-29476.

Bullock, George. MARIE CORELLI; THE LIFE AND
DEATH OF A BEST-SELLER. London: Constable,
[1940]. LC40-7742.

Carr, Kent. MISS MARIE CORELLI. London:
H.J. Drane, 1901. OCLC 8274470.

Coates, Thomas F. and R.S. Warren Bell. MARIE
CORELLI: THE WRITER AND THE WOMAN.
Philadelphia: G.W. Jacobs, [1903]. LC3-14283.

Masters, Brian. NOW BARABBAS WAS A ROTTER: THE
EXTRAORDINARY LIFE OF MARIE CORELLI. London:
H. Hamilton, 1978. LC78-307403.

Scott, William S. MARIE CORELLI; THE STORY OF A
FRIENDSHIP. London: Hutchinson, [1955].
LC56-3343L.

Vyver, Bertha. MEMOIRS OF MARIE CORELLI.
London: A. Rivers, Ltd., [1930]. LC30-32863.

Obituary
OUTLOOK 136 (30 Apr 1924), 722.
TIMES (LONDON) (22 Apr 1924), 18:4; tribute
(23 Apr), 20:2.

McKay, Mrs. Alfred Almond. See McKAY, ANNIE E.

MacKellar, Dorothea. See MACKELLAR, ISOBEL MARION DOROTHEA.

MACKELLAR, ISOBEL MARION DOROTHEA. Australia.
     Dorothea MacKellar

          Biography
MIAU

MACKENZIE, JEAN KENYON. 1874-1936. U.S.

          Biography
AWW   BURK   NAW   NCAB-28   WWNA   WWWA-1

          Obituary
CHRISTIAN CENTURY 53 (16 Sept 1936), 1238; (28
   Oct), 1438.
MISSIONARY REVIEW OF THE WORLD 59 (Oct 1936), 512.
NEWS WEEK 8 (12 Sept 1936), 27.
WILSON 11 (Oct 1936), 70.

MACKENZIE, SIBELL LILIAN BLUNT. 1878-1926. England.
     Countess of Cromartie
     Blunt is husband's name. He took her name.

          Biography
BRI   DIX   WWLA   WWWE

          Obituary
TIMES (LONDON) (23 Nov 1926), 19:2; (24 Nov),
   19:4.

Mackie, Pauline Bradford. See   CAVENDISH, PAULINE
BRADFORD (MACKIE) HOPKINS.

McKINNEY, ALICE JEAN CHANDLER (WEBSTER). 1876-1916.
U.S.
     Jean Webster

          Biography
AWW   BERE   BRO   BURK   DAB   DOY   HAOXA   KUJ1   KUT
NAW   REA   RIC   RICDA   TWCR   WARLC   WEBS   WOWWA
WWWA-1

Obituary
NY TIMES (12 June 1916), 11:4.

McKINNEY, ANNIE VALENTINE (BOOTH). U.S.

Biography
HINK   KNIB   WEBS   WWWA-5

McKINNEY, KATE (SLAUGHTER). B.1857. U.S.
    Katydid, pseud.

Biography
ALY   KNIB   WILA   WWNA   WWWA-4

MACKIRDY, OLIVE CHRISTIAN (MALVERY). d.1914.
    Mrs. Archibald MacKirdy
    Olive Christian Malvery

Autobiography
THE SOUL MARKET; with which is included "THE
    HEART OF THINGS," by Olive Christian Malvery.
    2d ed.   New York: McClure, Phillips, 1907.
    LC8-13767.

A YEAR AND A DAY, by Olive Christian Malvery.
    London: Hutchinson, 1912. OCLC 978596.

Biography
WWWL

Obituary
TIMES (LONDON) (5 Nov 1914), 11:4.

McKOWAN, EVAH MAY (CARTWRIGHT). b.1885. Canada.

Biography
WWNA

MacLagan,   Bridget,   pseud.   See   SPEARS,   MARY
    (BORDEN)   TURNER.

MACLANE

MACLANE, MARY. 1881-1929. U.S.

Biography

BURK   WWWA-1,2

Obituary

PUBLISHERS WEEKLY 116 (24 Aug 1929), 728-9.

McLAUREN, AMY. England.

Biography

WWWL

McLAURIN, KATE L. b.1885. U.S.
        m. Calvin

Biography

BURK   MAN

McLAWS, EMILY LAFAYETTE. 1821-1897. U.S.
        Lafayette McLaws

Biography

APP   BURK   DAB   KNIB   NCAB-4   PRE   TWCB   WOWWA
WWWA-H

McLaws, Lafayette. See McLAWS, EMILY LAFAYETTE.

MACLEAN, ANNIE MARION. d.1934. Canada.

Biography

AWW   MOR2   WOWWA   WWNA   WWWA-1

MACLEAN, CLARA VICTORIA (DARGAN). b.1841. U.S.

Biography

APP   KNIB   NCAB-7   WWWA-4

MACLEOD, DELLA CAMPBELL. U.S.

Biography

WOWWA

McLeod, Irene Rutherford. See DE SELINCOURT, IRENE RUTHERFORD (McLEOD).

MacLeod, Mrs. Alick, pseud. See MARTIN, CATHERINE EDITH MACAULEY (MACKAY).

MACMAHON, ELLA J. Ireland.

Biography

BRI   HAMM   LOGP   WWLA   WWWE   WWWL

McMANUS, CHARLOTTE ELIZABETH. Ireland.
L. McManus, pseud.

Biography

BRI   CLE

McManus, L., pseud. See McMANUS, CHARLOTTE ELIZABETH.

MacNab, Frances, pseud. See FRASER, AGNES.

MACNAMARA, RACHEL SWETE. Ireland.

Biography

BRI   WWWE

Macnaughtan, S. See MACNAUGHTAN, SARAH BROOM.

MACNAUGHTAN, SARAH BROOM. 1864-1916. Scotland.
S. Macnaughtan

Obituary
"Miss S. Macnaughtan." LIVING AGE 291 (14 Oct
1916), 119-23.
TIMES (LONDON) (29 July 1916), 11:2.

MACQUOID, KATHARINE SARAH (GADSDEN). 1824-1917.
England.

Biography
HAMM   WWWL

MACVANE, EDITH. b.1880. U.S.

Biography
WOWWA   WWWA-6

MADESANI, GRAZIA COSIMA (DELEDDA). 1871-1936.
Italy.
Grazia Deledda

Biography
BERE CAS CDME CHABI HAMM KU KUL MARB
MCCNP MDWB NOV OP PAC PEEU SEYS VIT WEBS

Balducci, Carolyn. A SELF-MADE WOMAN: BIOGRAPHY
OF NOBEL-PRIZE-WINNER GRAZIA DELEDDA. Boston:
Houghton Mifflin, 1975. LC75-17032R.
Juvenile literature.

Obituary
NY TIMES (17 Aug 1936), 19:3.
PUBLISHERS WEEKLY 130 (22 Aug 1936), 598.
TIMES (LONDON) (18 Aug 1936), 12:3.
WILSON 11 (Sept 1936), 8.

MADISON, LUCY FOSTER. 1865-1932. U.S.

Biography
WOWWA   WWWA-1

MADISON

Obituary
NY TIMES (17 Mar 1932), 24:6.
PUBLISHERS WEEKLY 121 (26 Mar 1932), 1490.

MAGOUN, JEANNE BARTHOLOW. b.1870. U.S.

Biography
WWWA-5

MAGRUDER, JULIA. 1854-1907. U.S.

Biography
APP AWW BD BURK DAB KUAA LIB NAW NCAB-8
RUT TWCB WARBD WWWA-1

Obituary
NY TIMES (10 June 1907), 7:6.

Main, Mrs. See LE BLOND, ELIZABETH ALICE FRANCES
(HAWKINS-WHITSHED) BURNABY MAIN.

Malet, Lucas, pseud. See HARRISON, MARY SAINT
LEGER (KINGSLEY).

MALLOWAN, AGATHA MARY CLARISSA (MILLER) CHRISTIE.
1891-1976. England.
Agatha Christie

Autobiography
AN AUTOBIOGRAPHY, by Agatha Christie. New York:
Dodd, Mead, c1977. LC77-11689.

COME, TELL ME HOW YOU LIVE. New York: Dodd,
Mead, [1976], c1946. LC76-359189.

Biography
ASH BERE BRO CAS CEL CHABI CON-19--20R
CONO CUR-1964 EMD HAMM HAOXE HAY KUAT KUT
KUTS LOF MANN MDWB MYE NCH NOV NPW PEE
RIC ROCK SHO TWCC TWCR WARLC WEBS WWWE

AGATHA CHRISTIE: FIRST LADY OF CRIME, edited by
H.R.F. Keating. New York: Holt, Rinehart and
Winston, [1977]. LC76-29907.

Feinman, Jeffrey. THE MYSTERIOUS WORLD OF AGATHA
CHRISTIE. New York: Award Books, 1975.
LC76-350500.

Gregg, Hubert. AGATHA CHRISTIE AND ALL THAT
MOUSETRAP. London: W. Kimber, 1980.
LC81-110086.

Mallowan, Max E. MALLOWAN'S MEMOIRS. New York:
Dodd, Mead, 1977. LC77-3658.

Mann, Jessica. DEADLIER THAN THE MALE: WHY ARE
RESPECTABLE ENGLISH WOMEN SO GOOD AT MURDER?
pp. 121-53. New York: Macmillan, c1981.
LC81-3760.

Murdoch, Derrick. THE AGATHA CHRISTIE MYSTERY.
Toronto; New York: Pagurian, c1976.
LC77-358644.

Robyns, Gwen. THE MYSTERY OF AGATHA CHRISTIE.
Garden City, N.Y.: Doubleday, 1978.
LC77-76259.

                        Obituary
BOOKSELLER (17 Jan 1976).
CON-61--64.
CHRISTIANITY TODAY 20 (13 Feb 1976), 28.
CUR-1976.
"Dame Agatha: Queen of the Maze." TIME 107 (26
Jan 1976), 75.
Kramer, P.G. "Mistress of Mystery." NEWSWEEK 87
(26 Jan 1976), 69.
Lowenthal, Max. "Agatha Christie, Creator of
Poirot, Dies." NY TIMES (13 Jan 1976), 1+.
NATIONAL REVIEW 28 (2 Feb 1976), 78.
NY TIMES OBITUARY INDEX. Vol. 2, pp. 28-30.
PUBLISHERS WEEKLY 209 (19 Jan 1976), 32.
SCHOOL LIBRARY JOURNAL (Feb 1976).
TIMES (LONDON) (13 Jan 1976), 16:6; profile
(18 Jan), 41.
WASHINGTON POST (13 Jan 1976).

MALVERY

Malvery, Olive Christian. See MACKIRDY, OLIVE CHRISTIAN (MALVERY).

MANDER, JANE. 1877-1949. New Zealand.
full name Mary Jane Mander

Biography
MYE   NPW   RIC   WARLC   WENW   WWWL

Turner, Dorothea. JANE MANDER. New York: Twayne, [1972]. LC76-120493.

MANIATES, BELLE KANARIS. d.1925. U.S.

Biography
ALY   BURK

MANN, MARY ELIZABETH (RACKHAM). 1848-1929. England.

Biography
BD   HAMM   WARLC   WWWL

Obituary
TIMES (LONDON) (15 July 1929), 19:2.

MANN, MARY (RIDPATH). b.1867. U.S.

Biography
BAN   WWWA-4

MANNING, FRANCES (DUNCAN). b.1877. U.S.
Frances Duncan

Biography
WOWWA   WWNA   WWWA-5

MANNING, MARIE. d.1945. U.S.
m. Gasch

Biography
ALY   AWW   BURK   DAB-S3   REA   WWWA-2

MANNING

Obituary
NEWSWEEK 26 (10 Dec 1945), 80.
TIME 46 (10 Dec 1945), 72.
WILSON 20 (Jan 1946), 328.

MANNIX, MARY ELLEN (WALSH). 1846-1939. U.S.

Biography
HO   LOGP

MANSFIELD, CHARLOTTE. 1881-1936. England.

Biography
WWWL

Obituary
TIMES (LONDON) (18 Feb 1936), 17:7.

Marbo, Camille, pseud.   See BOREL, MARGUERITE
(APPELL).

Marchant, Bessie.   See   COMFORT, BESSIE (MARCHANT).

MARKS, JEANNETTE AUGUSTUS. 1875-1964. U.S.

Biography
ALY   AWW   BURK   KUT   MAN   NCAB-B   REA   WOWWA
WWNA   WWWA-4

Obituary
NY TIMES (16 Mar 1964), 31:2.

Marlitt, E., pseud.   See   JOHN, EUGENIE.

MARLOWE, MARY (O'SHANASSY). Australia.

Biography
MIA   MIAU

Marryat, Florence. See LEAN, FLORENCE (MARRYAT) CHURCH.

MARSHALL, EMMA (MARTIN). 1830-1899. England.

Biography
BEL   BOASE-6   DNB-1   SHO

Marshall, Beatrice. EMMA MARSHALL, A
    BIOGRAPHICAL SKETCH. London: Seeley, 1900.
    LC01-28071.

Smith-Dampier, John L. EAST ANGLIAN WORTHIES.
    p. 132. Oxford: B. Blackwell, 1949.
    LC49-26023.

Obituary
ILLUS LONDON NEWS (13 May 1899), 677.
TIMES (LONDON) (5 May 1899), 10:4.

MARSHALL, FRANCES (BRIDGES). d.1920. England.
    Alan Saint Aubyn, pseud.

Biography
BEL

Obituary
TIMES (LONDON) (26 Oct 1920), 13:3.

MARSHALL, MARGUERITE MOOERS. 1887-1964. U.S.
    m. Dean

Biography
AWO   BURK   ROSS   WOMA   WOWWA   WWNA   WWWA-4

Obituary
NY TIMES (11 May 1964), 31:1.

MARSLAND, CORA. b.1859. U.S.

Biography
WOWWA   WWWA-4

MARTEL DE JANVILLE, SYBILLE GABRIELLE MARIE ANTOINETTE DE RIQUETTI DE MIRABEAU. 1849-1932. France.

      Sybille Gabrielle Martel De Janville
      Gyp, pseud.

Biography
BD CHABI CROS HAMM HAOXF HAR HEN WARBD
WEBS

Obituary
SAT REVIEW OF LIT 8 (16 July 1932), 839.

MARTIN, CATHERINE EDITH MACAULEY (MACKAY). 1847/48-1937. Australia.

      Mrs. Alick Macleod, pseud.

Biography
MIA MIAU MYE SER

MARTIN, GEORGE (MADDEN). 1866-1946. U.S.

Biography
AWO AWW BURG BURK KNIB MAN NAW NCAB-33
RICK RUT WOWWA WWNA WWWA-2

Obituary
NY TIMES (2 Dec 1946), 25:4.

Martin, H.R.   See MARTIN, HELEN (REIMENSNYDER).

MARTIN, HELEN (REIMENSNYDER). 1868-1939. U.S.

      H.R. Martin
      Helen Reimensnyder

Biography
AWO AWW KUT MAN MARBS OV OV2 WEBS WOWWA
WWWA-1

Obituary
NY TIMES (30 June 1939), 19:6.
PUBLISHERS WEEKLY 136 (22 July 1939), 237.
WILSON 14 (Sept 1939), 6.

MARTIN, MABEL WOOD (DOYLE). 1880-1956. U.S.

<u>Biography</u>
ALY   AWO   BURK   HINK   REA   WWWA-3

MARTIN, VIOLET FLORENCE. 1865-1915. Ireland.
Martin Ross, pseud.
See Also: SOMERVILLE, EDITH ANNA OENONE
AND VIOLET FLORENCE MARTIN.

<u>Biography</u>
BERE   BRO   CHA   CHABI   CLE   CRO   DIL   DNB-3
HAMM   HIG   KUAT   KUT   LAU   LES   MYE   NPW   PEE
SHO   WARLC   WEBS   WWWL

Somerville, Edith A. IRISH MEMORIES. New ed.
New York: Longmans, Green, 1925. LC26-6533R.

<u>Obituary</u>
TIMES (LONDON) (23 Dec 1915), 5:4.

MASON, CAROLINE (ATWATER). 1853-1939. U.S.
Alison Brooke, pseud.

<u>Biography</u>
ALY   AWO   BURK   NCAB-4   TWCA   WARBD   WOWWA   WWNA
WWWA-1

<u>Obituary</u>
NY TIMES (4 May 1939), 23:1.

MASON, GRACE (SARTWELL). b.1877. U.S.
m. Howes
<u>Biography</u>
AWO   WOWWA

MASSON, ROSALINE ORME. Scotland.

<u>Biography</u>
WWLA   WWWE   WWWL

MASTERSON, KATE. b.1870. U.S.

Biography
BURK   WOWWA   WWWA-5

Mathers, H.   See REEVES, HELEN   BUCKINGHAM (MATHERS).

Mathers, Helen.   See   REEVES, HELEN BUCKINGHAM (MATHERS).

MATHEWS, FRANCES AYMAR. 1865-1925. U.S.

Biography
AWW   BAN   BURK   WARBD   WOWWA   WWWA-2

MATHEWS, GERTRUDE (SINGLETON). 1881-1936. U.S.
        m. (1)Mathews (2)Shelby

Biography
BURK   WWWA-1

MATSON, SUSAN KEATING (GLASPELL) COOK. 1876-1948. U.S.
        Susan Glaspell

Biography
ADE   AMN   AWO   AWW   BERE   BURK   CHA   CHABI
DAB-S4   DR   HAMM   HAOXA   KUL   KUT   MAN   MAT   MICA
MYE   NAW   NCAB-15   NOV   REA   RICDA   WAR   WARLC
WEBS   WOWWA   WWNA   WWWA-2   WWWE   WWWT   YES-2

"Glaspell, Susan." In TWENTIETH-CENTURY AMERICAN DRAMATISTS. Vol. 7, Pt. 1, DICTIONARY OF LITERARY BIOGRAPHY. pp. 215-23. Detroit: Gale, 1981. LC81-564.

Waterman, Arthur E. SUSAN GLASPELL. New York: Twayne, [1966]. LC66-17062.

Obituary
NY TIMES (28 July 1948), 23:3.
NEWSWEEK 32 (9 Aug 1948), 52.

PUBLISHERS WEEKLY 154 (14 Aug 1948), 595.
TIME 52 (9 Aug 1948), 73.
TIMES (LONDON) (28 July 1948), 7:5.
WILSON 23 (Sept 1948), 10.

MATTHEWS, VICTORIA (EARLE). 1861-1907. U.S.
Victoria Earle

Biography
DANB   MAJ   NAW   PENN

Brown, Hallie Q., comp. HOMESPUN HEROINES AND
OTHER WOMEN OF DISTINCTION. pp. 208-16.
Freeport, N.Y.: Books for Libraries, 1971,
1926. LC70-152917.

Dannett, Sylvia G. PROFILES OF NEGRO WOMANHOOD.
pp. 288-9. Vol. 1. Yonkers, N.Y.: Educational
Heritage, [1964-66]. LC64-25013R.

Robinson, William H. EARLY BLACK AMERICAN
PROSE.... p. 159. Dubuque, Iowa: Brown, c1971.

Obituary
NY TIMES (11 Mar 1907), 7:6.

MAUD, CONSTANCE ELIZABETH. d.1929. England.

Obituary
TIMES (LONDON) (21 May 1929), 16:3.

MAULE, MARY KATHERINE (FINIGAN). b.1861? U.S.

Biography
BURK   WOWWA

MAXWELL, BEATRICE ETHEL HERON. d.1927.
name also appears as Heron-Maxwell

Biography
WWWL

Maxwell, Ellen Blackmar. See BARKER, ELLEN (BLACKMAR) MAXWELL.

MAXWELL, MARY ELIZABETH (BRADDON). 1837-1915.
England.
        M.E. Braddon
        Miss M.E. Braddon

Biography
ADE BD BEL BERE BRO CHA CHABI CON-108
DNB-3 EMD HAMM HAOXE JOHDB JOHH KUBA MDWB
MYE NCH NO NPW ROCK SHA SHO TWCC VIC
WAGCE WARBD WEBS WWWL

Wolff, Robert L. SENSATIONAL VICTORIAN: THE LIFE
AND FICTION OF MARY ELIZABETH BRADDON. New
York: Garland, 1979. LC76-52717.

Obituary
"Miss Braddon." BOOKMAN (NY) 41 (Mar 1915), 1-3.
NY TIMES (5 Feb 1915), 11:6.
TIMES (LONDON) (9 Feb 1915), 11:4.

MAY, GEORGIANA MARION (CRAIK). 1831-1895. England.
        Georgiana M. Craik
        Mrs. A.W. May

Biography
BOASE-4 CHA NCH WARBD

Obituary
TIMES (LONDON) (6 Nov 1895), 3:5.

May, Mrs. A.W. See MAY, GEORGIANA MARION (CRAIK).

May, Sophie, pseud. See CLARKE, REBECCA SOPHIA.

MAYNARD, SARA KATHERINE (CASEY). d.1945. England.
        Sadie Katherine Casey

Biography
BOOCA-3 HOE

Obituary
Malloy, J.I. CATHOLIC WORLD 162 (Jan 1946), 369.
WILSON 20 (Jan 1946), 328.

MAYNE, ETHEL COLBURN. 1870-1941. England.

Biography
MANBL MEL MICB NCH WARLC WEBS WWLA WWW-4
WWWE WWWL

Obituary
CUR-1941.
TIMES (LONDON) (2 May 1941), 7:5.

MAYO, ISABELLA (FYVIE). 1843-1914. Scotland.
Edward Garrett, pseud.

Autobiography
RECOLLECTIONS OF WHAT I SAW, WHAT I LIVED
THROUGH, AND WHAT I LEARNED, DURING MORE THAN
FIFTY YEARS OF SOCIAL AND LITERARY EXPERIENCE.
London: J. Murray, 1910. LCall-1550.

Biography
BD SHO WARBD WWWL

Obituary
TIMES (LONDON) (14 May 1914), 15:6.

MAYO, MARGARET LILIAN (CLATLIN). 1882-1951. U.S.

Biography
AWW BURK LOGP

Obituary
NY TIMES (26 Feb 1951), 23:1.

Mayor, F.M. See MAYOR, FLORA MACDONALD.

MAYOR, FLORA MACDONALD. 1872-1932. England.
  F.M. Mayor

      Biography
SHO

Meade, L. T., pseud. See SMITH, ELIZABETH
THOMASINA (MEADE).

Meade, Laura T., pseud. See SMITH, ELIZABETH
THOMASINA (MEADE).

Meade, Mrs. L.T., pseud. See SMITH, ELIZABETH
THOMASINA (MEADE).

Mears, A. Garland. See MEARS, AMELIA GARLAND.

MEARS, AMELIA (GARLAND). England.
  A. Garland Mears

      Biography
ODP

MEARS, MARY MARTHA. b.1876. U.S.

      Biography
BURK WWNA

MEIGS, CORNELIA LYNDE. 1884-1973. U.S.
  Adair Aldon, pseud.

      Biography
AWO AWW BURK CON-9--10R HOO KUJ1 KUJ2 KUL
REA SOME-6 WEBS WWWA-6

      Obituary
CON-45--48.
NY TIMES (15 Sept 1973), 34:5.
PUBLISHERS WEEKLY 204 (8 Oct 1973), 32.

MEISSNER, SOPHIE (RADFORD) DE. 1854-1957. U.S.

Biography
BURK   WWWA-4

Obituary
NY TIMES (20 Apr 1957), 17:2.

Mendl, Gladys, pseud.   See   SCHUETZE, GLADYS
HENRIETTA   (RAPHAEL).

Meredith, Ellis.   See   CLEMENT, ELLIS (MEREDITH).

Meredith, Isabel, pseud.   See   AGRESTI,   OLIVIA
FRANCES MADOX (ROSSETTI).

MERINGTON, MARGUERITE. d.1951. U.S.

Biography
AWW   BURK   WWWA-3

Obituary
NY TIMES (21 May 1951), 27:6.

MERRIMAN, EFFIE (WOODWARD). b.1857. U.S.
        m. (1)Merriman   (2)Fifield

Biography
WOWWA

METHLEY, VIOLET MARY. England.

Biography
WWWL

MEYER, ANNIE FLORANCE (NATHAN). 1867-1951. U.S.

Autobiography
IT'S BEEN FUN; AN AUTOBIOGRAPHY.   New York:
Schuman, [1951]. LC51-13631.

MEYER

Biography
ADE   ALY   AWO   BICA   BURG   BURK   DAB-S5   LOGP
NAWM   NCAB-42   REA   RUSB   TWCB   WEBS   WILA   WOMA
WOWWA   WWNA   WWWA-3

THREE OUTSTANDING WOMEN, MARY FELS, REBEKAH KOHUT
[and] ANNIE NATHAN MEYER. New York: Bloch,
1941. LC42-592.

Obituary
NY TIMES (24 Sept 1951), 27:1.
NEWSWEEK 38 (1 Oct 1951), 58.
TIME 58 (8 Oct 1951), 97.
WILSON 26 (Nov 1951), 202.

MEYER, LUCY JANE (RIDER). 1849-1922. U.S.

Biography
BICA   WOWWA   WWWA-1

Meynell, Viola. See DALLYN, VIOLA (MEYNELL).

Michaelis, Karin. See STANGELAND, KATHARINA MARIE
(BECH-BRONDUM) MICHAELIS.

MICHELSON, MIRIAM. 1870-1942. U.S.

Biography
BURK   REA   WOWWA   WWWA-2

MIDDLEMASS, JEAN. 1834-1919. England.

Biography
BEL   BLA   WWWL

Obituary
TIMES (LONDON) (7 Nov 1919), 15:5.

MIGHELS, ELLA STERLING (CLARK) CUMMINS. 1853-1934.
U.S.
        Mrs. Philip Verrill Mighels

Biography

BURK WWWA-2,4

Mighels, Mrs. Philip Verrill. See MIGHELS, ELLA
STERLING (CLARK) CUMMINS.

MILECETE, HELEN.
        Carleton-Milecete, joint pseud. with Susan
        Carleton Jones.

MILES, EMMA (BELL). 1879-1919. U.S.

Biography

THOI WOWWA WWWA-2

MILLER, ALICE (DUER). 1874-1942. U.S.

Biography

AUT AWO AWW BERE BURK CUR-1941 KUT MARBS
NAW NCAB-A OV OV2 REA WARLC WEBS WOWWA
WWNA WWWA-2

Miller, Henry W. ALL OUR LIVES. ALICE DUER
    MILLER. New York: Coward-McCann, [c1945].
    LC45-35102.

Obituary

CUR-1942.
NY TIMES (23 Aug 1942), 42:1.
NEWSWEEK 20 (31 Aug 1942), 6.
PUBLISHERS WEEKLY 142 (5 Sept 1942), 845.
TIME 40 (30 Aug 1942), 81.
WILSON 17 (Oct 1942), 78.

MILLER, ANNIE (JENNESS). b.1859. U.S.
        Mrs. Jenness Miller

Biography

WILA

MILLER, EMILY CLARK (HUNTINGTON). 1833-1913. U.S.

Biography
AWW BD BURK DAB KUAA LOGP NAW NCAB-10 ST
TWCB WARBD WILA WOWWA WWWA-1

MILLER, HARRIET (MANN). 1831-1918. U.S.
Olive Thorne Miller, pseud.

Biography
ALY AWW BD BURK COY DAB KUAA LOGP NAW
NCAB-9 TWCB WARBD WEBS WILA WOWWA WWWA-1

MILLER, MARY ELIZA BAKEWELL (GAUNT). 1872-1942.
Australia.
Mary Gaunt
Married a widower who supported her desire
to continue writing under her maiden name.

Biography
AUDB-8 HAMM MIA MIAU SER WWLA WWWE

Obituary
TIMES (LONDON) (5 Feb 1942), 7:5.

MILLER, MINNIE (WILLIS) BAINES-. b.1845. U.S.
Minnie Willis Baines

Biography
BURK COY WILA WOWWA WWWA-5

Miller, Mrs. Jenness. See MILLER, ANNIE (JENNESS).

Miller, Olive Thorne, pseud. See MILLER, HARRIET
(MANN).

MILLIN, SARAH GERTRUDE (LIEBSON). 1889-1968. South
Africa.

Autobiography
THE MEASURE OF MY DAYS. London: Faber and Faber,
[1955]. LC55-31893.

THE NIGHT IS LONG. London: Faber and Faber,
[1941]. LCa41-3660.

THE REELING EARTH. London: Faber and Faber,
[1945]. LC45-9625.

WORLD BLACKOUT. London: Faber and Faber, [1944].
LC44-5997.

Biography
BERE BRO CAS CON-102 FLE KUL KUT MANBL
MICB MOCL MYE NCH NOV PEE RIC ROS STA
WARLC WEBS WENW WWWE

Rubin, Martin. SARAH GERTRUDE MILLIN: A SOUTH
AFRICAN LIFE. Johannesburg: Ad. Donker, 1977.
LC78-310511.

Obituary
CON-93--96.
NY TIMES (12 July 1968), 31:2.
PUBLISHERS WEEKLY 194 (12 Aug 1968), 33.
OBIT2, 550-1.
TIMES (LONDON) (12 July 1968), 12:6.

MILLS, DOROTHY RACHEL MELISSA (WALPOLE). 1889-1959.
England.

Autobiography
A DIFFERENT DRUMMER; CHAPTERS IN AUTOBIOGRAPHY.
[London]: Duckworth, 1930. LC50-32944.

Biography
HAMM WWLA WWWE WWWL

Obituary
TIMES (LONDON) (8 Dec 1959), 15:1; tribute
(16 Dec), 13:3.

MILN, LOUISE (JORDAN). 1864-1933. U.S.
Mrs. George Crichton Miln

Biography
BURK KUAT KUT MARBS REA WEBS WWWL

MILN

Obituary
PUBLISHERS WEEKLY 124 (7 Oct 1933), 1232.

Miln, Mrs. George Crichton. See MILN, LOUISE (JORDAN).

MINER, LUELLA. 1861-1935. U.S.

Biography
COY WWWA-1

MINITER, EDITH MAY (DOWE). b.1869. U.S.

Biography
WOWWA WWWA-5

MIRRLEES, HOPE. England.

Biography
MANBL

Mitton, G.E. See SCOTT, GERALDINE EDITH (MITTON).

MOBERLY, CHARLOTTE ANNE ELIZABETH. 1846-1937.
England.
        Elizabeth Morison, pseud.

Biography
BRIT

MOLESWORTH, MARY LOUISA (STEWART). 1839/1842-1921.
Scotland.
        Mrs. Molesworth

Biography
ASH BD BRO CHA DOY GRET GRETB HAMM KUBA
KUJ1 LAS MYE NCH ROCK SHO WARBD WARLC
WEBS

Green, Roger L. MRS. MOLESWORTH. New York:
H.Z. Walck, [1964, c1961]. LC64-20839.

271

MOLESWORTH

Obituary
NY TIMES (22 July 1921), 11:6.
TIMES (LONDON) (22 July 1921), 13:6.

Molesworth, Mrs. See MOLESWORTH, MARY LOUISA (STEWART).

MONROE, ANNE SHANNON. 1877-1942. U.S.

Autobiography
THE WORLD I SAW. Garden City, N.Y.: Doubleday, Doran, 1928. LC28-29529.

Biography
AWO BURK NCAB-45 WWNA WWWA-2

Obituary
CUR-1942.
NY TIMES (20 Oct 1942), 21:2.
WILSON 17 (Dec 1942), 270.

MONROE, HARRIET (EARHART). 1842-1926. U.S.

Biography
ALY AWW NAW WEBS WILA WOWWA WWWA-1

MONSELL, MARGARET EMMA FAITH (IRWIN). 1889-1967. England.
M.E.F. Irwin
Margaret Irwin

Biography
ASH MYE TWCR WARLC WWWE WWWL

Obituary
OBIT2, 402.
TIMES (LONDON) (12 Dec 1967), 12:6.

MONTAGU, LILIAN HELEN. 1874-1963. England.
Lily H. Montagu

Obituary
TIMES (LONDON) (24 Jan 1963), 15:2.

Montagu, Lily H.   See   MONTAGU, LILIAN HELEN.

MONTAGUE, MARGARET PRESCOTT. 1878-1955. U.S.

Biography
AWO   BURK   KNIB   LIB-17   WOWWA   WWNA   WWWE

Obituary
NY TIMES (27 Sept 1955), 35:4.

MONTGOMERY, FLORENCE. 1843-1923. England.

Biography
WARBD

Obituary
TIMES (LONDON) (13 Oct 1923), 15:2.

Montgomery, K. L., joint pseud. of KATHLEEN and LETITIA MONTGOMERY.

MONTGOMERY, KATHLEEN. d.1960. Ireland.
            K. L. Montgomery, joint pseud. with
            Letitia Montgomery

Biography
WWWL

MONTGOMERY, LETITIA. d.1930. Ireland.
            K. L. Montgomery, joint pseud. with
            Kathleen Montgomery

Biography
WWWL

Obituary
TIMES (LONDON) (25 Oct 1930), 17:4.

Montgomery, Lucy Maud. See MACDONALD, LUCY MAUD (MONTGOMERY).

Montresor, F. F. See MONTRESOR, FRANCES
FREDERICA.

MONTRESOR, FRANCES FREDERICA. d.1934. England.
F.F. Montresor

Biography
WARBD

Obituary
TIMES (LONDON) (19 Oct 1934), 19:3.

MOODY, HELEN (WATTERSON). 1860-1928. U.S.

Biography
COY NCAB-22 WILA

MOORE, BERTHA PEARL. 1894-1925. U.S.
Bertha Pearl, pseud.

Biography
WWWA-1

MOORE, DOROTHEA MARY. b.1881.

Biography
WWWL

MOORE, E. HAMILTON. England.

Biography
WWWL

MOORE, EVELYN (UNDERHILL). 1875-1941. England.
Mrs. Stuart Moore
Evelyn Underhill, pseud.

Autobiography
THE LETTERS OF EVELYN UNDERHILL, edited with an
introduction by Charles Williams. Wilmington,
Del.: International Academic Pub., 1979, 1943.
LC79-11476.

Biography

BERE   BRO   CHA   KUT   MANBL   MDWB   MYE   NCH   RIC
WARLC   WEBS   WWWE   WWWL

Armstrong, Christopher, J.   EVELYN UNDERHILL,
   1875-1941: AN INTRODUCTION TO HER LIFE AND
   WRITING. Grand Rapids: Eerdmans, 1976, c1975.
   LC75-33401.

Cropper, Margaret.   LIFE OF EVELYN UNDERHILL.
   New York: Harper, [1958]. LC58-7092.
   Pub. in England as EVELYN UNDERHILL.

EVELYN UNDERHILL: TWO CENTENARY ESSAYS, by
   Michael Ramsey and A.M. Allchin.   Oxford:
   S.L.G. Press, 1977. LC77-374525.

Obituary
TIMES (LONDON) (18 June 1941), 7:4.

MOORE, JUSTINA.   d.1909. England.
         Martin J. Pritchard, pseud.

Biography
BEL

Moore, Mrs. Stuart.   See MOORE, EVELYN (UNDERHILL).

Mordaunt, Eleanor, pseud.   See   BOWLES,   EVELYN
   MAY (CLOWES) WIEHE.

Mordaunt, Elenor, pseud. See   BOWLES, EVELYN MAY
   (CLOWES) WIEHE.

Mordaunt, Elinor, pseud.   See   BOWLES, EVELYN MAY
   (CLOWES) WIEHE.

MORGAN, EMILY MALBONE.   1862-1937. U.S.

Biography
WWNA

Morison, Elizabeth, pseud. See MOBERLY, CHARLOTTE ANNE ELIZABETH.

MORLEY, MARGARET WARNER. 1858-1923. U.S.

Biography
ALY BURK DAB STOXC WARBD WOWWA WWWA-1

Obituary
NY TIMES (15 Dec 1923), 13:2.

Morris, Clara. See HARRIOTT, CLARA MORRIS.

MORRIS, E. O'CONNOR. 1861-1917. Ireland.

Biography
BRI

Morrison, Deborah, pseud. See CLARK, SUSIE CHAMPNEY.

MORROW, HONORE (MACCUE) WILLSIE. 1880?-1940. U.S.
    Honore Willsie

Biography
AWO BURK HAOXA KUL KUT MARBS NCAB-29 OV
OV2 REA TIT WEBS WWWA-1

Obituary
CUR-1940.
NY TIMES (13 Apr 1940), 17:3.
NEWSWEEK 15 (22 Apr 1940), 8.
PUBLISHERS WEEKLY 137 (20 Apr 1940), 1594.
WILSON 14 (June 1940), 706.

MORSE, LUCY (GIBBONS). 1839-1936. U.S.

Biography
NCAB-26 WARBD WWWA-1

MORSE, MARGARET FESSENDEN. b.1877. U.S.

WOWWA   WWWA-5   Biography

Mortlake,   G. N.,   pseud.   See   STOPES,   MARIE
CHARLOTTE   CARMICHAEL.

Morton,   Eleanor,   pseud.   See   STERN,   ELIZABETH
GERTRUDE (LEVIN).

MORTON, MARTHA. 1865-1925. U.S.

AWW   WILA   Biography

Obituary
NY TIMES (20 Feb 1925), 17:4.

MOSELEY, ELLA LOWERY. U.S.

WOWWA   Biography

MOSS, MARY. 1864-1914. U.S.

WOWWA   WWWA-1   Biography

MUCKLESTON, EDITH MARGARET (WHERRY). U.S.
Edith Wherry

Biography
ALY   AWO   HINK   WWNA   WWWE

Muhlbach,   Louise,   pseud.   See   MUNDT,   KLARA
(MUELLER).

MULHOLLAND, CLARA. d.1934. Ireland.

Biography

CRO   WWWL

Mulholland, Rosa.   See   GILBERT, ROSA (MULHOLLAND).

MULLINS, ISLA MAY (HAWLEY). 1859-1936. U.S.

Biography

ALY   BURK   WWNA   WWWA-1

Obituary

PUBLISHERS WEEKLY 129 (29 Feb 1936), 997.

Mumford, Ethel Watts. See   GRANT, ETHEL (WATTS)
MUMFORD.

MUNDT, KLARA (MUELLER). 1814-1873. Germany.
Louise Muhlbach, pseud.

Biography

ADE   BD   JOHDB   WARBD   WEBS

Obituary

NY TIMES (29 Sept 1873), 1:7.
TIMES (LONDON) (30 Sept 1873), 10:1.

MUNGER, DELL H. (STRICKLAND). b.1862. U.S.

Biography

WWWA-4

MUNN, MARGARET (CROSBY). U.S.
Biography

WOWWA

MUNN, MARGUERITE (BRYANT).   b.1870. England.
Marguerite Bryant
Mrs. Philip Munn

Biography
WOWWA   WWWE   WWWL

Munn, Mrs. Philip.   See   MUNN, MARGUERITE (BRYANT).

MURFREE, FANNY NOAILLES DICKINSON.   b.1845. U.S.

Biography
LIB   ROCK   RUB   SOU   ST   WARBD

MURFREE, MARY NOAILLES.   1850-1922. U.S.
Charles Egbert Craddock, pseud.

Biography
ADE   AMR   APP   AWW   BAS   BD   BERE   BURK   CHA   DAB
HAOXA   HARKF   KNIB   KUAA   LOGP   MYE   NAW   NCAB-2
NPW   ORG   PRE   REA   RICDA   RUT   ST   TWCB   WAGCA
WARBD   WEBS   WILA   WOWWA   WWWA-1   WYN

Cary, Richard.   MARY N. MURFREE.   New York:
Twayne, [1967].   LC67-24762.

Parks, Edd W.   CHARLES EGBERT CRADDOCK (MARY
NOAILLES MURFREE).   Port Washington, N.Y.:
Kennikat, [1972, c1941].   LC75-159098.

Ticknor, Caroline.   GLIMPSES OF AUTHORS.
pp. 179-81.   Freeport, N.Y.: Books for
Libraries, [1972, c1922].   LC70-167429.

MURPHY, EMILY (FERGUSON).   1868-1933. Canada.
Janey, Canuk, pseud.
Emily Ferguson

Autobiography
JANEY CANUCK IN THE WEST.   Toronto: McClelland
and Stewart, [1975].   LC77-355797.

MURPHY

Biography
INN   MDCB   MDWB   MOR2   RHO   STOXC   SY   WOWWA
WWNA

James, Donna. EMILY MURPHY. Don Mills, Ont.
   Fitzhenry & Whiteside, c1977. LC78-303915.

Sanders, Byrne H. EMILY MURPHY, CRUSADER ("JANEY
   CANUK"). Introduction by Nellie McClung.
   Toronto: Macmillan of Canada, 1945. LC46-4494.

_____. FAMOUS WOMEN: CARR, HIND, GULLEN,
   MURPHY. pp. 113-42. Toronto: Clarke, Irwin,
   1958. LC58-25398.

Obituary
CANADIAN AUTHOR 11 (Dec 1933), 11.
"The Passing of Janey Canuk." CANADIAN BOOKMAN
   15 (Nov 1933), 163.

MURPHY, EVA (MORLEY). b.1856. U.S.

Biography
HOO   WOWWA   WWWA-4

MURRAY, ROSALIND. b.1890. Scotland.
      m. Toynbee

Biography
OBRIR

MUZAKOVA, JOHANA (ROTTOVA). 1830-1899.
Czechoslovakia.
      Caroline Svetla, pseud.

Biography
CAS   SCHM

Nalkowska, Sofja Rygier. See NALKOWSKA, ZOFIA
RYGIER.

NALKOWSKA, ZOFIA RYGIER. 1885-1954. Poland.
Sofja Rygier Nalkowska
Sofja Rygier-Nalkowska

Biography
CAS CDME HAR MAT WEBS

Obituary
NY TIMES (29 Dec 1954), 23:4.

NEEDELL, MARY ANNA (LUPTON). 1830-1922. England.
Mrs. J.H. Needell

Biography
BD

Obituary
TIMES (LONDON) (1 Mar 1922), 7:5.

Needell, Mrs. J. H. See Needell, Mary Anna
(Lupton).

NEFF, ELIZABETH (HYER). d.1942. U.S.

Biography
COY WOWWA WWA-5

NELSON, KATHLEEN GRAY. U.S.

Biography
KNIB

NELSON, ROBERTA BERESFORD. 1864-1910. U.S.

Biography
COY

Nemcova, Bozena. See NEMEC, BARBORA (PANKLOVA).

NEMEC, BARBORA (PANKLOVA). 1820-1862.
Czechoslovakia.
Bozena Nemcova

Biography
Gregor, Frances. "A Biographical Sketch of the
Author." In THE GRANDMOTHER, by Bozena
Nemec. Chicago, A.C. McClurg, 1891. LC7-25782R.

Souickova, Milada. THE CZECH ROMANTICS.
pp. 129-65. 's-Gravenhase: Mouton, 1958.
LCa58-3867.

NEPEAN, EDITH (BELLIS). Wales.

Biography
HAMM   WWLA   WWWE   WWWL

Nesbit, E. See BLAND, EDITH (NESBIT).

Nethersole, S.C. See NETHERSOLE, SUSAN COLYER.

NETHERSOLE, SUSAN COLYER. b.1869. England.
S.C. Nethersole

Biography
WWWE

NEW, CATHERINE (MACLAEN). b.1870. Canada.

Biography
BAN   WOWWA   WWWA-5

NEWBERRY, FANNIE ELLSWORTH (STONE). 1848-1942. U.S.

Obituary
NY TIMES (25 Jan 1942), 41:2.
WILSON 16 (Mar 1942), 502.

NICHOLAS, ANNA. 1849-1929. U.S.

Biography
BAN WWWA-1

NICHOLSON, MEREDITH. 1866-1947. U.S.

Biography
ALY BAN BURK DAB-4 HAOXA KUL KUT MYE
NCAB-A REA WARD WARLC WEBS WWWA-2

Obituary
NY TIMES (22 Dec 1947), 21:1.

NICHOLSON, VICTORIA MARY SACKVILLE-WEST.
1892-1962. England.
Victoria Mary Sackville-West
V. Sackville West

Autobiography

DEAREST ANDREW: LETTERS FROM V. SACKVILLE-WEST
TO ANDREW REIBER, 1951-1962, edited by Nancy
MacKnight. New York: Scribner, c1979.
LC79-9244.

KNOLE AND THE SACKVILLES, by V. Sackville-West.
New York: Doran, [1923?]. OCLC 5020158.

Biography
BRO CEL CHABI CON-104 FLE KUL KUT LES
MANBL MARBS MDWB MICB NOV OV OVAM RIC
RULE SHO WAR WARLC WEBS WWLA WWWE

Church, Richard. "V. Sackville-West; a Poet in a Tradition." In EIGHT FOR IMMORTALITY. pp. 69-82. London: Dent, [1941]. LC41-20239.

Jullian, Philippe and John Phillips. THE OTHER WOMAN: A LIFE OF VIOLET TREFUSIS, INCLUDING PREVIOUSLY UNPUBLISHED CORRESPONDENCE WITH VITA SACKVILLE-WEST. Boston: Houghton Mifflin, 1976. LC76-25141.

Nicholson, Harold G. DIARIES AND LETTERS, edited by Nigel Nicholson. 3 vols. New York: Athenum, 1966-68. LC66-23571R.

Nicholson, Nigel. PORTRAIT OF A MARRIAGE. New York: Atheneum, 1973. LC73-80754.

Stevens, Michael. V. SACKVILLE-WEST: A CRITICAL BIOGRAPHY. New York: Scribners, [1974]. LC73-19357.

Trautmann, Joanne. THE JESSAMY BRIDES: THE FRIENDSHIP OF VIRGINIA WOOLF AND V. SACKVILLE-WEST. University Park: Administrative Committee on Research, Pennsylvania State Univ., 1973. LC74-621569.

Watson, Sara R. V. SACKVILLE-WEST. New York: Twayne, [1972]. LC77-169631.

Obituary

CON 93--96.
ILLUS LONDON NEWS 240 (9 June 1962), 941.
NY TIMES (3 June 1962), 88:3.
OBIT2, 698.
PUBLISHERS WEEKLY 181 (25 June 1962), 44.
TIME 79 (8 June 1962), 89.
TIMES (LONDON) (4 June 1962), 19:5; (11 June), 12:2.
WILSON 37 (Sept 1962), 18.

Nixon, Mary F. See ROULET, MARY F. (NIXON-).

NOBLE, ANNETTE LUCILE. 1844-1932. U.S.

Biography

APP   BURK   TWCB   WARBD   WARD   WOWWA   WWWA-1

Obituary

PUBLISHERS WEEKLY 122 (17 Dec 1932), 2254.

NOEL, AUGUSTA MARY (KEPPEL). 1838-1902. England.
Lady Augusta Noel

Biography

WWW-1

Noel, Lady   Augusta.   See NOEL,   AUGUSTA   MARY
(KEPPEL).

Norman, Mrs. George, pseud.   See   BLOUNT, MELESINA
MARY.

NORRIS, KATHLEEN (THOMPSON). 1880-1966. U.S.

Autobiography

FAMILY GATHERING.   Garden City, N.Y.: Doubleday,
1959. LC59-12638.

NOON; AN AUTOBIOGRAPHICAL SKETCH. Garden City,
N.Y.: Doubleday, Page, 1925. LC25-4227.

Biography

AUT   AWO   BERE   BURK   CEL   CEL2   CHABI   HAMM   HOE
KIL   KUL   MAN   MARBS   NAWM   NCAB-C   OV   OV2   REA
TWCR   WAR   WARLC   WEBS

Doubleday &   Co., Inc.   KATHLEEN NORRIS; THE
AUTHOR AND HER BOOKS. [Garden City, N.Y.,
Doubleday, Doran, 1933].
22 pages

Obituary

ANTIQUARIAN BOOKMAN (31 Jan 1966).
CON 25--28R.
NEW YORK HERALD TRIBUNE (19 Jan 1966).

NY TIMES (19 Jan 1966), 41:1.
NEWSWEEK 67 (31 Jan 1966), 61.
PUBLISHERS WEEKLY 189 (31 Jan 1966), 78.
TIME 87 (28 Jan 1966), 72.
TIMES (LONDON) (20 Jan 1966), 14:5.

NORRIS, MARY HARRIOTT. 1848-1919. U.S.

Biography
BURK   DAB   KUAA   WARBD

NORRIS, ZOE ANDERSON. d.1914. U.S.

Obituary
NY TIMES (14 Feb 1914), 11:5.

North, Leigh, pseud.   See PHELPS, ELIZABETH
STEWARD.

Noyes, Frances Newbold.   See   HART, FRANCES NEWBOLD
(NOYES).

OBENCHAIN, ELIZA CAROLINE (CALVERT). 1856-1936.
U.S.
       Eliza Calvert Hall, pseud.

Biography
BARN   BURK   KNIB   WWNA

OBER, SARAH ENDICOTT. 1854-1932. U.S.
      Huldah Herrick, pseud.

Biography
WWWA-4

O'BRIEN, FLORENCE ROMA MUIR WILSON. 1891-1930.
England.
      Romer Wilson, pseud.

Biography
BRO   KUAT   KUT   MICB   MYE   NCH   ROCK   WARLC   WEBS

Obituary
TIMES (LONDON) (5 Feb 1930), 16:3.

O'BRIEN, MARGARET ELIZABETH. 1870-1898. U.S.

Biography
ODP

O'BRIEN, MARY MARVIN (HEATON) VORSE. d.1955.
U.S.

Biography
WOWWA

O'Brien, Mrs.William. See O'BRIEN, SOPHIE
RAFFALOVICH.

O'BRIEN, SOPHIE (RAFFALOVICH). England.
Mrs. William O'Brien

Biography
BRI

O'CONNOR, ELIZABETH (PASCHAL). d.1931. U.S.
Mrs. T.P. C'Connor

Autobiography
I MYSELF, by Mrs. T.P. O'Connor. 3d ed. London:
Methuen, [1911]. LC11-14591.

O'Conner, Mrs. T. P. See O'CONNOR, ELIZABETH
(PASCHAL).

O'DONNELL, JESSIE FREMONT. 1860-1897. U.S.

Biography
AWW   ODP   WILA

OEMLER, MARIE (CONWAY). 1879-1932. U.S.

Biography
AWW   BURK   KUT   MARBS   OV2   WWNA   WWWA-1   WYN

Obituary
PUBLISHERS WEEKLY 121 (11 June 1932), 2355.

OHL, MAUDE ANNULET (ANDREWS). 1866-1943. U.S.
Annulet Andrews

Biography
KNIB   WILA

OLDER, CORA MIRANDA (BAGGERLY). 1873-1968. U.S.
Mrs. Fremont Older

Biography
ALY   AWO   AWW   BURK   HINK   WOWWA   WWWA-5

OLDER

Obituary
NY TIMES (29 Sept 1968), 80:3.

Older, Mrs. Fremont. See OLDER, CORA MIRANDA
(BAGGERLY).

OLIPHANT, BLOSSOM DRUM. U.S.
Blossom Drum

Biography
KNIB

OLIPHANT, MARGARET OLIPHANT (WILSON). 1828-1897.
Scotland.
Mrs. Oliphant
Mrs. M.O.W. Oliphant

Autobiography
AUTOBIOGRAPHY AND LETTERS OF MRS. MARGARET
OLIPHANT, edited by Mrs. Harry Coghill.
[Leicester]: Leicester Univ. Press, 1974.
LC74-183200.

THE DAYS OF MY LIFE. AN AUTOBIOGRAPHY. New York:
Harper, 1857. LC07-32618.

Biography
ASH BD BEL BERE BOASE-6 BRO CAS CHABI
CLARS COR DNB-1 FUR HAMM HAOXE JOHDB KUBA
MAGN MAO MDWB MYE NCH NO NOV NPW PEE
ROCK SHA SHA-A SHO VIC WAGCE WARBD WEBS

Colby, Vineta and Robert A. Colby. THE EQUIVOCAL
VIRTUE: MRS. OLIPHANT AND THE VICTORIAN
LITERARY MARKET PLACE. [Hamden, Conn.]: Archon
Books, 1966. LC66-12770.

Gwynn, Stephen L. "A Mother, Margaret Oliphant."
In SAINTS & SCHOLARS. pp. 221-56. London:
T. Butterworth, Ltd., [1929]. LC29-16693.

Monroe, Katharine. VICTORIAN WIVES. pp. 72-80.
New York:St. Martin's, [1974]. LC73-89048R.

O'Brien, Sophie R. "A Novelist of the Last
Century: Mrs. Oliphant." In UNSEEN FRIENDS.
pp. 34-67. New York: Longmans, Green, 1912.
LC12-26015.

Stebbins, Lucy P. A VICTORIAN ALBUM; SOME LADY
NOVELISTS OF THE PERIOD. pp. 155-91. New
York: AMS, 1966 [c1946]. LC76-182716.

Obituary
ATHENAEUM 110 (3 July 1897), 35.
CRITIC 31, n.s. 28 (3 July 1897), 8.
ILLUS LONDON NEWS (10 July 1897), 40.
NY TIMES (27 June 1897), 13:3.
TIMES (LONDON) (28 June 1897), 10:1.

Oliphant, Mrs. See OLIPHANT, MARGARET OLIPHANT
(WILSON).

Oliphant, Mrs. M.O.W. See OLIPHANT, MARGARET
OLIPHANT (WILSON).

OLIVER, AMY ROBERTA (RUCK). 1878-1978. England.
Mrs. Oliver Onions, pseud.
Berta Ruck

Autobiography
AN ASSET TO WALES, by Berta Ruck. London:
Hutchinson, 1970. LC76-557931.

A SMILE FOR THE PAST, by Berta Ruck. London:
Hutchinson, [1959]. LC59-65094.

A STORY-TELLER TELLS THE TRUTH: REMINISCENCES &
NOTES, by Berta Ruck. London: Hutchinson,
[1937]. LC38-1315.

A TRICKLE OF WELSH BLOOD, by Berta Ruck. London:
Hutchinson, 1967. LC67-108916.

Biography
BERE BRO CON-N5 HAMM KUT RIC ROCK TWCR
WARLC WEBS WWLA WWWE

OLIVER

Obituary
TIMES (LONDON) (12 Aug 1978), 14:7-8.

Oliver, Temple, pseud. See SMITH, JEANIE OLIVER
(DAVIDSON).

OLMSTEAD, FLORENCE. U.S.

Biography
AWO BURK WWNA

O'Neill, Moira, pseud. See SKRINE, NESTA
(HIGGINSON).

O'NEILL, ROSE CECIL. 1874-1944. U.S.
m. (1)Latham (2)Wilson

Biography
AWW BURK DAB-3 KUL KUT NAW VDW WEBS

McCanse, Ralph A. TITANS AND KEWPIES: THE LIFE
AND ART OF ROSE O'NEILL. New York: Vantage,
[1968]. LC68-1950.

Obituary
Walbridge, E. SAT REVIEW OF LIT 27 (3 June
1944), 28.
TIME 43 (17 Apr 1944), 75.

Onions, Mrs. Oliver, pseud. See OLIVER, AMY
ROBERTA (RUCK).

ORCUTT, EMMA LOUISE (FULLER). U.S.

Biography
WOWWA

Orczy, Baroness. See BARSTOW, EMMA MAGDALENA
ROSALIA MARIA JOSEFA BARBARA ORCZY.

Orczy, Baroness Emmuska. See BARSTOW, EMMA MAGDALENA ROSALIA MARIA JOSEFA BARBARA ORCZY.

ORR, CHRISTINE GRANT MILLAR. 1899-1963. Scotland.

Biography
WARLC   WWLA   WWWE

Obituary
TIMES (LONDON) (21 May 1963), 16:5.

ORRED, META.

Biography
JOHH2

Orzeszko, Eliza. See ORZESZKOWA, ELIZA (PAWLOWSKA).

ORZESZKOWA, ELIZA (PAWLOWSKA). 1841/42-1910. Poland.
Eliza Orzeszko

Biography
CAS   CDME   HAR   KUE   MDWB   PEEU   SCHM

OSGOOD, IRENE (DE BELLOT). 1875-1922. U.S.

Biography
BURK   WOWWA   WWWA-1   WWWL

Obituary
NY TIMES (13 Dec 1922), 21:5.

OSKISON, HILDEGARDE (HAWTHORNE). 1871-1952. U.S.
Hildegarde Hawthorne

Biography
AWO   AWW   BURK   KUJ1   KUJ2   REA   WWNA

Obituary
NY TIMES (11 Dec 1952), 33:1.

OSTRANDER, FANNIE ELIZA. d.1921. U.S.

Biography
ALY   WOWWA   WWWA-1

OSTRANDER, ISABEL EGENTON. 1883-1924. U.S.
          Robert Orr Chipperfield, pseud.
          David Fox, pseud.
          Douglas Grant, pseud.

Biography
BURK   WWWA-1

Ouida, pseud.   See DE LA RAMEE, MARIE LOUISE.

OVERTON, GWENDOLEN. b.1876. U.S.

Biography
WOWWA   WWWA-5

OVINGTON, MARY WHITE. 1865-1951. U.S.

Autobiography
THE WALLS CAME TUMBLING DOWN.   New York: Arno,
   1969, 1947. LC69-18543.

Biography
AWW   BURK   WWWA-3

Obituary
NY TIMES (16 July 1951), 21:4.

Owen, Caroline Dale, pseud.   See SNEDEKER, CAROLINE
DALE (PARKE).

OWEN, MARY ALICIA. 1858-1935. U.S.

Biography
AWW   BURK   KNIB   NCAB-13   WILA   WOWWA   WWWA-1

Page, Gertrude. See DOBBIN, GERTRUDE (PAGE).

PAGET, VIOLET. 1856-1935. England.
       Vernon Lee, pseud.

Biography
  ASH BD BERE BRO CHA CHABI COLSA CON-104
  DNB-5 HAOXE KUT LAU LES MANBL MCC MICB
  MYE NCH ROCK SHA SHA-A SHO WARBD WARLC
  WEBS WENW WWWL

Gunn, Peter. VERNON LEE: VIOLET PAGET, 1856-1935.
New York: Arno, 1975, c1964. LC75-12323.

Obituary
TIMES (LONDON) (14 Feb 1935), 17:4.

PAHLOW, GERTRUDE CURTIS BROWN. 1881-1937. U.S.

Biography
  ALY BURK COY WALD WWNA WWWA-1

PAINE, HARRIET ELIZA. 1845-1910. U.S.
       Eliza Chester, pseud.

Biography
  LOGP TWCB WWWA-1

PAINTER, LYDIA (HOYT) FARMER. 1842-1903. U.S.
       Lydia Hoyt Farmer.

Biography
  BURK COY NCAB-8 TWCB WARBD WILA WWWA-1

Obituary
NY TIMES (27 Dec 1903), 3:2.

PALMER, BELL (ELLIOTT). b.1873. U.S.

Biography
WWWA-5

Palmer, Lynde, pseud. See   PEEBLES, MARY LOUISE
(PARMELEE).

PANGBORN, GEORGIA (WOOD). b.1872. U.S.

Biography
AWO   BURK   WOWWA   WWWA-5

Pansy, pseud. See   ALDEN,   ISABELLA   (MACDONALD).

PANTON, JANE ELLEN (FIRTH). 1848-1923.

Autobiography
FRESH LEAVES AND GREEN PASTURES.   New York:
Bretano, 1909. LC9-25128.

LEAVES FROM A LIFE.   New York: Brentano's, 1908.
OCLC 3490303.

MORE LEAVES FROM A LIFE.   London: E. Nash, 1911.
OCLC 1539168.

PARDO BAZAN, EMILIA. 1852-1921.   Spain.
      m. Quiroga

Biography
BERE   CAS   CDME   CHABI   FLE   HAMM   HAR   KUE   MDWB
PEEU   SCHM   WARBD   WEBS   WWWL

Hemingway, Maurice.   "A Biographical Sketch."   In
EMILIA PARDO BAZAN: THE MAKING OF A NOVELIST.
pp. 163-4. New York: Cambridge Univ. Press,
1983. LC82-14609.

Newmark, Maxim.   DICTIONARY OF SPANISH
LITERATURE.   pp. 253-4.   New York:
Philosophical Library, [1956]. LC56-13978.

THE OXFORD COMPANION TO SPANISH LITERATURE,
edited by Philip Ward. pp. 442-3. Oxford
[Eng.]: Clarendon, 1978. LC78-325227.

Pattison, Walter T. EMILIA PARDO BAZAN. New
York: Twayne, [1971]. LC70-120497.

Obituary
Erskine, Beatrice. "Emilia Pardo Bazan."
CONTEMPORARY REVIEW (LONDON) 120 (Aug 1921),
240-4.
"A Great Spanish Author, Countess Bazan." LIVING
AGE 310 (13 Aug 1921), 433-4.
NY TIMES (13 May 1921), 15:6.
TIMES (LONDON) (14 May 1921), 9:4.

PARKER, FRANCES. b.1875. U.S.

Biography
WOWWA   WWWA-5

PARKER, LOTTIE (BLAIR). 1859?-1937. U.S.

Biography
AWW   BURK   LOGP   NCAB-10   WOWWA   WWWA-1

Obituary
NY TIMES (6 Jan 1937), 23:1.
PUBLISHERS WEEKLY 131 (30 Jan 1937), 537.

PARKER, MARY MONCURE (PAYNTER). 1862-1941. U.S.

Biography
WWNA

PARKES, ELIZABETH (ROBINS). 1862-1952. U.S.
C.E. Raimond, pseud.
Elizabeth Robins

Autobiography
BOTH SIDES OF THE CURTAIN, by Elizabeth Robbins.
London; Toronto: W. Heinemann, [1940].
LCa41-2948.

RAYMOND AND I, by Elizabeth Robbins. New York: Macmillan, 1956. LC56-10962L.

Biography
AWW BD BERE BURK CHA COY HAMM HAOXA KUT
LIB REA RICDA SHO WARLC WEBS WWWT

Obituary
NY TIMES (9 May 1952), 23:5.
OBIT1, 605.
TIMES (LONDON) (9 May 1952), 8:6.

PARMELE, MARY (PLATT). 1843-1911. U.S.

Biography
WWWA-1

PARR, LOUISA (TAYLOR). d.1903. England.
  Mrs. Parr

Biography
BLAP DNB-2

Obituary
TIMES (LONDON) (7 Nov 1903), 12:2.

Parr, Mrs. See PARR, LOUISA (TAYLOR).

PARR, OLIVE KATHARINE. 1874-1955. England.
  Beatrice Chase, pseud.

Biography
HOE WWWE WWWL

Green, Christina. BEATRICE CHASE, MY LADY OF
  THE MOOR. [2d ed.]. Newton Abbot: Ideford
  Publications, 1975. LC76-361671.
  17 pages
Obituary
NY TIMES (5 July 1955), 29:3.
TIMES (LONDON) (5 July 1955), 13:4.
WILSON 30 (Sept 1955), 20.

Paston, George, pseud. See SYMONDS, EMILY MORSE.

PATCH, KATE (WHITING). 1870-1909. U.S.

<u>Biography</u>
BURK WWWA-1

PATERSON, ISABEL (BOWLER). 1885-1961. U.S.

<u>Biography</u>
AWO BURK KUL KUT MYE WEBS

<u>Obituary</u>
NY TIMES (11 Jan 1961), 47:2.

Patrick, Diana, pseud. See WILSON, DESEMEA
(NEWMAN).

PATTERSON, MARJORIE. d.1948. U.S.

<u>Biography</u>
BURK WWNA

<u>Obituary</u>
NY TIMES (12 Mar 1948), 23:4.

Paulina Elizabeth Ottilia Louisa. See ELISABETH,
QUEEN CONSORT OF CHARLES I, KING OF RUMANIA.

Peacocke, Isabel Maud. See CLUETT, ISABEL MAUD
(PEACOCKE).

Peake, C.M.A. See PEAKE, CHARLOTTE M.A.
(BAYLIFF).

PEAKE, CHARLOTTE M.A. (BAYLIFF) b.1862. England.
C.M.A. Peake

<u>Biography</u>
WWLA WWWE

PEARD, FRANCES MARY. 1835-1923. England.

Biography
WARBD

Obituary
TIMES (LONDON) (3 Oct 1923), 17:6.

Pearl, Bertha, pseud. See MOORE, BERTHA PEARL.

PEATTIE, ELIA (WILKINSON). 1862-1935. U.S.

Biography
AWW   BURK   HOO   ST   TWCB   WARBD   WILA   WOWWA
WWWA-1

PECK, THEODORA AGNES. b.1882. U.S.

Biography
ALY   BURK   WOWWA   WWNA

Peck, Lady. See PECK, WINIFRED FRANCES (KNOX).

PECK, WINIFRED FRANCES (KNOX). 1882-1962.
Scotland.
Lady Peck

Autobiography
HOME FOR THE HOLIDAYS. London: Faber and Faber,
[1955]. LC56-16410.

A LITTLE LEARNING; OR, A VICTORIAN CHILDHOOD.
London: Faber and Faber, [1952]. LC52-42392.

Biography
BRIT   WARLC   WWWE

Obituary
OBIT2, 624.
TIMES (LONDON) (22 Nov 1962), 18:3; (4 Dec),
15:1.

PEEBLES, MARY LOUISE (PARMELEE). 1833-1915. U.S.
Lynde Palmer, pseud.

Biography
APP   NCAB-4   WOWWA   WWWA-1

Obituary
NY TIMES (26 Apr 1915), 9:6.

PEEKE, MARGARET BLOODGOOD (PECK). 1838-1908.
U.S.

Biography
COY   WILA   WWWA-1

PEEL, DOROTHY CONSTANCE (BAYLIFF). d.1934. England.
Mrs. C.S. Peel

Biography
WWLA   WWWE   WWWL

Obituary
TIMES (LONDON) (8 Aug 1934), 12:3.

Peel, Mrs. C.S.   See   PEEL, DOROTHY   CONSTANCE
(BAYLIFF).

PELTON, MABELL SHIPPIE CLARKE. b.1864.

Biography
KNIB

PENDER, MARGARET T. (O'DOHERTY). 1850?-1920.
Ireland.
Mrs. M.T. Pender

Biography
BRI   CLE   ODP

Pender, Mrs. M. T.   See   PENDER,   MARGARET T.
(O'DOHERTY).

PENDERED, MARY LUCY. 1858-1940. England.

Biography
WWLA WWWE

PENNELL, ELIZABETH (ROBINS). 1855-1936. U.S.

Biography
AWW BD BURK NAW NCAB-10 PRE WARBD WEBS
WWWA-1

Tinker, Edward L. THE PENNELLS. New York,
[1951]. LC51-5154.

Obituary
NY TIMES (8 Feb 1936), 15:1.

Pennington, Patience, pseud. See PRINGLE,
ELIZABETH WATIES (ALLSTON).

Penny, F.E. See PENNY, FANNY EMILY (FARR).

PENNY, FANNY EMILY (FARR). d.1939. India.
          F.E. Penny
          Mrs. Frank Penny

Biography
PARR WWWE WWWL

Obituary
TIMES (LONDON) (27 Dec 1939), 9:5.

Penny, Mrs. Frank. See PENNY, FANNY EMILY (FARR).

PENROSE, MARY ELIZABETH (LEWIS). b.1860. Ireland.
          Mrs. H.H. Penrose

Biography
BRI

Penrose, Mrs. H. H.   See   PENROSE,   MARY ELIZABETH
(LEWIS).

PERKINS, ROSE. 1856-1911.

Biography
WWWL

PERRIN, ALICE (ROBINSON).   1867-1934.   India.

Biography
HAMM   PARR   SHO   WWLA   WWWE

Obituary
TIMES (LONDON) (15 Feb 1934), 9:2.

PERRY, STELLA GEORGE (STERN).   b.1877.   U.S.

Biography
AWO   BURK   WOWWA   WWWA-3

PETERSEN, MARIE BJELKE. Australia.
Marie Bjelke-Petersen

Biography
MIA

Peterson, Maud Howard, pseud.   See   HOOPES, MARY
HOWARD (PETERSON).

PETTUS, MAIA.   1875-1956.   U.S.

Biography
KNIB   WOWWA   WWWA-3

PHELPS, ELIZABETH STEWARD.   d.1920.   U.S.
Leigh North, pseud.

Biography
BURK

Phelps, Elizabeth Stuart. See WARD, ELIZABETH STUART (PHELPS).

PICKARD, FLORENCE (WILLINGHAM). 1862-1930. U.S.

Biography
NCAB-B,27 WWNA WWWA-1

Pickering, Percival, pseud. See STIRLING, ANNA MARIA DIANA WILHELMINA (PICKERING).

PICKETT, LA SALLE CORBELL. 1848-1931. U.S.

Biography
BURK KNIB WILA WOWWA WWWA-1

Obituary
NY TIMES (23 Mar 1931), 21:3.

PICKTHALL, MARJORIE LOWRY CHRISTIE. 1883-1922.
Canada.

Biography
CHA CON-107 GARV KUT KUTS MANBL MDCB MOR2
MYE REA RHO SCHW STOXC WARLC WEBS WOWWA

Logan, J.D. MARJORIE PICKTHALL: HER POETIC
GENIUS AND ART. AN APPRECIATION AND AN
ANALYSIS OF AESTHETIC PARADOX. Halifax,
Canada: T.C.Allen, 1922. NUC.

Percival, Walter P. LEADING CANADIAN POETS.
pp. 168-76. Toronto: Ryerson, [1948]. LC48-7452.

Pierce, Lorne A. MARJORIE PICKTHALL, A BOOK OF
REMEMBRANCE. Toronto: Ryerson, [1925].
OCLC 676365.

Obituary
GLOBE (TORONTO) (20 Apr 1922); (27 Apr).
Also pub. in Logan, pp. 38-42.
MANITOBA FREE PRESS (WINNIPEG) (22 Apr 1922).
Also pub. in Logan, p. 43.

PICTON, NINA. U.S.
        Laura Dearborn, pseud.

                Biography
    ROCK

PINSENT, ELLEN FRANCES (PARKER). 1866-1949.
England.
        Dr. Richards, pseud.

                Obituary
    TIMES (LONDON) (12 Oct 1949), 4:6; (13 Oct), 4:2;
    (15 Oct), 7:5; tribute (21 Oct), 7:6.

Piper, Margaret R. See CHALMERS, MARGARET REBECCA
    (PIPER).

PIRKIS, CATHERINE LOUISA (LYNE). England.

                Obituary
    TIMES (LONDON) (5 Oct 1910), 11:3.

PITKIN, HELEN. b.1877. U.S.

                Biography
    KNIB

Pittman, H.D. See PITTMAN, HANNAH (DAVIESS).

PITTMAN, HANNAH (DAVIESS). 1840-1919. U.S.
        H.D. Pittman
        Mrs. H.D. Pittman

                Biography
    BURK KNIB WOWWA WWWA-4

Pittman, Mrs. H.D. See PITTMAN, HANNAH (DAVIESS).

PLANTZ, MYRA (GOODWIN). 1856-1914. U.S.

Biography
BICA   BOY   WOWWA   WWWA-1

Plympton, A.G.   See   PLYMPTON, ALMIRA GEORGE.

PLYMPTON, ALMIRA GEORGE.   1852-1939. U.S.
A.G. Plympton

Biography
BURK   WOWWA

POOL, MARIA LOUISE. 1841-1898.   U.S.

Biography
APP   BD   BURK   DAB   KUAA   NCAB-6   TWCB   WARBD
WWWA-H

Obituary
CRITIC 32, n.s. 29 (28 May 1898), 364.

POOR, AGNES BLAKE. 1842-1922. U.S.

Biography
BURK   NCAB-19   WARBD   WOWWA   WWWA-1

POPE, MARION (MANVILLE). b.1859. U.S.

Biography
AWO   WILA

PORTER, ELEANOR (HODGMAN). 1868-1920. U.S.

Biography
ALY   AMN   AWW   BERE   BICA   BRO   BURK   CHABI
CON-108   DOY   HAOXA   KUT   MYE   NAW   OV   OV2
NCAB-18   REA   RIC   TWCR   WARLC   WEBS   WWWA-1
WWWL

Russell, Foster W. MOUNT AUBURN BIOGRAPHIES. A
BIOGRAPHICAL LISTING OF DISTINGUISHED PERSONS
INTERRED IN MOUNT AUBURN CEMETERY....
pp. 132-3. [Cambridge, Mass.]: Proprietors of
the Cemetery of Mount Auburn, 1953. LC54-16598.

PORTER, GENE (STRATTON). 1868-1924. U.S.
Gene Stratton-Porter

Autobiography
HOMING WITH THE BIRDS; THE HISTORY OF A LIFETIME
OF PERSONAL EXPERIENCE WITH THE BIRDS, by Gene
Stratton-Porter. Garden City, N.Y.: Doubleday,
Page, 1919. LC19-15505.

Biography
ADE   ALY   AWW   BAN   BERE   BRO   BURK   CHABI
DAB-S1   DOY   HAMM   HAOXA   KUT   MYE   NAW   NCAB-15
NOV   OVA   OVAM   PEA   REA   RIC   RICDA   SOME-15
ST   TWCR   VDW   WARLC   WEBS   WOWWA

King, Rollin P. GENE STRATTON-PORTER, A LOVELY
LIGHT. Chicago: Adams, c1979. LC79-50501.

Meehan, Jeannette (Porter). LIFE AND LETTERS OF
GENE STRATTON-PORTER. Port Washington, N.Y.:
Kennikat, [1972]. LC77-160774.
First pub. in 1928 as: THE LADY OF THE
LIMBERLOST.

Richards, Bernard F. GENE STRATTON PORTER.
Boston: Twayne, 1980. LC79-24477.

Saxton, Eugene F. GENE STRATTON-PORTER; A LITTLE
STORY OF THE LIFE AND WORK AND IDEALS OF "THE
BIRD WOMAN," compiled from many intimate
records of the author's life by S.F.E. Garden
City, N.Y.: Doubleday, Page, [c1915].
LC15-16771.

Obituary
NY TIMES (8 12 1924), 2:2.
TIMES (LONDON) (8 Dec 1924), 16:4.

PORTER, REBECCA NEWMAN. b.1883. U.S.

Biography
BURK   WWNA   WWWE

PORTER, ROSE. 1845-1906. U.S.

Biography
AWW   BURK   NCAB-10   WILA   WWWA-1

POST, EMILY (PRICE). 1873-1960. U.S.

Biography
AWO   AWW   BERE   BRO   BURK   CEL   CON-103
CUR-1941   DAB-S6   HAOXA   MDWB   NAWM   NCAB-44
REA   VDW   WEBS   WOMA   WWWA-4   WWWE

Post, Edwin.   TRULY EMILY POST.   New York:
   Wagnalls, [1961]. LC61-7298.

Obituary
CON-89--92.
CUR-1960.
EDITOR AND PUBLISHER 93 (1 Oct 1960), 62.
NY TIMES (27 Sept 1960), 1:4.
NEWSWEEK 56 (10 Oct 1960), 30.
OBIT1, 581.
PUBLISHERS WEEKLY 178 (3 OCT 1960), 41.
TIME 76 (10 Oct 1960), 100.
TIMES (LONDON) (28 Sept 1960), 18:3.

POTTER, FRANCES BOARDMAN (SQUIRE). 1867-1914.
U.S.
            Frances Squire

Biography
BICA   NCAB-15   WWWA-1

Obituary
NY TIMES (26 Mar 1914), 11:5.

Potter, Margaret.   See BLACK, MARGARET HORTON
   (POTTER).

Potter, Margaret Horton. See Black, Margaret Horton (Potter).

Powell, Frances, pseud. See CASE, FRANCES POWELL.

POWERS, CAROL (HOYT). 1868-1940. U.S.

Biography
WOWWA   WWWA-1

Obituary
NY TIMES (9 June 1940), 44:3.

Praed, Mrs. Campbell. See PRAED, ROSE CAROLINE (MURRAY-PRIOR).

PRAED, ROSE CAROLINE (MURRAY-PRIOR). 1851-1935. Australia./England.
    Mrs. Campbell Praed

Biography
ASH   BD   BEI   BRO   BYR   CHA-3   HAMM   KUT   KUTS
MIA   MIAU   MYE   NCH   ROCK   ROD   SER   ST   WARBD
WEBS   WWW-3   WWWL

Pownall, Evelyn. A PIONEER DAUGHTER. New York: Oxford Univ. Press, 1968. LC76-469611.
    Juvenile literature; 32 pages.

Roderick, Colin A. IN MORTAL BONDAGE: THE STRANGE LIFE OF ROSA PRAED. Sydney: Angus and Robertson, 1948. OCLC 2570667.

Obituary
TIMES (LONDON) (15 Apr 1935), 16:3.

Pratt, Cornelia Atwood. See COMER, CORNELIA ATWOOD (PRATT).

PRATT, GRACE TYLER. U.S.

Biography

WOWWA

PRATT, LUCY. b.1874. U.S.

Biography

BURK   WWNA   WWWA-5

Prescott, E. Livingston, pseud.   See   JAY, EDITH KATHARINE SPICER.

PRICE, ELEANOR CATHERINE. England.

Biography

WWWL

Priceman, James, pseud.   See   KIRKLAND, WINIFRED MARGARETHA.

Prichard, Katharine Susannah.   See   THROSSELL, KATHARINE SUSANNAH (PRICHARD).

PRICHARD, SARAH JOHNSON.   1830-1909. U.S.

Biography

BURK   TWCB   WARBD   WWWA-1

PRINCE, HELEN CHOATE (PRATT).   b.1857. U.S.

Biography

BURK   TWCB   WARBD   WIN   WWWA-4

PRINDLE, FRANCES WESTON (CARRUTH).   1867-1934.
U.S.

Frances Weston Carruth

Biography

BURK   WOWWA   WWWA-4

PRINGLE, ELIZABETH WATIES (ALLSTON). 1845-1921.
U.S.
            Patience Pennington, pseud.

                    Biography
    NAW

                    Obituary
    GEORGETOWN (SO. CA.) TIMES (9 Dec 1921).

Pritchard, Martin J., pseud. See MOORE, JUSTINA.

Prothero John Keith, pseud. See CHESTERTON, ADA
    ELIZABETH (JONES).

PROUTY, OLIVE (HIGGINS). 1882-1974. U.S.

                    Autobiography
    PENCIL SHAVINGS; MEMOIRS. [Cambridge, Mass.]:
        Riverside, [1961]. LC62-1760.

                    Biography
    AWO AWW BERE BURK CON-11--12R KUT MARBS
    NCAB-57 OV2 REA WAR WWNA WWWA-6

                    Obituary
    CON-49--52.
    NY TIMES (26 Mar 1974), 44:4.
    NEWSWEEK 83 (8 Apr 1974), 43.
    WASHINGTON POST (28 Mar 1974).

Pryce, D. Hugh. See PRYCE, DAISY HUGH.

PRYCE, DAISY HUGH. Wales.
            D. Hugh Pryce

                    Biography
    WWWL (name appears as Price)

Pryde, Anthony, pseud. See WEEKES, AGNES RUSSELL.

                        311

Pryor, Mrs. Roger A.   See PRYOR, SARA AGNES (RICE).

PRYOR,   SARA   AGNES   (RICE).   1830-1912.   U.S.
Mrs. Roger A. Pryor

Biography
AWW   BURK   HINK   LIB   LOGP   NAW   RUT   WWWA-1

PUDDICOMBE,   ANNE   ADALIZA   (EVANS).   1836-1908.
Wales.
Allen Raine, pseud.

Biography
DNB-2

DICTIONARY OF WELSH BIOGRAPHY DOWN TO 1940,
edited by John E. Lloyd and R.T. Jenkins.
PP. 810-11.   London, 1959.   LC59-4309R.

Jones, Sally R.   ALLEN RAINE.   [Cardiff]: Univ.
of Wales Press, 1979.   LC80-451192.

Obituary
TIMES (LONDON) (23 June 1908), 13:3.
WWWL.

PULLEN,   ELISABETH   (JONES)   CAVAZZA.   U.S.

Biography
NCAB-8   WARBD   WOWWA   WWWA-5

PULVER,   MARY   BRECHT.   d.1926.   U.S.

Biography
BURG

PUNCHARD,   CONSTANCE   (HOLME).   1881-1955.   England.
Constance Holme

Biography
BRO   HAOXE   MYE   WARLC

Obituary
TIMES (LONDON) (20 June 1955), 11:4.

PUTNAM, NINA (WILCOX). 1888-1962. U.S.

Autobiography
LAUGHING THROUGH. BEING THE AUTOBIOGRAPHICAL
STORY OF A GIRL WHO MADE HER WAY. New York:
Sears, [c1930]. LC30-25657.

Biography
ALY AWO BURG BURK DAB-S7 KUT NCAB-46 WEBS
WOWWA WWNA WWWA-4

Obituary
NY TIMES (9 Mar 1962), 29:1.
NEWSWEEK 59 (19 Mar 1962), 80.
PUBLISHERS WEEKLY 181 (19 Mar 1962), 38.

- Q -

Queen of Rumania. See ELISABETH, QUEEN CONSORT
OF CHARLES I, KING OF RUMANIA.

Quinn, E. Hardingham, pseud. See SCOTT, PATRICIA
ETHEL (STONEHOUSE).

Quinn, Harlingham, pseud. See SCOTT, PATRICIA
ETHEL (STONEHOUSE).

Quinn, Tarella. See DASKEIN, TARELLA QUINN.

Ragsdale, Lulah. See RAGSDALE, TALLULAH.

RAGSDALE, TALLULAH. b.1866. U.S.
    Lulah Ragsdale

             Biography
AWO   LIB-17   WWNA   WWWA-3

Raimond, C. E., pseud. See PARKES, ELIZABETH
(ROBINS).

Raine, Allen, pseud. See PUDDICOMBE, ANNE ADALIZA
(EVANS).

RANDOLPH, EVELYN SAINT LEGER (SAVILE). England.
    Evelyn Saint Leger, pseud.

             Biography
WWWE

Ransom, Olive, pseud. See STEPHENS, KATE.

RAY, ANNA CHAPIN. 1865-1945. U.S.

             Biography
BURK   TWCB   WOWWA   WWWA-2

             Obituary
NY TIMES (14 Dec 1945), 27:5.
PUBLISHERS WEEKLY 149 (12 Jan 1946), 178.
WILSON 20 (Feb 1946), 392.

RAYMOND, EVELYN (HUNT). 1843-1910. U.S.

             Biography
BURK   HINK   KNIB   TWCB   WOWWA   WWWA-1

Rayner, E. See RAYNER, EMMA.

RAYNER, EMMA. d.1926. U.S.
        E. Rayner

                    Biography
    BURK WOWWA WWWA-1

RE, LUCY (BARTLETT).
        Lucy Re Bartlett
        name also appears as Re-Bartlett

                    Biography
    WWWL

                    Obituary
    TIMES (LONDON) (26 Apr 1922), 1:2; tribute
    (1 May), 25:6.

REA, HOPE. b.1860.

                    Biography
    WWWL

REA, LORNA. b.1897. England.

                    Biography
    KUT WARLC

REANEY, ISABEL (EDIS). b.1847.
        Mrs. G.S. Reaney

                    Biography
    WWWL

Reaney, Mrs. G.S. See REANEY, ISABEL (EDIS).

Redfield, Martin, pseud. See BROWN, ALICE.

REED

REED, FANNIE KIMBALL. 1870-1950. U.S.

Biography

COY

REED, HELEN LEAH. 1860?-1926. U.S.

Biography

ALY   BURK   WIN

Reed, Myrtle.   See McCULLOUGH,   MYRTLE (REED).

Reeve, Winnifred.   See BABCOCK, WINNIFRED (EATON).

Reeves, Amber.   See WHITE, AMBER (REEVES) BLANCO.

REEVES, HELEN BUCKINGHAM (MATHERS). 1853-1920.
England.
       David Lyall, pseud.
       H. Mathers
       Helen Mathers

Biography
BLA   CHA   EMD   KUBA   NCH   ROCK   SHO   WARBD   WEBS

Obituary
NY TIMES (16 Mar 1920), 9:4.
TIMES (LONDON) (13 Mar 1920), 18:2.

Reid, Christian, pseud.   See TIERNAN, FRANCES
CHRISTINE (FISHER).

REIFSNIDER, ANNA CYRENE (PORTER) ELLIS. 1850-1932.
U.S.
      Mrs. Calvin Kryder Reifsnider

Biography

NCAB-23

317

Reifsnider, Mrs. Calvin Kryder. See REIFSNIDER, ANNA CYRENE (PORTER) ELLIS.

Reimensnyder, Helen. See MARTIN, HELEN (REIMENSNYDER).

REMICK, GRACE MAY. U.S.

Biography
BURK WWWA-5

RENO, ITTI (KINNEY). b.1862. U.S.

Biography
AWW KNIB LOGP WILA WOWWA WWWA-4

REPPLIER, AGNES. 1855-1950. U.S.

Autobiography
EIGHT DECADES; ESSAYS AND EPISODES. Port
  Washington, N.Y.: Kennikat, [1970, c1937].
  LC72-91050.

Biography
ADE APP AWO AWW BERE BURK BURNT DAB-S4
HAL HAOXA HOE KUL KUT LOGP MAN MICA MYE
NAW NCAB-9,C REA RICDA WAG WARBD WARLC
WEBS WOWWA WWNA WWWA-3 WWWE

Stokes, George S. AGNES REPPLIER, LADY OF
  LETTERS. Westport, Conn.: Greenwood, [1970,
  c1949]. LC73-108400.

Witmer, Emma (Repplier). AGNES REPPLIER, A
  MEMOIR, by her niece. Philadelphia: Dorrance,
  [1957]. LC57-11237L.

Obituary
NY TIMES (16 Dec 1950), 17:1.
NEWSWEEK 36 (25 Dec 1950), 45.
PUBLISHERS WEEKLY 158 (30 Dec 1950), 2624.
TIME 56 (25 Dec 1950), 55.
TIMES (LONDON) (16 Dec 1950), 6:7; (19 Dec), 6:4.
WILSON 25 (Feb 1951), 412.

Revere, M.P., pseud. See WILLIAMSON, ALICE MURIEL (LIVINGSTON).

REYNOLDS, GERTRUDE M. (ROBINS). d.1939. England.
    Mrs. Baillie Reynolds
    G.M. Robins
    name appears also as Baillie-Reynolds

                Biography
ASH WWWE WWWL

Reynolds, Mrs. Baillie. See REYNOLDS, GERTRUDE M. (ROBINS).

RHOADES, CORNELIA HARSEN. 1863-1940. U.S.
    Nina Rhoades, pseud.

            Biography
BURK WWWA-1

            Obituary
CUR-41.
NY TIMES (29 Nov 1940), 21:2.

Rhoades, Nina. See RHOADES, CORNELIA HARSEN.

Rhone, Mrs. D.L. See RHONE, ROSAMOND (DODSON).

RHONE, ROSAMOND (DODSON). b.1855. U.S.
    Mrs. D.L. Rhone

            Biography
WOWWA WWWA-4

RHYS, GRACE (LITTLE). 1865-1929. Ireland.

            Biography
BRI

RICE

RICE, ALICE CALDWELL (HEGAN). 1870-1942. U.S.

Autobiography
THE INKY WAY. New York: D. Appleton-Century,
1940. LC40-27819.

Biography
ALY AWO AWW BERE BRO BURG BURK DAB-S3
HAMM HAOXA JOHDB KUAT KUT LIB MAN MARBS
NAW NCAB-14 OV OV2 REA RIC RICDA RICK RUT
SOU WARLC WEBS WOWWA WWNA WWWA-1 WYN

Obituary
CUR-1942.
NY TIMES (11 Feb 1942), 21:1.
NEWSWEEK 19 (23 Feb 1942), 7.
PUBLISHERS WEEKLY 141 (11 Apr 1942), 1419.
TIME 39 (23 Feb 1942), 78.
WILSON 16 (Apr 1942), 598.

RICE, RUTH LITTLE (MASON). 1884-1927. U.S.

Biography
WWNA

RICHARDS, CLARICE (ESTABROOK). b.1875. U.S.

Biography
COY

Richards, Dr., pseud. See PINSENT, ELLEN FRANCES
(DRAKE).

RICHARDS, LAURA ELIZABETH (HOWE). 1850-1943. U.S.

Biography
ALY AWO AWW BERE BOCCA BURG BURK DAB-3
HAOXA KUJ1 KUT LOGP NAW NCAB-15,39 REA
RICDA TWCB VDW WARBD WEBS WOWWA WWNA WWWA-2
YES-1

Obituary
CUR-1943.
PUBLISHERS WEEKLY 143 (23 Jan 1943), 356.
WILSON 17 (Mar 1943), 494.

RICHARDSON

RICHARDSON, ANNE STEESE (SAUSSER). 1865-1949.
U.S.

Biography
COY   WWWA-2

Obituary
NY TIMES (11 May 1949), 29:3.
WILSON 24 (Sept 1949), 12.

RICHARDSON, DOROTHY. 1875-1955. U.S.

Obituary
NY TIMES (29 Mar 1955), 29:2.

RICHARDSON, DOROTHY MILLER. 1873-1957. England.
        m. Odle

Biography
BERE   BRO   BURK   CAS   CHA   CHABI   CON-104   FLE
HAMM   HAOXE   KUAT   KUT   LAU   MAG   MANBL   MARBS
MDWB   MICB   MYE   NCH   NPW   PEE   RA   RIC   ROSS
SHO   WAGCE   WARLC   WEBS   WENW   WWWE

Fromm, Gloria G. DOROTHY RICHARDSON: A BIOGRAPHY.
  Urbana: Univ. of Illinois Press, c1977. LC77-8455.

Gregory, Horace. DOROTHY RICHARDSON; AN
  ADVENTURE IN SELF-DISCOVERY. New York: Holt,
  Rinehart and Winston, [1967]. LC67-15029.

Rosenberg, John. DOROTHY RICHARDSON. New York:
  Knopf, 1973. LC73-7259.
    Pub. in England as DOROTHY RICHARDSON, THE
    GENIUS THEY FORGOT: A CRITICAL BIOGRAPHY.
    LC73-165918.

Staley, Thomas F. DOROTHY RICHARDSON. Boston:
  Twayne, c1976. LC76-8009.

Obituary
NY TIMES (18 June 1957), 33:2.
OBIT1, 600.
TIMES (LONDON) (18 June 1957), 13:1.

RICHARDSON

Richardson,Henry Handel, pseud. See ROBERTSON, ETHEL FLORENCE LINDESAY (RICHARDSON).

RICHMOND, GRACE LOUISE (SMITH). 1866-1959. U.S.

Biography
ALY AWO AWW BRO BURK KUT MARBS OV OV2 WEBS WOWWA WWWA-3

Whitman, Willson. GRACE S. RICHMOND, BUILDER OF HOMES. Garden City, N.Y.: Doubleday, Doran, 1928. OCLC 1313447.

Obituary
NY TIMES (28 Nov 1959), 21:4.
PUBLISHERS WEEKLY 176 (14 Dec 1959), 25.
WILSON 34 (Jan 1960), 328.

RICKARD, JESSIE LOUISA (MOORE). b.1879. England.
Mrs. Victor Rickard

Biography
WWWE

Rickard, Mrs. Victor. See RICKARD, JESSIE LOUISA (MOORE).

Rickert, Edith. See RICKERT, MARTHA EDITH.

RICKERT, MARTHA EDITH. 1871-1938. U.S.
Edith Rickert

Biography
BURK NAW REA WEBS WWWA-1

Obituary
NY TIMES (24 May 1938), 17:2.

RIDDELL, CHARLOTTE ELIZA LAWSON (COWAN). 1832-1906.
Ireland.
          Mrs. J.H. Riddell

Biography
ASH BD BEL BLA BRI CLE CRO DAB-2 FUR
HAMM MYE NCH ROCK WARBD WEBS WWWL

Ellis, Stewart M. "Mrs. J.H. Riddell: the
   Novelist of the City and of Middlesex." In
   WILKIE COLLINS, LE FANU, AND OTHERS. pp. 266-
   335. Freeport, N.Y.: Books for Libraries,
   [1968]. LC68-29203.

Obituary
TIMES (LONDON) (26 Sept 1906), 8:3.

Riddell, Mrs. J.H.   See RIDDELL, CHARLOTTE ELIZA
   LAWSON (COWAN).

RIDDING, LAURA ELIZABETH. 1849-1939. England.

Biography
WWWL

Obituary
TIMES (LONDON) (23 May 1939), 18:2.

RIDLEY, ALICE (DAVENPORT). d.1945. England.
          Lady Ridley

Obituary
TIMES (LONDON) (8 June 1945), 4:4; (9 June), 7:5;
   (27 June), 7:5.

RIGGS, KATE DOUGLAS (SMITH) WIGGIN. 1856-1923.
U.S.
          Kate Douglas Wiggin

Autobiography
MY GARDEN OF MEMORY: AN AUTOBIOGRAPHY, by Kate
   Douglas Wiggin. Boston: Houghton Mifflin,
   1923. LC23-15164.

Biography
ADE APP AWW BD BERE BRO BURG BURK CHA
CHABI DAB DOY HAL HAMM HAOXA HARKF HUN
KU KUJ1 KUAT KUT LOGP MAN MARBS MIG MYE
NAW NCAB-6 OV OV2 PRE REA RICDA TWCB VDW
WAGCA WARBD WARLC WEBS WILA WOWWA WWWA-1
WWWL YES-1

International Kindergarten Union. Committee of
  Nineteen. PIONEERS OF THE KINDERGARTEN IN
  AMERICA. New York: Century, [c1924].
  LC24-9353.

Mason, Miriam E. YOURS WITH LOVE, KATE. Boston:
  Houghton Mifflin, 1952. LC52-5907L.

Rather, Lois. MISS KATE, KATE DOUGLAS WIGGIN IN
  SAN FRANCISCO. Oakland, Calif.: Rather, 1980.
  LC80-118249.

Smith, Nora A. KATE DOUGLAS WIGGIN AS HER SISTER
  KNEW HER. Boston: Houghton Mifflin, 1925.
  LC25-22403.

Obituary
NY TIMES (25 Aug 1923), 7:5.
OUTLOOK 135 (5 Sept 1923), 9-10.
TIMES (LONDON) (25 Aug 1923), 10:4.

RINEHART, MARY (ROBERTS). 1876-1958. U.S.

Autobiography
MY STORY; A NEW EDITION AND SEVENTEEN NEW YEARS.
  New York: Arno, 1980, c1948. LC79-8806.

Biography
APPS AWO AWW BERE BREI BRO BURK CON-108
DAB-S6 EMD HAMM HAOXA HAY JOHDB KUL KUT
LOGP LOV MANA MARBS MAT MYE NAWM NCAB-25,C
NOV NPW OV OV2 OVA OVEWH PEA REA RIC TAV
TWCC TWCR VDW WAGCA WAR WARLC WEBS WOWWA
WWNA WWWA-3 WWWT

Cohn, Jan. IMPROBABLE FICTION: THE LIFE OF MARY
  ROBERTS RINEHART. Pittsburgh: Univ. of
  Pittsburgh Press, c1980. LC79-3997.

Disney, Dorothy C. and Milton Mackaye. MARY
ROBERTS RINEHART. New York: Rinehart, [1948?].
OCLC 7764282.

Doran, George H., Co. MARY ROBERTS RINEHART; A
SKETCH OF THE WOMAN AND HER WORK. New York:
G.H. Doran, [1925?] OCLC 2367782.
44 pages

Obituary
ILLUS LONDON NEWS 233 (4 Oct 1958), 573.
NY TIMES (23 Sept 1958), 1+.
NEWSWEEK 52 (6 Oct 1958), 65.
OBIT1, 601-2.
PUBLISHERS WEEKLY 174 (13 Oct 1958), 36.
SATURDAY EVENING POST 231 (25 Oct 1958), 136.
TIME 72 (6 OCT 1958), 86.
TIMES (LONDON) (24 Sept 1958), 13:2.
WILSON 33 (Nov 1958), 200.

Rion, Hanna. See VER BECK, HANNA (RION).

Rita, pseud. See HUMPHREYS, ELIZA MARGARET J.
(GOLLAN).

Rives, Amelie. See TROUBETZKOY, AMELIE (RIVES)
CHANLER.

Rives, Hallie Erminie. See WHEELER, HALLIE ERMINIE
(RIVES).

ROBERTS, CLARA (LEMORE). d.1898. U.S.
Clara Lemore

Biography
BOASE-6

Obituary
ATHENAEUM #3668 (12 Feb 1898), 217.

ROBERTS, INA BREVOORT (DEANE). b.1874. U.S.

Biography
WOWWA WWWA-5

ROBERTS, MARGARET. 1833-1919. England.

Biography
BD WARBD

Obituary
TIMES (LONDON) (18 Jan 1919), 11:2.

ROBERTSON, ALICE ALBERTHE. b.1871. U.S.
Berthe Saint Luz, pseud.

Biography
ROCK

ROBERTSON, ETHEL FLORENCE LINDESAY (RICHARDSON).
1870-1946. England.
Henry Handel Richardson, pseud.

Autobiography
LETTERS OF HENRY HANDEL RICHARDSON TO NETTIE
PALMER, edited by Karl-Johan Rossing.
Cambridge: Harvard University Press, [1953].
LC53-12091.
43 pages

MYSELF WHEN YOUNG, by Henry Handel Richardson.
Together with an essay on THE ART OF HENRY
HANDEL RICHARDSON, by J.G. Robertson. London:
W. Heinemann, [1948]. LC49-17545.

Biography
BERE BRO CAS CHABI CON-105 DNB-S5 FLE HAMM
HAOXE JONES KUL KUT KUTS LAU MAG MCW MDWB
MIA MIAU MICB MOCL MYE NCH NPW PEE RIC
SEYS SHO WAGCE WARLC WEBS WENW WWW-4

Elliott, William D. HENRY HANDEL RICHARDSON
(ETHEL FLORENCE LINDESAY RICHARDSON). Boston:
Twayne, c1975. LC75-12692.

Green, Dorothy. ULYSSES BOUND; HENRY HANDEL
RICHARDSON AND HER FICTION. Canberra:
Australian National Univ. Press, 1973.
LC72-87433.

Kramer, Leonie J. HENRY HANDEL RICHARDSON.
New York: Oxford Univ. Press, [1967].
LC68-85777.
   30 pages

Palmer, Nettie. HENRY HANDEL RICHARDSON, A
STUDY. Folcroft, Pa: Folcroft, 1979, 1950.
LC79-25820.

Purdie, Edna and Olga M. Roncoroni. eds. HENRY
HANDEL RICHARDSON: SOME PERSONAL IMPRESSIONS.
Sydney: Angus and Robertson, [1957].
LC58-27540L.

Obituary
AGE (MELBOURNE) (21 Mar 1946), 1.
ARGUS (MELBOURNE) (21 Mar 1946), 5.
CUR-1946.
ILLUS LONDON NEWS 208 (30 Mar 1946), 350.
NY TIMES (21 Mar 1946), 25:5; (22 Mar), 20.
PUBLISHERS WEEKLY 149 (4 May 1946), 2459.
SYDNEY MORNING HERALD (21 Mar 1946), 1-2.
TIME 47 (1 Apr 1946), 90.
TIMES (LONDON) (21 Mar 1946), 7:6.
WILSON 20 (May 1946), 632.

Bibliography
Howells, Gay. HENRY HANDEL RICHARDSON 1870-1946;
A BIBLIOGRAPHY TO HONOUR THE CENTENARY OF HER
BIRTH. Canberra: National Library of
Australia,1970. LC76-591037.

Robertson, Frances Forbes. See HARROD, FRANCES
(FORBES-ROBERTSON).

Robins, Elizabeth. See PARKES, ELIZABETH (ROBINS).

Robins, G.M. See REYNOLDS, GERTRUDE M. (ROBINS).

ROBINSON, SUZANNE (ANTROBUS). U.S.
Suzanne Antrobus

Biography
WARBD

RODEN, ADA MARIA (JENYNS) JOCELYN. b.1860.
Mrs. Robert Jocelyn

Biography
WWWL

Rodziewicz, Marya.   See   RODZIEWICZOWNA, MARIA.

RODZIEWICZOWNA, MARIA. 1863-1944. Lithuania.
Marya Rodziewicz

Biography
CAS   COL

Roe, V.E.   See   ROE, VINGIE EVE.

ROE, VINGIE EVE. 1879-1958. U.S.
m. Lawton
V.E. Roe

Biography
BURK   MAR   WWWA-3

ROGERS, GRACE DEAN (MACLEOD). 1865-1958. Canada.

Biography
MDCB   MOR   MOR2   RHO   WOWWA

ROHLFS, ANNA KATHARINE (GREEN). 1846-1935. U.S.
Anna Katharine Green
Mrs. Charles Rohlfs

Biography
APP AWW BD BERE BURG BURK DAB-S1 EMD
HAOXA HARKF HAY JOHDB KUL KUT LOGP MARBS
NAW NCAB-9 NOV OV OV2 PRE REA TWCC WARBD
WARLC WEBS WILA WOWWA WWNA WWWA-1 WWWE

Obituary
NEWSWEEK 5 (20 Apr 1935), 24.
PUBLISHERS WEEKLY 127 (20 Apr 1935), 1599.

Rohlfs, Mrs. Charles. See ROHLFS, ANNA KATHARINE
(GREEN).

ROLAND, ALICE KATE. 1853-1915? U.S.

Biography
KNIB

ROLLINS, ALICE MARLAND (WELLINGTON). 1847-1897.
U.S.

Biography
APP BD BURK DAB NCAB-8 TWCB WARBD WILA
WWWA-H

ROLLINS, CLARA HARRIOT (SHERWOOD). b.1874. U.S.

Biography
WWWA-5

ROOF, KATHARINE METCALF. U.S.

Biography
BURK

Roosevelt, Blanche, pseud. See MACCHETTA, BLANCHE
ROOSEVELT (TUCKER).

ROSE, HELOISE (DURANT). U.S.

Biography
AWO   BURK   WWWA-5

ROSEBORO', VIOLA. 1857-1945. U.S.

Biography
BURK   KNIB   WOWWA

Graham, Jane K.   VIOLA, THE DUCHESS OF NEW DORP;
A BIOGRAPHY OF VIOLA ROSEBORO'. [Danville?
Ill., 1955].   LC55-13808.

Obituary
NY TIMES (30 Jan 1945), 19:3.

ROSMAN, ALICE GRANT. 1887-1930. England./Australia.

Biography
BRO   KUT   MIA   MIAU   WWWE

Obituary
BOSTON TRANSCRIPT (5 July 1930).
WILSON 4 (Jun 1930), 491.

Ross, Martin, pseud.   See   MARTIN, VIOLET FLORENCE.

ROSSETTI, CHRISTINA GEORGINA. 1830-1894. England.

Autobiography
THE FAMILY LETTERS OF CHRISTINA GEORGINA
ROSSETTI; WITH SOME SUPPLEMENTARY LETTERS AND
APPENDICES, edited by William Michael Rossetti.
New York: Haskell House, 1968, 1908. LC68-24915.

Biography
ADE   BD   BERE   BOASE   BRO   CAS   CHA   CHABI   DNB
GRE   HAMM   HAOXE   JBA   KRO   KUBA   MAG   MAGN   MCW
MDWB   MOO   NCH   PEE   RA   SCHM   SHA   SHA-A   SHO
SOME-20   WARBD   WEBS   WENW

Battiscombe, Georgina. CHRISTINA ROSSETTI. London: Pub. for the British Council and the National Book League by Longmans, Green, [1965]. LC66-70588.

_____. CHRISTINA ROSSETTI, A DIVIDED LIFE. New York: Holt, Rinehart and Winston, 1981. LC81-47451R.

Bell, Mackenzie. CHRISTINA ROSSETTI; A BIOGRAPHICAL AND CRITICAL STUDY. [New York: AMS, 1973, 1898]. LC70-148747.

Bellas, Ralph A. CHRISTINA ROSSETTI. Boston: Twayne, c1977. LC76-29711.

Birkhead, Edith. CHRISTINA ROSSETTI AND HER POETRY. [New York: AMS, 1972, 1930]. LC75-148751.

Boyle, Edward. BIOGRAPHICAL ESSAYS, 1790-1890. pp. 193-203. Freeport, N.Y.: Books for Libraries, [1968]. LC68-54331.

BRITISH WRITERS, edited by Ian S. Scott-Kilvert. Vol. 5. pp. 247-60. New York: Scribner, c1982. LC78-23483.

Cary, Elisabeth L. THE ROSSETTIS: DANTE GABRIEL AND CHRISTINA. New York: G.P. Putnam's Sons, 1900. LC16-24505.

Packer, Lona M. CHRISTINA ROSSETTI. Berkeley: Univ. of Calif. Press, 1963. LC63-21221.

_____. THE ROSSETTI-MACMILLAN LETTERS. Berkeley: Univ. of Calif. Press, 1963. LC63-21222.
   Letters used by the author in preparing her biography of Rossetti.

Proctor, Ellen A. A BRIEF MEMOIR OF CHRISTINA G. ROSSETTI. Norwood, Pa.: Norwood, 1977, 1895. LC77-2556.

Rossetti, William M. SOME REMINISCENCES OF WILLIAM MICHAEL ROSSETTI. 2 vols. New York: AMS, [1970, 1906]. LC75-132386.

Sandars, Mary F. THE LIFE OF CHRISTINA ROSSETTI. Westport, Conn.: Greenwood, 1980. LC71-141488.

Sawtell, Margaret. CHRISTINA ROSSETTI: HER LIFE AND RELIGION. Philadelphia: R. West, 1977. LC77-28834.

Shove, Fredegond. CHRISTINA ROSSETTI: A STUDY. Norwood, Pa.: Norwood, 1977, 1931. LC77-27942.

Stuart, Dorothy M. CHRISTINA ROSSETTI. London: Macmillan, c1930. LC31-26878. 200 pages

_____. CHRISTINA ROSSETTI. Norwood, Pa.: Norwood, 1978, 1931. LC78-849. 18 pages

Thomas, Eleanor W. CHRISTINA GEORGINA ROSSETTI. New York: Columbia Univ. Press, 1931. LC31-29780.

Troxell, Janet C., ed. THREE ROSSETTIS; UNPUBLISHED LETTERS TO AND FROM DANTE GABRIEL, CHRISTINA, WILLIAM. pp. 138-80. Cambridge: Harvard Univ. Press, 1937. LC38-1069.

Weintraub, Stanley. FOUR ROSSETTIS: A VICTORIAN BIOGRAPHY. New York: Weybright and Talley, c1977. LC76-21341.

Wilde, Justine F. CHRISTINA ROSSETTI, POET AND WOMAN. Nijkerk: Drukkerij C.C. Callenbach, 1923. LC24-21720.

Winwar, Frances. POOR SPLENDID WINGS; THE ROSSETTIS AND THEIR CIRCLE. Boston: Little, Brown, 1933. LC33-252225R.

Zaturenska, Marya. CHRISTINA ROSSETTI, A PORTRAIT WITH BACKGROUND. New York: Macmillan, 1949. LC49-11708.

ROSSETTI

Obituary
ATHENAEUM 105 (5 Jan 1895), 16-18.
CRITIC 26, n.s. 23 (12 Jan 1895), 16, 34;
  (21 Jan), 5-12.
DIAL 18 (16 Jan-1 Feb 1895), 37-9, 69-70.

Bibliography
Crump, Rebecca W. CHRISTINA ROSSETTI: A
  REFERENCE GUIDE. Boston: G.K. Hall, c1976.
  LC75-28008.

ROULET, MARY F. (NIXON-). d.1930. U.S.
        Mary F. Nixon

Biography
LOGP

ROUSE, ADELAIDE LOUISE. d.1912. U.S.

Biography
  BURK   WWWA-1

ROWE, HENRIETTA (GOULD). 1835-1910. U.S.

Biography
  BURK   WWWA-1

ROWLAND, HELEN. 1875-1950. U.S.
        m. Hill-Brereton [AWO]   Lutz [WOWWA]
        Helen Rowland Lutz

Biography
  AWO   BURK   REA   ROSS   WOWWA

ROWLAND, K. ALICE. U.S.
        Lenore, pseud.

Biography
  RUT

Rowlands, Effie Adelaide, pseud.   See ALBANESI,
  EFFIE ADELAIDE MARIA.

ROY, LILLIAN ELIZABETH (BECKER). 1868-1932. U.S.

Biography
WWWA-1

Ruck, Berta. See OLIVER, AMY ROBERTA (RUCK).

Ruffin, M.E. Henry. See RUFFIN, MARGARET ELLEN (HENRY).

RUFFIN, MARGARET ELLEN (HENRY). 1857-1941. U.S.
        Margaret Henry-Ruffin
        M.E. Ruffin

Biography
BURK KNIB LOGP WOWWA WWWA-5

Runkle, Bertha. See BASH, BERTHA (RUNKLE).

RUSSEL, FLORENCE (KIMBALL). b.1873. U.S.

Biography
WOWWA

RUSSELL, DORA. England.

Biography
BLAP WARBD

RUSSELL, MARY ANNETTE (BEAUCHAMP) ARNIM RUSSELL.
1866-1941. England.
        Alice Cholmondeley, pseud.
        Elizabeth, pseud.

Autobiography
ALL THE DOGS OF MY LIFE, by Elizabeth. London;
   Toronto: Heinemann, [1936]. LC36-33439.

Biography
ADE BERE BRO CHA COOPA HAMM KUT MARBS MYE
NCH RIC WARLC WEBS

De Charms, Leslie. ELIZABETH OF THE GERMAN
GARDEN; A BIOGRAPHY. Garden City, N.Y.:
[c1958]. LC A59-8624.

Swinnerton, Frank. FIGURES IN THE FOREGROUND;
LITERARY REMINISCENCES, 1917-1940. pp. 52-62.
Freeport, N.Y.: Books for Libraries, [1970,
c1963]. LC73-117850.

Obituary
COMMONWEAL 33 (28 Feb 1941), 461.
CUR-1941.
NY TIMES (10 Feb 1941), 17.
PUBLISHERS WEEKLY 139 (22 Feb 1941), 918.
TIMES (LONDON) (11 Feb 1941), 7:4; tributes
(22 Feb), 7:5; (25 Feb), 7:5; (26 Feb), 7:6.
WILSON 15 (Mar 1941), 554.

Russell, Lindsay, pseud. See SCOTT, PATRICIA
ETHEL (STONEHOUSE).

Russell, Patricia Lindsay, pseud. See SCOTT,
PATRICIA ETHEL (STONEHOUSE).

Russell, Raymond, pseud. See FEARING, LILIAN
BLANCHE.

Rutledge, Marice. See HALE, MARICE RUTLEDGE
(GIBSON).

RYAN, MARAH ELLIS (MARTIN). 1860?-1934. U.S.

Biography
BURK   TWCW   WILA   WOWWA   WWWA-1,4

Ryce, John, pseud. See BROWNE, ALICE M.

Rygier-Nalkowska, Sofja. See NALKOWSKA, ZOFIA
RYGIER.

RYLAND, CALLY THOMAS. U.S.

BURK   KNIB   WOWWA <u>Biography</u>

RYLEY, MADELEINE LUCETTE. 1868-1934. U.S.

AWW <u>Biography</u>

Sackville-West, Victoria. See NICHOLSON, VICTORIA
MARY SACKVILLE-WEST.

SADLIER, ANNA THERESA. 1854-1932. Canada.

Biography
APP AWW BRI HOE MOR2 WARBD WOWWA

Saint Aubyn, Alan, pseud. See MARSHALL, FRANCES
(BRIDGES).

Saint Felix, Marie, pseud. See LYNCH, HARRIET
LOUISE (HUSTED).

Saint Leger, Evelyn, pseud. See RANDOLPH, EVELYN
SAINT LEGER (SAVILE).

Saint Luz, Berthe, pseud. See ROBERTSON, ALICE
ALBERTHE.

SALE, EDITH (TUNIS). U.S.

Biography
KNIB

SAMPSON, EMMA (SPEED). 1868-1947. U.S.

Biography
BURK NCAB-37 SOU WEBS WWNA WWWA-2

SAMPTER, JESSIE ETHEL. 1883-1938. U.S.

Biography
NAW

Strauss, Bertha B. WHITE FIRE: THE LIFE AND
WORKS OF JESSIE SAMPTER. New York: Arno, 1977
[1956]. LC77-70663.

Obituary
NY TIMES (26 Nov 1938), 16:3.

SANBORN, KATHERINE ABBOTT. 1839-1917. U.S.

Autobiography
MEMORIES AND ANECDOTES, by Kate Sanborn. New
York: G.P. Putnam's Sons, 1915. LC15-23325.

Biography
APP BD BURK DAB LOGP NCAB-9 TWCB WARBD
WIN WOWWA WWWA-1

[Sanborn, Edwin W.]. KATE SANBORN, JULY 11,
1839, JULY 9, 1917. Boston: McGrath-Sherill,
1918. LC20-381.

Obituary
NY TIMES (10 July 1917), 13:5.

SANBORN, MARY FARLEY (SANBORN). 1853-1941. U.S.

Biography
ALY BURK WOWWA WWWA-3

SANDERS, HELEN (FITZGERALD). b.1883. U.S.

Biography
WOWWA

Sandys, Oliver, pseud. See EVANS, MARGUERITE
FLORENCE HELENE (JERVIS) BARCLAY.

Sanford, M. Bouchier. See SANFORD, MARY BOUCHIER.

SANFORD, MARY BOURCHIER. Canada.
M. Bouchier Sanford

Biography

MOR   MOR2   STOXC

SANGSTER, MARGARET ELIZABETH (MUNSON). 1838-1912.
U.S.

Autobiography

AN AUTOBIOGRAPHY, FROM MY YOUTH UP, PERSONAL
  REMINISCENCES. New York: Arno, 1980 [c1909].
  LC79-8812.

Biography

ADE   APP   AWO   AWW   BD   BURK   DAB   HAL   KUAA
LOGP   NCAB-6   PRE   REA   TWCB   WARBD   WEBS   WILA
WWWA-1

Obituary

CON-105.
NY TIMES (5 June 1912), 11:5.

SATTERLEE, ANNA ELIZA (HICKOX). b.1851. U.S.

Biography

HINK   WWNA

Saunders, Margaret Elsie (Crowther) Baillie-.   See
  BAILLIE-SAUNDERS, MARGARET ELSIE (CROWTHER).

SAUNDERS, MARGARET MARSHALL. 1861-1947. Canada.
Marshall Saunders, pseud.

Biography

ADE   AWO   BURK   CAS   HAMM   HAOXA   HARKF   KUJ1
KUT   MDCB   MOR   MOR2   MORGA   RHO   STOXC   SY
THOMC   WARBD   WOWWA   WWNA   WWW-4   WWWA-2   WWWE
WWWL

Obituary

NY TIMES (17 Feb 1947), 19:4.
TIMES (LONDON) (18 Feb 1947), 6:5.
WILSON 21 (Apr 1947), 572.

Saunders, Marshall, pseud. See SAUNDERS, MARGARET MARSHALL.

Savi, E.W. See SAVI ETHEL WINIFRED (BRYNING).

SAVI, ETHEL WINIFRED (BRYNING). 1865-1954. England. India.
E.M. Savi

Autobiography
MY OWN STORY. New York: Hutchinson, [1947]. LC48-26232.

Biography
HAMM WARLC WWLA WWW-5

Obituary
TIMES (LONDON) (7 Oct 1954), 11:3.

SAWYER, RUTH. 1880-1970. U.S.
m. Durand

Biography
ALY AWW BURK CON-73--76 KUJ2 KUT SOME-17 WEBS WWNA WWWA-5

AMERICAN WRITERS FOR CHILDREN, 1900-1960. Vol. 22, DICTIONARY OF LITERARY BIOGRAPHY. pp. 294-9. Detroit: Gale, 1983. LC83-14199.

SAXBY, JESSIE MARGARET (EDMONDSTON). 1842-1940. Scotland.

Biography
WWWE

SAYLOR, EMMA ROSALYN (SUTEMEIER). B.1863. U.S.

Biography
HINK

SCARFOGLIO, MATILDE (SERAO). 1856-1927. Italy.
Matilde Serao

Biography
BD   BERE   CAS   CDME   HAMM   HAR   JOHDB   PEEU
WARBD   WEBS

Gisolfi, Anthony M.   THE ESSENTIAL MATILDE SERAO.
New York: Las Americas, 1968. LC68-4386.

James, Henry.   NOTES ON NOVELISTS.   pp. 294-313.
New York: C. Scribner's Sons, 1914. LC14-18367.

Ojetti, Ugo.   AS THEY SEEMED TO ME, translated
by Henry Furst.   pp. 208-14.   Freeport, N.Y.:
Books for Libraries, 1968 [1928].   LC68-54364.

Obituary
NATION 125 (10 Aug 1927), 125.
NY TIMES (28 July 1927), 19:3.
TIMES (LONDON) (27 July 1927), 13:7.

SCHAUFFLER, RACHEL CAPER. b.1876. U.S.

Biography
COY   WOWWA   WWWA-5

SCHERR, MARIE. U.S.
Marie Cher, pseud.

Biography
AWO   BURK   ROCK

Schock, Georg, pseud.   See LOOSE, KATHARINE RIEGEL.

SCHOONMAKER, NANCY (MUSSELMAN). 1873-1965. U.S.

Biography
AWO   WWNA   WWWA-4

**SCHREINER, OLIVE EMILIE ALBERTINA (SCHREINER)
CRONWRIGHT.** 1855-1920. South Africa.
m. Crownwright who took her name

341

Ralph Iron, pseud.

Autobiography
THE LETTERS OF OLIVE SCHREINER, 1876-1920, edited by S.C. Cronwright-Schreiner. Westport, Conn.: Hyperion Press, 1976. LC74-33937.

OLIVE SCHREINER; A SELECTION, edited by Uys Krige. Cape Town, New York: Oxford Univ. Press, 1968. LC74-401357.

Biography
ADE BD   BERE BRIT BRO CAS   CHABI COLSA
CON-105   DELL DSAB-1 HAMM HAOXE JOHDB KUAT
KUT LAU MAG MCC MDWB MOCL MYE NCH NOV
NPW PEE RIC ROS ROSE SHO STA VIC WAGCE
WARBD WARLC WEBS WELL WENW

Berkman, Joyce A. OLIVE SCHREINER: FEMINISM ON THE FRONTIER. St. Alban's, Vt.: Eden Press Women's Publications, c1979. LC78-74842.

Buchanan-Gould, Vera. NOT WITHOUT HONOUR; THE LIFE AND WRITINGS OF OLIVE SCHREINER. New York: Hutchinson, [1948]. LC50-3152.

Cronwright-Schreiner, Samuel C. THE LIFE OF OLIVE SCHREINER. New York: Haskell House, 1973, 1924. LC72-2122.

First, Ruth and Ann Scott. OLIVE SCHREINER. New York: Schocken, 1980. LC80-13190.

Friedlander, Zelda. UNTIL THE HEART CHANGES, A GARLAND FOR OLIVE SCHREINER. [Cape Town]: Tafelberg-Uitgewers, 1967. LC67-99843.

Gregg, Lyndall (Schreiner). MEMORIES OF OLIVE SCHREINER. London: W.&R. Chambers, [1957]. LC58-26290/L.

Harris, Frank. CONTEMPORARY PORTRAITS, (FOURTH SERIES), pp. 291-5. New York: Brentano's, [c1923], LC23-18138.

Hobman, Daisy L. OLIVE SCHREINER, HER FRIENDS AND TIMES. London: Watts, [1955]. LC55-31042.

Lawrence, Margaret. THE SCHOOL OF FEMININITY; A
BOOK FOR AND ABOUT WOMEN AS THEY ARE INTERPRETED
THROUGH FEMININE WRITERS OF YESTERDAY AND TODAY.
pp. 126-56. Port Washington, N.Y.: Kennikat,
[1966, c1936]. LC66-25924R.

Meintjes, Johannes. OLIVE SCHREINER; PORTRAIT OF
A SOUTH AFRICAN WOMAN. [Johannesburg]:
H. Keartland, [1965]. LC66-57992.

Rasmussen, R. Kent. HISTORICAL DICTIONARY OF
RHODESIA/ZIMBABWE. p.290. Metuchen, N.J.:
Scarecrow, 1979. LC78-23671.

Stern, Elizabeth G. THE WOMEN IN GANDHI'S LIFE.
pp. 61-73, 91-101. New York: Dodd, Mead,
[1953]. LC52-14160/L.

Obituary
NY TIMES (13 Dec 1920), 15:6.
TIMES (LONDON) (13 Dec 1920), 16:4.

Bibliography
Davis, Roslyn. OLIVE SCHREINER 1920-1971: A
BIBLIOGRAPHY. Johannesburg: Univ. of the
Witwatersrand, Dept. of Bibliography,
Librarianship and Typography, 1972. LC73-166962.

Schubin, Ossip, pseud. See KIRSCHNER, LULA.

SCHUETZE, GLADYS HENRIETTA (RAPHAEL). b.1884.
England.
        Henrietta Leslie, pseud.
        Gladys Mendl, pseud.

Autobiography
GO AS YOU PLEASE; MEMORIES OF PEOPLE AND PLACES.
London: Macdonald, [1946]. LCa47-3490.

... MORE HA'PENCE THAN KICKS; BEING SOME THINGS
REMEMBERED, by Henrietta Leslie. London:
Macdonald, [1943]. LCa43-2793.

Biography
KUAT KUT WWLA WWWE WWWL

SCHWARTZ, JULIA AUGUSTA. b.1873. U.S.

Biography
BURK   WOWWA   WWWA-5

SCIDMORE, ELIZA RUHAMAH. 1856-1928. U.S.

Biography
ALY   BICA   BURK   DAB   KUAA   LOGP   TIT   TWCB
WARBD   WEBS   WWWA-1

SCOTT, CATHARINE AMY (DAWSON). 1863-1934. England.
C.A. Dawson-Scott

Biography
ADC   HAMM   WWLA   WWWE

Obituary
PUBLISHERS WEEKLY 126 (17 Nov 1934), 1840.
TIMES (LONDON) (6 Nov 1934), 9:4.

Scott, E.C.   See   SCOTT, ELLEN (CORRIGAN).

SCOTT, ELLEN (CORRIGAN). 1862-1936. U.S.
E.C. Scott

Biography
BURK   WWNA   WWWA-1

SCOTT, FRANCES.

Biography
WOWWA

SCOTT, GERALDINE EDITH (MITTON). d.1955. England.
G.E. Mitton

Biography
HAMM   WWLA   WWWE   WWWL

Obituary
TIMES (LONDON) (27 Apr 1955), 15:2.

Scott, Leader, pseud.   See BAXTER, LUCY E. (BARNES).

SCOTT, PATRICIA ETHEL (STONEHOUSE). 1870-1949. Australia.
> E. Hardingham Quinn, pseud.
> Harlingham Quinn, pseud.
> Lindsay Russell, pseud.
> Patricia Lindsay Russell, pseud.

Biography
MIA   MIAU   WWWL

SCUDDER, VIDA DUTTON. 1861-1954. U.S.

Autobiography

JOURNEYS: AUTOBIOGRAPHICAL WRITINGS BY WOMEN, edited by Mary G. Mason and Carol H. Green. pp. 146-63. Boston: G.K. Hall, 1979. LC79-10726.

ON JOURNEY. New York: E.P. Dutton, [c1937]. LC37-27231.

Biography
APP   AWO   BURK   DAB-5   LOGP   NCAB-4   REA   TWCB
WAG   WARBD   WEBS   WIN   WWNA   WWWE   WWWL

Allen, Devere, ed. ADVENTUROUS AMERICANS. pp. 277-89. New York: Farrar & Rinehart, [c1932]. LC32-5281.

Corcoran, Theresa. VIDA DUTTON SCUDDER. Boston: Twayne, c1982. LC82-3095.

Frederick, Peter J. KNIGHTS OF THE GOLDEN RULE: THE INTELLECTUAL AS CHRISTIAN SOCIAL REFORMER IN THE 1890S. pp. 115-40. Lexington: Univ. Press of Kentucky, c1976. LC76-9497.

Mann, Arthur. YANKEE REFORMERS IN THE URBAN AGE: SOCIAL REFORM IN BOSTON, 1880-1900. pp.217-28. New York: Harper & Row, 1954. LC54-5020.

SCUDDER

<u>Obituary</u>
NY TIMES (11 Oct 1954), 27:6.
PUBLISHERS WEEKLY 166 (27 Nov 1954), 2119.
WILSON 41 (9 Feb 1953), 57.

SEABROOK, PHOEBE HAMILTON. U.S.

<u>Biography</u>
KNIB

SEAMAN, AUGUSTA (HUIELL). 1879-1950. U.S.

<u>Biography</u>
AWW   BURK   KUJ1   REA   WEBS   WWNA   WWWA-3

<u>Obituary</u>
NY TIMES (5 June 1950), 23:6.
PUBLISHERS WEEKLY 157 (24 June 1950), 2743.
WILSON 25 (Sept 1950), 12+.

SEARS, CLARA ENDICOTT. 1863-1960. U.S.

<u>Biography</u>
BICA   BURK   NCAB-47   WWNA

O'Brien, Harriet E.   LOST UTOPIAS ... RESCUED
   FROM OBLIVION, RECORDED AND PRESERVED BY CLARA
   ENDICOTT SEARS ON PROSPECT HILL....   pp. 56-62.
   Boston: Walton, c1929. LC30-1914.

<u>Obituary</u>
NY TIMES (26 Mar 1960), 21:1.

SEAWELL, MOLLY ELLIOT. 1860-1916. U.S.

<u>Biography</u>
APP   AWW   BURK   DAB   HARKF   JOHDB   KUT   LIB   LOGP
NCAB-7   RUT   SOU   TWCB   WARBD   WEBS   WILA   WOWWA

<u>Obituary</u>
NY TIMES (16 Nov 1916), 11:5.

Sedgwick, Anne Douglas. See   DE SELINCOURT, ANNE
   DOUGLAS (SEDGWICK).

SEEGMILLER, WILHELMINA. 1866-1913. U.S.

BAN   WWWA-1

Biography

Seranus, pseud. See HARRISON, SUSIE FRANCES (RILEY).

Serao, Matilde. See SCARFOGLIO, MATILDE (SERAO).

Sergeant, Adeline. See SERGEANT, EMILY FRANCES ADELINE.

SERGEANT, EMILY FRANCES ADELINE. 1851-1904.
England.
Adeline Sergeant

Biography
BD   BLA   CHA   DNB-S2   KUBA   NCH   SHO

Obituary
NY TIMES (6 Dec 1904), 9:3.
TIMES (LONDON) (6 Dec 1904), 6:3.

SETON, JULIA. b.1862. U.S.
m. (1)Knapp (2)Sears--separated took
her maiden name

Biography
AWO   NCAB-16   WWNA   WWWA-4

SEYMOUR, BEATRICE KEAN (STAPLETON). d.1955.
England.

Biography
BRO   KUT   MICB   MYE   NCH   WARLC   WEBS   WWW-5
WWWE   WWWL

Obituary
TIMES (LONDON) (2 Nov 1955), 11:3.

SHAFER, SARA (ANDRERW). d.1913. U.S.

Biography

BAN   WOWWA   WWWA-1

SHARBER, KATE (TRIMBLE). b.1883. U.S.

Biography

WOWWA

SHARKEY, EMMA AUGUSTA (BROWN). b.1858. U.S.
E. Burke Collins, pseud.

Biography

WILA

SHARP, EVELYN JANE. 1869-1955. England.
m. Nevinson

Autobiography
UNFINISHED ADVENTURE; SELECTED REMINISCENCES FROM
AN ENGLISHWOMAN'S LIFE. London: John Lane;
[1933]. LC33-38218.

Biography
BRIT   HAMM   WWLA   WWWE   WWWL

Obituary
ILLUS LONDON NEWS 227 (2 July 1955), 31.
NY TIMES (22 June 1955), 29:3.
OBIT1, 639-40.
TIMES (LONDON) (21 June 1955), 13:1.
WILSON 30 (Sept 1955), 30.

SHARP, KATHARINE (DOORIS). 1845-1935. U.S.

Biography

COY   ODP

SHAW, ADELE MARIE. 1865?-1941. U.S.

Biography
ALY   AWO   BURK   WOWWA   WWNA

SHAW

Obituary
NY TIMES (5 Dec 1941), 23:2.

SHEARD, VIRGINIA (STANTON). 1865?-1943. Canada.
Virna Sheard

Biography
GARV   MDCB   MOR2   STOXC   THOMC   WOWWA

Sheard, Virna. See SHEARD, VIRGINIA.

SHEFFIELD, RENA CARY. 1878/79-1948. U.S.

Biography
WOWWA

Obituary
NY TIMES (12 Aug 1948), 21:3.

Sheldon, Mrs. Georgie, pseud. See DOWNS, SARAH
ELIZABETH (FORBUSH).

SHELDON,   RUTH   LOUISE   GIFFORD. 1846-1926. U.S.

Biography
COY

SHEPHERD,   ELIZABETH   LEE   (KIRKLAND). 1872-1936.
U.S.
Odette Tyler, pseud.

Biography
KNIB   WOWWA   WWWA   WWWT

SHERWOOD,   MARGARET   POLLOCK. 1864-1955. U.S.
Elizabeth Hastings, pseud.

Biography
AWO   BURK   WOMA   WOWWA   WWNA   WWWA-3   WWWE

SHEPHERD

Obituary
NY TIMES (26 Sept 1955), 23:4.
TIMES (LONDON) (27 Sept 1955), 11:2.

SHIELDS, GERTRUDE MARGARET. b.1890. U.S.

Biography
THOI   WWNA

Sholl, A.M.   See   SHOLL, ANNA MACCLURE.

SHOLL, ANNA MACCLURE. 1867?-1956. U.S.
        Geoffrey Corson, pseud.
        A.M. Sholl

Biography
BURG   WOWWA

Obituary
NY TIMES (3 Apr 1956), 29:6.

SHORT, ELEANOR TALBOT (KINKEAD). U.S.
        Eleanor Talbot Kinkead
        Nellie Talbot Kinkead
        Mrs. Thompson Short

Biography
BURK   KNIB   WOWWA   WWNA

Short, Mrs. Thompson. See   SHORT, ELEANOR TALBOT (KINKEAD).

SHORTALL, KATHERINE.

Autobiography
A "Y" GIRL IN FRANCE; LETTERS OF KATHERINE
    SHORTALL.   Boston: R.G. Badger, c1919.
    LC20-2357.

SHORTER, DORA MARY (SIGERSON). 1866-1918. Ireland.
        Dora Sigerson

Biography
BRI   BRO   CHA3   CLE   CRO   DIL   KUAT   KUT   KUTS
MAGN   ODP   RIC   SHA-A   WARBD   WEBS   WWWL

SHUEY, LILLIAN (HINMAN). 1853-1921. U.S.

Biography
HINK   WWWA-4

SHULER, MARJORIE. U.S.

Biography
WWNA

SICHEL, EDITH HELEN. 1862-1914.

Biography
WWWL

SICKERT, ELLEN MELICENT (COBDEN). 1848-1914.
        Miles Amber, pseud.
        Ellen Melicent Cobden

Biography
WWWL

SIDGWICK, CECILY (ULLMANN). d.1934. England.
        Mrs. Andrew Dean, pseud.
        Mrs. Alfred Sidgwick

Obituary
PUBLISHERS WEEKLY 126 (25 Aug 1934), 603.
TIMES (LONDON) (11 Aug 1934), 12:2.

SIDGWICK, ETHEL. 1877-1970. England.

Biography
BRI   BRO   CHA   KUT   MANBL   MARBS   MICB   MYE   NCH
WARLC   WWLA

SIDGWICK

Obituary
TIMES (LONDON) (1 May 1970), 12:7.

Sidgwick, Mrs. Alfred. See SIDGWICK, CECILY (ULLMANN).

Sidney, Margaret, pseud. See LOTHROP, HARRIET MULFORD (STONE).

Sigerson, Dora. See SHORTER, DORA MARY (SIGERSON).

Silberrad, U.L. See SILBERRAD, UNA LUCY.

SILBERRAD, UNA LUCY. 1872-1955. England.
        U.L. Silberrad

Biography
WARLC   WWLA

Obituary
ILLUS LONDON NEWS 227 (10 Sept 1955), 427.
TIMES (LONDON) (2 Sept 1955), 11:5.

Sime, J.G. See SIME, JESSIE GEORGINA.

SIME, JESSIE GEORGINA. b.1880. Canada.
        J.G. Sime

Autobiography
IN A CANADIAN SHACK. London: L. Dickson,
    [c1937]. LC38-14218.

Biography
HAOXA   STOXC   THOMC

Sinclair, B.M. See SINCLAIR, BERTHA (MUZZY).

SINCLAIR

SINCLAIR, BERTHA (MUZZY). 1874?-1940. U.S.
m. (1)Bower (2)Sinclair (3)Cowan
B.M. Bower, pseud.
B.M. Sinclair

Biography
AWO AWW BURK KUT MARBS REA ROCK TWCW
WARLC WWNA WWWA-1 WWWE

Obituary
CUR-1940.
NY HERALD TRIBUNE (24 July 1940).
NY TIMES (24 July 1940), 21:5.
NEWSWEEK 16 (5 Aug 1940), 7.
PUBLISHERS WEEKLY 138 (3 Aug 1940), 321.

SINCLAIR, MAY. 1870-1946. England.

Biography
ADC ASH BERE BRO CAS CHA CON-104 COOPE
DIX FLE HAMM JOHDB KUL KUT KUTS LAU MAG
MANBL MARBS MICB MYE NCH NPW SHO WAGCE
WARLC WEBS WELL WWWE WWWL

Boll, Theophilus E. MISS MAY SINCLAIR; NOVELIST;
A BIOGRAPHICAL AND CRITICAL INTRODUCTION.
Rutherford [N.J.]: Fairleigh Dickinson Univ.
Press, [1973]. LC72-414.

Zegger, Hrisey D. MAY SINCLAIR. Boston: Twayne,
c1976. LC76-18853.

Obituary
CUR-1946.
NY TIMES (15 Nov 1946), 23:3.
TIME 48 (25 Nov 1946), 100.
TIMES (LONDON) (14 Nov 1946), 7:5.
WILSON 21 (Jan 1947), 330.

SINGLETON, ESTHER. 1865-1930. U.S.

Biography
ALY AWW BURK DAB PRE TWCB WOWWA WWNA
WWWA-1 WWWL

SINGLETON

Obituary
PUBLISHERS WEEKLY 118 (19 July 1930), 262.

SINGMASTER, ELSIE. 1879-1958. U.S.
m. Lewars

Biography
AMN AWO AWW BURK HAOXA KUAT KUJ1 KUT MAG
MAN MARBS NCAB-C OV2 REA WAR WEBS WOWWA
WWNA WWWA-3

Obituary
NY TIMES (1 Oct 1958), 37:2.
PUBLISHERS WEEKLY 174 (27 Oct 1958), 35.

SIVITER, ANNA (PIERPONT). 1859-1932. U.S.

Biography
ALY TWCB WOWWA WWNA WWWA-1

Skene, F.M.F.   See   SKENE, FELICIA MARY FRANCES.

SKENE, FELICIA MARY FRANCES. 1821-1899. England.
F.M.F. Skene

Biography
BOASE-6 BRO DNB-1 MAGN

O'Brien, Sophie R. "Felicia Skene." In UNSEEN
FRIENDS. New York: Longmans, Green, 1912.
LC12-26015.

Rickards, Edith C. FELICIA SKENE OF OXFORD; A
MEMOIR. London: J. Murray, 1902. LC2-20999R.

Obituary
ILLUS LONDON NEWS (14 Oct 1899), 529; portrait
(21 Oct), 569.
TIMES (LONDON) (10 Oct 1899), 4:2.

SKINNER, CONSTANCE LINDSAY. 1879/1882-1939. U.S.

Biography
AWW   BURK   DODD   FUL   HAOXA   JBA   KUL   KUT   MYE
NAW   NCAB-E   PRE   THOMC   WWNA   WWWA-1   YES-1

CONSTANCE LINDSAY SKINNER, AUTHOR AND EDITOR:
   SKETCHES OF HER LIFE AND CHARACTER ..., edited
   by Ann H. Eastman. Blacksburg, Va.: Women's
   National Book Assoc., 1980. LC79-28680.

Obituary
LIBRARY JOURNAL 64 (15 Apr 1939), 313.
NY TIMES (28 Mar 1939), 24:2.
PUBLISHERS WEEKLY 135 (1 Apr 1939), 1289.
TIME 33 (10 Apr 1939), 72.
WILSON 13 (May 1939), 580.

SKINNER, HENRIETTA CHANNING (DANA). 1857-1928.
U.S.

Biography
AWW   TWCB   WOWWA   WWNA   WWWA-1

SKRAM, BERTHA AMALIE (ALVER) MULLER. 1846-1905.
Norway/Denmark.
              m. (1)Muller   (2)Skram

Biography
BEY   CAS   CDME   HAN   HAR   KUE   MDWB   WEBS

SKRINE, NESTA (HIGGINSON). England.
         Moira O'Neill, pseud.

Biography
BRI   WEBS

SLEIGHT, MARY BREACK. d.1928. U.S.

Biography
BURK   TWCB   WOWWA

SLOSSON, ANNIE (TRUMBULL). 1838-1926. U.S.

<u>Biography</u>
AWW   BURK   WARBD   WOWWA   WWWA-1

Smedley, Constance.   See   ARMFIELD, ANNE CONSTANCE
(SMEDLEY).

SMITH, ANNIE H. 1850-1909. U.S.

<u>Biography</u>
KNIB

SMITH, ANNIE S. (SWAN). 1859-1943. Scotland.
          David Lyall, pseud.
          Mrs. Burnett Smith
          Annie S. Swan

<u>Autobiography</u>
THE LETTERS OF ANNIE S. SWAN, edited by Mildred
   R. Nicoll.   London: Hodder and Stoughton,
   [1945].   LC46-15010.

MY LIFE; AN AUTOBIOGRAPHY.   London: Ivor
   Nicholson and Watson, 1934.   LC A35-1281.

<u>Biography</u>
BLA   BLAP   BRO   CHA   CHABI   HAMM   TWCR   WARLC

<u>Obituary</u>
CHRISTIAN SCIENCE MONITOR (10 July 1943), 15.
NY TIMES (19 June 1943), 13:7.

SMITH, CICELY FOX. d.1954. England.

<u>Biography</u>
WWLA   WWWE

<u>Obituary</u>
TIMES (LONDON) (9 Apr 1954), 10:6.

SMITH, CONSTANCE ISABELLA STUART. d.1930. England.

Obituary
TIMES (LONDON) (29 Mar 1930), 17:1; tribute
(31 Mar), 19:2; (1 Apr), 11:6.

SMITH, ELIZABETH THOMASINA (MEADE). 1854-1914.
Ireland.
   L.T. Meade, pseud.
   Laura T. Meade, pseud.
   Mrs. L.T. Meade, pseud.

Biography
BLAP BRI CLE CRO DOY EMD GRETB HAMM ROCK
TWCC

Obituary
TIMES (LONDON) (28 Oct 1914), 5:5.

Smith, Emma Pow. See BAUDER, EMMA POW (SMITH).

Smith, Essex, pseud. See HOPE, FRANCES ESSEX
THEODORA.

SMITH, GERTRUDE. 1860-1917. U.S.

Biography
BURK WOWWA WWWA-1

SMITH, HARRIET (LUMMIS). d.1947. U.S.

Biography
AWO BURK WOWWA WWWA-2

Obituary
NY TIMES (10 May 1947), 13:3.

SMITH, JEANIE OLIVER (DAVIDSON). 1836-1925. U.S.
   Temple Oliver, pseud.

Biography
WILA WOWWA WWNA WWWA-1

SMITH, MARION COUTHOUY. d.1931. U.S.

Biography
ALY   WOWWA   WWNA   WWWA-1

SMITH, MARY E. 1849?-1918. U.S.
        Christine Faber, pseud.

Obituary
NY TIMES (25 May 1918), 13:5.

SMITH, MARY ELIZABETH. 1880-1915. U.S.

Biography
WOWWA   WWNA   WWWA-1

SMITH, MINNA CAROLINE. b.1860. U.S.

Biography
WOWWA   WWWA-1

Smith, Mrs. Burnett.   See SMITH, ANNIE S. (SWAN).

SMITH, NORA ARCHIBALD. 1859-1934. U.S.

Biography
ALY   BURK   KUJ1   NAW   NCAB-26   REA   TWCB   WOWWA
WWWA-1

Obituary
PUBLISHERS WEEKLY 125 (10 Feb 1934), 696.

SMITH, SARA TRAINER. d.1899. U.S.

Biography
AWW

SMITH, SARAH. 1832-1911. England.
        Hesba Stretton, pseud. (Hesba--initials
        of her 5 sisters; Stretton--where she
        lived)

SMITH, SARAH

Biography
CHA   DAB-2   GRETB   HAMM   MYE   NCH   WARLC   WEBS

Obituary
TIMES (LONDON) (10 Oct 1911), 9:3.

Smith, Sheila Kaye.   See   FRY, SHEILA KAYE (SMITH).

SMITHSON, ANNIE MARY PATRICIA. 1883-1948. Ireland.

Autobiography
MYSELF, AND OTHERS. AN AUTOBIOGRAPHY.   Dublin:
   Talbot, [1944].   LC45-19712.

Biography
BRI   CLE   WWWE

SNEDEKER, CAROLINE DALE (PARKE). 1871-1956. U.S.
   Caroline Dale Owen, pseud.
   Mrs. Charles H. Snedeker

Biography
AWW   BAN   BURK   COY   KUJ1   KUJ2   WA   WOWWA   WWNA
WWWA-3   WWWE   YES-2

Obituary
HORN BOOK 32 (Apr 1956), 85.
PUBLISHERS WEEKLY 169 (11 Feb 1956), 923.
WILSON 30 (Apr 1956), 593.

SNEDEKER, FLORENCE WATTERS. d.1893.
   Mrs. Charles H. Snedeker

Obituary
CRITIC 22, n.s. 19 (20 May 1893), 335.

Snedeker, Mrs. Charles H.   See   SNEDEKER, CAROLINE
   DALE (PARKE).

SOMERSET, ISABELLA CAROLINE (SOMERS-COCKS).
   1851-1921. England.
   Lady Henry Somerset

SOMERSET

Biography
WEBS

Bolton, Sarah K. FAMOUS LEADERS AMONG WOMEN.
    pp. 250-71. Freeport, N.Y.: Books for
    Libraries, [1972, 1895]. LC76-38745.

Fitzpatrick, Kathleen. LADY HENRY SOMERSET.
    London: J. Cape, 1923. LC24-8583.

Obituary
NY TIMES (12 Mar 1921), 11:6.
TIMES (LONDON) (14 Mar 1921), 16:3.

Somerset, Lady Henry. See SOMERSET, ISABELLA
    CAROLINE (SOMERS-COCKS).

Somerville, E.Oe. See SOMERVILLE, EDITH ANNA
    OENONE.

SOMERVILLE, EDITH ANNA OENONE. 1858-1949. Ireland.
        E.Oe. Somerville
        See also SOMERVILLE, EDITH ANNA OENONE AND
        VIOLET FLORENCE MARTIN.

Biography
BERE BOY BRI BRO CAS CHA CLE DIL HAMM
HAOXE HIG HOE KUAT KUT LAU LES MDWB MYE
NCH NPW PEE SHO WARLC WEBS WWW-4 WWWE
WWWL

Cummins, Geraldine D. DR. E.Oe. SOMERVILLE; A
    BIOGRAPHY. Being the 1st biography of the
    leading member of the famous literary partner-
    ship of E. Oe. Somerville and Martin Ross.
    London: Dakers, [1952]. LC52-68252.

Obituary
ILLUS LONDON NEWS 215 (15 Oct 1949), 568.
NY TIMES (10 Oct 1949), 23:5.
PUBLISHERS WEEKLY 156 (3 Dec 1949), 2285.
TIMES (LONDON) (10 Oct 1949), 7:5.
WILSON 24 (Dec 1949), 264.

SOMERVILLE, EDITH ANNA OENONE and VIOLET FLORENCE MARTIN.

Biography
Collis, Maurice. SOMERVILLE AND ROSS: A
   BIOGRAPHY. London: Faber, 1968. LC68-118569.

Cronin, John. SOMERVILLE AND ROSS. Lewisburg
   [Pa.]: Bucknell Univ. Press, [1972].
   LC78-126031.

Powell, Violet G. THE IRISH COUSINS: THE BOOKS
   AND BACKGROUND OF SOMERVILLE AND ROSS. London:
   Heinemann, 1970. LC75-504027.

Robinson, Hilary. SOMERVILLE AND ROSS: A
   CRITICAL APPRECIATION. New York: St. Martin's,
   1980. LC80-44.

SOMERVILLE AND ROSS: A SYMPOSIUM. Belfast:
   Queen's Univ. (Institute of Irish Studies),
   [1969]. LC74-410748.

Somerville, Henry, pseud. See HUMPHREYS, MARY GAY.

SOUTHWORTH, EMMA DOROTHY ELIZA (NEVITTE).
   1819-1899. U.S.
         Mrs. E.D.E.N. Southworth

Biography
APP AWW BD BERE BURK DAB HAOXA KNIB KUAA
LOG NAW NCAB-1 PAP PRE REA ROCK RUB RUT
SOU TWCB VDW WARBD WEBS WILA WWWA-1

Boyle, Regis L. MRS. E.D.E.N. SOUTHWORTH,
   NOVELIST. Washington: Catholic Univ. of
   America Press, 1939. LC30-32645.

Obituary
NY TIMES (1 July 1899), 7:5.
TIMES (LONDON) (3 July 1899), 12:4.

Southworth, Mrs. E.D.E.N. See SOUTHWORTH, EMMA
DOROTHY ELIZA (NEVITTE).

SPARHAWK, FRANCES CAMPBELL. b.1847. U.S.

Biography
ALY BD BURK NCAB-10 WARBD WILA WOWWA WWNA
WWWA-4

SPEARS, MARY (BORDEN) TURNER. 1886-1968. England.
      m. (1)Turner (2)Spears
      Mary Borden
      Bridget MacLagan, pseud.
      Lady Spears

Autobiography
JOURNEY DOWN A BLIND ALLEY, by Mary Borden. New
    York: Harper, [1946]. LC46-6919.

Biography
AWO BRO CON-P1 HAMM KUL KUT KUTS MARBS
OV2 WARLC WWNA WWW-6 WWWA-5 WWWE WWWL

Obituary
CON-25--28R.
NY TIMES (3 Dec 1968), 50:4.
PUBLISHERS WEEKLY 194 (30 Dec 1968), 49.
TIMES (LONDON) (3 Dec 1968), 10:7; (5 Dec), 13:7.
WASHINGTON POST (4 Dec 1968).

SPENDER, EMILY. 1841-1922. England.

Biography
WARBD

Obituary
TIMES (LONDON) (4 Apr 1922), 16:5.

SPENDER, LILIAN (HEADLAND). 1835-1895. England.
      Mrs. J. Kent Spender

Biography
BOASE DNB HAMM

Obituary
SKETCH (LONDON) (22 May 1895), 180.
TIMES (LONDON) (6 May 1895), 10:4.

Spender, Mrs. J. Kent. See SPENDER, LILIAN (HEADLAND).

SPIELMANN, MABEL HENRIETTA (SAMUEL). 1862-1938. England.

Biography
WWLA   WWWE

Obituary
TIMES (LONDON) (2 May 1938), 18:3.

SPOFFORD, HARRIET ELIZABETH (PRESCOTT). 1835-1921. U.S.

Biography
APP   AWW   BD   BURK   CHA   DAB   HAL   HAOXA   JOHDB
KUAA   LOGP   MYE   NAW   NCAB-4   PRE   REA   RICDA
TWCB   WARBD   WEBS   WILA   WOWWA   WWWA-1

SPRENT, MABEL. Australia.
            m. Taylor

Biography
MIA

SPRINGER, FLETA CAMPBELL. U.S.

Biography
MAR

Squire, Frances. See POTTER, FRANCES BOARDMAN (SQUIRE).

STACPOOLE, MARGARET (ROBSON) DE VERE. d.1934. England.

Obituary
TIMES (LONDON) (9 Jan 1934), 12:5.

STAHR, FANNY (LEWALD). 1811-1889. Germany.
Fanny Lewald

Biography
GAR   HAR   JOHDB   MDWB   WARBD   WEBS

Obituary
TIMES (LONDON) (6 Aug 1889), 3:4; (7 Aug), 8:4.

Stairs, Gordon, pseud. See AUSTIN, MARY (HUNTER).

Stangeland, Karin Michaelis. See STANGELAND,
KATHARINA MARIE (BECH-BRONDUM) MICHAELIS.

**STANGELAND,   KATHARINA   MARIE (BECH -BRONDUM)
MICHAELIS.** 1872-1950. Denmark.
Karin Michaelis
Karin Michaelis Stangeland

Biography
BERE   CAS   FLE   HAMM   HAR   KUT   PEEU   RIC   WARLC
WEBS   WWLA   WWNA

Claudi, Jorgen. CONTEMPORARY DANISH AUTHORS ...,
translated by Jorgen Andersen and Aubrey Rush.
pp. 49-51. Copenhagen: Danske Selskab, 1952.
LC52-14932L.

Obituary
NY TIMES (12 Jan 1950), 28:2.
PUBLISHERS WEEKLY 157 (11 Feb 1950), 909.
TIMES (LONDON) (12 Jan 1950), 6:5.
WILSON 24 (Mar 1950), 456.

STANLEY, CAROLINE (ABBOT). 1849-1919. U.S.

Biography
WOWWA   WWWA-1

STANLEY, DOROTHY (TENNANT). d.1926. England.
  Lady Stanley

Obituary
  TIMES (LONDON) (6 Oct 1926), 14:5.

Stanley, Lady. See STANLEY, DOROTHY (TENNANT).

Stanley-Wrench, Mollie. See WRENCH, MOLLIE LOUISE
  (GIBBS) STANLEY-.

STANNARD, HENRIETTA ELIZA VAUGHAN (PALMER).
  1856-1911. England.
    John Strange Winter, pseud.

Biography
  BD BLA CHA DNB-2 HAMM KUBA NCH WARBD
  WARLC WEBS WWWL

Obituary
  TIMES (LONDON) (15 Dec 1911), 13:2.

Stanton, Coralie, pseud. See HOSKEN, ALICE CECIL
  (SEYMOUR).

STAPLETON, PATIENCE. 1863-1893. U.S.

Biography
  NCAB-38

STEEL, FLORA ANNIE (WEBSTER). 1847-1929. Scotland.
    Mrs. F.A. Steel

Autobiography
  THE GARDEN OF FIDELITY, BEING THE AUTOBIOGRAPHY
  OF FLORA ANNIE STEEL, 1847-1929. London,
  Macmillan, 1930, 1929. LC30-12267.

Biography
  ADE BD BERE CHA DNB-4 HAOXE JOHDB KUT LAU
  MARBS NCH PARR SHO WARBD WARLC WEBS WWW-3

Diver, Maud. THE ENGLISHWOMAN IN INDIA.
Edinburgh: Blackwood, 1909. OCLC 4254305

Patwardhan, Daya. A STAR OF INDIA (FLORA ANNIE
STEEL, HER WORKS AND TIMES). [Bombay]: A.V.
Griha Prakashan Poona, [1963]. LC SA64-8310.

Powell, Violet G. FLORA ANNIE STEEL: NOVELIST OF
INDIA. London: Heinemann, 1981. LC81-161139.

Obituary
GLASGOW HERALD (16 Apr 1929).
SPECTATOR (5 May 1929), (11 May).
TIMES (LONDON) (15 Apr 1929), 14:4, 19:1;
(19 Apr), appreciation 12:4.

Steel, Mrs. F. A. See STEEL, FLORA ANNIE
(WEBSTER).

STEELE, FRANCESCA MARIA. 1848-1931. England.
Darley Dale, pseud.

Biography
WWLA WWNA WWW-3 WWWE WWWL

Obituary
TIMES (LONDON) (21 Aug 1931), 12:2.

STEELE, ROWENA (GRANICE). 1824?-1900. U.S.

Biography
HINK WILA

STEIN, GERTRUDE. 1874-1946. U.S.

Autobiography
THE AUTOBIOGRAPHY OF ALICE B. TOKLAS.... New
York: Harcourt, Brace, [c1933]. LC33-22918.

DEAR SAMMY: LETTERS FROM GERTRUDE STEIN AND ALICE
B. TOKLAS, edited with a memoir by Samuel M.
Steward. Boston: Houghton Mifflin, 1977.
LC77-3519.

EVERYBODY'S AUTOBIOGRAPHY. New York: Cooper
  Square Publishers, 1971 [c1937]. LC70-159032.
  Sequel to AUTOBIOGRAPHY OF ALICE B. TOKLAS.

TWO: GERTRUDE STEIN AND HER BROTHER, AND OTHER
  EARLY PORTRAITS, 1908-12. Freeport, N.Y.:
  Books for Libraries, [1969, c1951].
  LC74-103667R.

WARS I HAVE SEEN. New York: Random, [1945].
  LC45-2075.

Biography

AMWRP AW AWO AWW BERE BRO BURK CAS CHA
CHABI CON-104 DAB-S4 FLE HAMM HAOXA HAOXE
HINK KRO KU KUL KUT LOGG MAO MAT MCW
MDWB MICA MYE NAW NCAB-38,D NOV NPW PEA
RA RCW REA RIC RICDA RICEW RULE SEYS STOD
VDW WARLC WEBS WENW WWNA WWWA-2 WWWL

Anderson, Sherwood. SHERWOOD ANDERSON/GERTRUDE
  STEIN: CORRESPONDENCE AND PERSONAL ESSAYS,
  edited by Ray L. White. Chapel Hill: Univ. of
  North Carolina Press, [1972]. LC72-78152.

Bridgman, Richard. GERTRUDE STEIN IN PIECES.
  New York: Oxford Univ. Press, 1971. LC71-123609.

Brinnin, John. THE THIRD ROSE: GERTRUDE STEIN
  AND HER WORLD. Gloucester, Mass.: P. Smith,
  1968, [c1959]. LC68-7882.

GERTRUDE STEIN, A COMPOSITE PROTRAIT, edited by
  Linda Simon. New York: Avon, 1974. LC74-19905.

Gould, Jean. AMERICAN WOMEN POETS: PIONEERS OF
  MODERN POETRY. pp.66-83. New York: Dodd,
  Mead, c1980. LC79-25670.

Greenfield, Howard. GERTRUDE STEIN; A BIOGRAPHY.
  New York: Crown, [1973]. LC72-92385.

Harrison, Gilbert A. "A RARE PRIVILEGE, THIS, OF
  BEING AN AMERICAN": A PERSONAL NOTE ON GERTRUDE
  STEIN. [Los Angeles: Friends of the UCLA
  Library, 1974]. LC76-373551R.
    15 pages

Hobhouse, Janet. EVERYBODY WHO WAS ANYBODY: A BIOGRAPHY OF GERTRUDE STEIN. New York: Putnam, 1975. LC75-10844.

Hoffman, Frederick J. GERTRUDE STEIN. Minneapolis: Univ. of Minnesota Press, [1961]. LC61-62617.

Hoffman, Michael. GERTRUDE STEIN. Boston: Twayne, c1976. LC76-2661.

Imbs, Bravis. CONFESSIONS OF ANOTHER YOUNG MAN. New York: Henkle-Yewdale House, [1936]. LC36-17990.

Longstreet, Stephen. WE ALL WENT TO PARIS; AMERICANS IN THE CITY OF LIGHT, 1776-1971. pp. 242-56+. New York: Macmillan, [1972]. LC78-165572.

Mellow, James R. CHARMED CIRCLE: GERTRUDE STEIN AND COMPANY. New York: Praeger, [1974]. LC73-7473.

Powell, Lawrence C. FROM THE HEARTLAND: PROFILES OF PEOPLE AND PLACES OF THE SOUTHWEST AND BEYOND. pp. 160-7. Flagstaff [Ariz.]: Northland, c1976. LC75-43347R.

Rather, Lois. GERTRUDE STEIN AND CALIFORNIA. Oakland, Calif.: Rather, 1974. LC74-181509.

Rogers, William G. GERTRUDE STEIN IS GERTRUDE STEIN IS GERTRUDE STEIN: HER LIFE AND WORK. New York: Crowell, [1973]. LC72-7555.

_____. WHEN THIS YOU SEE REMEMBER ME: GERTRUDE STEIN IN PERSON. Westport, Conn.: Greenwood, [1971, c1948]. LC72-139145.

Rose, Francis C. GERTRUDE STEIN AND PAINTING. London: Book Collecting and Library Monthly, 1968. LC73-355333.

Saarinen, Aline B. THE PROUD POSSESSORS; THE LIVES, TIMES, AND TASTES OF SOME ADVENTUROUS AMERICAN ART COLLECTORS. pp. 174-205. New York: Random House, [1958]. LC58-9890.

STEIN

Simon, Linda. THE BIOGRAPHY OF ALICE B. TOKLAS. Garden City, N.Y.: Doubleday, 1977. LC76-23798.

Sorell, Walter. THREE WOMEN: LIVES OF SEX AND GENIUS. pp. 71-128. Indianapolis: Bobbs-Merrill, c1975. LC74-17644.

Sprigge, Elizabeth. GERTRUDE STEIN: HER LIFE AND WORK. New York: Harper, [1957]. LC56-12229.

Toklas, Alice B. STAYING ON ALONE; LETTERS OF ALICE B. TOKLAS, edited by Edward Burns. New York: Liveright, [1973]. LC73-82424.

_____. WHAT IS REMEMBERED. New York: Holt, Rinehart and Winston, [1963]. LC63-7274.

Untermeyer, Louis. MAKERS OF THE MODERN WORLD; THE LIVES OF NINETY-TWO WRITERS ... WHO FORMED THE PATTERN OF OUR CENTURY. pp. 458-67. New York: Simon and Schuster, 1955. LC54-12364.

Wickes, George. AMERICANS IN PARIS. pp. 15-64. New York: Da Capo, c1980. LC80-18371.

Wilson, Ellen J. THEY NAMED ME GERTRUDE STEIN. New York: Farrar, Straus and Giroux, [1973]. LC73-76223.

Obituary
ART DIGEST 20 (1 Aug 1946), 13.
CUR-1946.
NATION 163 (10 Aug 1946), 142-3.
NY TIMES (28 July 1946), 40:1; portrait, 39.
NEW YORKER 22 (10 Aug 1946), 41-43.
NEWSWEEK 28 (5 Aug 1946), 54.
PUBLISHERS WEEKLY 150 (3 Aug 1946), 484-5.
TIME 48 (5 Aug 1946), 87.
TIMES (LONDON) (29 July 1946), 6:5.
WILSON 21 (Sept 1946), 10.

Bibliography
Liston, Maureen R. GERTRUDE STEIN: AN ANNOTATED CRITICAL BIBLIOGRAPHY. Kent, Ohio: Kent State Univ. Press, c1979. LC78-21971.

Wilson, Robert A., Comp. GERTRUDE STEIN: A
BIBLIOGRAPHY. New York: Phoenix Bookshop,
1974. LC73-85937.

Stephens, Ethel Stefana. See DROWER, ETHEL STEFANA
(STEVENS).

STEPHENS, KATE. 1853-1938. U.S.
Olive Ransom, pseud.

Biography
ALY   BICA   BURK   NAW   NCAB-B   WOWWA   WWNA   WWWA-1

Obituary
NY TIMES (13 May 1938), 19:5.
PUBLISHERS WEEKLY 133 (28 May 1938), 2096.
SCHOOL AND SOCIETY 47 (28 May 1938), 698.

Stephenson, Cora Bennett. See CLARE, CORA ESTELLA
BENNETT (STEPHENSON).

STERLING, SARA HAWKS. U.S.

Biography

WOWWA

Stern, E. G. See STERN, ELIZABETH GERTRUDE
(LEVIN).

STERN, ELIZABETH GERTRUDE (LEVIN). 1890-1954. U.S.
Eleanor Morton, pseud.
E.G. Stern

Autobiography
I AM A WOMAN AND A JEW. New York: Arno, 1969
[c1926]. LC69-18791.

MY MOTHER AND I, by E.G. Stern. New York:
Macmillan, 1917. LC17-16442.

Biography
AWO   AWW   BURK   NCAB-39   WOMA   WWWA-3

STERN

Obituary
NY TIMES (10 Jan 1954), 86:1.

Stern, G. B. See HOLDSWORTH, GLADYS BRONWYN (STERN).

Sterne, Stuart, pseud. See BLOEDE, GERTRUDE.

STERRETT, FRANCES ROBERTA. 1869-1947. U.S.

Biography
ALY   AWO   BURK   WWNA   WWWA-2

Stetson, Charlotte Perkins. See GILMAN, CHARLOTTE (PERKINS) STETSON.

STETTHEIMER, ETTIE. d.1955. U.S.
      Henrie Waste, pseud.

Obituary
NY TIMES (3 June 1955), 23:2.

Stevens, E. S. See DROWER, ETHEL STEFANA (STEVENS).

Stevens, Sheppard, pseud. See STEVENS, SUSAN SHEPPARD (PIERCE).

STEVENS, SUSAN SHEPPARD (PIERCE). b.1862. U.S.
      Sheppard Stevens, pseud.

Biography
KNIB   WWWA-4

STEWART, EDITH ANNE. b.1883. Scotland.
      m. Robertson

Biography
WWWE

STILLMAN, ANNIE RAYMOND. b.1855. U.S.

Biography

KNIB

STIRLING, ANNA MARIA DIANA WILHELMINA (PICKERING).
1865-1965. England.
        Percival Pickering, pseud.

Autobiography
LIFE'S LITTLE DAY, SOME TALES AND OTHER
    REMINISCENCES, by A.M.W. Stirling. New York,
    Dodd, Mead, 1924. OCLC 359787.

LIFE'S MOSAIC: MEMORIES, CANNY AND UNCANNY, by
    A.M.W. Stirling. London: Unicorn Press, 1934.
    OCLC 2289516.
    Continuation of LIFE'S LITTLE DAY.

A SCRAPHEAP OF MEMORIES. London: P.R. Macmillan,
    [1960]. LC60-2510.

Biography

CON-P1 WARLC

Obituary
TIMES (LONDON) (12 AUG 1965), 10:4.

STOCK, ETTA FLORENCE (KNIGHTENGALE). b.1858. U.S.

Biography

WWNA

STOCK, GERTRUDE GEORGINA (DOUGLAS). 1842-1893.
England.

Biography

BOASE-5

STOCKLEY, CYNTHIA. 1877?-1936. Rhodesia.
full name Lilian Julia (Webb) Stockley
Browne
m. (1)Stockley (2)Browne
Cynthia Stockley Browne
name also appears as Pelham-Browne

Biography
BRO DSAB-3 ROS ROSE WWWE WWWL

Obituary
TIMES (LONDON) (16 Jan 1936), 9:4.

Stolzenberg, Betsey (Riddle) Von Hutten Zum. See
HUTTEN ZUM STOLZENBERG, BETSEY (RIDDLE) VON.

Stone, Jane, pseud. See TRIMBLE, JESSIE.

STOPES, MARIE CHARLOTTE CARMICHAEL. 1880-1958.
England.
m. (1)Gates--annuled (2)Verdon-Roe--
retained her maiden name
G.N. Mortlake, pseud.

Biography
CHABI HAMM MDWB WARLC WEBS WWWE WWWL

Briant, Keith. PASSIONATE PARADOX; THE LIFE OF
MARIE STOPES. New York: Norton, [1962].
LC62-10094.

Hall, Ruth. PASSIONATE CRUSADER: THE LIFE OF
MARIE STOPES. New York: Harcourt Brace
Jovanovich, c1977. LC77-73054.

Maude, Aylmer. THE AUTHORIZED LIFE OF MARIE C.
STOPES. London: Williams and Williams, 1924.
LC26-22228.

_____. MARIE STOPES: HER WORK AND PLAY. New
York: G.P. Putnam, 1933. LC33-27401.
Incorporatés material used in THE AUTHORIZED
LIFE OF MARIE C. STOPES.

STOPES

Obituary
NY TIMES (3 Oct 1958), 29:1.
OBIT1, 674-5.
TIMES (LONDON) (3 Oct 1958), 13:1; (8 Oct), 13:2.

STORER, MARIA (LONGWORTH) NICHOLS. 1849-1932. U.S.
    m. (1)Nichols (2)Storer

Biography
COY NCAB-11 WARLC WOWWA WWWA-1

STRAHAN, KAY (CLEAVER). 1888-1941. U.S.

Biography
AWO BIN BURK WWNA WWWA-1

Strain, E. H. See STRAIN, EUPHANS H.
    (MACNAUGHTON).

STRAIN, EUPHANS H. (MACNAUGHTON). d.1934. Ireland.
    E.H. Strain

Biography
BRI

Obituary
TIMES (LONDON) (20 Mar 1934), 19:3.

STRATTON, JENNIE M. U.S.

Biography
COY

Stratton-Porter, Gene. See PORTER, GENE(STRATTON).

STRAUSS, JULIET VIRGINIA (HUMPHREYS). 1863-1918.
U.S.

Biography
BAN NCAB-2 WWWA-3

STRAUSS

Obituary
LADIES HOME JOURNAL 35 (Dec 1918), 20.

STREET, LILIAN. d.1936. England.

Obituary
TIMES (LONDON) (25 MAR 1936), 21:4.

Stretton, Hesba, pseud. See SMITH, SARAH.

STRICKLAND, TERESA HAMMOND. U.S.

Biography
WOWWA

Strong, Hero, pseud. See JONES, CLARA AUGUSTA.

Strong, Isobel, pseud. See FIELD, ISOBEL
(OSBOURNE) STRONG.

STROTHER, EMILY (VIELE). b.1865. U.S.

Biography
WOWWA

Stuart, Eleanor, pseud. See CHILDS, ELEANOR STUART
(PATTERSON).

Stuart, Esme, pseud. See LEROY, AMELIE CLAIRE.

STUART, RUTH (McENERY). 1849-1917. U.S.

Biography
ADE   AWW   BD   BURK   DAB   HAL   HAOXA   HARKF   JOHDB
KUAA   LIB   LOGP   NAW   NCAB-4   PRE   REA   RUB   SOU
TWCB   WARBD   WEBS   WOWWA   WWWA-1

Obituary
NY TIMES (8 May 1917), 11:5; (13 May), VII 188:2.

Stuyvesant, Alice, pseud. See WILLIAMSON, ALICE
MURIEL (LIVINGSTON).

SULLIVAN, ELIZABETH (HIGGINS). b.1874. U.S.
Elizabeth Higgins

Biography
WOWWA WWWA-5

SULLIVAN, MAY KELLOGG. U.S.

Autobiography
A WOMAN WHO WENT TO ALASKA. Boston: J.H. Earle,
[c1902]. LC02-29911.
Two trips covering 18 months in Alaska.

Sumner, Helen L.   See WOODBURY, HELEN LAURA
(SUMNER).

SURGHNOR, MRS. M.F. b.1833. U.S.

Biography
KNIB

Sutherland, Joan, pseud. See KELLY, JOAN COLLINGS
(SUTHERLAND).

SUTTNER, BERTHA FELICIE SOPHIE (KINSKY) VON.
1843-1914. Germany.

Autobiography
MEMOIRS OF BERTHA VON SUTTNER; THE RECORDS OF AN
EVENTFUL LIFE. New York: Garland, 1972,
[c1910]. LC75-147458.

Biography
ADE CAS CHABI GAR HAMM KU KUE MCC MDWB
OP SCHM WEBS WWWL

Kempf, Beatrix. WOMAN FOR PEACE: THE LIFE OF
BERTHA VON SUTTNER, translated by R.W. Last.
Park Ridge, N.J.: Noyes, [1973, c1972].
LC72-87475.
Pub. in England as SUFFRAGETTE FOR PEACE....
LC72-170725.

Lengyel, Emil. AND ALL HER PATHS WERE PEACE: THE
LIFE OF BERTHA VON SUTTNER. Nashville: T.
Nelson, c1975. LC75-19293R.

Pauli, Hertha E. CRY OF THE HEART; THE STORY OF
BERTHA VON SUTNER, translated by Richard and
Clara Winston. New York: I. Washburn, [1957].
LC57-6608.

Playne, Caroline E. BERTHA VON SUTTNER AND THE
STRUGGLE TO AVERT THE WORLD WAR. London: G.
Allen and Unwin, 1936. LC37-2335.

Tauschinski, Oskar J. PEACE IS MY MESSAGE: LIFE
AND WORK OF BERTHA SUTTNER, translated by Harry
Crawshaw. Wien: Oesterreichischer
Bundesverlag, [1964]. LC72-220398.

Wintterle, John and Richard S. Cramer. PORTRAITS
OF NOBEL LAUREATES IN PEACE. pp. 25-30.
London and New York: Abelard-Schuman, [1971].
LC79-105263R.
    juvenile literature

                    Obituary
LITERARY DIGEST 49 (4 July 1914), 29-32.
NATION 98 (25 June 1914), 745-6.
TIMES (LONDON) (24 June 1914), 10:4.
"A Woman and the Nobel Prize." OUTLOOK (NY) 107
    (4 July 1914), 512.

Svetla, Caroline, pseud. See   MUZAKOVA, JOHANA
    (ROTTOVA).

Swan, Annie S.   See   SMITH, ANNIE S. (SWAN).

Sylvia, Carmen, pseud. See   ELISABETH, QUEEN
CONSORT OF CHARLES I, KING OF RUMANIA.

SYMONDS, EMILY MORSE. d.1936. England.
George Paston, pseud.

Biography
CHA   WARLC   WWWT

Obituary
TIMES (LONDON) (12 Sept 1936), 14:2.

SYRETT, NETTA. d.1943. England.

Autobiography
THE SHELTERING TREE.... London: G. Bles, [1939].
LC39-24616.

Biography
WWWE   WWWL

Obituary
NY TIMES (19 Dec 1943), 48:6.
TIMES (LONDON) (18 Dec 1943), 6:5.

TABER, LOUISE EDDY. b.1890. U.S.

Biography
ALY   HINK

TABER, MARY JANE HOWLAND. b.1834. U.S.

Biography
WOWWA   WWWA-4

Tadema, Laurence Alma-. See ALMA-TADEMA, LAURENCE,
MISS.

TAGGART, MARION AMES. 1866-1945. U.S.

Biography
BURK   HOE   WOWWA   WWWA-5

Obituary
Malloy, J.I. CATHOLIC WORLD 160 (Mar 1945), 561.
NY TIMES (21 Jan 1945), 40:3.

TAIT, EUPHEMIA MARGARET. England.
        John Ironside, pseud.

Biography
WWWE

TALCOTT, HANNAH ELIZABETH (BRADBURY). 1827-1893.
U.S.

Biography
AWW

TAPPAN, EVA MARCH. 1854-1930. U.S.

Biography
ALY   AWW   BURK   DAB   KUJ1   KUT   NAB   NAW   NCAB-22
REA   TWCB   WARBD   WOWWA   WWNA   WWWA-1

Obituary
PUBLISHERS WEEKLY 117 (8 Feb 1930), 753.

TARBELL, IDA MINERVA. 1857-1944. U.S.

Autobiography
ALL IN THE DAY'S WORK: AN AUTOBIOGRAPHY.
   Washington: Zenger, 1975, c1939. LC75-35979.

Biography
ADE   APPS   AWO   AWW   BERE   BURG   BURK   DAB-S3
HAMM   HAOXA   KU   KUT   MAN   MDWB   MYE   NAW
NCAB-14   REA   RICDA   VDW   WARBD   WEBS   WOMA
WOWWA   WWNA   WWWA-2   WWWL

Conn, Frances. G.   IDA TARBELL, MUCKRAKER.
   Nashville, T. Nelson, [1972]. LC78-181678.

Cook, Fred J.   THE MUCKRAKERS: CRUSADING
   JOURNALISTS WHO CHANGED AMERICA.   pp. 65-96.
   Garden City,   N.Y.: Doubleday. LC71-168287.

Fleming, Alice M.   IDA TARBELL; FIRST OF THE
   MUCKRAKERS.   New York: Crowell, [1971].
   LC76-139103.

Garraty, John A., ed.   THE UNFORGETTABLE
   AMERICANS.   pp. 292-7.   Great Neck, N.Y.:
   Channel, [1960]. LC60-15694.

Hazeltine, Alice I.   WE GREW UP IN AMERICA;
   STORIES OF AMERICAN YOUTH TOLD BY THEMSELVES.
   pp. 55-64.   New York: Abingdon, 1954.
   LC55-5052.
      Selections from ALL IN A DAYS WORK.

Reifert, Gail and Eugene M. Dermody.   WOMEN WHO
   FOUGHT: AN AMERICAN HISTORY.   pp. 183-4.
   Norwalk, Calif.: Dermody, c1978. LC78-106358.

Thomas, Benjamin P. PORTRAIT FOR POSTERITY;
LINCOLN AND HIS BIOGRAPHERS. Freeport, N.Y.:
Books for Libraries, [1972, c1947]. LC72-38318.

Tomkins, Mary E. IDA M. TARBELL. New York:
Twayne, [1974]. LC73-22293.

Obituary
AMERICAN HISTORICAL REVIEW 49 (Apr 1944), 604-5.
CUR-1944.
NATION 158 (15 Jan 1944), 59.
NY TIMES (7 Jan 1944), 17:1.
NEWSWEEK 23 (17 Jan 1944), 10.
PUBLISHERS WEEKLY 145 (29 Jan 1944), 504.
TIME 43 (17 Jan 1944), 92.
TIMES (LONDON) (7 Jan 1944), 6:7.

Tasma, pseud. See COUVREUR, JESSIE CATHERINE
(HUYBERS).

TAYLOR, C. BRYSON. b.1880. U.S.

Biography
WOWWA

TAYLOR, KATHARINE HAVILAND. 1888-1941. U.S.

Biography
AWO   BURK   WWNA   WWWA-1

Taylor, M. Imlay. See TAYLOR, MARY IMLAY.

TAYLOR, MARY IMLAY. 1878-1938. U.S.
M. Imlay Taylor

Biography
ALY   BURK   WOWWA   WWNA   WWWA-1

Obituary
NY TIMES (29 Aug 1938), 13:4.
PUBLISHERS WEEKLY 134 (1 Oct 1938), 1291.

TCHERNINE, ODETTE. England.

Biography

WWWE

TEAL, ANGELINE (GRUEY). 1842-1913. U.S.

Biography

BAN   COY

TENCH, MARY FRANCES ALICIA. England.

Biography

BRI   WWWL

TERHUNE, MARY VIRGINIA (HAWES). 1830-1922. U.S.
Marion Harland, pseud.

Autobiography

MARION HARLAND'S AUTOBIOGRAPHY. New York: Arno,
1980 [c1910]. LC79-8816.

Biography

ADE   APP   AWW   BD   BOLS   BURK   DAB   HAL   HAOXA
JOHDB   KNIB   KUAA   LOGP   NAW   NCAB-2   ORG   PAP
PRE   REA   RICDA   TWCB   WARBD   WARD   WEBS   WILA
WOWWA   WWWA-1

Obituary

"Marion Harland." OUTLOOK (NEW YORK) 131
(14 June 1922), 286-7.
NY TIMES (4 June 1922), 28:3.
REVIEW OF REVIEWS 66 (July 1922), 27.

TESKEY, ADELINE MARGARET. d.1924. Canada.

Biography

MDCB   MOR2   STOXC   WOWWA

Teters, Wilbertine. See WORDEN, WILBERTINE
(TETERS).

TEUFFEL, BLANCHE WILLIS (HOWARD) VON. 1847-1898.
U.S.
Blanche Willis Howard

Biography
BD   BURK   DAB   HAL   HAOXA   JOHDB   KUAA   NAW
NCAB-1   STOX2   WARBD   WILA

Obituary
ATHENAEUM 112 (22 Oct 1898), 571.

THACKER, MAY DIXON. b.1876. U.S.
Biography
BURK   WOWWA

Thanet, Octave, pseud.   See   FRENCH, ALICE.

THAYER, EMMA (HOMAN). 1842-1908. U.S.
Biography
PRE   TWCB   WARBD   WWWA-1

THAYER, EMMA REDINGTON (LEE). 1874-1973.   U.S.
Lee Thayer, pseud.

Biography
AWO   BURK   CON-P1   EMD   WWNA   WWWA-5   WWWE

Obituary
CON-45--48.
NY TIMES (20 Nov 1973), 42:3.
WASHINGTON POST (22 Nov 1973).

Thayer, Lee, pseud. See   THAYER, EMMA REDINGTON
(LEE).

Thomas, Annie.   See   CUDLIP, ANNIE HALL (THOMAS).

THOMPSON, LILIAN IRENE (TURNER). Australia.
Lilian Turner
Sister of Ethel Turner Curlewis.

Biography
MIA   MIAU

THOMPSON, MARAVENE (KENNEDY). U.S.

Biography
BURG   BURK

Thorne, Kate, pseud. See JONES, CLARA AUGUSTA.

Thorne, Marion, pseud. See THURSTON, IDA
(TREADWELL).

THROSSELL, KATHARINE SUSANNAH (PRICHARD).
1884-1969. Australia.
Katharine Susannah Prichard

Autobiography
CHILD OF THE HURRICANE: AN AUTOBIOGRAPHY, by
Katherine Susannah Prichard. Sydney, Australia:
Angus and Robertson, 1963. OCLC 7223813.

Biography
BRO   CON-Pl   JONES   MIA   MIAU   MICB   RIC   WEBS
WWLA   WWWE   WWWL

Drake-Brockman, Henrietta F. KATHARINE SUSANNAH
PRICHARD. New York: Oxford Univ. Press,
[1967]. LC68-82315.

Hetherington, John A. FORTY-TWO FACES. pp. 7-12.
Freeport, N.Y.: Books for Libraries, [1969,
c1962]. LC73-75719.

Throssell, Ric. WILD WEEDS AND WIND FLOWERS:
THE LIFE AND LETTERS OF KATHARINE SUSANNAH
PRICHARD. London: Angus & Robertson, 1975.
LC76-367192.

WESTRALIAN PORTRAITS, edited by Lyall Hunt.
pp. 199-206. Nedlands, W.A.: Univ. of Western
Australia Press, 1979. LC79-670403.

THRUSTON, LUCY MEACHAM (KIDD). b.1862. U.S.

Biography
BURK   LIB   TWCB   WOWWA   WWNA   WWWA-4

Thurston, I.T.   See   THURSTON, IDA (TREADWELL).

THURSTON, IDA (TREADWELL). 1848-1918. U.S.
Marion Thorne, pseud.
I.T. Thurston

Biography
LOGP   WWWA-1

THURSTON, KATHERINE CECIL (MADDEN). 1875-1911.
Ireland.

Biography
BOY   BRI   CHABI   CLE   CRO   DNB-2   WWWL

Obituary
"The Late Katherine Cecil Thurston."   HARPERS
WEEKLY 55 (16 Sept 1911), 21.
TIMES (LONDON) (7 Sept 1911), 7:2.

TICKNOR, CAROLINE. 1866-1937. U.S.

Biography
AWO   AWW   BD   BURK   REA   TWCB   WARBD   WIN   WOWWA
WWNA   WWWA-1

Obituary
NY TIMES (12 May 1937), 23:2.

TIERNAN, FRANCES CHRISTINE (FISHER). 1846-1920.
U.S.
Christian Reid, pseud.

Biography

AWW   BOOCA-4   BURK   DAB   JO   JOHDB   LIB   LOGP
NAW   NCAB-20   RICDA   RUT   WARBD   WOWWA   WYN

Becker, Kate H.   BIOGRAPHY OF CHRISTIAN REID.
   [Belmont, N.C., 1941]. LC44-23088.

Walser, Richard G.   PICTUREBOOK OF TAR HEEL
   AUTHORS. p. 9. Raleigh, N.C.: State Dept.
   of Archives and History, 1957. OCLC1277314.

Tinayre, Marcelle, pseud. See   TINAYRE, MARGUERITE
   SUZANNE MARCELLE (CHASTEAU).

TINAYRE, MARGUERITE SUZANNE MARCELLE (CHASTEAU).
   1877?-1948. France.
            Marcelle Tinayre, pseud.

Biography

DUC   HAMM   HAR   HOL   WEBS

Whale, Winifred S.   FRENCH NOVELISTS OF TODAY.
   Second Series. pp. 43-94. London, New York:
   John Lane, 1915. LC15-25109.

Tincker, M.A.   See   TINCKER, MARY AGNES.

TINCKER, MARY AGNES. 1831-1907. U.S.
            M.A. Tincker

Biography

APP   AWW   BD   BURK   DAB   NCAB-8   TWCB   WARBD
WWWA-1

Tinker, Beamish, pseud. See HARWOOD, FRYNIWYD
   TENNYSON (JESSE).

TODD, MARGARET GEORGINA. 1859-1918. Scotland.
            Graham Travers, pseud.

Biography

WARLC

Obituary
TIMES (LONDON) (5 Sept 1918), 9:5.

TOMPKINS, ELIZABETH KNIGHT. b.1865. U.S.

Biography
WWWA-4

TOMPKINS, JULIET WILBOR. 1871-1956. U.S.
     m. Pottle

Biography
AWO   BURG   HINK   WOMA   WWWA-3   WWWE

Obituary
NY TIMES (30 Jan 1956), 27:2.

TOWNESEND, FRANCES ELIZA (HODGSON) BURNETT.
1849-1924. U.S.
     Frances Hodgson Burnett

Autobiography
THE ONE I KNEW THE BEST OF ALL, by Frances
  Hodgson Burnett. New York: Arno, 1980 [c1893].
  LC79-8779.

Biography
ADE   AML   APP   AWW   BD   BERE   BRO   BURK   CHA
CHABI   CON-108   DAB   DIX   DOY   GRETB   HAL   HAMM
HAOXA   HAOXE   HARKF   HIND   JOHDB   KU   KUAT   KUJ1
KUT   LAS   LIB   LOGP   MAN   MAY   MDWB   MYE   NAW
NCAB-1,20   NPW   OV   OV2   PEA   PEE   PRE   REA   RUT
SHO   SOU   TWCB   WA   WAGCA   WARBD   WARLC   WEBS
WILA   WOWWA   WWWA-1   WWWL   WWWT   YES-2

Burnett, Constance B. HAPPILY EVER AFTER; A
  PORTRAIT OF FRANCES HODGSON BURNETT. New
  York: Vanguard, [1965]. LC65-17370.

Burnett, Vivian. THE ROMANTICK LADY (FRANCIS
  HODGSON BURNETT) THE LIFE STORY OF AN
  IMAGINATION. New York: C. Scribner's Sons,
  1927. LC27-23018.

Thwaite, Ann. WAITING FOR THE PARTY; THE LIFE OF
   FRANCES HODGSON BURNETT, 1849-1924. New York:
   Scribner, [1974]. LC74-7794.

Obituary
NY TIMES (30 Oct 1924), 19:1; (2 Nov), 7:1.
TIMES (LONDON) (30 Oct 1924), 14:4, 16:4.

TOWNSEND, VIRGINIA FRANCES. 1836-1920. U.S.

Biography
APP   BD   BURK   DAB   NCAB-13   TWCB   WARBD   WOWWA
WWWA-4

TOWNSHEND, DOROTHEA (BAKER).

Biography
WWWL

TOZIER, JOSEPHINE. b.1863. U.S.

Biography
BURK   WWWA-4

TRAIL, FLORENCE. 1854-1944. U.S.

Biography
APP   KNIB   WILA

TRAIN, ELIZABETH PHIPPS. b.1856. U.S.

Biography
BURK   TWCB   WARBD   WIN   WOWWA   WWWA-4

TRAIN, ETHEL (KISSAM). 1875-1923. U.S.

Biography
BURK   WWWA-1

TRASK, KATE (NICHOLS). 1853-1922. U.S.
     m. (1)Trask (2)Peabody
     Katrina Trask

Biography
AWW BURK NAW NCAB-11 WARBD WEBS WOWWA
WWWA-1

Obituary
NY TIMES (9 Jan 1922), 17:1+.
REVIEW OF REVIEWS 65 (Mar 1922), 246.
SOUTHERN WORKMAN 51 (Feb 1922), 51-52.

Trask, Katrina. See TRASK, KATE (NICHOLS).

Travers, Graham, pseud. See TODD, MARGARET
GEORGINA.

Travers, John, pseud. See BELL, EVA MARY
(HAMILTON).

TRIMBLE, JESSIE. 1873-1957. U.S.
     Jane Stone, pseud.

Obituary
NY TIMES (17 Apr 1957), 31:3.

TROLLOPE, FRANCES ELEANOR (TERNAN). 1834-1913.
England.

Biography
CHA NCH

TROUBETZKOY, AMELIE (RIVES) CHANLER. 1863-1945.
U.S.
     Amelie Rives
     Princess Troubetzkoy

Biography
ADE APP AWO AWW BD BURG BURK CLARI HAOXA
JOHDB KUT LIB LOGP NAW NCAB-1,B REA RUB

RUT SOU TWCB WARBD WARD WARLC WEBS WOWWA
WWWA-2 WWWE

Taylor, Welford D. AMELIE RIVES (PRINCESS
TROUBETZKOY). New York: Twayne, [1973].
LC72-3232.

Obituary
"Amelie Rives, Authoress, Dies, Aged 81."
RICHMOND TIMES-DISPATCH (17 June 1945), B-14.
"Amelie Rives, Gifted Virginia Woman Dies."
RICHMOND NEWS LEADER (16 June 1945), 9.
CUR-1945.
NY TIMES (17 June 1945), 26:3.
PUBLISHERS WEEKLY 148 (7 July 1945), 47.
WILSON 20 (Sept 1945), 8.

Bibliography
Longest, George C. THREE VIRGINIA WRITERS: MARY
JOHNSTON, THOMAS NELSON PAGE, AND AMELIA RIVES
TROUBETZKOY: A REFERENCE GUIDE. pp. 149-84.
Boston: G.K. Hall, c1978. LC77-9566R.

Troubetzkoy, Princess. See TROUBETZKOY, AMELIE
(RIVES) CHANLER.

TROUBRIDGE, LAURA (GURNEY). England.
Lady Trowbridge

Autobiography
MEMORIES AND REFLECTIONS. London: Heinemann,
1925. LC25-19177.

Biography
WWWE

TROUT, GRACE (WILBUR). d.1955. U.S.

Biography
BICA NCAB-B WOWWA WWWA-3

Trowbridge, Lady. See TROUBRIDGE, LAURA
(GURNEY).

TRUMBULL, ANNIE ELIOT. 1857-1949. U.S.
      Annie Eliot, pseud.

Biography
BURK   WARBD   WOWWA   WWWA-2

Obituary
NY TIMES (24 Dec 1949), 15:1.

TUCKER, CHARLOTTE MARIA. 1821-1893. England.
      A.L.O.E., pseud. (A Lady of England)

Biography
BOASE   BUC   DNB   DOY   HAMM   KUBA   NCH   SHO   WEBS

Giberne, Agnes. A LADY OF ENGLAND: THE LIFE AND
   LETTERS OF CHARLOTTE MARIA TUCKER. New York:
   A.C. Armstrong & Son, 1895. LC29-39108.

Obituary
TIMES (LONDON) (29 Dec 1893), 8:3.

TUPPER, EDITH SESSIONS. d.1927. U.S.

Biography
BURK

TURCZYNOWICZ, LAURA (BLACKWELL) DE GOZDAWA.

Autobiography
WHEN THE PRUSSIANS CAME TO POLAND; THE
   EXPERIENCES OF AN AMERICAN WOMAN DURING THE
   GERMAN INVASION. New York: G.P. Putnam's Sons,
   [c1916]. LC17-207.

TURNBULL, DORA AMY (ELLES) DILLON. 1878-1961.
England.
      Mrs. G.F. Dillon
      Patricia Wentworth, pseud.

Biography
EMD   KUTS   RIC   ROCK   TWCC   WARLC   WWWE

TURNBULL

Obituary
NY TIMES (1 Feb 1961), 35:2.
PUBLISHERS WEEKLY 179 (13 Feb 1961), 130.
TIMES (LONDON) (31 Jan 1961), 17:6.

TURNBULL, FRANCESE HUBBARD (LITCHFIELD).
1845?-1927. U.S.
        Mrs. Lawrence Turnbull

Biography
WOWWA   WWWA-1

TURNBULL, MARGARET. d.1942. U.S.

Biography
AWO   BURK   WWNA   WWWA-2

Obituary
NY TIMES (13 June 1942), 15:6.

Turnbull, Mrs. Lawrence. See TURNBULL, FRANCESE
HUBBARD (LITCHFIELD).

Turner, Ethel Sybil. See CURLEWIS, ETHEL SYBIL
TURNER.

Turner, Lilian. See THOMPSON, LILIAN IRENE
TURNER.

Turner, Mary (Borden). See SPEARS, MARY (BORDEN)
TURNER.

TURPIN, EDNA HENRY LEE. 1869-1952. U.S.

Biography
ALY   AWO   BURK   WOMA   WWNA   WWWA-3   WWWE

TUTTIETT, MARY GLEED. 1847-1923. England.
Maxwell Gray, pseud.

Biography
BD   CHA   HAMM   JOHDB   WARBD   WWWL

Obituary
BOOKMAN (LONDON) 65 (Nov 1923), 103.
TIMES (LONDON) (22 Sept 1923), 7:3.

TUTTLE, MARGARETTA MUHLENBERG (PERKINS). 1880-1958.
U.S.

Biography
ALY   AWO   BURK   COY   WEBS   WOWWA   WWWE

TWEEDALE, VIOLET (CHAMBERS). 1862?-1936. England.

Biography
WWWE

Obituary
TIMES (LONDON) (16 Dec 1936), 16:5.

TWEEDIE, ETHEL BRILLIANA (HARLEY). d.1940. England.
Mrs. Alec Tweedie

Autobiography
ME AND MINE; A MEDLEY OF THOUGHTS AND MEMORIES,
by Mrs. Alec-Tweedie.... London: Hutchinson,
[1932]. LC32-19700.

MY LEGACY CRUISE (THE PEAK YEAR OF MY LIFE), by
Mrs. Alec-Tweedie. London: Hutchinson, [1936].
NUC.

MY TABLE-CLOTHS; A FEW REMINISCENCES, by Mrs.
Alec Tweedie. New York: Doran, 1916.
LC17-16197.

THIRTEEN YEARS OF A BUSY WOMAN'S LIFE, by Mrs.
Alec Tweedie. New York: John Lane, 1912.
LC12-29124.

TIGHT CORNERS OF MY ADVENTUROUS LIFE, by Mrs.
Alec-Tweedie. London: Hutchinson, [1933].
LC35-2717.

A WOMAN ON FOUR BATTLE-FRONTS, by Mrs. Alec-
Tweedie. Leeds, London: Beck and Inchbold,
[1919]. LC23-5431.

Biography
HAMM WWLA WWWE WWWL

Obituary
CUR-1940.
NY TIMES (16 Apr 1940), 23:5.
TIMES (LONDON) (20 Apr 1940), 200:1.

Tweedie, Mrs. Alec. See TWEEDIE, ETHEL BRILLIANA
(HARLEY).

TYBOUT, ELLA MIDDLETON. U.S.

Biography
BURK WOWWA

Tyler, Odette, pseud. See SHEPHERD, ELIZABETH LEE
(KIRKLAND).

TYLER, THERESE PAULINE (COLES). b.1884. U.S.

Biography
WOWWA

Tynan, Katharine. See HINKSON, KATHARINE (TYNAN).

Tytler, Sarah, pseud. See KEDDIE, HENRIETTA.

ULLMAN, ALICE (WOODS). 1871-1959. U.S.
        Alice Woods

Biography
BAN   WOWWA   WWWA-5

Obituary
NY TIMES (25 July 1959), 17:3.

Underhill, Evelyn, pseud.   See MOORE, EVELYN
(UNDERHILL).

UNDERWOOD, EDNA (WORTHLEY). b.1873. U.S.

Biography
APP-S   AWO   BURK   WOMA   WWNA   WWWL

Craine, Carol W. MRS. UNDERWOOD: LINGUIST,
    LITTERATEUSE. [Hays: Fort Hays Kansas State
    College], 1965 [c1964]. LC64-63576R.

URNER, MABEL HERBERT. 1881-1957. U.S.

Biography
AWO   WOWWA   WWWA-3

Vacaresco, Helene. See VACARESCU, ELENA.

VACARESCU, ELENA. 1868-1947. Rumania.
    Helene Vacaresco

              Biography
  HAR   WEBS   WWLA   WWWL

             Obituary
  NY TIMES (18 Feb 1947), 26:3.
  TIMES (LONDON) (18 Feb 1947), 6:5.
  WILSON 21 (Apr 1947), 572.

VAIZEY, JESSIE (BELL) MANSERGH. 1857-1917. England.
    Mrs. George De Horne Vaizey

             Biography
  BRI   TWCR

Vaizey, Mrs George De Horne. See VAIZEY, JESSIE
  (BELL) MANSERGH.

Vaka, Demetra. See BROWN, DEMETRA (VAKA).

Valentine, Jane, pseud. See MEEKER, NELLIE J.

VALLINGS, GABRIELLE FRANCESCA LILIAN MAY. b.1886.
  England.

             Biography
  WWWE

Van Anderson, Helen. See GORDON, HELEN (VAN METRE)
  VAN ANDERSON.

Vandegrift, Margaret, pseud. See JANVIER, MARGARET THOMSON.

VANDERCOOK, MARGARET O'BANNON (WOMACK). b.1876. U.S.

Biography
AWO   BURK   WWNA

Van Deventer, E. M.   See   VAN DEVENTER,   EMMA MURDOCH.

Van Deventer, E. Murdoch. See VAN DEVENTER, EMMA MURDOCH.

VAN DEVENTER, EMMA MURDOCH. fl.1879-1912. U.S.
        Lawrence L. Lynch, pseud.
        E.M. Van Deventer
        E. Murdoch Van Deventer

Biography
    EMD

VAN DE WATER, VIRGINIA BELLE (TERHUNE). 1865-1945. U.S.

Biography
    ALY   AWO   BURK   WOWWA   WWNA   WWWA-2

Obituary
    TIME 46 (29 Oct 1945), 74.

VAN DRESSER, JASMINE STONE. b.1875. U.S.

Biography
    WWNA   WWWA-6

Van Hoesen, Antoinette. See   WAKEMAN, ANTOINETTE PRUDENCE (VAN HOESEN).

Van Saanen, Marie Louise, pseud. See HALE, MARICE
RUTLEDGE (GIBSON).

VAN SLINGERLAND, NELLIE BINGHAM. b.1850. U.S.
      Neile Bevans, pseud.

Biography

WOWWA   WWWA-4

VAN SLYKE, LUCILLE (BALDWIN). b.1880. U.S.

Biography

ALY   WWWA-6

VAN VORST, BESSIE (MACGINNIS). 1873-1928. U.S.
      Mrs. John Van Vorst

Biography

AWW   BURK   WOWWA   WWWA-1

VAN VORST, MARIE LOUISE. 1867-1936. U.S.
      m. Cagiati

Autobiography

WAR LETTERS OF AN AMERICAN WOMAN. New York: J.
Lane, 1916. LC16-6225.

Biography

AWW   BURK   NAW   WOWWA   WWWA-1

Obituary

NY TIMES (18 Dec 1936), 25:5.
PUBLISHERS WEEKLY 131 (2 Jan 1937), 43.
WILSON 11 (Jan 1937), 296.

Van Vorst, Mrs. John.   See VAN VORST, BESSIE
(MACGINNIS).

VAUGHN, KATE (BREW). 1874-1933. U.S.

Biography

WWNA

VER BECK, HANNA (RION). 1875-1924. U.S.
Hanna Rion

Biography
WWWA-1

Obituary
NY TIMES (6 May 1924), 21:5.

VERMILYE, KATE (JORDAN). 1862-1926. U.S.
Kate Jordan
Mrs. F.M. Vermilye

Biography
ALY BURG BURK DAB

Vermilye, Mrs. F.M. See VERMILYE, KATE (JORDAN).

VERY, LYDIA LOUISA ANNA. 1823-1901. U.S.

Biography
APP BURK DAB HAOXA KUAA NCAB-6 WARBD WWWA-1

Viebig, Clara. See COHN, CLARA (VIEBIG).

Von Heyking, Elisabeth Auguste (Von Flemming). See
HEYKING, ELISABETH AUGUSTE (VON FLEMMING) VON.

Von Hillern, Wilhelmine (Birch). See HILLERN,
WILHELMINE (BIRCH) VON.

Von Hutten, Baroness. See HUTTEN ZUM STOLZENBERG,
BETSEY (RIDDLE) VON.

Von Hutten, Bettina. See HUTTEN ZUM STOLZENBERG,
BETSEY (RIDDLE) VON.

Von Suttner, Bertha Felicie Sophie (Kinsky). See
SUTTNER, BERTHA FELICIE SOPHIE (KINSKY) VON.

Von Teuffel, Blanche Willis (Howard). See TEUFFEL,
    BLANCHE WILLIS (HOWARD) VON.

Voynich, E.L. See VOYNICH, ETHEL LILLIAN (BOOLE).

VOYNICH, ETHEL LILLIAN (BOOLE). 1864-1960. England.
    E.L. Voynich

Biography
BERE   BURK   COU   NCH   SHO   WARLC   WEBS

Obituary
CON-104.
NY TIMES (9 July 1960), 25:3.
PUBLISHERS WEEKLY 178 (8 Aug 1960), 41.
TIME 76 (8 Aug 1960), 82.

WAGGAMAN, MARY TERESA MACKEE. 1846-1931. U.S.

Biography
BOCCA-1   BURK   DAB

WAGNALLS, MABEL. 1871-1946. U.S.
m. Jones

Biography
ALY   AWO   BURK   COY   TWCB   WOWWA   WWNA

Wait, Frona Eunice, pseud. See   COLBURN, FRONA
EUNICE WAIT (SMITH).

WAKEMAN, ANTOINETTE PRUDENCE (VAN HOESEN). b.1856.
U.S.
Antoinette Van Hoesen

Biography
WILA   WOWWA   WWWA-4

WALDEN, ANN BREVOORT (EDDY). 1872-1962. U.S.
Ann Devoore

Biography
WWWA-5

Walford,   L. B.   See   WALFORD,   LUCY   BETHIA
(COLQUHOUN).

WALFORD, LUCY BETHIA (COLQUHOUN). 1845-1915.
Scotland.
L.B. Walford

Autobiography
MEMORIES OF VICTORIAN LONDON, by L.B. Walford.
London: E. Arnold, 1912. LC13-35392.

RECOLLECTIONS OF A SCOTTISH NOVELIST, by
L.B. Walford. New York: Longmans, Green,
1910. OCLC 563997.

Biography
BD   BLA   NCH   SHA-A   SHO   WARBD   WWWL

WALL, MARY. England.

Biography
WWWE

WALLACE, ELIZABETH. 1866-1960. U.S.

Biography
BICA   WOWWA   WWWA-3

Obituary
NY TIMES (13 Apr 1960), 40:1.

Waller, M.E.   See   WALLER, MARY ELLA.

WALLER, MARY ELLA. 1855-1938. U.S.
M.E. Waller

Biography
AWW   BURK   KUT   OV   OV2   REA   WARLC   WWWA-1

Obituary
NY TIMES (15 June 1938), 23:6.
PUBLISHERS WEEKLY 134 (2 July 1938), 41.

WALLING, ANNA STRUNSKY. 1879-1964. U.S.

Biography
ALY   WWWA-1

WALTON, ELEANOR GOING. U.S.

Biography
WWWA-5

WALTZ, ELIZABETH (CHERRY). 1866-1903. U.S.

Biography
BURK   COY   KNIB   WWWA-1

Obituary
NY TIMES (20 Sept 1903), 7:6.

WALWORTH, JEANNETTE RITCHIE (HADERMANN). 1837-1918.
U.S.
        Mrs. J.H. Walworth

Biography
AWW   BURK   DAB   KNIB   NCAB-8   WARBD   WILA   WWWA-4

Walworth,   Mrs.   J.H.   See   WALWORTH,   JEANNETTE
RITCHIE   (HADERMANN).

Ward, A.B.   See   BAILEY, ALICE (WARD).

Ward, E., pseud.   See   GREEN, EVELYN EVERETT-.

WARD, ELIZABETH STUART (PHELPS). 1844-1911. U.S.
        Mary Adams, pseud.
        Elizabeth Stuart Phelps

Autobiography
CHAPTERS FROM A LIFE, by Elizabeth Stuart Phelps.
  Boston: Houghton Mifflin, 1896. LC04-17208R.

Biography
ADE   APP   AWW   BD   BEL   BURKE   DAB   HAL   HAMM
HAOXA   HARKF   JOHDB   KUAA   LOGP   MYE   NAW   NCAB-9
PRE   REA   RICDA   ROCK   TWCB   WARBD   WEBS   WILA
WIN   WWWA-1

Bennett, Mary A.   ELIZABETH STUART PHELPS.
  Philadelphia: Univ. of Pennsylvania Press,
  1939. LC39-16781.

Kessler, Carol F.   ELIZABETH STUART PHELPS.
  Boston: Twayne, c1982. LC82-11836.

Petty, Sallie D. FAMOUS AUTHORS, THEIR LIVES AND WORKS. pp. 45-46. 2d ed. Friend, Neb.: Studio News, 1948. OCLC 6521732.

Obituary
NY TIMES (29 Jan 1911), II 11:1.

WARD, FLORENCE GANNON HANFELD. b.1860.
Mrs. J. Carlton Ward

Biography
AWO BURK HOO WWWA-3

WARD, FLORENCE JEANNETTE (BAIER). 1886-1959. U.S.

Biography
WWWL

WARD, JOSEPHINE MARY (HOPE-SCOTT). 1864-1932. England.
Mrs. Wilfrid Ward

Biography
HOE

Obituary
CATHOLIC WORLD 136 (Jan 1933), 490.
TIMES (LONDON) (21 Nov 1932), 19:2; (25 Nov), 19:4.

WARD, MARY AUGUSTA (ARNOLD). 1851-1920. England.
Mrs. Humphry Ward

Autobiography
A WRITER'S RECOLLECTIONS. [Folcroft, Pa.]: Folcroft, 1973, 1918. LC73-16312.

Biography
ADE BD BEL BENN BERE BRIT BRO CAS CHA CHABI COLSA COU DNB-3 FUR HAL HAMM HAOXE HINA JOHDB KUT LAU MAGN MDWB MYE NCH NO NOV NPW PEE SER SHA SHA-A SHO VIC WAGCE WARBD WARLC WEBS WENW WWWL

Gwynne, Stephen L. MRS. HUMPHRY WARD. New York: Holt, [191-?]. OCLC 3508428.

Jones, Enid H. MRS. HUMPHRY WARD. New York: St. Martin's, [1973]. LC73-80643.

Smith, Esther M. MRS. HUMPHRY WARD. Boston: Twayne, 1980. LC79-24476.

Trevelyan, Janet P. THE LIFE OF MRS. HUMPHRY WARD, by her daughter. New York: Dodd, [1923]. LC47-39797.

Obituary
Harris, Muriel. "Mrs. Humphry Ward." NORTH AMERICAN REVIEW 211 (June 1920), 818-25.
"Mrs. Humphry Ward." LITERARY DIGEST 65 (1 May 1920), 40-41.
NY TIMES (25 Mar 1920), 11:5.
"Passing of Mrs. Humphry Ward." LIVING AGE 305 (15 May 1920), 415-18.
TIMES (LONDON) (25 Mar 1920), 16:3.

Ward, Mrs. Humphry. See WARD, MARY AUGUSTA (ARNOLD).

Ward, Mrs. J. Carlton. See WARD, FLORENCE GANNON HANFELD.

Ward, Mrs. Wilfrid. See WARD, JOSEPHINE MARY (HOPE-SCOTT).

Warden, Florence, pseud. See JAMES, FLORENCE ALICE (PRICE).

WARING, MALVINA SARAH (BLACK). 1842-1930. U.S.

Biography
KNIB   WOWWA   WWWA-3

WARNER, ANNA BARTLETT. 1827-1915. U.S.

Biography
ADE APP AWW BURK DAB KUAA MYE NAW NCAB-4
PAP PRE REA WARBD WEBS WOWWA WWWA-1

Baker, Mabel. LIGHT IN THE MORNING: MEMORIES OF
SUSAN AND ANNA WARNER. [West Point, N.Y.]:
Constitution Island Assoc., 1978. LC78-72491.

Foster, Edward H. SUSAN AND ANNA WARNER.
Boston: Twayne, c1978. LC78-2431.

Stokes, Olivia E. LETTERS AND MEMORIES OF SUSAN
AND ANNA BARTLETT WARNER. New York: G.P.
Putnam's Sons, 1925. LC25-27795.

Obituary
NY TIMES (23 Jan 1915), 11:4.

Bibliography
Sanderson, Dorothy H. THEY WROTE FOR A LIVING: A
BIBLIOGRAPHY OF THE WORKS OF SUSAN BOGERT WARNER
AND ANNA BARTLETT WARNER. West Point, N.Y.:
Constitution Island Assoc., 1976. LC76-11294.

Warner, Anne. See FRENCH, ANNE RICHMOND (WARNER).

WARREN, CONSTANCE MARTHA (WILLIAMS). b.1877. U.S.

Biography
WOWWA

WARREN, CORNELIA. 1857-1921. U.S.

Biography
WIN WOWWA WWWA-5

WARREN, MAUDE LAVINIA (RADFORD). 1875-1934. U.S.

Biography
BURK WOWWA WWWA-1

Warwick, Anne, pseud. See CRANSTON, RUTH.

WASHBURNE, MARION (FOSTER). b.1863. U.S.

Biography
WOWWA

Waste, Henrie, pseud. See STETTHEIMER, ETTIE.

Watanna, Onoto, pseud. See BABCOCK, WINNIFRED (EATON).

WATSON, ELIZABETH SOPHIA (FLETCHER). d.1918.
Deas Cromarty, pseud.

Biography
WWWL

WATSON, MARY DEVEREUX). d.1914. U.S.
M. Devereux
Mary Devereux

Biography
BURK   COY   WOWWA   WWWA-1

WATSON, VIRGINIA CRUSE. b.1872. U.S.
Roger West, pseud.

Biography
AWO   WWNA

WATTS, MARY (STANBERY). 1868-1958. U.S.

Biography
BURK   COY   HAOXA   KUT   MAN   MARBS   NCAB-C   OV
OV2   REA   WOWWA   WWNA   WWWA-4

Obituary
NY TIMES (23 May 1958), 23:1.

WEAVER, BAILLE GERTRUDE RENTON (COLMORE). England.
G. Colmore, pseud.

Biography
ROCK

WEAVER, EMILY POYNTON. 1865-1943. Canada.

Biography
MDCB   MOR   MOR2   STOXC   WOWWA

Obituary
NY TIMES (12 Mar 1943), 17:5.

Webb, Gladys Mary.   See   WEBB, MARY GLADYS
(MEREDITH).

WEBB, MARY GLADYS (MEREDITH). 1881/83-1927. England.
Gladys Mary Webb

Biography
ADC   BERE   BRO   CAS   CHABI   HAMM   HAOXA   KUAT
KUT   KUTS   LAU   MAG   MANBL   MICB   MYE   NCH   NOV
PEE   RA   RIC   SHO   WAGCE   WEBS   WWWL

Addison, Hilda. MARY WEBB: A SHORT STUDY OF HER
LIFE AND WORK. [London]: C. Palmer, 1931.
OCLC 2731075.

Byford-Jones, W. SHROPSHIRE HAUNTS OF MARY WEBB.
2d ed. Shrewsbury: Wilding, 1948. OCLC 654247.

Coles, Gladys M. THE FLOWER OF LIGHT: A
BIOGRAPHY OF MARY WEBB. London: Duckworth,
1978. LC78-323267.

Moult, Thomas. MARY WEBB: HER LIFE AND WORK.
London: J. Cape, [1932]. LC33-27031.

Steff, Bernard. MY DEAREST ACQUAINTANCE: A
BIOGRAPHICAL SKETCH OF MARY AND HENRY WEBB.
Ludlow: King's Bookshop, 1977. LC77-377889.

Wrenn, Dorothy P. GOODBYE TO MORNING; A
  BIOGRAPHICAL STUDY OF MARY WEBB. Shrewsbery
  [Eng.]: Wilding, 1964. LC66-6045.

WEBLING, PEGGY. England.

Autobiography
PEGGY: THE STORY OF ONE SCORE YEARS AND TEN.
  London: Hutchinson, [1924]. OCLC 3334226.

Biography
HAMM   WWWE

Webster, Jean. See McKINNEY, ALICE JEAN CHANDLER
  (WEBSTER).

Weekes, A.R. See   WEEKES, AGNES RUSSELL.

WEEKES, AGNES RUSSELL. b.1880.   England.
        Anthony Pryde, pseud.
        A.R. Weekes

Biography
KUT   MARBS   WWWE   WWWL

WEIMAN, RITA. 1889-1954. U.S.
        m. Marks

Biography
BURK   REA   WWNA   WWWA-3   WWWE   WWWL

WELLMAN, RITA (MCCANN). b.1890. U.S.

Biography
BURK   MAN

WELLS, CAROLYN. 1862-1942. U.S.
        m. Houghton
        Rowland Wright, pseud.

Autobiography
THE REST OF MY LIFE. Philadelphia: J.B.
Lippincott, [c1937]. LC37-30710.

Biography
ALY AMH AWO AWW BERE BRO BURG BURK EMD
HAY KUT MARBS NAW NCAB-13 REA RIC TWCB
TWCC WARBD WEBS WOWWA WWNA WWWA-2

Masson, Thomas L. OUR AMERICAN HUMORISTS.
pp. 305-23. New and enl. ed. Freeport, N.Y.:
Books for Libraries Press, [1966, 1931].
LC 67-23245.

Obituary
CUR-1942.
NY TIMES (27 Mar 1942), 23:1.
NEWSWEEK 19 (6 Apr 1942), 8.
PUBLISHERS WEEKLY 141 (4 Apr 1942), 1332.
TIME 39 (6 Apr 1942), 64.
WILSON 16 (May 1942), 692.

Wentworth, Patricia, pseud. See TURNBULL, DORA AMY
(ELLES) DILLON.

WERNER, ALICE. 1859-1935. South Africa.
Biography
WEBS

Werner, E., pseud. See BUERSTENBINDER, ELISABETH.

West, Kenyon, pseud. See HOWLAND, FRANCES LOUISE
(MORSE).

WEST, LILLIAN (CLARKSON). b.1869. U.S.
Biography
WOWWA

West, Rebecca, pseud. See FAIRFIELD, CICILY ISABEL
ANDREWS.

West, Roger, pseud. See WATSON, VIRGINIA CRUSE.

West, V. Sackville. See NICHOLSON, VICTORIA MARY
    SACKVILLE-WEST.

Westover, Cynthia M. See ALDEN, CYNTHIA MAY
    (WESTOVER).

WETMORE, ELIZABETH (BISLAND). 1861-1929. U.S.
    Elizabeth Bisland

Biography
BD BUCK LIB WARBD WILA WOWWA WWNA WWWA-1

WHARTON, ANNE HOLLINGSWORTH. 1845-1928. U.S.

Biography
ADE APP BURK DAB NCAB-13 PRE TWCB WARBD
WEBS WOWWA WWWA-1

WHARTON, EDITH NEWBOLD (JONES). 1862-1937. U.S.

Autobiography
A BACKWARD GLANCE. New York: D. Appleton-
    Century, 1934. LC34-10082.

"The Writing of Ethan Frome." In BREAKING INTO
    PRINT; ... A SELECT GROUP OF AUTHORS TELLS OF
    THE DIFFICULTIES OF AUTHORSHIP AND HOW SUCH
    TRIALS ARE MET, TOGETHER WITH BIOGRAPHICAL
    NOTES ..., compiled by Elmer Adler.
    pp. 187-91. Freeport, N.Y.: Books for
    Libraries, [1968]. LC68-55840.

Biography
ADE AMN AMR AMWRP APPS ASH AUC AW AWW
BERE BRO BROOK BURK CAS CHA CHABI CON-104
DAB-S2 FLE HAMM HAOXA HAOXE HINA JENS JES
JOHDB KRO KU KUL KUT LOGG LOGP LOV MAG
MAO MARBS MCW MDWB MILA MON MORG MYE NAW
NCAB-14 NOV NPW OVA PEA PRE RA REA RIC
RICDA SCHM SEYS TWCB VDW WAGCA WARBD WARLC
WEBS WENW WOWWA WWNA WWWA-1 WWWE

Andrews, Wayne, ed. "The World of Edith Wharton: Fragments of a Biography in Progress." In THE BEST SHORT STORIES OF EDITH WHARTON. pp. vii-xxvii. New York: C. Scribner's Sons, [1958]. LC58-10825.

Auchincloss, Louis. EDITH WHARTON. Minneapolis: Univ. of Minnesota Press, [1961], LC61-63841L. Also pub. in SEVEN MODERN AMERICAN NOVELISTS, edited by William Van O'Connor. pp. 11-45. Minneapolis: Univ. of Minnesota Press, [1964]. LC64-18175.

_____. EDITH WHARTON; A WOMAN IN HER TIME. New York: Viking, [1971]. LC77-146606.

Bell, Millicent. EDITH WHARTON AND HENRY JAMES, THE STORY OF THEIR FRIENDSHIP. New York: G. Braziller, [1965]. LC65-10196.

Chanler, Margaret T. AUTUMN IN THE VALLEY. Boston: Little, Brown, 1936. LC36-30939R.

Coolidge, Olivia. EDITH WHARTON, 1862-1937. New York: Scribner, [1964]. LC64-16181. juvenile literature

Griffith, Grace K. THE TWO LIVES OF EDITH WHARTON. New York: Appleton-Century, [1965]. LC65-5135.

Lawson, Richard H. EDITH WHARTON. New York: Ungar, c1977. LC77-40.

Lewis, Richard W. EDITH WHARTON: A BIOGRAPHY. New York: Harper & Row, [1975]. LC74-1833.

Longstreet, Stephen. WE ALL WENT TO PARIS; AMERICANS IN THE CITY OF LIGHT, 1776-1971. pp. 201-16. New York: Macmillan, [1972]. LC78-165572.

Lovett, Robert M. EDITH WHARTON. Philadelphia: R. West, 1977, [c1925]. LC77-28804.

Lubbock, Percy. PORTRAIT OF EDITH WHARTON. New York: Appleton-Century, 1947. LC47-31175.

McDowell, Margaret. EDITH WHARTON. Boston:
Twayne, c1976. LC75-44094R.

Quinn, Arthur H. EDITH WHARTON. Norwood, Pa.:
Norwood, 1976, 1938. LC76-9780.

_____, ed. "Introduction." In AN EDITH WHARTON
TREASURY. pp. v-xxvii. New York: Appleton-
Century-Crofts, [1950], LC50-2775.

Wolff, Cynthia G. A FEAST OF WORDS: THE TRIUMPH
OF EDITH WHARTON. New York: Oxford Univ.
Press, 1977. LC76-42678.

Obituary
COMMONWEAL 26 (27 Aug 1937), 412.
LONDON MERCURY 36 (Sept 1937), 417.
NY TIMES (13 Aug 1937), 17:1.
NEWSWEEK 10 (21 Aug 1937), 5.
PUBLISHERS WEEKLY 132 (21 Aug 1937), 575-6.
TIME 30 (23 Aug 1937), 53.
TIMES (LONDON) (14 Aug 1937), 12:3; tribute
(17 Aug), 15:2.

Bibliography
Brenni, Vito J. EDITH WHARTON: A BIBLIOGRAPHY.
Morgantown: West Virginia Univ. Library, 1966.
LC66-24417.

Springer, Marlene. EDITH WHARTON AND KATE
CHOPIN: A REFERENCE GUIDE. Boston: G.K. Hall,
c1976. LC76-1831.

WHEELER, HALLIE ERMINIE (RIVES). 1876-1956. U.S.
Hallie Erminie Rives
Mrs. Post Wheeler

Autobiography
Wheeler, Post and Hallie Rives. DOME OF MANY-
COLOURED GLASS. Garden City, N.Y.: Doubleday,
1955. LC55-6486.

Biography
BURK   DAB-S6   KNIB   WARBD   WOWWA

WHEELER

Obituary
CUR-1956.
NY TIMES (18 Aug 1956), 17:3.
NEWSWEEK 48 (27 Aug 1956), 75.
WILSON 31 (Oct 1956), 126-7.

WHEELER, HARRIET MARTHA. 1858-1924. U.S.

Obituary
NY TIMES (10 Apr 1924), 23:4.

Wheeler, Mrs. Post. See WHEELER, HALLIE ERMINIE
(RIVES).

Wherry, Edith. See MUCKLESTON, EDITH MARGARET
(WHERRY).

WHITAKER, LYDIA. U.S.

Biography
BAN

WHITCOMB, JESSIE (WRIGHT). b.1864. U.S.
         Elvirton Wright, pseud.
         Jessie E. Wright

Biography
WOWWA

WHITE, AMBER (REEVES) BLANCO. 1887-1982. New
Zealand.
         Amber Reeves

Biography
WHO'S WHO-1982 WWWE

Obituary
CON-105.
TIMES (LONDON) (6 Jan 1982), 10:6.

WHITE

WHITE, CAROLINE (EARLE). 1833-1916. U.S.

Biography
BURK   WWWA-1

WHITE, ELIZA ORNE. 1856-1947. U.S.

Biography
ALY   AWO   AWW   BD   BURK   KUJ1   KUJ2   NAW   NCAB-13
TWCB   WARBD   WIN   WOWWA   WWWA-2   YES-2

WHITE, GRACE (MILLER). d.1965. U.S.

Biography
BURK

WHITE, NANA (SPRINGER). 1873/74-1956. U.S.
        Adele Garrison, pseud.

Obituary
NY TIMES (4 Dec 1956), 39:2.

WHITEHOUSE, FLORENCE (BROOKS). 1869/70-1945. U.S.

Biography
WOWWA   WWWA-5

Obituary
NY TIMES (23 Jan 1945), 19:1.

WHITELEY, ISABEL (NIXON). 1859-1935. U.S.

Biography
WWWA-5

Whitelock, L. Clarkson.   See   WHITELOCK, LOUISE
(CLARKSON).

WHITELOCK, LOUISE (CLARKSON). b.1865. U.S.
L. Clarkson Whitelock

Biography
BURK   KNIB   ROCK   WARBD

WHITING, LILIAN. 1855/1859-1942. U.S.
full name Emily Lilian Whiting

Biography
ALY   AWO   AWW   BD   BURK   HAMM   LOGP   NAW   NCAB-9
WARBD   WILA   WOWWA   WWNA   WWWA-2

Obituary
NY TIMES (1 May 1942). 19:2.
WILSON 16 (Jun 1942), 788.

WHITNEY, ADELINE DUTTON (TRAIN). 1824-1906. U.S.
Mrs. A.D.T. Whitney

Biography
APP   AWW   BD   BURK   DAB   HAL   KUAA   NAW   NCAB-2
TWCB   WARBD   WEBS   WILA   WIN   WWWA-1

Obituary
NY TIMES (22 Mar 1906), 9:5.

WHITNEY, GERTRUDE CAPEN. 1861-1941. U.S.
Mrs. George Erastus Whitney

Biography
AWO   BURK   WOWWA   WWNA   WWWA-1

Obituary
NY TIMES (23 May 1941), 21:4.

Whitney, Mrs. A.D.T. See WHITNEY, ADELINE DUTTON
(TRAIN).

Whitney, Mrs. George Erastus. See WHITNEY,
GERTRUDE CAPEN.

WIDDEMER, MARGARET. 1880-1978. U.S.
    m. Schauffer

Autobiography
GOLDEN FRIENDS I HAD; UNREVISED MEMORIES OF
   MARGARET WIDDEMER. Garden City, N.Y.:
   Doubleday, 1964. LC64-19258.

Biography
ALY AWO BERE BURK CON-N4 HAOXA KUT KUTS
MYE OV2 REA WEBS WWNA WWWL

Overton, Grant M. MARGARET WIDDEMER. New York:
   Farrar & Rinehart, Inc., [c1930]. NUC.

Obituary
CON-77--80.
NY TIMES (15 July 1978), 20:4.

Wiggin, Kate Douglas. See RIGGS, KATE DOUGLAS
(SMITH) WIGGIN.

WIGHT, EMMA HOWARD. U.S.

Biography
WILA

WILCOX, ELLA (WHEELER). 1850-1919. U.S.

Autobiography
THE STORY OF A LITERARY CAREER. Holyoke, Mass.:
   E. Towne, [1905]. LC05-8346R.

THE WORLDS AND I. New York: Arno, 1980, c1918.
   LC79-8823.

Biography
ADE ALY APP AWW BD BRO BURK CHA CHABI
DAB HAMM HAOXA HAOXE KUAA LOGP MCC MYE
NAW NCAB-11 PEA PRE REA SCHM TIT VDW
WARBD WARLC WEBS WILA WOWWA WWWA-1

State Historical Society of Wisconsin.
   DICTIONARY OF WISCONSIN BIOGRAPHY. pp. 376.
   Madison, 1960. LC60-63043.

WILCOX

Obituary
LITERARY DIGEST 63 (22 Nov 1919), 32-33.
NY TIMES (31 Oct 1919), 13:3.
TIMES (LONDON) (31 Oct 1919), 15:4.

WILCOX, MARRION. 1858-1926. U.S.

Biography
ALY   BURK   ROCK   WARBD   WWNA   WWWA-1

Wilkins, Mary E.   See   FREEMAN, MARY ELEANOR
(WILKINS).

Wilkinson,   Florence.   See   EVANS,   FLORENCE
WILKINSON.

WILKINSON, MARGUERITE OGDEN (BIGELOW). 1883-1928.
U.S./Canada.
        Marguerite Ogden Bigelow

Biography
BURG   KUT   MAN   NCAB-21   REA   WEBS   WWNA   WWWA-1

Obituary
Monroe, H.   POETRY 31 (Mar 1928), 332-4.
WOMAN'S JOURNAL n.s. 13 (Feb 1928), 28.

Willcocks, M.P.   See   WILLCOCKS, MARY PATRICIA.

WILLCOCKS, MARY PATRICIA. b.1869. England.
        M.P. Willcocks

Biography
WEBS   WWLA   WWWE

Williams, Margery. See   BIANCO, MARGERY (WILLIAMS).

WILLIAMS, MARTHA (COLLINS) McCULLOCH. U.S.

Biography
ALY   BURK   KNIB   WARBD   WOWWA   WWWA-5

WILLIAMS

Williams, Robert Dolly, pseud. See BLACK, MARGARET HORTON (POTTER).

Williamson, A.M. See WILLIAMSON, ALICE MURIEL (LIVINGSTON).

WILLIAMSON, ALICE MURIEL (LIVINGSTON). 1869-1933. England.
    Marquesa D'Alpens, pseud.
    Dona Teresa De Savallo
    M.P. Revere, pseud.
    Alice Stuyvesant, pseud.
    A.M. Williamson
    Mrs. C.N. Williamson
    Mrs. Harcourt Williamson

Autobiography
THE INKY WAY. London: Chapman & Hall, 1931. LC31-9802.

Biography
KUT TWCR WARLC WEBS

Obituary
PUBLISHERS WEEKLY 124 (30 Sept 1933), 1142.
TIMES (LONDON) (26 Sept 1933), 19:1.

Williamson, Mrs. C.N. See WILLIAMSON, ALICE MURIEL (LIVINGSTON).

Williamson, Mrs. Harcourt. See WILLIAMSON, ALICE MURIEL (LIVINGSTON).

Willsie, Honore. See MORROW, HONORE (MACCUE) WILLSIE.

Willy, Colette, pseud. See DE JOUVENAL, SIDONIE GABRIELLE (COLETTE) GAUTHER-VILLARS.

WILSON, AUGUSTA JANE (EVANS). 1835-1909. U.S.

Biography

BURK DAB-S3 JONE KUAA LIB LOGP NAW NCAB-4
ORG PAP REA RUB RUT SOU TWCB WARBD WEBS
WWWA-1 WYN

Fidler, William P. AUGUSTA EVANS WILSON,
1835-1909, A BIOGRAPHY. University, Ala.:
Univ. of Alabama Press, 1951. LC52-102.

Williams, Benjamin B. A LITERARY HISTORY OF
ALABAMA: THE NINETEENTH CENTURY. pp. 183-94.
Rutherford [N.J.]: Fairleigh Dickinson Univ.
Press, 1979. LC76-50286.

Obituary

NY TIMES (10 May 1909), 9:3.
TIMES (LONDON) (13 May 1909), 13:3.

WILSON, DESEMEA (NEWMAN).
        Diana Patrick, pseud.
                Biography

WWWE

WILSON, LEONA (DALRYMPLE). b.1884. U.S.
        Leona Dalrymple

Biography

BURK WWNA

Wilson, Romer, pseud. See O'BRIEN, FLORENCE ROMA
MUIR WILSON.

WINN, MARY POLK. U.S.

Biography

KNIB

WINSLOW, HELEN MARIA. 1851-1938. U.S.

Biography
ALY   AWO   AWW   BURK   LOGP   NCAB-B   ROSS   WARBD
WILA   WOWWA   WWNA   WWWA-1

Obituary
NY TIMES (28 Mar 1938), 15:3.

WINSLOW, ROSE GUGGENHEIM. b.1881. U.S.
        Jane Burr, pseud.

Biography
BURK

WINSTON, ANNIE STEGER. d.1927. U.S.

Biography
WOWWA   WWWA-1

WINTER, ALICE VIVIAN (AMES). 1865-1944. U.S.

Biography
ALY   AWO   BICA   BURK   NAW   WOWWA   WWNA   WWWA-2

WINTER, ELIZABETH (CAMPBELL). 1841-1922. U.S.
        Isabella Castelar, pseud.

Biography
BURK   WOWWA   WWWA-1

Winter, John Strange, pseud.   See   STANNARD,
    HENRIETTA ELIZA VAUGHAN (PALMER).

Winterton, Mark, pseud.   See   KIDD, BEATRICE ETHEL.

WOLF, EMMA. 1865-1932. U.S.

Biography
BURK   WARBD   WOWWA   WWNA   WWWA-4

WOLFENSTEIN, MARTHA. 1869-1906. U.S.

Biography

COY

WOOD, EDITH (ELMER). 1871-1945. U.S.

Biography

AWO   BURK   DAB-3   LOGP   NAW   WOWWA   WWNA   WWWA-2

Obituary

JOURNAL OF HOME ECONOMICS 37 (Jun 1945), 375.
SURVEY 81 (May 1945), 155.

WOOD, JOANNA E. d.1919. Canada.

Biography

MOR2   MORGA   STOXC   WOWWA

Wood, L.C.   See   WOOD, LYDIA COPE (COLLINS).

WOOD, LYDIA COPE (COLLINS). b.1845. U.S.
        L.C. Wood

Biography

WOWWA

WOODBURY, HELEN LAURA (SUMNER). 1876-1933. U.S.
        Helen L. Sumner

Biography

DAB   NAW   PRE   WWNA   WWWA-1

Obituary

NY TIMES (12 Mar 1933), 29:2.

WOODGATE, MILDRED VIOLET. b.1904. England.

Biography

AWWW   CON-11--12R

Woodman, H. Rea. See WOODMAN, HANNAH REA.

WOODMAN, HANNAH REA. 1870-1951. U.S.
      H. Rea Woodman

Biography
   AWO

Obituary
   NY TIMES (15 May 1951), 31:3.

Woodroffe, Daniel, pseud. See WOODS, MRS. JAMES
   CHAPMAN.

Woodrow, Mrs. Wilson. See WOODROW, NANCY MANN
   (WADDEL).

WOODROW, NANCY MANN (WADDEL). 1870-1935. U.S.
      Mrs. Wilson Woodrow

Biography
   BURG BURK COY NAW WEBS

Obituary
   NY TIMES (8 Sept 1935), 38:1.
   PUBLISHERS WEEKLY 128 (14 Sept 1935), 831.

WOODRUFF, HELEN (SMITH). 1888-1924. U.S.

Biography
   ALY WOWWA WWWA-1

WOODRUFF, JANE (SCOTT). U.S.

Biography
   WOWWA

WOODRUFF, JULIA LOUISA MATILDA (CURTISS).
1833-1909. U.S.
      W.M.L. Jay, pseud.

Biography
BURK   WWWA-1   WWWE

Woods, Alice. See ULLMAN, ALICE (WOODS).

WOODS, KATHARINE PEARSON. 1853-1923. U.S.

Biography
AWW BD BURK LIB NAW TUR WARBD WOWWA WWWA-1

Turner, Ella M., comp. and ed. STORIES AND VERSE
   OF WEST VIRGINIA. pp. 301-3. Richwood, W.Va.:
   Comstock, 1974. LC78-111733.

Obituary
NY TIMES (20 Feb 1923), 17:3.

WOODS, MARGARET LOUISA (BRADLEY). 1856-1945.
England.

Biography
BD BRI BRO CHA MYE NCH SHA SHA-A SHO
WARBD WARLC WEBS WWWE

Obituary
NY TIMES (2 Dec 1945), 46:4.
TIMES (LONDON) (3 Dec 1945), 7:5; (4 Dec), 6:6.
WILSON 20 (Feb 1946), 392.

Woods, Mrs. J.C. See WOODS, MRS. JAMES CHAPMAN.

WOODS, MRS. JAMES CHAPMAN.
      Daniel Woodroffe, pseud.
      Mrs. J.C. Woods

Biography
WWWE

WOODS, VIRNA. 1864-1903. U.S.

Biography
BD BURK CHA COY DAB KRO KUJ1 MIG MYE NAW
NCAB-11 PRE REA WARBD WILA WWWA-1

Obituary
NY TIMES (7 Mar 1903), 9:5.

WOOLF, ADELINE VIRGINIA (STEPHEN). 1882-1941.
England.
     Virginia Woolf

Autobiography
BOOKS AND PORTRAITS: SOME FURTHER SELECTIONS FROM
   THE LITERARY AND BIOGRAPHICAL WRITINGS OF
   VIRGINIA WOOLF, edited by Mary Lyon. New
   York: Harcourt Brace Jovanovich, 1978, c1977.
   LC77-85206.

THE DIARY OF VIRGINIA WOOLF, edited by Anne O.
   Bell. New York: Harcourt Brace Jovanovich,
   c1977-. LC77-73111.
     Vol. 1--1915-19.   Vol. 2--1920-24.
     Vol. 3--1925-30.   Vol. 4--1931-35.

LETTERS: VIRGINIA WOOLF AND LYTTON STRACHEY,
   edited by Leonard Woolf and James Strachey.
   New York: Harcourt, Brace, [c1956]. LC56-11962.

THE LETTERS OF VIRGINIA WOOLF, edited by Nigel
   Nicolson. 6 vols. New York: Harcourt Brace
   Jovanovich, 1975-1980. LC75-25538.
     First pub. as:
     Vol. 1--THE FLIGHT OF THE MIND 1888-1912.
     Vol. 2--THE QUESTION OF THINGS HAPPENING
       1912-1922.
     Vol. 3--A CHANGE OF PERSPECTIVE 1923-1928.
     Vol. 4--A REFLECTION OF THE OTHER PERSON
       1929-31.
     Vol. 5--SICKLE SIDE OF THE MOON 1932-35.
     Vol. 6--LEAVE THE LETTERS TILL WE'RE DEAD
       1936-41.

MOMENTS OF BEING: UNPUBLISHED AUTOBIOGRAPHICAL
WRITINGS, edited with an introduction and notes
by Jeanne Schulkind. New York: Harcourt Brace
Jovanovich, 1976. LC76-27410.

A WRITER'S DIARY: BEING EXTRACTS FROM THE DIARY
OF VIRGINIA WOOLF, edited by Leonard Woolf.
New York: Harcourt, Brace, [c1954]. LC54-5257.

Biography
BEAT   BERE   BRO   CAS   CHA   CHABI CHU   CON-104
DUN   FLE   HAOXE KRO   KUL   KUT   LES   MAG   MANBL
MAO   MARBS MCW   MDWB MICB MON   MYE   NCH   NOV
NPW   PEE   RA   RCW   RIC   SEYS   SHO   WAGCE WARLC
WEBS   WENW

Bell, Clive. OLD FRIENDS: PERSONAL
RECOLLECTIONS. New York: Harcourt, Brace,
[1957, c1956]. LC57-13597.

Bell, Quentin. BLOOMSBURY. New York: Basic
Books, [1969, c1968]. LC69-16313.

_____. VIRGINIA WOOLF; A BIOGRAPHY. New York:
Harcourt Brace Jovanovich, [1972]. LC72-79926.

Bell, Vanessa S. NOTES ON VIRGINIA'S CHILDHOOD:
A MEMOIR. New York: F. Hallman, 1974.
LC74-5246.
Originally written for the Memoir Club after
the death of Virginia Woolf.

Brewster, Dorothy. VIRGINIA WOOLF. [New York]:
New York Univ. Press, 1962. LC62-19050L.

Daiches, David. VIRGINIA WOOLF. [Rev. ed.   New
York: New Directions, 1963]. LC62-16926L.

Gadd, David. THE LOVING FRIENDS: A PORTRAIT
OF BLOOMSBURY. New York: Harcourt Brace
Jovanovich, [1975], c1974. LC74-26596.

Gorsky, Susan R. VIRGINIA WOOLF. Boston:
Twayne, 1978. LC78-8045.

Guiguet, Jean. VIRGINIA WOOLF AND HER WORKS, translated by Jean Stewart. New York: Harcourt, Brace & World, [1966, c1965]. LC66-3717.

Johnson, Manly. VIRGINIA WOOLF. pp. 1-24. New York: F. Ungar, [1973]. LC72-79944.

Kennedy, Richard. A BOY AT THE HOGARTH PRESS. London: Whittington, 1972. LC72-169577R.

Lehmann, John. VIRGINIA WOOLF AND HER WORLD. London: Thames and Hudson, c1975. LC75-330614.

Love, Jean O. VIRGINIA WOOLF: SOURCES OF MADNESS AND ART. Berkeley: Univ. of Calif. Press, c1977-. LC76-48004.

Marder, Herbert. FEMINISM AND ART; A STUDY OF VIRGINIA WOOLF. Chicago: Univ. of Chicago Press, [1968]. LC68-16704.

Maurois, Andre. POINTS OF VIEW; FROM KIPLING TO GRAHAM GREENE. New York: Ungar, [1968]. LC68-20517.

Meaker, Marijane. SUDDEN ENDINGS. Greenwich, Conn.: Fawcett, c1964. LC64-16211.

Moffat, Mary J. and Charlotte Painter, comps. REVELATIONS: DIARIES OF WOMEN. pp. 225-36. New York: Random House, [1974]. LC74-8040.

Nathan, Monique, ed. VIRGINIA WOOLF. New York: Grove, [1961]. LC61-5530.

Newton, Deborah. VIRGINIA WOOLF. [Folcroft, Pa.]: Folcroft, 1973, 1946. LC73-1254.

Noble, Joan R. RECOLLECTIONS OF VIRGINIA WOOLF. New York: W. Morrow, 1972. LC72-5595.

Pippett, Aileen. THE MOTH AND THE STAR; A BIOGRAPHY OF VIRGINIA WOOLF. Boston: Little, Brown, [c1955]. LC55-7465.

Poole, Roger. THE UNKNOWN VIRGINIA WOOLF.
New York: Cambridge Univ. Press, 1978.
LC78-3458R.

Rose, Phyllis. WOMAN OF LETTERS: A LIFE OF
VIRGINIA WOOLF. New York: Oxford Univ. Press,
1978. LC77-16489.

Rosenthal, Michael. VIRGINIA WOOLF. pp. 1-34.
New York: Columbia Univ. Press, 1979.
LC79-12161.

Spater, George AND IAN PARSONS. A MARRIAGE OF
TRUE MINDS: AN INTIMATE PORTRAIT OF LEONARD AND
VIRGINIA WOOLF. New York: Harcourt Brace
Jovanovich, 1977. LC77-73062.

Trautmann, Joanne. THE JESSAMY BRIDES: THE
FRIENDSHIP OF VIRGINIA WOOLF AND V. SACKVILLE-
WEST. University Park: Administrative
Committee on Research, Pennsylvania State
Univ., c1973. LC74-621569.

Trombley, Stephen. ALL THAT SUMMER SHE WAS MAD:
VIRGINIA WOOLF FEMALE, VICTIM OF MALE MEDICINE.
New York: Continuum, 1982. LC81-19439.
   Pub. in England as 'ALL THAT SUMMER SHE WAS
MAD': VIRGINIA WOOLF AND HER DOCTORS.

Woolf, Leonard. BEGINNING AGAIN: AN
AUTOBIOGRAPHY OF THE YEARS 1911 TO 1918. New
York: Harcourt Brace Jovanovich, [1975], 1964.
LC75-9848.

_____. DOWNHILL ALL THE WAY: AN AUTOBIOGRAPHY
OF THE YEARS 1919 TO 1939. New York:
Harcourt Brace Jovanovich, 1975, c1967.
LC75-9821.

_____. THE JOURNEY NOT THE ARRIVAL MATTERS: AN
AUTOBIOGRAPHY OF THE YEARS 1939 TO 1969. New
York: Harcourt Brace Jovanovich, 1975, c1969.
LC75-9822.

Woodring, Carl R. VIRGINIA WOOLF. New York:
Columbia Univ. Press, 1966. LC66-19554.

Obituary

"Artist Vanishes." TIME 37 (14 Apr 1941), 34+.
CUR-1941.
"Missing." NEWSWEEK 17 (14 Apr 1941), 12.
NEW REPUBLIC 104 (14 Apr 1941), 487.
PUBLISHERS WEEKLY 139 (12 Apr 1941), 1559.
Roberts, R.E. "Virginia Woolf: 1882-1941." SAT
   REVIEW OF LIT 23 (12 Apr 1941), 12+.
Shillito, E. "Tragic Death of Novelist."
   CHRISTIAN CENTURY 58 (7 May 1941), 632.
"Suicide Note." TIME 37 (5 May 1941), 97.
TIMES (LONDON) (3 Apr 1941), 7:4; tribute
   (9 Apr), 7:5.
WILSON 15 (May 1941), 710.

WOOLSEY, SARAH CHAUNCEY. 1835-1905. U.S.
   Susan Coolidge, pseud.

Biography

BD   BRO   BURK   CHA   COY   DAB   DOY   KUAA   KUJ1
MYE   NAW   NCAB-11   PRE   REA   WARBD   WEBS   WILA
WWWA-1

Obituary

NY TIMES (10 Apr 1905), 9:5.

WOOLSON, CONSTANCE FENIMORE. 1840-1894. U.S.

Autobiography

CONSTANCE FENIMORE WOOLSON. FIVE GENERATIONS
   (1785-1923) ... WITH EXTRACTS FROM THEIR LETTERS
   AND JOURNALS ..., edited by Clara Benedict.
   London: Ellis, [1932]. LC32-22803R.
      "Includes a sketch of the author from Henry
      James's 'PARTIAL PORTRAITS,' extracts from
      her letters, short stories, and reflections,
      thoughts and criticisms from her note-books."

Biography

ADE   AML   AMR   APP   BD   BERE   BROOK   BURK   CAS
COY   DAB   HAOXA   KIR   KUAA   MYE   NAW   NCAB-1   NPW
PEA   PRE   REA   TWCB   WAGCA   WARBD   WEBS   WILA
WWWA-H

Kern, John D. CONSTANCE FENIMORE WOOLSON,
LITERARY PIONEER. Philadelphia, Univ. of
Pennsylvania Press, 1934. LC34-3295.

Moore, Rayburn S. CONSTANCE FENIMORE WOOLSON.
New York: Twayne, [1963]. LC62-19478L.

Obituary
CRITIC 24, n.s. 21 (3 Feb 1894), 73-74.
DIAL 16 (1 Feb 18940, 92.
HARPER'S WEEKLY 38 (3 Feb 1894), 113; (10 Feb),
130.
NY TIMES (25 Jan 1894), 2:5; (27 Jan), 8:6;
(28 Jan), 3:1; (1 Feb), 5:2.
OUTLOOK 49 (3 Feb 1894), 210.

Worboise, Emma Jane. See GUYTON, EMMA JANE
(WORBOISE).

WORDEN, WILBERTINE (TETERS). d.1949. U.S.
            Wilbertine Teters

Biography
COY

WORKMAN, MARY CHRISTIANA (SHEEDY). 1859-1926. U.S.
            Mrs. Hanson Workman

Biography
COY

Workman, Mrs. Hanson. See WORKMAN, MARY CHRISTIANA
(SHEEDY).

WRENCH, MOLLIE LOUISE (GIBBS) STANLEY. England.
            Mollie Stanley-Wrench
            Mrs. Stanley Wrench

Biography
WWLA   WWWE   WWWL

Wright, Elvirton, pseud. See WHITCOMB, JESSIE (WRIGHT).

WRIGHT, HELEN SAUNDERS (SMITH). b.1874. U.S.

Biography
AWO   BURK   WOWWA   WWWA-5

Wright, Jessie E. See WHITCOMB, JESSIE (WRIGHT).

WRIGHT, JULIA (MACNAIR). 1840-1903. U.S.

Biography
APP   AWW   BURK   WARBD   WILA   WWWA-1

WRIGHT, LOUISE SOPHIE (WIGFALL). 1846-1915. U.S.
Mrs. D.G. Wright

Biography
KNIB   WOWWA   WWWA-4

WRIGHT, MABEL (OSGOOD). 1859-1939. U.S.
Barbara, pseud.

Biography
ADE   ALY   AWW   BURK   NAW   NCAB-12   PRE   ROCK
WARBD   WEBS   WWWA-1   WWWL

WRIGHT, MARY (TAPPAN). 1851-1917. U.S.

Biography
BURK   WIN   WOWWA   WWWA-1

Wright, Mrs. D.G.   See WRIGHT, LOUISE SOPHIE (WIGFALL).

Wright, Rowland, pseud. See WELLS, CAROLYN.

WYATT, EDITH FRANKLIN. 1873-1958. U.S.

Biography
ALY   AUT   AWO   AWW   BURK   WOWWA   WWWA-3

Wylie, I.A.R.   See   WYLIE, IDA ALEXA ROSS.

WYLIE, IDA ALEXA ROSS. 1885-1959. England.
  I.A.R. Wylie

Autobiography
MY LIFE WITH GEORGE, AN UNCONVENTIONAL
 AUTOBIOGRAPHY, by I.A.R. Wylie.   New York:
 Random, [c1940].   LC40-27793.

Biography
BRO   KUT   LES   PARR   SHO   WARLC   WEBS   WWWA-3
WWWE   WWWL

Obituary
NY TIMES (5 Nov 1959), 35:1.
NEWSWEEK 54 (16 Nov 1959), 79.
PUBLISHERS WEEKLY 176 (23 Nov 1959), 31.
TIME 74 (16 Nov 1959), 93.
TIMES (LONDON) (5 Nov 1959), 17:2.
WILSON 34 (Jan 1960), 328.

Wylwynne, Kythe, pseud.   See   HYLAND, M.E.F.

Wynman, Margaret, pseud. See   DIXON, ELLA HEPWORTH.

Wynne, May, pseud.   See   KNOWLES, MABEL   WINIFRED.

- X -

X., pseud. See ARMFIELD, ANNE CONSTANCE (SMEDLEY).

- Y -

YEIGH, KATE (WESTLAKE). 1856-1906. Canada.

Biography
MDCB   STOXC

YEZIERSKA, ANZIA. 1885-1970. U.S.

Autobiography
"Hester Street." In AUTOBIOGRAPHIES OF AMERICAN
JEWS, compiled by Harold U. Ribalow.
pp. 446-59. Philadelphia: Jewish Publication
Society of America, 1965. LC65-17047.

RED RIBBON ON A WHITE HORSE. New York: Persea
Books, 1981, c1950. LC81-80749.

Biography
AWO   AWW   BURK   COOPA   HAOXA   KUT   MARBS   NAWM
REA   SCHW   WEBS   WWNA

Schoen, Carol. ANZIA YEZIERSKA. Boston: Twayne,
c1982. LC81-24080.

Obituary
NY TIMES (23 Nov 1970), 40:2.

YONGE, CHARLOTTE MARY. 1823-1901. England.

Biography
ADE   BD   BEL   BERE   BRIT   BRO   CAS   CHA   CHABI
DAB-S2   DOY   GRET   GRETB   HAMM   HAOXE   JOHDB

JOHW KUBA KUJ1 MAGN MDWB MYE NCH NO NPW
PEE SHA SHA-S SHO SOME-17 VIC WAGCE WARBD
WEBS

Battiscombe, Georgina. CHARLOTTE MARY YONGE; THE
    STORY OF AN UNEVENTFUL LIFE. London:
    Constable, [1943]. LC43-3712.

Coleridge, Christabel R. CHAROLTTE MARY YONGE,
    HER LIFE AND LETTERS. Detroit: Gale, 1969,
    1903. LC77-75961.

Mare, Margaret L. and Alicia C. Percival.
    VICTORIAL BEST-SELLER; THE WORLD OF CHARLOTTE
    M. YONGE. Port Washington, N.Y.: Kennikat,
    [1970, 1947]. LC70-103202.

Romanes, Ethel D. CHARLOTTE MARY YONGE, AN
    APPRECIATION. London: A.R. Mowbray, 1908.
    LC W10-278.

Obituary
TIMES (LONDON) (26 Mar 1901), 7:4.

Yorke, Curtis, pseud. See LEE, SUSAN RICHMOND.

Young, E.H. See YOUNG, EMILY HILDA.

YOUNG, EMILY HILDA. 1880-1949. Ireland.
        m. Daniell
        E.H. Young

Biography
BRO CHA KUL KUT MARBS MICB NCH WARLC WEBS
WWW-4

Obituary
CUR-1941.
TIMES (LONDON) (9 Aug 1949), 4:5; (10 Aug), 7:5.

Young, F.E. Mills. See YOUNG, FLORENCE ETHEL
MILLS.

YOUNG, FLORENCE ETHEL MILLS. 1875-1954. England.
F.E. Mills Young

Biography
WWWE   WWWL

YOUNG, JULIA EVELYN (DITTO). b.1857. U.S.

Biography
BURK   WARBD   WILA   WWWA-4

YOUNG, MARTHA. b.1868. U.S.

Biography
ALY   BURK   KNIB   WILA   WOWWA   WWNA

YOUNG, MARY STUART (WELLER). b.1847. U.S.

Biography
WOWWA

Young, R.E.   See   YOUNG, ROSE EMMET.

YOUNG, ROSE EMMET. 1869-1941. U.S.
R.E. Young

Biography
BURK   WOWWA   WWNA   WWWA-1

Obituary
CUR-1941.
NY TIMES (8 July 1941), 19:2.
WILSON 16 (Sept 1941), 6.

Yver, Colette, pseud.   See   HUZARD, ANTOINETTE (DE
BERGEVIN).

Zack, pseud. See KEATS, GWENDOLINE.

ZANGWILL, EDITH (AYRTON). d.1945. England.

Biography
WWWE

Obituary
TIMES (LONDON) (8 May 1945), 8:5.

ZOLLINGER, GULIELMA. 1856-1917. U.S.

Biography
KUJ1   KUJ2   WWWA-1

INDEX

441

INDEX

INDEX

445

INDEX

INDEX

INDEX

448

INDEX

449

INDEX

INDEX

451

INDEX

INDEX

INDEX

INDEX

INDEX